Heritage Preservation

Bhabatosh Chanda · Subhasis Chaudhuri
Santanu Chaudhury
Editors

Heritage Preservation

A Computational Approach

Editors
Bhabatosh Chanda
Electronics and Communication
  Sciences Unit
Indian Statistical Institute
Kolkata, West Bengal
India

Santanu Chaudhury
CSIR-CEERI
Pilani, Rajasthan
India

Subhasis Chaudhuri
Department of Electrical Engineering
Indian Institute of Technology Bombay
Mumbai, Maharashtra
India

ISBN 978-981-13-3924-0   ISBN 978-981-10-7221-5   (eBook)
https://doi.org/10.1007/978-981-10-7221-5

Preface

Heritage records the history of our world—social, religious, ecological, cultural, and political. It represents the footprint of the temporal evolution of civilizations and ecosystems. As it is inherited from the past, it should be bestowed on the future for the benefit of subsequent generations. It is the legacy of tangible artifacts (e.g., monuments, statues, manuscripts, and paintings) and intangible elements (e.g., customs, religion, culture, legends, and history). The vulnerability of heritage items to the harmful effects of climate change, pollution, natural and man-made disasters, neglect, infiltration of new ideas and practices, vandalism, and even mass tourism is becoming more and more evident over the years. Thus, preservation, renovation, restoration, and management of heritage items have become an important task nowadays. However, the physical renovation and restoration work may cause damage to otherwise undamaged part of the artifacts and may fail to provide the flavor of history. Sometimes, this loss may be irrecoverable. Second, the heritage artifacts may not be physically accessible for renovation and restoration work due to various reasons. So, a plausible solution might be restoring and reconstructing the damaged artifacts digitally using computational methods without any physical embodiment. Being re-rectifiable as well as inexpensive, the digital preservation, restoration, and reconstruction of heritage items have become an active research field. Heritage, both tangible and intangible, may also be recorded, represented, and archived in digital space conveniently by means of appropriate computational methods. This handling of heritage items in digital space is popularly known as *digital heritage preservation* and is an emerging area of research in *computational techniques.*

This book presents a balanced treatment of heritage preservation problems and state-of-the-art digital techniques to achieve their novel and useful solutions. It covers the methods starting from data acquisition and digital imaging to computational methods for recreation of original (pre-damaged) look of heritage artifacts. Case studies are almost equally drawn from the tangible and non-tangible heritage which is multi-dimensional as well as rich. Authors of the articles have been working in their respective fields for years and have presented their working experience and methods so lucidly that these can be easily implementable. Both methods and results are illustrated with a large number of color images.

This book consists of sixteen articles covering five major aspects of digital heritage research, namely (i) digital system for heritage preservation including data acquisition, (ii) signal and image processing, (iii) audio and video processing, (iv) image and video database, and (v) architectural modeling and visualization. The first aspect is covered by the first three articles written by Georgopoulos (Article 1), MacDonald (Article 2), and Yao et al. (Article 3). In Article 1, technological advances in digital heritage preservation are briefly presented and explained. It also presents the currently available digital documentation techniques along with the contemporary nondestructive techniques for cultural heritage pathology diagnosis and conservation. Digital heritage requires the represented physical objects to look realistic when viewed on a display screen. Article 2 presents a new method for estimating the reflectance distribution function from a set of images taken in an illumination dome. Surface normal and albedo are calculated by regressing over a subset of the intensity at each pixel. Ground truth collection and large data analysis and evaluation are the important tasks for developing methods for digital heritage. Article 3 presents an open, cross-platform, effective, and extensible GUI annotation tool, known as Epix, for that purpose. This tool can also be used for multiple research purposes, including Euclidean epipolar error measurement and 3D distance measurement. Signal and image processing aspects are dealt in the next five articles written by Madhu and Joshi (Article 4), Kumar et al. (Article 5), Frohlich et al. (Article 6), Sreeni and Chaudhuri (Article 7), and Mukherjee and Sural (Article 8). The problems dealt here range from single-image super-resolution (SR) using deep learning framework (Article 4) to source-constrained exemplar-based inpainting for restoring images of old degraded cave paintings (Article 5), from fusion of 3D and 2D visual data for colorizing the point cloud from multiple cameras with application to old churches (Article 6) to haptic rendering of object described by a dense, oriented point cloud data without a pre-computed polygonal mesh (Article 7). Finally, Article 8 presents an ontology-based approach to retrieve structurally and semantically similar images from heritage image dataset. Articles 9, 10, 11, and 12 cover the audio and video processing aspects of digital heritage. Article 9 (written by Mandal et al.) develops a formal model for the *Ragas*, consequently classifies the *Ragas*, and evaluates music scores based on the *Ragas*. Like music, films are also important media for cultural heritage. A unified approach for detecting some of the most commonly appearing noise artifacts in heritage movies and restoring them to achieve a superior visual quality for viewing and archival is presented in Article 10 (written by Bhattacharya et al.). Next two articles written by Mohanty et al. (Article 11) and Mullik et al. (Article 12) deal with dance, more specifically Bharatanatyam, and its various components such as hand gestures, facial expressions, and dynamic body postures are called *Adavus*. Benchmark dataset is an essential part of evaluating computer vision algorithms. Articles 13 and 14, respectively, present two novel datasets: (i) an image dataset of different temples in Bishnupur suitable for evaluating computer vision techniques such as 3D reconstruction, image inpainting, texture classification, and content-specific figure spotting and retrieval (written by

Ghorai et al.) and (ii) a novel dataset for evaluating computer vision method for recognition of *Sattriya* dance hand gestures (written by Devi et al.). Finally, last two articles cover architectural modeling and visualization aspects. Article 15 outlines the process and methodology of arriving at visualizations of clothing style of Vijayanagara period through study and analysis of textual narratives, murals, stucco work, and relief work of this period, while Article 16 presents a thorough study, documentation, analysis of design elements, and 3D virtual modeling as well as reconstruction of the Krishna temple complex at Hampi, Karnataka, India.

In essence, this book is a comprehensive representation of various aspects and state-of-the-art methodologies suitable for heritage preservation through computational approach. We express our utmost gratitude to the contributors for sharing their experience through these articles. We are thankful to the reviewers without whose support it would not be possible to select the high-quality works for this book. We are thankful to Saurabh Kumar of IIT Bombay for helping us on handling the Web interface for all communication and review activities of the submitted manuscripts. Some of these articles are extended versions of the papers presented in the Workshop on Digital Heritage organized in association with Indian Conference on Computer Vision, Graphics and Image Processing held at Guwahati in December 2016. We are also thankful to the organizers of the conference and the workshop. Last but not least, we are grateful to the editorial team of Springer who has persuaded and helped to bring this book into existence. Editors gratefully acknowledge the support of DST, Ministry of Science and Technology, Government of India, in this endeavor.

Kolkata, India   Bhabatosh Chanda
Mumbai, India   Subhasis Chaudhuri
Pilani, India   Santanu Chaudhury

Contents

About the Editors

Bhabatosh Chanda is a Professor at the Indian Statistical Institute, Kolkata, India. His research interests include image and video processing, pattern recognition, computer vision, and mathematical morphology. He has published more than 200 articles in refereed journals and conferences, authored 2 books, and edited 5 books. He received the Indian National Science Academy 'Young Scientist Medal' in 1989, the Institution of Engineers (India) 'Computer Engineering Division Medal' in 1998, the 'Vikram Sarabhai Research Award' in 2002, and the 'IETE-Ram Lal Wadhwa Gold Medal' in 2007. He is a Fellow of the Institute of Electronics and Telecommunication Engineers (FIETE), National Academy of Science, India (FNASc.), Indian National Academy of Engineering (FNAE), and the International Association of Pattern Recognition (FIAPR).

Subhasis Chaudhuri holds the KN Bajaj Chair Professorship at the Indian Institute of Technology Bombay and is a J.C. Bose national fellow. He works in the area of image processing, computer vision, and haptics. He has published 300 papers in various journals and conferences, as well as 6 monographs in his area of research. He has also served on the editorial board of several international journals, including *IEEE T-PAMI* and *IJCV*. He is a recipient of the Shanti Swarup Bhatnagar Prize in Engineering Sciences. He is a Fellow of the IEEE and the Science Academies in India.

Santanu Chaudhury is currently the Director of the CSIR-CEERI, Pilani, and a Professor in the Department of Electrical Engineering, Indian Institute of Technology Delhi (IIT Delhi). He was also the Dean of Undergraduate Studies at IIT Delhi. He was Schlumberger as well as Dhananjoy Chair Professor at IIT Delhi. His research interests include computer vision, robotics, embedded systems, and machine learning. He has published more than 250 research papers in international journals and conference proceedings and a number of patents. He has been on the program committee of a number of international conferences like ICCV, ACCV,

ICPR, ICVGIP, and PReMI. He was awarded the INSA Medal for Young Scientists in 1993 and received the CDAC-ACCS Award for his scientific achievements in 2012. He is a Fellow of the Indian National Academy of Engineering, the National Academy of Sciences, India, and the International Association of Pattern Recognition.

Contemporary Digital Technologies at the Service of Cultural Heritage

Andreas Georgopoulos

1 Introduction

Cultural heritage is recognized by all civilized countries of the world as the most important carrier of historical memory for mankind. However, it is nor respected and protected as it should be in all cases. Hence, cultural heritage is in great danger as it may be destroyed, lost, altered, forgotten for a number of reasons. The main sources of danger are natural hazards, violent actions, such as wars, terrorism, etc., looting, illicit trafficking, vandalism, modern construction activities, globalization, modern way of life and indifference, urban population growth and many more. In Fig. 1, some examples of such destructions are depicted.

Consequently, their thorough study, preservation and protection are an obligation of our era to mankind's past and future. Respect towards cultural heritage has its roots already in the era of the Renaissance. During the nineteenth century, archaeological excavations became common practice, while they matured in the twentieth century. Over the recent decades, international bodies and agencies have passed resolutions concerning the obligation for protection, conservation and restoration of monuments. The Athens Convention (1931), The Hague Agreement (1954), the Chart of Venice (1964) and the Granada Agreement (1985) are some of these resolutions in which the need for the full documentation of the monuments is also stressed, as part of their protection, study and conservation. Nowadays, all countries of the civilized world are using all their scientific and technological efforts towards protecting and conserving the monuments within or even outside their borders assisting other countries. These general tasks include geometric recording, risk assessment, monitoring, restoring, reconstructing and managing cultural heritage. Indeed, it was in the Venice Charter (1964) that the necessity of the geometric documentation of cultural heritage was

A. Georgopoulos (✉)
Laboratory of Photogrammetry, NTUA, Athens, Greece
e-mail: drag@central.ntua.gr

© Springer Nature Singapore Pte Ltd. 2018
B. Chanda et al. (eds.), *Heritage Preservation*,
https://doi.org/10.1007/978-981-10-7221-5_1

Fig. 1 Destruction of cultural heritage (natural hazards, looting and violent actions)

first set as a prerequisite. In Article 16 it is stated '... *In all works of preservation, restoration or excavation, there should always be precise documentation in the form of analytical and critical reports, illustrated with drawings and photographs...*'.

1.1 Interdisciplinary Cooperation

Traditionally, scientists specialized in monument maintenance were also responsible for their geometric documentation. These experts mainly belonged to the field of archaeology and architecture. However, over the past decades more and different specialists developed an interest in the monuments, as they proved definitely able to contribute to their study, maintenance and care [4]. Among them are surveyors, photogrammetrists and geomatics engineers in general, as the technological advances have enabled them to produce interesting, alternative and accurate geometric documentation products. Until the end of the nineteenth century, architectural heritage had been a matter of national concern only and most of the laws regarding the protection of historic buildings, in Europe at least, date back to that period. Countless associations existed in each country, but their scope never went beyond national borders. Cultural internationalism, as we know it today, was an outcome of the First World War, with the creation of the League of Nations, and most of all of the Second World War, with the creation of the United Nations Organisation and the establishment of the UNESCO. The Athens Conference (1931) on restoration of historic buildings was organized by the International Museums Office, and the Athens Charter, drafted

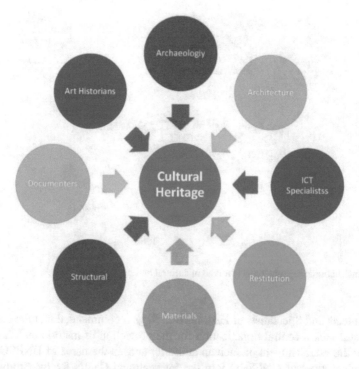

Fig. 2 The interdisciplinary contribution to cultural heritage

by Le Corbusier at the fourth Assembly of the International Congresses on Modern Architecture (1933) was published anonymously in Paris in 1941 both represent a major step in the evolution of ideas because they reflect a growing consciousness among specialists all over the world, introducing for the first time in history the concept of international heritage.

Today, this way of thinking is slowly changing and the traditionally involved scientists, like archaeologists and architects, tend to accept and recognize the contribution of other disciplines to the agenda of cultural heritage. Hence, it is rapidly becoming an interdisciplinary and intercultural issue (Fig. 2) [4].

UNESCO (1946) and the Council of Europe have formed specialized organizations for taking care of mankind's cultural heritage. ICOMOS (International Council for Monuments and Sites) is the most important one, but also CIPA Heritage Documentation (International Committee for Architectural Photogrammetry), ISPRS (International Society for Photogrammetry & Remote Sensing), ICOM (International Council for Museums), ICCROM (International Centre for the Conservation and Restoration of Monuments) and UIA (International Union of Architects) are all involved in this task (Fig. 3). The Venice Charter was conceived from the necessity to form a union of specialists of conservation and restoration independent of the already existing associations of museologists, ICOM. In 1957, in Paris, the First Congress

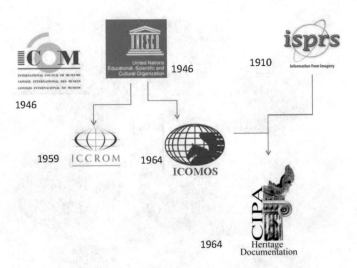

Fig. 3 International organizations involved in cultural heritage

of Architects and Specialists of Historic Buildings recommended that the countries which still lack a central organization for the protection of historic buildings provide for the establishment of such an authority and, in the name of UNESCO, that all member states of UNESCO join the International Centre for the Study of the Preservation and Restoration of Cultural Property (ICCROM) based in Rome [4].

ICCROM is an intergovernmental organization dedicated to the conservation of cultural heritage. Its members are individual states which have declared their adhesion to it. It exists to serve the international community as represented by its Member States, which currently number 133. It is the only institution of its kind with a worldwide mandate to promote the conservation of all types of cultural heritage, both movable and immovable. The decision to found the International Centre for the Study of the Preservation and Restoration of Cultural Property was made at the 9th UNESCO General Conference in New Delhi in 1956, at a time of mounting interest in the protection and preservation of cultural heritage. It was subsequently established in Rome in 1959 at the invitation of the Government of Italy. ICCROM aims at improving the quality of conservation practice as well as raising awareness about the importance of preserving cultural heritage. The Second Congress of Architects and Specialists of Historic Buildings, in Venice in 1964, adopted 13 resolutions, the first one being the International Restoration Charter, better known as Venice Charter, and the second one, put forward by UNESCO, provided for the creation of the International Council on Monuments and Sites (ICOMOS).

1.2 CIPA Heritage Documentation

CIPA Heritage Documentation was founded in 1964 as an International Scientific Committee (ISC) of ICOMOS and ISPRS (International Society for Photogrammetry and Remote Sensing) and hence is a dynamic international organization that has twin responsibilities: keeping up with technology and ensuring its usefulness for cultural heritage conservation, education and dissemination [4]. These two sometimes conflicting goals are accomplished in a variety of ways, through (cipa.icomos.org)

- Encouraging and promoting the development of principles and good practices for recording, documentation and information management of cultural heritage;
- Leading and participating in international training programs for conservation and informatics professionals, students and site personnel;
- Advising government bodies, regional authorities, nonprofit groups and institutions on tools, technology and methods for using technology;
- Sponsoring an international network of professionals in both the fields of technology and cultural heritage for scientific research but also applied practical experience;
- Providing a platform through the biannual International Conference for the exchange of ideas, best practices as well as scientific research papers.

In the recent past, CIPA undertook the RECORDIM initiative, recognizing that there are critical gaps in the fields of heritage recording, documentation and information management between those who provide information for conservation and those who use it, i.e. providers and users of contemporary documentation information. In response, the International Council on Monuments and Sites (ICOMOS), the Getty Conservation Institute (GCI) and CIPA together created the RecorDIM (for Heritage Recording, Documentation and Information Management) Initiative partnership [4]. The purpose of the initiative (started in 2002 and closed on 2007) was to bring information users and providers together to identify the nature of the gaps between them, to develop strategies to close the gaps and to recommend a framework for action.

The involvement of contemporary Digital Technologies (ICT) in the domain of cultural heritage has increased the gap between providers, i.e. those who master these techniques and are able to apply them and the users, i.e. those scholars traditionally concerned with the cultural heritage. This gap was caused mainly due to the mistrust of the latter towards contemporary technologies and lately ICT. However systematic efforts have been applied, like CIPA's RecorDIM (http://cipa.icomos.org/index.php?id=43) which have managed to narrow if not bridge this gap.

This current effort concerned with the 3D virtual reconstruction of monuments is motivated exactly by this endeavour to bridge this gap. This will only be done through a deep understanding of each other's needs and through the proper exploitation of ICT with the benefit of cultural heritage always in mind. In addition, the notion of virtual reconstruction is introduced and its use for bringing the reconstructed monuments into a museum environment is investigated [4].

This interdisciplinary approach to the issue of cultural heritage has opened vast new possibilities and led to new alternative products for the benefit of monuments. These new possibilities include, among others, the production of 3D models, virtual reconstructions, virtual restorations, monitoring of constructions and the applications of serious games for educational and dissemination purposes.

Digital surveying and geometric documentation of cultural heritage require the cooperation of several disciplines and expertise in order to produce results that sufficiently satisfy the highly demanding environment of conservation, restoration, research and dissemination. It should not escape our attention that resources are frequently inadequate while the infrastructure used (equipment, hardware and software) is expected to achieve the maximum possible benefit.

2 Digitization of Cultural Heritage

Nowadays, the rapid advances in digital technology also referred to as Information Communication Technologies (ICT) have provided scientists with new powerful tools. We are now able to acquire, store, process, manage and present any kind of information in digital form [4]. This may be done faster, more completely and it may ensure that this information may be easily available for a larger base of interested individuals. Those digital tools include instrumentation for data acquisition, such as scanners, digital cameras, digital total stations etc., software for processing and managing the collected data and of course computer hardware, for running the software, storing the data and presenting them in various forms.

The introduction of digital technologies has already altered the way we perceive fundamental notions like *indigenous, artefact, heritage, 3D space, ecology*, etc. At the same time, they tend to transform the traditional work of archaeologists and museums as they are so far known. In other words, DT redefines the relationship to CH, as they enable universal access to it and they also connect cultural institutions to new 'audiences'. Finally, they appeal to new generations, as the latter is, by default, computer literate. In this way, we experience a 'democratization' of cultural information across geographic, religious, cultural and scientific borders [4]. Cultural heritage is nowadays, an international, interdisciplinary and intercultural responsibility.

The introduction of digital technologies may contribute to all traditional steps of archaeological practice. It goes without saying that the degree of contribution of ICT is different in the various stages and in the various cases. Modern technologies of remote sensing and archaeological prospection assist the touchless and rapid detection of objects of interest. Spectroradiometers or ground penetrating radars or even the simple processing of multispectral satellite images may easily lead to the rapid location of underground or submerged objects of interest. Contemporary noncontact survey technologies, such as photogrammetry, terrestrial laser scanning and digital imaging, may be used to produce accurate base maps for further study, or 3D virtual renderings and visualizations. The collected data may be stored in interactive databases, georeferenced or not, and be managed according to the needs of the experts. Finally, ICT may assist in the presentation stage, by producing virtual models, which may be displayed in museums or be included in an educational gamification, or serve purposes of enabling handicapped persons to admire the treasures of the World's cultural heritage [4].

The use of digital technologies in preservation and curation in general of cultural heritage is also mandated by UNESCO. With the *Charter on the Preservation of the Digital Cultural Heritage* [25], this global organization proclaims the basic principles of digital cultural heritage for all civilized countries of the world. At the same time, numerous international efforts are underway with the scope to digitize all aspects of cultural heritage, be it large monuments, or tangible artefacts or even intangible articles of the world's legacy.

The impact of digital technologies on the domain of cultural heritage has increased the speed and automation of the procedures which involve processing of the digital data and presentation of the results. At the same time, accuracy and reliability have been substantially enhanced. However, most important is the ability to provide to the users new and alternative products, which include two-dimensional and three-dimensional products, such as orthophotos and 3D models. 3D modelling, on the other hand, is the process of virtually constructing the three-dimensional representation of an object. The use of 3D models is highly increased nowadays in many aspects of everyday life (cinema, advertisements, games, museums, medicine, etc.). All in all, the digitization of the world's cultural heritage whether it is tangible or intangible is now possible.

3 ICT at the Service of CH

The integrated documentation of monuments includes the acquisition of all possible data concerning the monument and which may contribute to its safeguarding in the future. Such data may include historical, archaeological, architectural information, but also administrative data, past drawings, sketches, photos, etc. [4]. Moreover, these data also include metric information which defines the size, the form and the location of the monument in 3D space and which document the monument geometrically. The geometric documentation of a monument, which should be considered as an integral part of the greater action, the integrated documentation of cultural heritage may be defined as [24]:

- The action of acquiring, processing, presenting and recording the necessary data for the determination of the position and the actual existing form, shape and size of a monument in the three-dimensional space at a particular given moment in time.
- The geometric documentation records the present of the monuments, as this has been shaped in the course of time and is the necessary background for the studies of their past, as well as the care of their future.

For the geometric recording, several recording methods may be applied, ranging from the conventional simple topometric methods, for partially or totally uncontrolled surveys, to the elaborated contemporary surveying and photogrammetric ones, for completely controlled surveys. The simple topometric methods are applied only when the small dimensions and simplicity of the monument may allow it when an uncontrolled survey is adequate, or in cases when a small completion of the fully controlled methods is required. Surveying and photogrammetric methods are based on direct measurements of lengths and angles, either on the monument or on images thereof. They indirectly determine three-dimensional point coordinates in a common reference system and ensure uniform and specified accuracy. Moreover, they provide adaptability, flexibility, speed, security and efficiency. All in all, they present undisputed financial merits, in the sense that they are the only methods, which may surely meet any requirements with the least possible total cost and the biggest total profit. To this measurement, group belong complicated surveying methods with total stations, 3D image based photogrammetric surveys and terrestrial laser scanners (TLS). All these methods manage to collect a huge number of points in 3D space, usually called point cloud, in a very limited time frame.

All these techniques can be categorized in different ways. The experience shows that the most efficient method is to characterize them by the scale at which they can be used as well as by the number of measurements they can be used during data acquisition. Practically, this means that they are related to the object size as well as to the complexity of the object. Böhler and Heinz (1999) proposed and developed a system to summarize all existing techniques in terms of scale and object complexity. This is adapted to include modern technologies and is shown in Fig. 4 [21].

According to this figure, the metric surveying techniques are organized considering the scale of the outcome which is a function of the object size and the representation based on the required details. The complexity of the survey can be conveyed by the number of recorded points. In practice, this ranges from one single point describing the geographic location of a single cultural heritage object, to some thousands of points (e.g. a single CAD drawing of a simple monument) or to a few millions of points (e.g. a point cloud) for the detailed representation of a cultural heritage site.

Recording techniques are based on devices and sensors which perform the necessary measurements either directly on the object, or indirectly by recording energy reflected from the object. In the latter category, one may broadly distinguish between active and passive sensors. Active sensors send their own radiation to the object and record the reflectance, while passive ones rely on the radiation sent to the object from some other source. Usually, the latter are image-based sensors, which record the visible light reflected from the objects of interest.

The terrestrial image-based survey comprises all those methods, techniques and technologies that are using images in order to extract metric and thematic information from the object imaged. Within this section, the most important image-based digital technologies supporting the digital surveying and documentation of cultural heritage will be discussed and presented. The main concern will be given to digital cameras and sensors, especially the new entries, the contribution of the Unmanned Air Vehicle

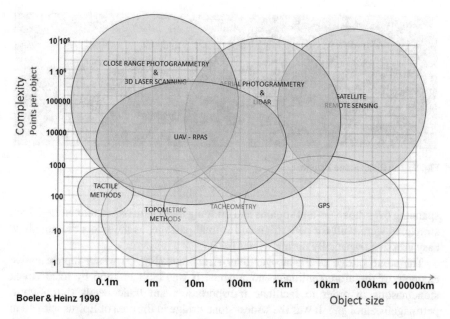

Boeler & Heinz 1999

Fig. 4 Three-dimensional survey techniques characterized by scale and object size and complexity

(UAV) or Remotely Piloted Aircraft Systems (RPAS) or Unmanned Aerial Systems (UAS), but also the useful role that Image Assisted Total Station (IATS) technologies are playing in the recording, monitoring and documentation of cultural heritage.

4 Selected Examples

In order to illustrate the above, some representative examples of cultural heritage digitization will be presented They include (1) the successful attempt to digitize a collapsed traditional stone bridge for assisting the restoration study, (2) the complete geometric documentation of a prominent Athens monument based entirely on image-based techniques and (3) the implementation of an HBIM system for cultural heritage.

4.1 The Restoration of a Collapsed Bridge[1]

A variety of arched stone bridges exist in the Balkan area, built mainly in the eighteenth and nineteenth centuries or even earlier. Just in the Epirus region in northwestern Greece, there are more than 250 magnificent examples of such historic structures

---

[1] Adapted from [5].

Fig. 5 The Plaka Stone Bridge

spanning over the rivers and streams and bridging them with one to four arches. Such structures were built for pedestrian and animal passage, as the rivers did not allow easy crossing, especially during winter [12].

The stone bridge of Plaka over river Arachthos (Fig. 5) was a representative example of the aforementioned monuments. It was built in 1866 by local Greek stonemasons in order to facilitate transportation and trade needs (http://www.petrinagefiria.uoi.gr/). It was the widest stone bridge in the area of Epirus with 40 m span and the biggest single-arch bridge in the Balkans with a height of 20 m (Fig. 5). Next, to the main arch, there were two smaller ones 6 m wide, the so-called relief arches [20].

Apart from its significant size and age, the stone bridge of Plaka was a renowned stone bridge in Greece because of its emblematic historic meaning. First, it was the border between free Greece and the occupied part of Greece by the Ottoman Empire between 1881 and 1912. During World War II, the bridge was bombed by the German army with partial damages. At the same period, representatives of the various armed groups of Greek Resistance signed the Treaty of Plaka on this very bridge.

Before the implementation of any actions, a thorough geometric documentation is necessary, as clearly dictated by the Venice Charter (1964). For that purpose, the Laboratory of Photogrammetry undertook two tasks (a) to produce digital three-dimensional drawings from a documentation study conducted in 1984 using traditional surveying techniques [9] and (b) to produce a textured three-dimensional model of the Plaka Stone Bridge in order to geometrically document its shape and size before the collapse. This 3D model would be produced from existing images taken by visitors of the bridge over the years. These documentation products will form the basis for any eventual reconstruction study [20] (Fig. 6).

Common image-based 3D modelling of the current state of a monument requires data acquisition in the field. Surveying, photogrammetry and laser scanning techniques can be combined to produce a full and accurate 3D model of the object. Such approaches cannot be applied in cases of sudden loss of cultural heritage objects due to a number of reasons such as fire, earthquakes, floods, looting, armed conflict, terrorism, attacks, etc.

Fig. 6 The remains of the bridge after destruction (http://epirusgate.blogspot.gr/2015/02/blog-post_32.html)

Modern photogrammetry and computer vision techniques manage to create useful and accurate 3D models of objects of almost any size and shape, by combining robust algorithms and powerful computers. Multiple images depicting the object from different viewpoints are needed and the so-called SfM and MVS procedures are implemented. These images do not necessarily need to have been captured by calibrated cameras, though. Compact or even mobile phone cameras can also be used. Moreover, capturing geometry is nowadays flexible, in contrast with the traditional strict stereo-normal case of the past. A variety of recent studies are examining the creation of 3D models of cultural heritage objects and sites with the use of SfM algorithms [1, 10, 17, 18]. The lack of images or other surveying data in lost cultural heritage objects has led to the use of random, unordered images acquired from the web. However, few projects, many of them EU funded, make use of data available on the web for such a purpose. Some recent studies are dealing with the 4D (space-time) virtual reconstruction of cultural heritage objects using web-retrieved images [11, 14, 19]. An approach for diachronic virtual reconstruction of lost heritage based on historical information integrated with real metric data of the remains was proposed by Guidi and Russo [7].

For image-based virtual reconstruction, many images from different points of view are required. As already implemented in similar cases in the past, the contribution of people that have visited the area for tourism or other reasons and have taken pictures was sought. Crowdsourcing has already been used for applications in the cultural heritage domain [16]. However, none of the similar actions produced a metric product like the present one.

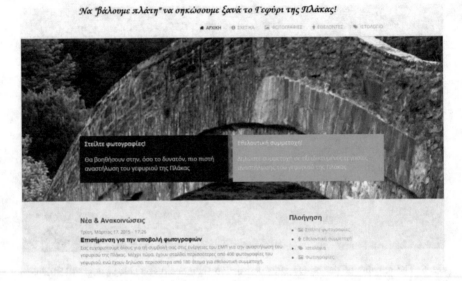

Fig. 7 Homepage of the crowdsourcing webpage

The key aspects of a project like the present one, concerning crowdsourcing information can be summarized as follows:

- The project has a time limit.
- The contribution of the users is of one type of content, i.e. images or video sequences.
- Special information (metadata) about the viewpoint of the images, the equipment used or the time taken could be useful.

To provide a suitable framework for the above, a website has been developed using the Drupal CMS (Fig. 7). Drupal is a Content Management System (CMS) with proper functions for community websites and has been used for educational and research crowdsourcing purposes [8, 15]. More specifically, the website developed includes five sections: (a) a news and announcements page, (b) a general info page, (c) a submit content (images) page, (d) a submit page for volunteers and (e) a blog page. To collect the images, the 'submit images' page is the only section utilized, since it also provides the required information to the contributors [20].

Within the first month of its operation, the website has been visited around 2800 times. More than 470 images were uploaded to the platform during these sessions by more than 130 contributors. Apart from the uploaded content, approximately 200 images and 15 videos were collected through other means, mainly by ordinary mail delivery, by contacting the contributors.

Fig. 8 Dense point cloud after PMVS software (VisualSfM)—51 images

The majority of the collected images were of high resolution, correctly focused and without significant perspective or optical distortions. However, we had to cope with some special challenges in order to exploit as much as possible the rest of the images, which had many different problems. In addition, the majority of the collected photos were taken facing upstream and mainly from the east riverside due to landscape inaccessibility. This causes gaps and difficulties for the algorithm to converge to a stable geometry. After a thorough and careful sorting, it was established that less than 60 images fulfil the needs of the project in terms of viewpoint, image resolution, lighting conditions, occlusions, etc., which corresponds to 10% of the total contributions [20].

The selected data have been processed using commercial as well as free software. VisualSfM is a free GUI application for 3D reconstruction that implements SfM and PMVS along with other tools [2, 3, 28–30]. In this case study, a dense point cloud was produced by 51 images (Fig. 8).

In order to improve the results, a masking procedure was applied to the images while processed in Agisoft PhotoScan. Therefore, background elements that are subjected to temporal changes and obstacles (people, trees, mountains, etc.) have been excluded from photo-alignment. This results in less noisy dense point clouds (Fig. 9). A mesh has also been created, followed by the texturing procedure (Fig. 10).

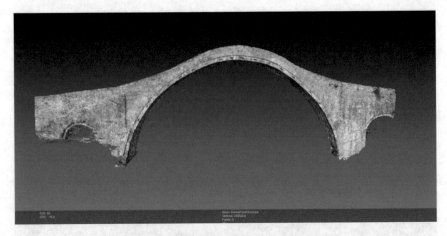

Fig. 9 Dense point cloud produced in Agisoft PhotoScan—56 images

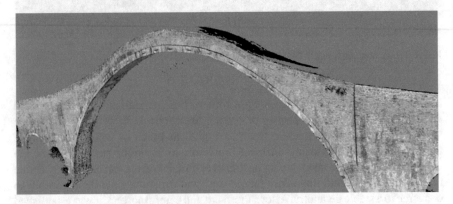

Fig. 10 A view of the textured mesh created in Agisoft PhotoScan

The experts working for the restoration proposal needed also the documentation of the current situation. Hence during a campaign some months ago, data was collected for the creation of the 3D models of the remaining pedestals. They were imaged with a high-resolution DSLR and some Ground Control Points (GCP) were measured. Using again SfM/MVS software, the three-dimensional models were produced (Fig. 11) and served as a detailed geometric basis for the restoration proposal.

It should be stressed that the wide promotion of the 3×3 Rules proposed by CIPA [27] and revised in 2013, available at the relevant webpage (www.cipa.icomos.org) would ensure the existence of more useful images and related metadata for the Plaka Stone Bridge, as the public would be more aware of the eventual future significance of their souvenir images. This may be useful in the future for other monuments in similar situations [20].

Fig. 11 3D models of the remaining parts of the bridge

4.2 Virtual Restoration

The monument of Zalongon is situated on top of an 80 m high and steep cliff about 30 km north of Preveza. The sculpture is about 18 m long and 15 m high and is a composition of several female figures. Although fairly recent, the sculpture has suffered severely from frost and strong winds and tourists inscribing their names on the monument's surface. For its complete restoration, a detailed and accurate geometric documentation and a three-dimensional model of the construction were required. Given the size and complexity of the monument, contemporary digital techniques were employed for this purpose [26].

The most interesting product, possible only with the use of contemporary digital methods, was the 3D model. For the creation of the surface of the 3D model, all of the original scans were registered into a common reference system by applying a method that was specially developed. The creation of high resolution textured 3D models is undoubtedly a nontrivial task as it requires the application of advanced data acquisition and processing techniques, such as geodetic, photogrammetric, scanning, programming, surfacing, modelling, texturing and mosaicking [4].

For achieving restoration, the basic steps are: identifying the destroyed parts, interact with the 3D model and extract the geometry of the parts to be restored, insert them virtually into the 3D model and finally assess the result, before a final decision. In the present case, the main points of interest were, of course, the destroyed figureheads, but there were also many other damages to be restored (Fig. 12).

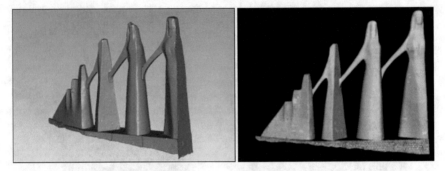

Fig. 12 Virtual restoration of the Zalongon monument

4.3   Virtual Museums

Developing and displaying a museum in a virtual environment has some advantages especially concerning the preservation and promotion of cultural heritage but also the development of tourism and the promotion of the touristic product. Virtual museums are important to both the visitors and the museums themselves and their curators. The majority of the museums only exhibit a small part of their collection due to the lack of space and of course due to the fact that some objects are extremely valuable or fragile [13]. In a virtual and interactive environment, the visitor is able to interact with the digitized exhibits and learn all the essential, historical information about them. Moreover, in a virtual environment, the visitor can view a virtual reconstruction of important objects, buildings and archaeological sites that may no longer exist are damaged or access to them is not permitted. Moreover, collections may also be displayed made of objects that are spread in various museums around the world [5].

The digitization of cultural heritage helps to preserve, store, renew, retrieve and make it accessible for a wider audience in a more appealing and contemporary way, especially to people with special abilities or people that may never have the chance to visit the real museum [23]. The wide use of Internet, social media and websites can make the digitized content of a museum more accessible and transport it to everyone all around the world. It is important to mention the result of Colorado University research according to which 70% of a total of 223 million people who visit a museum website would subsequently be more likely to go and also visit the real museum [6]. This means that the virtual museum functions in a complementary manner to the real museum. Finally, in virtual museum exhibitions, the visitor is able to fully control the navigation as well as to freely explore, move around, manipulate the exhibits and create his/her own, unique virtual experience or collection of 3D digital exhibits even from different museums. It is obvious that every effort and innovation that concerns the digitization of cultural heritage and the development of virtual museums and applications is a complicated, difficult, controversial task with many advantages and can only benefit and offer both the museums and the visitors. Especially in Greece,

65% of the tourists make an online search of their destination and 45% of them are interested in cultural heritage, monuments, museums and archaeological sites [5].

The Virtual Museum of the Stoa of Attalos is an application where the visitor is able to make a tour in the museum on his own, explore it, interact with the exhibits, rotate them and learn all the necessary information about them. The development of this application took into consideration various aspects such as the requirements' analysis, the architectural design, the planning of the exhibits' presentation, the user interaction, the programming process and the evaluation of the final product [13].

As far as the Virtual Museum of the Stoa of Attalos is concerned, the virtual environment hosts some of the exhibits which can be found on the ground floor of the Stoa of Attalos, in the Ancient Agora of Athens. For this project, 16 of the exhibits were chosen from the south part of the colonnade of the museum and the most important concern was to produce accurate, realistic and appealing 3D models that can be used in virtual applications, especially in a short period of time. That is why photogrammetric methods and 3D surveys were used for the mass production of the exhibits' 3D models and the development of the virtual museum. In order to process the data and build the accurate, textured 3D models of the exhibits PhotoScan Professional® v.1.1 software by Agisoft was used [5].

The application is available in Greek and English. In the beginning of the virtual tour, the visitor has the chance to read the instructions that are available in order to freely navigate in the environment and understand the options and opportunities he/she has in the virtual museum (Fig. 13). The parameters that concern the movement, speed, rotation, height vision and behaviour of the visitor were extremely important in order to make the navigation friendly and easy for the visitor, as the majority of them may not have any previous experience with this kind of applications or even with the use of computers [5].

Moreover, the ambience and the depth of field were properly adjusted in order to have a more clear and realistic view of the exhibits, which is also important to the visitor and his/her virtual experience in the museum. The visitor has the chance to learn and find out more information about the exhibits that attract and interest him/her simply by clicking on them (Fig. 14). Moreover, the visitor is able to rotate the exhibits while the panel with the information appears on the right part of the screen. In that way, the visitor is able to manipulate, closely examine and observe the details of every exhibit and at the same time learn not only the available information of the small panel that exists in the real museum, but also further information about it. The curator of the museum has the opportunity to choose the information that will be available to the visitor and this is one of the advantages of this kind of applications. Finally, the last element that was added in the virtual environment was a mini-map to help the visitor move around and navigate in the environment without feeling disorientated, simply by offering him/her a view of the virtual museum from the top [5].

Fig. 13 The environment of the virtual museum

Fig. 14 The virtual museum with all included elements

5 Concluding Remarks

With the presentation of a few characteristic implementation examples, it has been shown that digital contemporary technologies can contribute decisively to the conservation of cultural heritage. The final products are 3D models and virtual restorations or reconstructions of monuments that do not exist today or are at risk. Consequently, digital technologies and interdisciplinary synergies are of utmost importance. Equally important are the discussions and suggestions of scientists who have studied the monuments from a historical and archaeological point of view, proving once again that such interventions are a multidisciplinary process.

Virtual reconstructions, virtual restorations, monitoring and 3D models on the other hand support many other disciplines involved in cultural heritage. They help architects and structural engineers in their work for monuments especially in cases of restoration, anastylosis, etc. Archaeologists and conservationists have a very good tool at their disposal for their studies. Many applications can be generated from a virtual reconstruction like virtual video tours of the monument for educational and other purposes for use by schools, museums and other organizations, for incorporation into a geographical information system (GIS) for archaeological sites, for the design of virtual museums and the creation of numerous applications for mobile devices (e.g. mobile phones, tablets, etc.).

References

1. Barsanti, S.G., Guidi, G.: 3D digitization of museum content within the 3D-ICONS project. ISPRS Ann. Photogram. Remote Sens. Spat. Inf. Sci. II-5 W **1**, 151–156 (2013)
2. Furukawa, Y., Ponce, J.: Accurate, dense, and robust multiview stereopsis. IEEE Trans. Pattern Anal. Mach. Intell. **32**(8), 1362–1376 (2010)
3. Furukawa, Y., Curless, B., Seitz, S.M., Szeliski, R.: Towards internet-scale multi-view stereo. In: 2010 IEEE Conference on Computer Vision and Pattern Recognition (CVPR), pp. 1434–1441. IEEE (2010)
4. Georgopoulos, A.: Non-contact contemporary techniques for geometric recording of Cultural Heritage. In: Aggelis et al. (eds.) Emerging Technologies in Non-Destructive Testing IV. Taylor & Francis Group, London, ISBN 978-1-138-02884-5 (2015)
5. Georgopoulos, A., Kontogianni, G., Koutsaftis, Ch., Skamantzari, M.: Serious games at the service of cultural heritage and tourism. In: Proceedings IACUDIT Conference, May 2016, Athens (to appear in International Journal of Cultural and Digital Tourism) (2016)
6. Griffiths, J-M., King D.W.: Physical spaces and virtual visitors: the methodologies of comprehensive study of users and uses of museums. In: Trant, J., Bearman, D. (eds.) Proceedings of the International Cultural Heritage Informatics Meeting (ICHIM07). Archives & Museum Informatics, Toronto. Retrieved from http://www.archimuse.com/ichim07/papers/griffiths/griffiths. html, 24 Oct 2007
7. Guidi, G., Russo, M.: Diachronic 3D reconstruction for lost Cultural Heritage. ISPRS-Int. Arch. Photogram. Remote Sens. Spat. Inf. Sci. **3816**, 371–376 (2011)
8. Kaliampakos, D., Benardos, A., Mavrikos, A., Panagiotopoulos, G.: The underground atlas project. Tunn. Undergr. Space Technol. (accepted for Publication) (2015)
9. Karakosta, E., Papanagiotou, B., Tragaris, N., Chatzigeorgiou, Th., Arampatzi, O., Doggouris, S., Mpalodimos, D-D.: Plaka Bridge: survey-check for vertical deformations, diploma thesis, National Technical University of Athens (1984)
10. Kersten, T. P., Lindstaedt, M.: Image-based low-cost systems for automatic 3D recording and modelling of archaeological finds and objects. In: Progress in Cultural Heritage Preservation, pp. 1–10. Springer Berlin Heidelberg (2012)
11. Kyriakaki, G., Doulamis, A., Doulamis, N., Ioannides, M., Makantasis, K., Protopapadakis, E., Hadjiprocopis, A., Wenzel, K., Fritsch, D., Klein, M., Weinlinger, G.: 4D reconstruction of tangible cultural heritage objects from web-retrieved images. Int. J. Herit. Digit. Era **3**(2), 431–452 (2014)

12. Leftheris, B.P., Stavroulaki, M.E., Sapounaki, A.C., Stavroulakis, G.E.: Computational Mechanics for Heritage Structures. WIT Press, Southampton (2006)
13. Lepouras, G., Katifori, A., Vassilakis, C., Haritos, D.: Real exhibitions in a virtual museum. Arch. J. Virtual Real. **7**(2), 120–128 (2004)
14. Makantasis, K., Doulamis, A., Doulamis, N., Ioannides, M., Matsatsinis, N.: Content-based filtering for fast 3D reconstruction from unstructured web-based image data. In: Digital Heritage. Progress in Cultural Heritage: Documentation, Preservation, and Protection, pp. 91–101. Springer International Publishing (2014)
15. Munoz-Torres, M.C., Reese, J.T., Childers, C.P., Bennett, A.K., Sundaram, J.P., Childs, K.L., Anzola, J.M., Milshina, N., Elsik, C.G.: Hymenoptera Genome Database: integrated community resources for insect species of the order Hymenoptera. Nucleic Acids Res. **39**, D658–D662 (2011)
16. Oomen, J., Aroyo, L.: Crowdsourcing in the cultural heritage domain: opportunities and challenges. In: Proceedings of the 5th International Conference on Communities and Technologies, Brisbane (Australia), 19 June–2 July 2011
17. Remondino, F., Del Pizzo, S., Kersten, T.P., Troisi, S.: Low-cost and open-source solutions for automated image orientation–a critical overview. In: Progress in Cultural Heritage Preservation, pp. 40–54. Springer Berlin Heidelberg (2012)
18. Santagati, C., Inzerillo, L., Di Paola, F.: Image-based modelling techniques for architectural heritage 3D digitalization: limits and potentialities. Int. Arch. Photogram. Remote Sens. Spat. Inf. Sci. **5**(w2), 555–560 (2013)
19. Santos, P., Serna, S.P., Stork, A., Fellner, D.: The potential of 3D internet in the cultural heritage domain. In: 3D Research Challenges in Cultural Heritage, pp. 1–17. Springer Berlin Heidelberg (2014)
20. Stathopoulou, E.K., Georgopoulos, A., Panagiotopoulos, G., Kaliampakos, D.: 3D visualisation of lost cultural heritage objects using crowdsourcing the international archives of the photogrammetry, remote sensing and spatial information sciences, volume XL-5/W7. In: 2015 25th International CIPA Symposium, 31 Aug–04 Sept 2015, Taipei, Taiwan (2015)
21. Stylianidis, E., Georgopoulos, A.: Digital surveying in cultural heritage: the image-based recording and documentation approaches. In: Ippolito, A., Cigola, M. (eds.) Handbook of Research on Emerging Technologies for Digital Preservation and Information Modeling. IGI Global Publishing (2016)
22. Stylianidis, E., Remondino, F. (eds.): 3D Recording, Documentation and Management of Cultural Heritage, p. 388. Whittles Publishing. ISBN 978-184995-168-5 (2016)
23. Sylaiou, S., Liarokapis, F., Kotsakis, K., Patias, P.: Virtual museums, a survey and some issues for consideration. Arch. J. Cult. Herit. **10**, 520–528 (2009). Elsevier, ISSN: 1296-2074
24. UNESCO: Photogrammetry Applied to the Survey of Historic Monuments, of Sites and to Archaeology. UNESCO editions (1972)
25. UNESCO: Guidelines for the Preservation of Digital Heritage, CI-2003/WS/3 (2003)
26. Valanis, A., Tapinaki, S., Georgopoulos, A., Ioannidis, C.: High-resolution textured models for engineering applications. In: Proceedings XXII CIPA Symposium, Kyoto, Japan, 11–15 Oct 2009
27. Waldhäusl, P., Ogleby, C.L.: 3 × 3 rules for simple photogrammetric documentation of architecture. Int. Arch. Photogram. Remote Sens. **30**, 426–429 (1994)
28. Wu, C.: SiftGPU: A GPU implementation of scale invariant feature transform (SIFT). http://cs.unc.edu/~ccwu/siftgpu (2007)
29. Wu, C., Agarwal, S., Curless, B., Seitz, S.M.: Multicore bundle adjustment. In: 2011 IEEE Conference on Computer Vision and Pattern Recognition (CVPR), pp. 3057–3064. IEEE June 2011
30. Wu, C.: Towards linear-time incremental structure from motion. In: 2013 International Conference on 3D Vision-3DV 2013, pp. 127–134. IEEE, June 2013

Visual Realism in Digital Heritage

Lindsay W. MacDonald

1 Materiality and Appearance

Central to the visitor experience in any museum or gallery is looking at objects in the collections. An object is a relic of a particular time and place, crafted using contemporary techniques and representing the prevailing social values. Coming face to face with an ancient artefact, one cannot help but be moved by its materiality and the realisation that this object was there in the past and is still here now. If only it could tell its story of all that it had witnessed over the centuries! The materiality of an object is one of the ways that it conveys authenticity: signs of toolmarks, decoration, and texture of the substrate show how it was made; signs of granularity, wear, damage, cracking, weathering and decay show its degradation with the passage of time. All combine to give the impression that it is the 'real thing'. Even if one cannot touch the object and feel its tactile qualities, the patina of age somehow transforms its degraded nature into something evocative, even romantic, adding to its charm and visual power. The appearance of the object is inseparable from its 'pastness' [1]. It follows that in any visualisation of a cultural heritage object, the patina needs to be reproduced accurately, or at least in a way that is convincing. Two key aspects are colour and specularity.

In a traditional museum or gallery, the actual objects are on display and visitors can walk around them and view them from many angles under the prevailing room illumination. In digital media, however, a representation of the object is shown through some form of display, usually at a remote location away from the museum, and what the observer sees is a product of the digital processing at every stage (Fig. 1). This is a modality of media communication [2] in which the quality of experience depends on both the quality of reproduction of the object and the quality of the script, as well

L. W. MacDonald (✉)
3DImpact Research Group, Faculty of Engineering, University College London, London, UK
e-mail: lindsay.macdonald@ucl.ac.uk

© Springer Nature Singapore Pte Ltd. 2018
B. Chanda et al. (eds.), *Heritage Preservation*,
https://doi.org/10.1007/978-981-10-7221-5_2

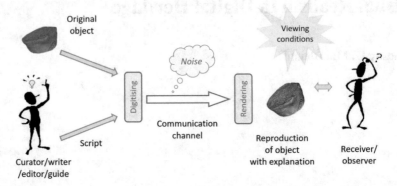

Fig. 1 A model of digital heritage, in which the observer sees a reproduction of an object, communicated through a digital channel with a scripted explanation

as the viewing conditions. The communication is between people and is centred on the object, analogous to a visitor listening to a human guide in a gallery, but mediated by technology.

The role of the observer is central to any display or presentation. In the context of the graphic arts, there are broadly two types of objectives in colour reproduction: accurate and pleasing [3]. An accurate colour reproduction should match the original to the extent that when the two objects are placed side-by-side under the same illumination they look the same, at least to the majority of observers (Fig. 2). In the case of fine art reproduction this is a rare case, because the original is generally not available for comparison [4].

A pleasing reproduction is not necessarily accurate but adjusts the tone, colour and sharpness in a way that is preferred. In the processing of photographic prints from film negatives, it was standard practice by Kodak and others to adjust the chromaticity of blue sky, green grass and skin tones to make them more like the ideal

Fig. 2 Side-by-side comparison of two reproductions (right) with the original painting on the wall of the National Gallery, London, during the MARC project in 1993. The painting *The Adoration of the Kings* is a fragment of an altarpiece by the Master of Liesborn c.1470, catalogue NG258

(prototypical) memory colours expected by the consumer. Thus the print of a painting that one might buy online, or even in the gallery shop, is generally not an accurate match to the original but is enhanced to be more attractive in a way that conforms to popular imagination. Colour management enables this to be done in a systematic way through different 'rendering intents'. In electronic media, such as television and computer displays and mobile media, naturalness is important. In psychophysical experiments, observer preferences for brightness rendering and chromatic rendering of images invariably tend toward greater contrast and higher colour saturation [5].

Colour stimulus is determined as the product of the spectral power distribution of the illumination, the spectral reflectance factor of the surface, and the spectral sensitivity of the observer. Because human vision is trichromatic, with three classes of photoreceptor in the retina, the CIE system of colorimetry reduces the computation to three numbers at each point, the so-called tristimulus values [6]. But this convenient reduction of dimensionality disguises the underlying spectral reality. It leads to metameric differences in colour perception between environments with different light sources, between observers with different visual sensitivities, and between humans and cameras. For best representation of any coloured object, especially for cultural heritage purposes, the reflectance spectrum of the surface should be captured as accurately as possible, by multispectral sampling in sufficiently many bands to capture all spectral frequencies present in the colourants [7]. For paintings, this facilitates identifying pigments, quantifying fading and predicting colour appearance under various illumination sources [8].

The difficulty with pleasing reproduction of imagery is that everyone may have a different individual preference. On the World Wide Web, moreover, there is very little control over the colour reproduction of images for either digitisation or display. As an example, Fig. 3 shows renderings of *La Nascita di Venere* found at a dozen different web sites, and it is very difficult to say which, if any, is 'correct'. Some of

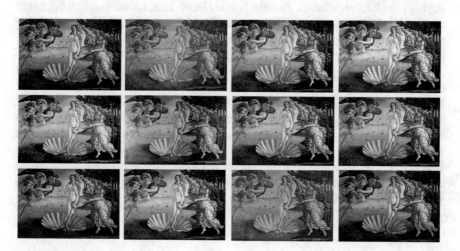

Fig. 3 Twelve versions on the Web of *La Nascita di Venere* by Sandro Botticelli (1483–85)

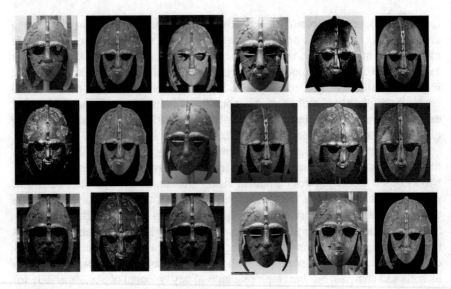

Fig. 4 Images of the Sutton Hoo Anglo-Saxon helmet, on display in the British Museum, London, found at 18 web sites

these images even seem to have been scanned from printed halftone pictures, which themselves may not have been properly colour-managed.

The problem is compounded with three-dimensional objects. Even when photographs are taken from the same viewpoint in the same location, the appearance of the image is strongly dependent on the quality of the lighting, the surface properties and the spectral sensitivity of the camera. The interaction between the illumination (directional or diffuse, daylight or artificial) and the surface (matte or gloss or metallic) is particularly significant. Take the Sutton Hoo helmet, for example, on display in a gallery at the British Museum, where there is a mixture of daylight, room lighting and spotlights on the object, all with different spectral power distributions. Every image taken by every visitor with every kind of camera may be different (Fig. 4).

Objects are usually digitised and processed with the simplifying assumption that the surface is Lambertian, i.e. that the incident light is reflected diffusely with equal intensity in all directions. In fact for the majority of materials this is not true. Most surfaces have a sheen or gloss, which causes light to be reflected more strongly in one direction. Point sources of light are reflected as localised specular highlights from shiny surfaces. Much of the skill of the professional photographer lies in the selection and arrangement of light sources to produce the desired rendering of the object's form and features. These factors are well illustrated in the imaging and visualisation of coins.

2 Photography of Coins

In the documentation of coins, images provide additional information besides the written description, conveying both the visual design and the state of preservation. Traditionally coins have been photographed by numismatists as 2D monochrome images, and these are of great qualitative value. But unless a standardised configuration of illumination is employed, it is difficult to use the images for quantitative analysis and comparison. For imaging of premodern coins, for example, numismatic photographers have sometimes employed a light source inclined at an angle from the optical axis of the camera. This has the advantage of reducing the direct specular reflections from the metallic surface, but it produces bright reflections from gradients on one side of relief features and shadows on the other. This asymmetrical rendering, which depends on both illumination and viewing angles, makes it difficult to decide whether two coins were minted by the same die.

The intensity, direction and number of light sources usually vary from one studio to another, leading to differences in the shadows cast, the contrast between bright and dark regions and the rendering of surface texture. Different lighting directions may make small patterns on the coin, such as inscriptions and symbols, look very different, and highlight arising from specularity of the metallic surface may affect the image quality, especially when automatic exposure correction is enabled in the camera. More fundamentally, the projection of 3D object onto 2D image means that valuable information about the object is discarded, making it more difficult to analyse distortions arising from the striking of the coin in the die and also of subsequent wear and corrosion [9].

Because of the relatively small size, shallow relief and metallic specularity of most coins, special techniques are needed for photography. In addition to a copystand and a good macro lens, careful attention needs to be paid to the geometry of the incident illumination. In general, the raised areas of the surface need to be rendered in the image by tones different from those of the ground plane of the coin. This cannot be achieved by a single light source at an oblique angle, because for a shiny surface the light is reflected away from the camera, making it appear too dark. Moreover, the reflection from the leading edge of each surface feature becomes an over-exposed specular highlight, while the trailing edge is cast into shadow. The resulting image is harsh in contrast and the gradients are strongly directional, and fine surface texture may be exaggerated.

Hoberman, writing in the days of analogue photography, gave the following advice [10]: 'The object should be to illuminate the coin with maximum visual impact, to reproduce it accurately, and to accentuate its beauty. One should endeavour to reproduce maximum gradation of tone and in the case of colour film to record its subtle hues'. He noted the importance of shadow as well as light, 'for without light there is no visual image and without shadow there is no visual form'. He recommended axial illumination, i.e. parallel to the optical axis and perpendicular to the plane of the coin, produced by a single studio flashlight beamed upwards into a downward-facing silvered umbrella reflector (Fig. 5). The effect is to foreshorten

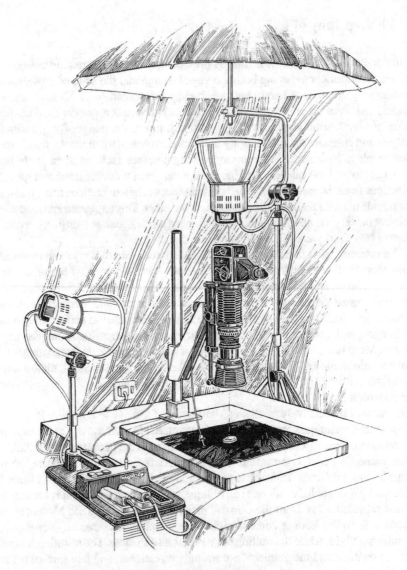

Fig. 5 Photographic setup for axial illumination of a coin (from Hoberman)

the shadows at the boundaries of surface features and to produce 'a subtle moulding effect similar to the bright haze of an overcast noon sky'.

Another traditional technique used by professionals is to illuminate the coin via a periscope arrangement, in which the camera views it through a plate of glass or a half-silvered mirror (Fig. 6). Only rays reflected parallel to the optical axis are captured, resulting in an image that is light in horizontal surfaces of the coin and dark in inclined surfaces, i.e. the outlines of relief features. Conversely, a different apparatus with a

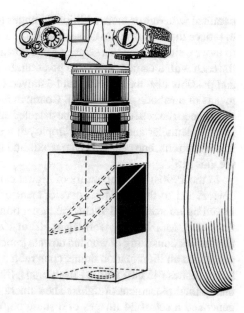

Fig. 6 Setup with half-silvered mirror for photography of coins (from Hawkins and Avon)

white paper cone enables the sloping sides of features to be illuminated without frontal light, resulting in an image with light outlines and dark surfaces [11].

More recently, Goodman has noted that illumination from a high angle, i.e. as near as possible to axial, improves the relief, helps to prevent dark spots, makes details more vibrant and enhances lustre [12]. Single lights, especially those closer to a point source, produce higher contrast in the image, whereas multiple lights, or those emitting over a larger area, produce a more diffused light and therefore lower the image contrast. He distinguishes between three classes of coins, which he calls low, medium and high contrast, according to their degree of metallic specularity, corresponding to normal coins in circulation (low contrast), new coins (medium contrast) and brilliant proof coins (high contrast). For these, he recommends illumination by one, two and three lights, respectively, adding a diffused light where needed to soften the shadows in the image.

3 Dome Photography

The angle at which each illuminating ray strikes the surface of a material affects the intensity of the reflected ray, and hence the intensity at that location of the image from a given viewpoint. By capturing a series of images with illumination from known directions, a richer representation of the object surface can be obtained than from a single image. The concept of using an array of lights to illuminate an object from different directions emerged during the 1980s through research in the 'photometric stereo' technique, also known as 'shape from shading', to determine the surface normal vector at each point. Although this process can in theory be achieved with only three images so solve for the three unknowns at each pixel, better results are obtained with one or more additional images to provide some redundancy and hence to reduce the sensitivity to noise. One way to achieve this in the image acquisition is to move a single lamp to a sequence of known coordinate positions, taking an image for each with a camera at a fixed position. In an automated system the light source, and possibly also the camera, can be moved to a series of programmed positions by means of a robotic actuator [13]. Coleman and Jain showed how by using a fourth image specular reflections could be detected and removed from the computation [14]. Later Rushmeier and Bernadini employed a simple rig with five tungsten lamps in fixed positions, one near the camera axis and four separated approximately 45° from the axis [15].

In the 1990s, the availability of digital cameras and light-emitting diode (LED) devices led to the industrial development of illumination arrays in several fields, including microscopy [16] and the inspection of objects in machine vision applications [17]. Malzbender, working at HP in 1998, experimented with an icosahedral framework consisting of wooden dowels joined using hot melt glue. Subsequently he developed an illumination dome, constructed from an acrylic hemisphere of diameter 18 inches (45 cm) with 24 flash lights. Simulated annealing was applied to find the optimal placement of lights. The camera, fixed at the 'north pole' of the dome, generated a set of 24 images of a static object in the equatorial plane, all in pixel register, but with a different direction of incident illumination in each image. He demonstrated a fitting technique known as polynomial texture mapping (PTM) for the interactive visualisation of objects with surface relief, such as fossils, and ancient artefacts, such as inscribed clay tablets [18].

PTM was applied to Roman and medieval coins from the collection at the monastery of St. Bernard [19]. The system consisted of a template for 24 light positions in a hemispherical array surrounding the coin, a fibre optic directional light source, and a computer-controlled camera. The study concluded that PTMs provide an interactive experience of a more complete data set than traditional numismatic documentation and that they offer a more informed method for generating images that convey numismatic ideas. Moreover, a strong affinity was found between structured light 3D acquisition and PTM imaging, in relation to surface normal vectors and bidirectional reflectance distribution functions (BRDFs), suggesting that high-quality numismatic documentation could be produced through the joint application of these techniques. PTM was later used for presenting a collection of coins for public display through an interactive kiosk at the National Museum of San Matteo in Pisa [20]. The objective of the project was to enable the virtual manipulation of the coins for detailed inspection, and thereby to reveal their features in an easy and understandable way. The collection included both gold coins with highly specular surfaces and bronze coins that were more opaque and presented patinas resulting from various degradation processes.

The dome imaging system at UCL enables sets of images of an object to be taken with illumination from different directions (Fig. 7). A hemisphere of 1030 mm diameter is fitted with 64 flash lights, calibrated so that the geometric centroid of every light source is known to within 3 mm [21]. A Nikon D200 digital camera mounted at the 'north pole' captures a series of 64 colour images, each illuminated by flashlight

Fig. 7 Illumination dome at UCL, showing the flash lights mounted on individual circuit boards, arranged in five horizontal tiers

from a different direction, all in pixel register. This opens the way for characterising the texture, geometry and gloss of the object surface and for visualising its appearance under any direction of illumination. Previous publications have explained how the image sets may be used for PTM [22], virtual exhibitions [23] and 3D surface reconstruction [24].

In the present study, an ancient silver coin (Fig. 8) has been used as the test object. This particular coin is a rare Roman Republic denarius serratus dated to 118 BC, minted in Narbo (now Narbonne) France to celebrate the defeat of the Gauls by the Roman Republican Army. The obverse shows the goddess Roma, and the reverse a naked warrior riding in a chariot, identified as Bituitus, King of the Averni tribe of the Gauls. The coin was found by amateur archaeologist James Balme in a field near Warburton, Cheshire, during investigations into the possible site of a Roman fortlet, and it has been featured on Time Team and various TV documentaries [25].

Fig. 8 Obverse and reverse of a Roman denarius, taken by a Nikon 200 camera, illuminated by a single flashlight from the right side at an elevation of 60°

It is recorded in the Portable Antiquities Scheme (PAS) [26]. The weight of the coin is 3.4 grammes, and its diameter is 19 mm. Before imaging it was partially cleaned, to give a bright silver finish in the raised areas.

An interesting feature of the coin is a number of punched countermarks on both faces. Such marks did not come into use until the start of the Augustine imperial era (27 BC). There were several reasons why a Roman coin might be countermarked during this period [27]: (1) To extend the geographical area in which it would be accepted as legal tender; (2) To continue in use a coin which had been in circulation for a considerable period of time; and (3) To designate a new authority usurping the coins of another for their own use. All three of these reasons might apply in this case.

For photography of this coin in the UCL dome, a Nikkor 200 mm macro lens was employed, giving an image of the coin of approximate dimensions 1250 (W) × 1180 (H) pixels, corresponding to a surface sampling of 66 pixels/mm, i.e. each pixel represents a span of 16 μm on the surface of the coin. With the 64 flash lights, a set of 64 images was captured, each illuminated from a different direction. The lightness of the images increases with increasing angle of elevation of the light source (Fig. 9).

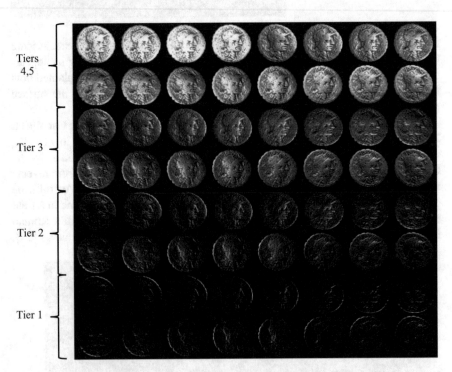

Fig. 9 Montage of 64 images of the obverse of the Roman denarius, taken by a Nikon D200 camera in the UCL dome, illuminated by each of the 64 flashlights arranged in five tiers. The image brightness decreases with angle of elevation of the light source, shown from top of the figure (highest angles in Tiers 4, 5) to the bottom (lowest angles in Tier 1)

Fig. 10 (left) mean of images from top 4 flashlights; (centre) mean of 64 images taken in dome; (right) weighted sum of 60% of the specular image plus 40% of the overall mean image

By digital processing (in Matlab), it is possible to construct any weighted sum of the images, and hence to emulate the conventional photographic lighting configurations described above. For example, the image produced by the recommended axial illumination (Fig. 5) can be formed as the mean of the four images corresponding to the four lights nearest the camera, with elevation approximately 80° (first four images in the top row of Fig. 9). The image produced by diffuse (i.e. omnidirectional) illumination is approximated as the mean of all 64 images. A weighted sum of the two, with 60% of the specular image plus 40% of the overall mean image, retains the shadowed outlines around the surface features, softened to reduce contrast (Fig. 10).

4 Image Processing

The difficulty with silver and other metals, and indeed with all shiny and glossy materials, is that they reflect strongly in the specular direction. So in the vector of 64 intensity values for any pixel, there are a few values much larger than the others, corresponding to positions where the surface normal is close to the bisector of the angle between the illumination vector (toward the light) and the view vector (toward the camera). This results in images with high dynamic range where a few pixels may be 10 times greater in value than the majority. The two sides of the coin in this study have been cleaned, and so are reasonably bright, but they do not have the mirror-like quality of newly minted coins. Close examination shows signs of wear, pitting, scratches, corrosion and tarnishing of their surface, contributing to the patina, all of which cause some scattering of the reflected rays and diminution of their intensity.

The images of the coin were captured with the lens aperture set to f/8 to achieve a good exposure while minimising overexposure and maximising depth of focus. They were converted from raw (NEF format) files by DCRAW to linear 16-bit per channel (range 0–65535) and stored as TIFF files. Figure 11 (left) shows the intensity distribution by lamp number for a single pixel on Roma's cheek in the coin obverse. There are three peaks where the pixel intensities reach values in the range 3000–4500 but most others are less than 500. The magenta curve shows what the intensities would

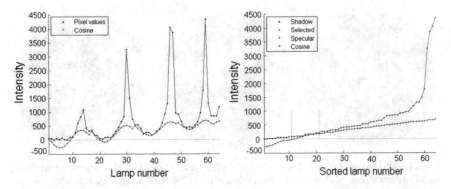

Fig. 11 Intensity distributions for a single pixel: (left) in lamp order; (right) sorted

be for a perfectly matte (Lambertian) surface with the same albedo and normal angle. It is clear that the specular peaks are much greater in intensity than the cosine, but elsewhere they are similar. Thus, the metallic silver surface is similar at most angles to the equivalent matte surface, except for bright highlights at a few angles.

The image processing method is to identify from the sorted intensity distribution a range of values between the shadow and specular regions, which are taken to be representative of the non-specular 'body colour' of the object, illustrated by the sequence of blue dots in Fig. 11 (right). Then using the principle of 'shape from shading', a regression is performed on the corresponding lamp vectors to estimate the most probable direction of the surface normal at that pixel [28]. This 'bounded regression' procedure is actually performed on a 3×3 pixel neighbourhood (9×64 = 576 values in total), taking a weighted sum of the R, G, B channels. The albedo is the magnitude of the normal vector, and its appearance is surprisingly dark and low in contrast (Fig. 12 left), representing the diffuse 'base colour' of the silver. The tarnished (oxidised) regions are much more conspicuous than in the original images (Fig. 8). The surface normal vectors are represented by the standard false-colour encoding scheme with the N_x normal values in red, N_y in green and N_z in blue.

The second stage of processing is to determine the specular vector at each pixel, i.e. the direction of maximum specular reflectance. First the ratio, or specular quotient, is calculated between the actual intensity value and the diffuse component for each lamp. This would be the black value divided by the magenta value for each of the 64 points in Fig. 11 (left). For semi-matte surfaces, the quotient values are typically in the range 0.5–2.5, but for high gloss and shiny metallic surfaces they may be much larger. In this case, the maximum value over the image of the coin is 518, which is indicative of the high dynamic range of the imagery. To facilitate the computation, a compression function is applied to the quotient by a power function with fractional exponent. In this case, an exponent of 0.7 has been used, giving a maximum compressed quotient value of 108. A weighted sum is made of all the normalised lamp vectors above a threshold of 0.2 and within 50° of the normal vector, using the magnitude of the quotient as the weighting factor.

Fig. 12 Albedo and normals of the coin, derived from processing the sets of 64 images

One might suppose that the specular angle should be exactly double that of the normal, as it would be for a perfect mirror surface, but in fact there is a great deal of variation. This is caused not only by noise, but also by the fixed sampling positions of the flash lights on the dome. Moreover granularity and surface imperfections, such as scratches and dust, cause perturbations in the direction of strongest reflectance. The scatter is clear when the specular angle with respect to the Z-axis is plotted against the normal angle for 10,000 points randomly selected throughout the image of coin obverse (Fig. 13 left). Instead of lying along the line of slope 2 they are spread over a wide range of angles, both greater than and less than the normal angle. Plotting the specular angle and normal angle at each pixel along a horizontal section (Fig. 13 right) shows that the two angles are closely correlated, and the specular angle is always greater but somewhat less than double the value of the normal angle and there is a good deal of random variation.

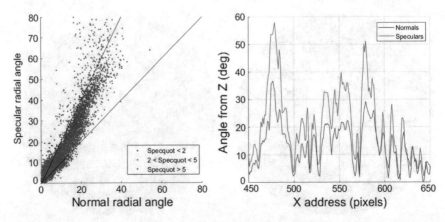

Fig. 13 (left) Specular versus normal angles for 10,000 random pixels in coin obverse; (right) Specular and normal angles for each pixel on a horizontal cross section

The specular colour at each pixel is computed from the colours of the selected specular values, using the same weighting factors derived from the specular quotients. The resulting colours over the image are shown in Fig. 14 (right) and it is apparent that the colour balance is slightly cyanic in the highlights, corresponding to the metallic silver, and orange in the shadows, corresponding to the tarnish. The relationship between the colours can be seen by scatter plotting corresponding values for a random selection of 10,000 points throughout the image area. In Fig. 15, the albedo colours are shown as black dots and the specular colours as red dots in a normalised R, G, B cube. Also shown are lines representing the first principal component of each cluster of points, which tend in slightly different directions. The albedo is below neutral on the blue axis, meaning that it appears yellowish, but the specular is above neutral and therefore more bluish. Note that all images were taken with the Nikon camera as NEF files (raw mode), not auto-white, and that the images were corrected to ensure that equal values of R, G, B would correspond to neutral grey, before the image processing was undertaken. The two principal component vectors in RGB colour space (denoted by the black and red lines in Fig. 15) may be considered as

Fig. 14 Specular components for coin obverse: (left) normals; (centre) quotient; (right) colour

Fig. 15 Scatter plot in RGB
cube of albedo and specular
colours and principal
components

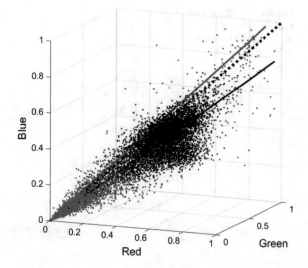

equivalent respectively to the body and interface colours identified by Shafer [29] in
his proposal for a dichromatic model of reflection from a material surface.

5   Specular Modelling

To achieve visual realism, the computer-generated rendering of an object needs to be
plausible. Ideally, it should be identical to a view of the real object from any angle
for a given illumination environment; at least it should give a realistic impression
of a similar object made of the same material. For this purpose the specularity and
sheen are critical. The aim is therefore to model the luminance variation at each
point on the surface of the coin as a function of illumination angle, in such a way
that the reconstructed images are indistinguishable from the original photographs.
This would enable views of the object to be 'relit' for arbitrary illumination angles,
in between those of the lamps in the dome, and for multiple sources of illumination.

A complete model would accommodate the bidirectional reflectance distribution
function (BRDF), with four degrees of freedom, specifying the reflectance of the
surface at any viewpoint when illuminated from any direction. In the case of dome
imaging, however, the viewpoint is fixed with the camera always at the 'north pole'
of the hemisphere and the object lying horizontally in the equatorial plane. So the
problem is simplified to finding a two-dimensional function of the reflectance factor
toward the camera, given the surface normal and lamp vectors. A further simplification is to assume that the function of reflectance is isotropic and therefore rotationally
symmetric, i.e. dependent only on the radial angle ω from the peak but not on the
phase angle φ around the peak. The required function needs to be positive, continuous
and monotonic, with a peak at $\omega = 0$ and asymptotic to zero as $\omega \rightarrow 90°$.

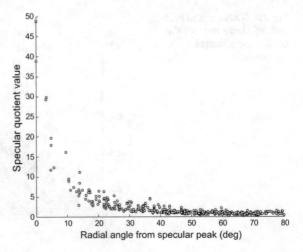

Fig. 16 Distribution of specular quotients in a 3×3 pixel region as a function of radial angle

Plotting the specular quotient values against radial angle ω from the specular peak (Fig. 16) at a single pixel shows the distribution for the metallic surface of the coin, with large values at small angles falling to a 'knee' between 10° and 20° followed by a long tail out to 90°, asymptotic to unity. Analysis of the intensity of the specular peak for various materials in image sets gathered from the UCL dome has suggested that they are best fitted by the Lorentzian function, which has a narrower peak and broader flanks than a Gaussian. The model adopted initially [30] was a sum of two components, a Lorentzian peak and a linear flank, each with two parameters for amplitude and scaling:

$$f(\omega) = \frac{p_a}{1 + (\omega/p_s)^2} + (f_a\omega + f_s), \qquad (1)$$

where $\omega = \text{acosd}(\mathbf{L} \cdot \mathbf{S})$ is the angle in degrees between lamp and specular vectors.

An alternative approach has been developed and is presented here for the first time, namely to model the specular reflectance distribution by a modified Lorentzian function, again in the form of a curved peak plus a linear flank:

$$f(\omega) = \frac{p_a}{1 + (\omega/p_s)^{p_e}} + \left(1 - \frac{\omega}{180}\right) \qquad (2)$$

This distribution is characterised at each pixel in terms of three parameters: p_a is the amplitude, p_s is the scale and p_e is an exponent. The flank is not fitted to the distribution of quotient values, but is assumed to be an invariant cone of value 1 at the apex and 0.5 at 90° from the specular vector. In this model, denoted the 'power Lorentzian', the exponent p_e of the peak term is not a constant value = 2, as for a standard Lorentzian function, but can vary over the range 1–10. The influence of the scale and exponent parameters on the function's shape is shown in Fig. 17. Increasing the scale value p_s reduces the sensitivity to x and causes the curve to be flattened and

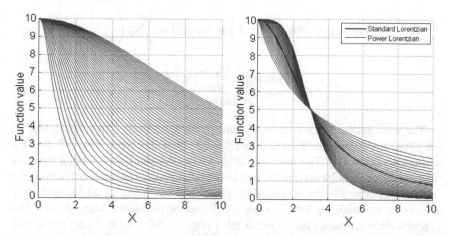

Fig. 17 Influence of two parameters on the power Lorentzian function: (left) scale p_s over range [1, 10] in steps of 0.2, with constant exponent $p_e = 2$; (right) exponent p_e over range [1, 4] in steps of 0.1, with constant scale $p_s = 3$. The red curve is the standard Lorentzian with $p_e = 2$

stretched horizontally (Fig. 17 left); increasing the exponent p_e broadens the peak and reduces the flank (Fig. 17 right).

The peak function of Eq. 2 can be rewritten more compactly as

$$y = \frac{a}{1 + (x/s)^p} \tag{3}$$

and inverted to give

$$\frac{x}{s} = \left(\frac{a}{y} - 1\right)^{1/p} \tag{4}$$

The principle of fitting the peak function to the distribution of specular quotient values at a pixel is to construct the curve through three control points derived from determining the x values corresponding to y values with amplitudes of a_0, a_1 and a_2, as described below. The parameters s and p are then calculated as follows. For the first control point $y_0 = a_0 = a$, the peak amplitude. For the second control point $y_1 = a_1$ and it follows from Eq. 4 that

$$s = x_1 / \left(\frac{a}{a_1} - 1\right)^{1/p} \tag{5}$$

Hence the exponent p can be determined:

$$x_1 / \left(\frac{a}{a_1} - 1\right)^{1/p} = x_2 / \left(\frac{a}{a_2} - 1\right)^{1/p} \tag{6}$$

$$\therefore \log (x_1) - \frac{1}{p}\log \left(\frac{a}{a_1} - 1\right) = \log (x_2) - \frac{1}{p}\log \left(\frac{a}{a_2} - 1\right)$$

$$\therefore p = \frac{\log \left(\frac{a}{a_2} - 1\right) - \log \left(\frac{a}{a_1} - 1\right)}{\log (x_2) - \log (x_1)} \tag{7}$$

The relationship of three control points to the function is illustrated in Fig. 18 for parameter values $a = 10$, $s = 3$ and $p = 2.5$. Note that when $a_1 = a/2$ then $s = x_1$ (independent of p). The radii x_1 and x_2 are determined for each pixel from the distribution of specular quotient values in the polar plane. The angle of the specular vector is translated to the centre of the plane, and the angles of all incident lamp vectors are translated by the same amount. When the procedure is applied to the 64 specular quotient values for a typical pixel (Fig. 19 left), the resulting curve with parameter values $a = 9.7$, $s = 14.5$ and $p = 1.76$ is seen to be a good fit.

To determine the parameter values, Delaunay triangulation is applied to the two-dimensional distribution of points on the polar plane. When plotted as a mesh in 3D, with quotient value on the Z axis, the distribution forms a polyhedral central peak surrounded by an irregular flank (Fig. 19 right). Then a convex hull is fitted at two heights corresponding to 0.5 and 0.2 times the peak amplitude, and the mean radii of these two hulls provide the x values of the control points for fitting the power Lorentzian function (Fig. 18). With one parameter each convex hull is approximated by a circle (shown in red in Fig. 19 right). By extending the fitting to two parameters it could be approximated by an ellipse, and with three parameters by a rotated ellipse.

The fitting procedure can be performed for every pixel individually, but with a maximum of 64 points the distribution is rather sparse, especially for small radial angles near the peak, as shown in Fig. 19 left. More points can be included by fitting to the nine pixels in a 3×3 neighbourhood (Fig. 16), which in effect applies

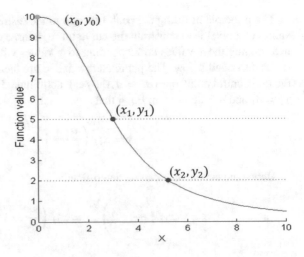

Fig. 18 Three control points for the power Lorentzian function, with $a_1 = a/2$ and $a_2 = a/5$

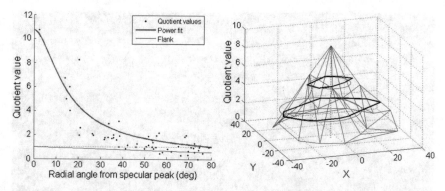

Fig. 19 (left) Lorentzian fitting of specular intensity for one pixel as a function of radial angle; (right) Profile modelled on the polar angle plane, fitting to a 3D Delaunay triangulation

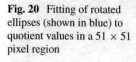

Fig. 20 Fitting of rotated ellipses (shown in blue) to quotient values in a 51 × 51 pixel region

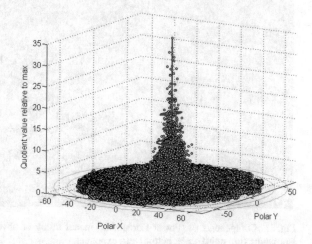

a box smoothing filter to the specular quotient array. For a homogeneous surface, where the surface specularity is constant over an area, the fitting can be performed for a much larger number of points, to give a more accurate characterisation of the reflectance distribution of the surface relative to the specular angle. Figure 20 shows the accumulated quotient values in a 51 × 51 pixel region, plotted in the polar plane relative to the specular angle. This was done by translating the distribution of 64 quotient values at each pixel so that the specular angle lies at the origin of the polar plane. Also shown in Fig. 20 is a series of rotated ellipses fitted to the distribution at amplitudes in 10% steps of the maximum. By separating out the distributions in each range of angles of the incident light, a more complete specular specification may be obtained, essentially two of the four dimensions of the BRDF.

Fitting the set of images of the coin obverse gives the three components of Fig. 21, expressed as images. The amplitude parameter p_a is high in the shiny silver regions and low in the tarnished regions of the coin; the scale p_s and exponent p_s parameters are both high in the dark recessed regions of the coin, and low in the elevated shiny

Fig. 21 Components of 'Power Lorentzian' model fitting of obverse coin image set: (top left) amplitude; (top right) scale; bottom left) exponent; (bottom right) false-colour combination

regions. Combining the three parameters into a false-colour image (p_a in R, p_s in G, p_e in B) indicates the high degree of correlation between the scale and exponent parameters, suggesting that they could be merged into a single parameter.

6   Image Rendering

The complete model for rendering images under a single light source adds the diffuse and specular terms:

$$I = \mathbf{L} \cdot \mathbf{N} A_{rgb} + (f(\omega) - 1) S_{rgb} A_m / S_m \qquad (8)$$

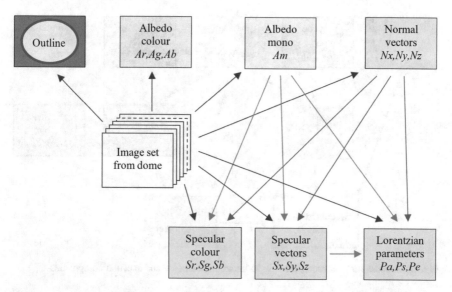

Fig. 22 Process flow for extracting diffuse and specular components from original image set

where A_{rgb} is the albedo colour, S_{rgb} is the specular colour, A_m is the monochrome albedo (weighted sum of the R,G,B channels of A_{rgb}), and S_m is the monochrome specular intensity.

The procedures for analysis and rendering are shown diagrammatically in Figs. 22 and 23, respectively. The diffuse image is characterised by eight coefficients: the albedo colour, normal vectors, monochrome albedo and outline mask. In addition, the specular image is characterised by a further nine coefficients: the specular colour, specular normal vectors and the Lorentzian parameter values. The image rendering process uses the light vector with the sixteen coefficient values for each pixel to reconstruct both diffuse and specular components.

This procedure gives images that are realistic in appearance and a good match to actual photographs. It is important to recognise that the specular reflection is not isolated at the specular peak angle, but extends over a wide range of angles. Without this broad flank in the specular reflectance distribution the rendering would be darker with scattered pinpoint highlights and would not be realistic. Figure 24 juxtaposes the actual photographic image taken in the dome illuminated by lamp 35 (to the northwest at an elevation of approximately 40°) with the images rendered by Eq. 8, based on both the old and new versions of the Lorentzian model (Eqs. 1 and 2). Although not identical, the two modelled images resemble the original photograph in terms of the overall tonality and distribution of highlights. The improvement in realism is remarkable when compared with the simple Lambertian model, where the intensity at each point is simply the product of the albedo and the cosine of the incident light vector with the surface normal. The new power Lorentzian model gives

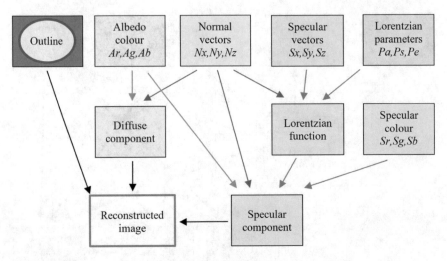

Fig. 23 Process flow for reconstructing an image from diffuse and specular components

a smoother rendering of the surface, compared with the previous cluster Lorentzian model which gives a more granular appearance.

Visual realism may be achieved by careful modelling of the specularity of the surface. Because the specular model is based on a continuous function of angle, images can be rendered for a virtual light source at any position in the hemisphere. Moreover, because the power Lorentzian in Eq. 2 is a continuous function of angle, the object can be rendered with the light at any position in the enclosing hemisphere. This enables an animation to be generated by a series of frames with a scripted trajectory of the coordinates of the lamp as it moves in an arc over the enclosing hemisphere [23].

Thus the colour of the Roman coin can be represented as a sum of two components: a dark slightly orange 'body colour', the albedo corresponding to the diffuse reflectance from the material, plus a bright slightly cyan-tinged highlight with a well-defined angular distribution around the specular peak. A more complete model for metallic surfaces would need to take into account the Fresnel effect, which causes the spectrum of the reflected light to flatten at angles of incidence greater than 70°.

Acknowledgements This research was carried out under the auspices of the European COST Action TD1201 Colour and Space in Cultural Heritage (COSCH). The purpose of the study of Roman coins was to apply a number of techniques to record silver coins, to compare and evaluate the results, and to test methods for 3D visualisation and presentation of multimodal results. Thanks to Dr. Anna Bentkowska for oversight of the research programme and to Prof. Stuart Robson and Dr. Mona Hess for support within UCL. Thanks also to Tom Malzbender for notes about the development of his illumination dome.

Fig. 24 Rendering of coin images illuminated by a single lamp: (top left) photographic image; (top right) power Lorentzian model; (bottom left) previous cluster Lorentzian model; (bottom right) Lambertian model

References

1. Holtorf, C.: On pastness: a reconsideration of materiality in archaeological object authenticity. Anthropol. Q. **86**(2), 427–443 (2013)
2. MacDonald, L.W.: Colour image engineering for multimedia systems. Ch. 11 In: MacDonald, L.W., Luo, M.R. (eds.) Colour Imaging: Vision and Technology, pp. 191–214. Wiley, Chichester (1999)
3. Hunt, R.W.G.: The Reproduction of Colour, 6th edn., pp. 163–179. Wiley, Chichester (2004)
4. MacDonald, L.W., Morovič, J., Saunders, D.: Evaluation of colour fidelity for reproductions of fine art paintings. Museum Manage. Curatorship **14**(3), 253–281 (1995)
5. Yendrikhovskij, S., MacDonald, L.W., Bech, S., Jensen, K.: Enhancing colour image quality in television displays. Imaging Sci. J. **47**(4), 197–211 (1999)
6. Schanda, J.: Colorimetry: Understanding the CIE System, pp. 30–33. Wiley, Hoboken, NJ (2007)

7. MacDonald L.W., Westland S., Shaw J.: Colour image reproduction: spectral versus spatial. In: Proceedings of the International Symposium on Multispectral Imaging and Color Reproduction for Digital Archives, pp. 81–91. Chiba University, Japan (1999)
8. Saunders, D., Cupitt, J., Padfield, J.: Digital imaging of easel paintings, Ch. 19. In: MacDonald, L.W. (ed.) Digital Heritage: Applying Digital Imaging to Cultural Heritage, pp. 521–548. Elsevier, Oxford (2006)
9. Howgego, C.J.: The potential for image analysis in numismatics, Ch. 11. In: Bowman, A.K., Brady, M. (eds.) Images and Artefacts of the Ancient World, pp. 109–113. British Academy, London (2005)
10. Hoberman, G.: The Art of Coins and Their Photography, pp. 340–342. Lund Humphries, London (1981)
11. Hawkins A., Avon, D.: Photography: The Guide to Technique, pp. 229–231. Blandford Press, Poole (1979)
12. Goodman, M.: Numismatic Photography, 2nd edn., pp. 49–54. Zyrus Press, Irvine, CA (2009)
13. Sakane, S., Sato, T.: Automatic planning of light source and camera placement for an active photometric stereo system. In: Proceedings of the IEEE Conference on Robotics and Automation, pp. 1080–1087 (1991)
14. Coleman, E.N., Jain, R.: Obtaining 3-dimensional shape of textured and specular surfaces using four-source photometry. Comput. Graph. Image Process. **18**(4), 309–328 (1982)
15. Bernardini, F., Rushmeier, H.E.: The 3D model acquisition pipeline. Comput. Graph. Forum **21**(2), 149–172 (2002)
16. Koch, K.P., Prinz, R.: Illuminating arrangement for illuminating an object with incident light. US Patent 5,038,258. Carl-Zeiss-Stiftung (1991)
17. Tait, R.W., Lewin, A.D., DeYong, M.R.: Light array system and method for illumination of objects imaged by imaging systems. US Patent 6,161,941. Intelligent Reasoning Systems Inc. (2000)
18. Malzbender, T., Gelb, D., Wolters, H.: Polynomial texture maps. Proc. ACM Siggraph **28**, 519–528 (2001)
19. Mudge, M., Voutaz, J.-P., Schroer, C., Lum, M.: Reflection transformation imaging and virtual representations of coins from the hospice of the grand St. Bernard. In: Proceedings of the 6th International Symposium on Virtual Reality, Archaeology and Cultural Heritage (VAST), pp. 29–39, Pisa, Italy (2005)
20. Palma, G., Siotto, E., Proesmans, M., Baldassari, M., Baracchini, C.. Batino, S., Scopigno R.: Telling the story of ancient coins by means of interactive RTI images. In: Proceedings of the Conference on Computer Applications and Quantitative Methods in Archaeology (CAA), pp. 177–185. Southampton (2012)
21. MacDonald, L.W., Hosseininaveh Ahmadabadian, A., Robson, S.: Determining the coordinates of lamps in an illumination dome. In: Proceedings of the SPIE Conference on Videometrics, Range Imaging, and Applications XIII, SPIE vol. 9528–18, Munich, June (2015)
22. MacDonald, L.W., Robson, S.: Polynomial texture mapping and 3D representation. In: Proceedings of the ISPRS Conferece on Close-Range Image Measurement Techniques, Newcastle, UK (2010)
23. MacDonald, L.W., Hindmarch, J., Robson, S., Terras, M.: Modelling the appearance of heritage metallic surfaces. In: Proceedings of the ISPRS Conference on Close-Range Photogrammetry, Riva, Italy (2014)
24. MacDonald, L.W., Moitinho de Almeida, V., Hess, M.: Three-dimensional reconstruction of Roman coins from photometric image sets. J. Electron. Imaging **26**(1) (2017)
25. http://youtu.be/byN7n7MPSAc, www.youtube.com/watch?v=7EFudYrrZM4
26. Portable Antiquities Scheme (PAS). http://finds.org.uk/database/artefacts/record/id/142280
27. Baker, R.: The countermarks found on Ancient Roman Coins: a brief introduction. ACTA ACCLA. Retrieved from http://www.accla.org/actaaccla/baker2.html, Aug (2004)
28. MacDonald, L.W.: Representation of cultural objects by image sets with directional illumination. In: Proceedings of the 5th Computational Color Imaging Workshop (CCIW). LNCS, St. Etienne, France, Mar 2015, vol. 9016, pp. 43–56. Springer, Heidelberg (2015)

29. Shafer, S.A.: Using color to separate reflection components. Color Res. Appl. **10**(4), 210–218 (1985)
30. MacDonald, L.W.: Colour and directionality in surface reflectance. In: Proceedings of the Artificial Intelligence and the Simulation of Behaviour (AISB). Goldsmiths College, London (2014)

EpiX: A 3D Measurement Tool for Heritage, Archeology, and Aerial Photogrammetry

Shizeng Yao, Hang Yu, Hadi AliAkbarpour, Guna Seetharaman and Kannappan Palaniappan

1 Introduction

With the advent of affordable imaging devices and efficient processing algorithms, the use of images as the main investigation tools has become very popular even outside scientific communities [1]. Cultural heritage is no exception to this developing phenomenon. Cultural heritage is a broad concept that covers a diverse legacy passed down from previous generation, and it is always at risk of perishing due to time, natural phenomena, or terrorist attacks [2]. To preserve this precious digital information, many groups have developed three-dimensional (3D) or four-dimensional (4D) reconstruction applications [3–5]. However to successfully apply those applications, it is required to have accurate 3D location of salient features of objects from sequential images, and precise metadata for multiple camera views are extremely important information. In most important computer vision tasks including Structure from Motion (SfM), 3D reconstruction, and multi-target tracking, precise metadata is of critical value as the observed imagery itself [6]. Currently, the task of generating the ground truth for targets in sequential image datasets is performed manually using electronic pen or mouse to roughly click on data images or achieved using certain basic annotation tool [7], which may consume a large amount of time. It is inherently difficult and expensive to execute a ground-truthing process on a large collection of

S. Yao (✉) · H. Yu (✉) · H. AliAkbarpour (✉) · K. Palaniappan (✉)
Department of Electrical Engineering and Computer Science,
University of Missouri, Columbia, MO 65211, USA
e-mail: syyh4@mail.missouri.edu

H. Yu
e-mail: hy2vf@mail.missouri.edu

H. AliAkbarpour
e-mail: aliakbarpourh@missouri.edu

K. Palaniappan
e-mail: palaniappank@missouri.edu

G. Seetharaman (✉)
US Naval Research Laboratory, Washington D.C., USA
e-mail: guna.seetharaman@nrl.navy.mil

© Springer Nature Singapore Pte Ltd. 2018
B. Chanda et al. (eds.), *Heritage Preservation*,
https://doi.org/10.1007/978-981-10-7221-5_3

aerial wide-area motion imagery, WAMI. Several practical issues, for example, the subjective nature of GUI based tagging, parasitic inaccuracies in the GPS (location) and IMU (orientation) measurements, and lack of up to date baseline GIS data—all compound the challenge.

EpiX is a cross-platform measurement application that helps researchers to conduct such tasks in a very short amount of time by creatively utilizing computer vision theories. There are three embedded functions in EpiX: ground truth collecting, Euclidean epipolar error measurement, three-dimensional distance measurement, and one on-developing function: automatic feature tracking and error measurement for camera parameters. Each of the four functions help with a specific problem in WAMI.

Related Works Several annotation tools for similar purposes have been exclusively designed and developed for certain specific applications. VpView [8] was developed by Kitware Inc. to visualize and analyze threat detection in wide-area motion imagery and it allows users to click on certain location on the image to mark and collect one single ground truth point per click. It is simple and effective especially for short image sequences with lower image resolution, but it consumes huge amount of time if applied on long image sequences with wide-area motion imagery since it cannot adopt any information from previous images and thus researchers have to keep changing image scale to find the exact same feature point location.

LabelMe developed by Russel et al. [9] is a WEB-based image annotation tool that allows researchers to label images and share the annotation with the world. It is simple and lightweight, sufficient for image annotation, but again it is not suitable for WAMI since it was designed for small objects labeling and not effective for wide-area motion imagery. A outdoor field annotation tool designed by Eren and Balcisoy [7] is another image annotation tool for outdoor field works. It provides a novel annotation technique based on three-dimensional geometric regions and a fast modeling workflow based on building blocks to allow researchers to create models based on images. Though it is effective and sufficient in modeling area, for collecting ground truth purpose, it is not efficient enough.

In this paper, we focus on the application of EpiX and the computer vision theories behind each function. The rest of this paper is organized as follows: Sect. 2 introduces the problem statement that researchers are facing to. Section 3 presents the 3D computer vision theories behind EpiX, including three-dimensional Epipolar Geometry and Bundle Adjustment. Section 4 presents the three embedded functions in EpiX and corresponding experimental results. The on-developing function is given in Sect. 5 and Sect. 6 concludes the paper with some future work.

2   Problem Statement

Megapixel-sized images have become much more prevalent over the past decade in a variety of domains including medicine, space, satellite, and defense. Consequently, the need of accurate ground truth and precise metadata for computer vision tasks on megapixel-sized image, such as accuracy evaluation of object tracking in WAMI, large city-scale 3D reconstruction, has been a critical demand of research.

Right now collection of ground truth for megapixel-sized image is performed manually or based on certain basic annotation tool. To label ground truth for WAMI, researchers have to keep adjusting image scale, changing from different regions of focus, searching for the same target, and distinguishing the target from distractors for each individual frame through the whole sequence, which may take a huge amount of time, due to large object displacements caused by low frame rate sampling, massive contents due to wide-area coverage and substantial repetitive texture. In EpiX, users only need to label two initial ground truth points, and then EpiX will help them to autofocus on the region of interest for all rest of the frames within the sequence with the same image scale, utilizing epipolar geometry. In this case, user does not need to spend long time in finding the same region, same image scale, and same ground truth point along thousands of frames in a sequence. In our experiment, users only need 2 s on average to label one ground truth point using EpiX, while they spend almost 10 s on average using other tools, like VpView [8].

The second problem many researchers are facing is, when received megapixel-sized images with corresponding camera metadata, such as camera intrinsic and extrinsic parameters, longitude/latitude information, and focal length information, there is no intuitive way to evaluate whether the metadata is valid or not. Using invalid metadata may cause critical problems, such as failure in 3D reconstruction, and failure in Bundle Adjustment. Using EpiX, researchers could be able to evaluate the camera metadata very efficiently and intuitively based on Euclidean error measurement function.

Distance information is very important for most of the outdoor field works, such as photogrammetry or geographic surveying. Currently, those information can be only achieved by manually measured in actual location. Imagine a rescue excavations for urban archeology is taking place: there is limited time and manpower before construction work starts and traditional techniques do not suffice. While with EpiX, researchers could achieve 3D distance information very quickly be using the 3D distance measurement function. This function is based on the triangulation theory [10], and able to calculate the real 3D distance without reaching the actual location, which is much more convenient for researchers.

Each annotation tool has its strengths, some creates better visualization [8], and some may emphasize on smart device use [9]. To best of our knowledge, EpiX is the most efficient annotation tool for the three tasks above. We are also developing more features for EpiX, and the new use of EpiX would support more useful tools for management of WAMI data.

3   Epipolar-Based Annotation Tool

The main 3D computer vision theory behind EpiX is 3D Epipolar Geometry, which is creatively utilized to expedite the process of ground truth collection, error measurement, and 3D distance measurement. Given a pair of images of a static scene

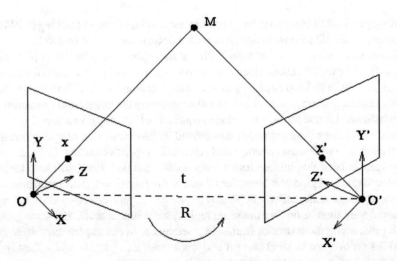

Fig. 1 The Euclidean relationship between the two view-centered coordinate systems. Given **x** in one image and the metadata of the imaging instance, the location of **x** is constrained to the line uniquely characterized by **x**. Thus, if a user interactively picks **x**, then, a smart GUI will cue the selection of **x'** by drawing the epipolar line instantiated by **x**

acquired from two distinct locations, and the observed location of an object point in one image, its corresponding position in the second image is constrained to a line, based on a well-known result called the *epipolar lines*. It is specified by a matrix called the *fundamental matrix*. By computing the fundamental matrix between two images, one can analyze the three-dimensional structure of the scene [11].

As can be seen in Fig. 1, two cameras are looking at the same 3D point from two different views. Epipolar geometry is about the intrinsic projective geometry between two views. More concretely, it describes the geometric relations between the three-dimensional points and their projections onto the two-dimensional images, and also the geometric relations between the projected two-dimensional points themselves. Our purpose of using epipolar geometry is to find the corresponding points among images of the same scene but different views, and we will explain this geometric theory closely regarding to this objective.

Point Correspondence The first principle of epipolar geometry is triangulation. Given a single image, the three-dimensional location of any visible object point must lie on the straight line that passes through the center of projection and the image of the object point. The determination of the intersection of two such lines generated from two independent images is called triangulation.

Clearly, the determination of the scene position of an object point through triangulation depends upon matching the image location of the object point in one image to the location of the same object point in the other image. The process of establishing such matches between points in a pair of images is called correspondence.

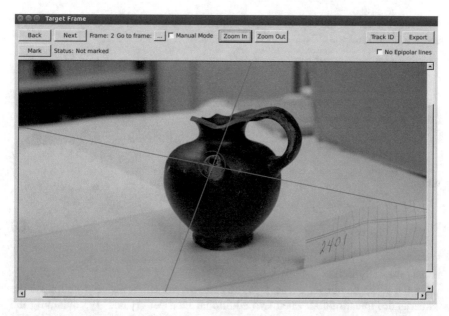

Fig. 2 Multiple epipolar lines intersect on target frame: target frame is the second frame in data sequence, epipolar lines computed from frame 1 and frame 10 are marked in blue, correspondence (intersection of two epipolar lines) is marked by a red circle

At first it might seem that correspondence requires a search through the whole image, but the epipolar constraint reduces this search to a single line. To see this, we consider Fig. 1 again.

The epipole is the intersection of the line and image plane. Thus the epipole is the image, in one camera, of the optical center of the other camera. The epipolar plane is the plane defined by a three-dimensional point M and the optical centers O and O'. The epipolar line is the straight line of intersection of the epipolar plane with the image plane. It is the image in one camera of a ray through the optical center and image point in the other camera. All epipolar lines intersect at the epipole.

Thus, a point **x** in one image generates a line in the other on which its corresponding point **x'** must lie. We see that the search for correspondences is thus reduced from a region to a line. This property affords huge help to researchers in finding correspondences since we could draw multiple epipolar lines on the target frame based on initial reference frames and due to the constrain, all the lines should intersect on the same point, which is the correspondence on current frame. This is illustrated in Fig. 2.

To calculate depth information from a pair of images, we need to compute the epipolar geometry. In the calibrated environment, we capture this geometric constraint in an algebraic representation known as the essential matrix. In the uncalibrated environment, it is captured in the fundamental matrix.

With two views, the two camera coordinate systems are related by a rotation R and a translation t:

$$x' = Rx + t \tag{1}$$

Since in Fig. 1 we could observe that $\mathbf{Ox}$, $\mathbf{O'x'}$, and $\mathbf{OO'}$ are coplanar, this relationship can be written as

$$x'^T E x = 0 \tag{2}$$

where

$$E = \begin{bmatrix} 0 & -t_Z & t_Y \\ t_Z & 0 & -t_X \\ -t_Y & t_X & 0 \end{bmatrix} \cdot R \tag{3}$$

is the essential matrix.

In the example above, we assume the cameras are calibrated. Now suppose the cameras are uncalibrated. Then two additional matrices A_1 and A_2 containing the internal parameters of the two cameras are needed to transform the normalized coordinates into pixel coordinates:

$$\begin{aligned} \bar{x} &= A_1 x \\ \bar{x}' &= A_2 x' \end{aligned} \tag{4}$$

This yields the following equation based on Eq. 2:

$$\bar{x}'^T F \bar{x} = 0, \tag{5}$$

where $F = A_2^{-T} E A_1^{-1}$ is the more recently discovered Fundamental matrix.

In EpiX, due to the uncalibrated cameras, fundamental matrix is what we used to compute corresponding epipolar lines. Although we have illustrated the epipolar lines could help to find correspondence on target frame, we have not introduced how to compute a epipolar line from a known point, and the following part will explain this concept.

Given a point m_1 that has coordinates (u_1, v_1) in the reference frame, based on the fundamental constrains we just presented, its correspondence m with coordinates (u, v) and the fundamental matrix are related by

$$(u \ v \ 1) \, F \begin{pmatrix} u_1 \\ v_1 \\ 1 \end{pmatrix} = 0, \tag{6}$$

where u_1, v_1 and F are known entities, u and v are unknown variables. After solving Eq. 6, we could get a relationship between u and v for correspondence m, which is the equation of a line in the second target plane. It is the epipolar line on which correspondence must lie.

EpiX uses the formula above to compute the epipolar lines lying on target frame based on the locations of preselected ground truth points on two reference frames, and recognizes the intersection as the correspondence.

4 Experiments

Quantitative evaluation in both wide-area motion imagery and cultural heritage dataset is a challenging task. A dataset may contain up to tens of thousands of images with megapixel resolution, making it extremely difficult to collect ground truth for such dataset. EpiX is an effective GUI application that helps researchers to conduct such tasks in a very short amount of time by creatively utilizing computer vision theories. There are three embedded main functions in EpiX, Ground Truth Collection, Euclidean Epipolar Error Measurement, and 3D Distance Measurement. Each of the three functions helps with a specific problem in WAMI. In this chapter, we will review each of those functions in details and show some experimental results for each of them (Fig. 3).

We applied EpiX on three datasets, including two WAMI datasets: Louisiana dataset and Albuquerque dataset, and one cultural heritage dataset: Roman pottery dataset.

The sample aerial WAMI data were collected (by Transparent Sky [12]) using an aircraft with onboard pose sensors flying over five different urban areas including downtown Albuquerque, NM. Images with resolution 6600 * 4400 are taken consecutively between a very short time interval. During one flight, the number of images taken can go up to a few thousand frames.

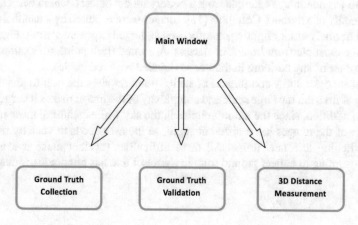

Fig. 3 Structure of EpiX

Fig. 4 Roman pottery dataset, serial number: 2401

The reason we chose the two WAMI datasets, especially Louisiana dataset was because the island, lsle de Jean Charles, Louisiana, is disappearing, due to rising sea levels. The coastal island has lost 98% of its land since 1955 and right now a football field of land, on average, falls into the Gulf each hour. The latest scientific evidence suggests seas could rise 2 m by the end of the century, which could drown this entire island into the Pacific. To reserve the precious heritage information, we applied our experiments on Louisiana dataset.

Figure 4 is one image example from a pottery model dataset, which was captured by University of Missouri, Columbia [13]. Images were captured by a handheld camera with normal outdoor lighting, autofocused and fixed exposure setting. Figure 5 is one image example from Louisiana dataset. A ground truth point, for example, can be the corner of any building in the image (labeled with red circle).

To locate the x and y coordinates of such a point requires the user to identify the building at first, but the large scale and complexity of the image makes it very hard to do so. In addition, since the aircraft circles in the sky while capturing these images, each one of the images has a different angle, so the user needs to visually re-adapt after switching to a new frame. All these difficulties together make it extremely time-consuming to collect ground truth in a dataset that has hundreds of images.

Fig. 5 Louisiana dataset—WAMI imagery of Jean Charles Island, recently identified to be in eminent danger of ocean warming [14]. Upper left image is the original image, and a region of interest is marked with a red rectangle. Upper right, bottom left, and bottom right images are zoomed-in subregions from original image. A ground truth point can be the corner of a house, marked with red circle in bottom left image

4.1 Autofocusing with EpiX

As we mentioned in this chapter, in EpiX, epipolar geometry is creatively utilized to expedite the process of ground truth collection, and each fundamental matrix between each pair of images in used to calculate the epipolar line in the target image from a reference image.

Utilizing Epipolar Lines for Autofocusing Function The idea of autofocusing is to use two images to generate epipolar lines on the rest of the images in the entire dataset, the two intersecting lines will visually guide the user to the target point, and the intersection of the two lines will serve as the pre-calculated ground truth point. According to epipolar geometry, any of the two frames can be used to generate the guiding lines, however, in practice, it is better to use two frames that are taken at two very different time points during the flight so that the two epipolar lines will intersect at a larger angle. In this way, it is easier for the user to observe the intersection point.

Epix was programmed to calculate which frames are the first and the middle frames when the user load the dataset into memory, and put those two frames to the control board. The example below is our Albuquerque, New Mexico dataset. It has 215 frames, so frame 1 and frame 108 are chosen to be the reference frames. The user need to manually mark the ground truth point on frame 1 and frame 108, and

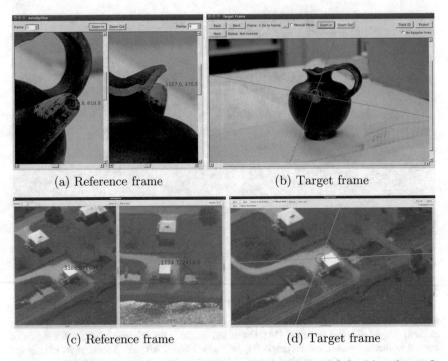

(a) Reference frame   (b) Target frame

(c) Reference frame   (d) Target frame

Fig. 6 Autofocusing function Interface, **a** and **b**: pottery dataset, **c** and **d**: Louisiana dataset. In reference frames (**a**) and (**c**), two corresponding ground truth points are marked with red dots and locations. In target frames (**b**) and (**d**), two computed epipolar lines are shown in blue, and correspondence is marked with red circle

Epix will use this information to generate epipolar lines on the rest of the images. As shown in the figure below, when switching to a new frame, the intersection of two lines marks the target point, and the view is zoomed to a reasonable degree. If the user agrees with the automatically marked point, he can directly click the Next Frame button, and the coordinates of the automatically marked point will be saved as the result. And, of course, if the user is not satisfied with it, he can always manually correct the location.

In addition, when switching from the current frame to another one, EpiX calculates the difference between the coordinates of the two target points, and translates the view-port so that the interest area will always stay in the middle. In this way, the user only spends a few seconds on each frames, and the overall execution time will be largely reduced by hours.

Figure 6 shows an example of utilizing epipolar lines for autofocusing function. Two red points on left image represent two preselected corresponding ground truth points, which are matched to each other, on frame 1 and middle frame of whole image sequence, separately (see Fig. 6a, c). Then based on those preselected two points pixel coordinate information and corresponding camera parameters, EpiX is

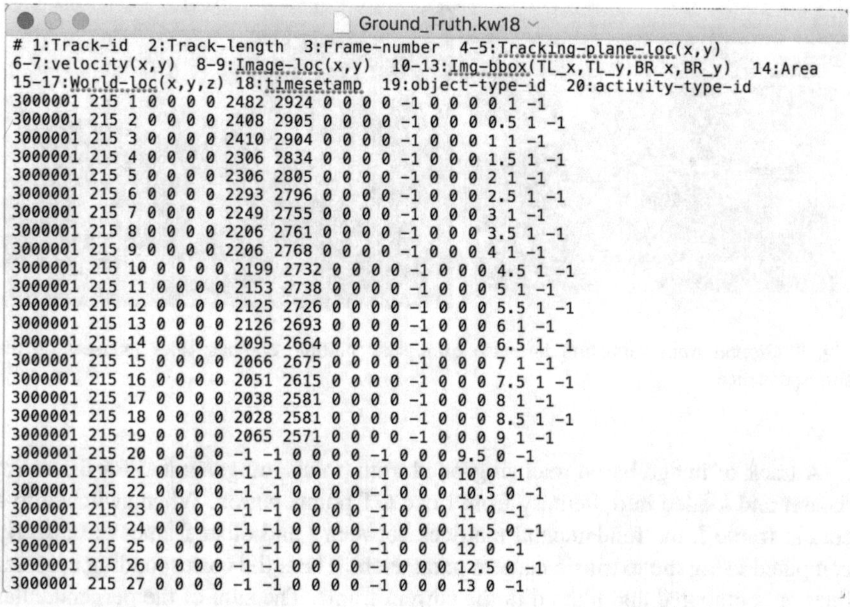

```
●  ●  ●                    📄 Ground_Truth.kw18 ⌄
# 1:Track-id  2:Track-length  3:Frame-number  4-5:Tracking-plane-loc(x,y)
6-7:velocity(x,y)  8-9:Image-loc(x,y)  10-13:Img-bbox(TL_x,TL_y,BR_x,BR_y)  14:Area
15-17:World-loc(x,y,z) 18:timesetamp  19:object-type-id  20:activity-type-id
3000001 215 1 0 0 0 0 2482 2924 0 0 0 0 -1 0 0 0 0 1 -1
3000001 215 2 0 0 0 0 2408 2905 0 0 0 0 -1 0 0 0 0.5 1 -1
3000001 215 3 0 0 0 0 2410 2904 0 0 0 0 -1 0 0 0 1 1 -1
3000001 215 4 0 0 0 0 2306 2834 0 0 0 0 -1 0 0 0 1.5 1 -1
3000001 215 5 0 0 0 0 2306 2805 0 0 0 0 -1 0 0 0 2 1 -1
3000001 215 6 0 0 0 0 2293 2796 0 0 0 0 -1 0 0 0 2.5 1 -1
3000001 215 7 0 0 0 0 2249 2755 0 0 0 0 -1 0 0 0 3 1 -1
3000001 215 8 0 0 0 0 2206 2761 0 0 0 0 -1 0 0 0 3.5 1 -1
3000001 215 9 0 0 0 0 2206 2768 0 0 0 0 -1 0 0 0 4 1 -1
3000001 215 10 0 0 0 0 2199 2732 0 0 0 0 -1 0 0 0 4.5 1 -1
3000001 215 11 0 0 0 0 2153 2738 0 0 0 0 -1 0 0 0 5 1 -1
3000001 215 12 0 0 0 0 2125 2726 0 0 0 0 -1 0 0 0 5.5 1 -1
3000001 215 13 0 0 0 0 2126 2693 0 0 0 0 -1 0 0 0 6 1 -1
3000001 215 14 0 0 0 0 2095 2664 0 0 0 0 -1 0 0 0 6.5 1 -1
3000001 215 15 0 0 0 0 2066 2675 0 0 0 0 -1 0 0 0 7 1 -1
3000001 215 16 0 0 0 0 2051 2615 0 0 0 0 -1 0 0 0 7.5 1 -1
3000001 215 17 0 0 0 0 2038 2581 0 0 0 0 -1 0 0 0 8 1 -1
3000001 215 18 0 0 0 0 2028 2581 0 0 0 0 -1 0 0 0 8.5 1 -1
3000001 215 19 0 0 0 0 2065 2571 0 0 0 0 -1 0 0 0 9 1 -1
3000001 215 20 0 0 0 0 -1 -1 0 0 0 0 -1 0 0 0 9.5 0 -1
3000001 215 21 0 0 0 0 -1 -1 0 0 0 0 -1 0 0 0 10 0 -1
3000001 215 22 0 0 0 0 -1 -1 0 0 0 0 -1 0 0 0 10.5 0 -1
3000001 215 23 0 0 0 0 -1 -1 0 0 0 0 -1 0 0 0 11 0 -1
3000001 215 24 0 0 0 0 -1 -1 0 0 0 0 -1 0 0 0 11.5 0 -1
3000001 215 25 0 0 0 0 -1 -1 0 0 0 0 -1 0 0 0 12 0 -1
3000001 215 26 0 0 0 0 -1 -1 0 0 0 0 -1 0 0 0 12.5 0 -1
3000001 215 27 0 0 0 0 -1 -1 0 0 0 0 -1 0 0 0 13 0 -1
```

Fig. 7 Example of a kw18 file

able to compute and indicate the two corresponding epipolar lines on target frame, which is frame 2 in this example. The intersection of those two epipolar lines, marked be a red circle on right image, is the estimated matched ground truth point and marked automatically with a green cycle (see Fig. 6b, d).

Export Collected Data EpiX exports collected ground truth data into kw18 format [15], which is defined by Kitware Inc. Fields name of the format can be modified according to need meanwhile the number of columns should remains the same so that the file can be read by all the other software from Kitware Inc. In EpiX, the most important data recorded in the file are the coordinates of the ground truth points (Fig. 7).

4.2 Euclidean Epipolar Error Measurement

In aerial WAMI, the fast Bundle Adjustment for Sequential imagery (BA4S) pipeline [16] is used for refinement of noisy camera metadata measurements available from IMU and GPS sensors. Re-projection error is commonly used for the evaluation of such systems, however, its not an appropriate measure for BA4S since outliers, in this case, have not been not eliminated. In Epix we introduce a pixel-based error measure called Euclidean Epipolar Error (EEE) [17] to evaluate the quality of refined camera parameters.

(a)   **(b)**

Fig. 8 Ground truth validation interface examples: multiple epipolar lines intersect on the correspondence

A track of image-based manual ground truth points are generated for the entire dataset and loaded into memory from Load GT points button. When switched to a certain frame l, the fundamental matrices between l and other frames are directly computed using the extrinsic camera parameters. Then, the corresponding epipolar lines are computed and plotted in the current frame. The sum of the perpendicular Euclidean distances between each epipolar lines and the ground truth point of the current frame divided by the number of frames is the error measurement, and it is displayed on the current frame near the ground truth point. Two examples of ground truth validation can be found in Fig. 8a, b.

4.3 3D Distance Measurement

Another useful function in EpiX is distance measurement. This function recovers distance information between points in 3D space.

Same as the previous functions in EpiX, after loading metadata into the program memory for the target dataset, the user can open the control panel to begin operation. Our distance measurement is based on the triangulation function in OpenCV. This function reconstructs the 3D coordinates of a point by using its observations with two cameras under stereo setting [18]. Even though our aerial images are not taken with stereo cameras, we have the camera pose information when each image was taken, so it can be treat as equivalent.

Multi-pair Measurement As shown in Fig. 9a, b, two images in the dataset are presented to the user from the left to the right on the control panel, and all the user have to do it to use the mouse to mark the target points in both of the images. Multiple pair of points can be measured at the same time as shown below. Each pair will be connected by by red lines, and the points are marked with numbers so there is no visual confusion. The results are shown on the right side of the control panel, including the XYZ coordinates of the points and the distances. They can be shown

Fig. 9 Multi-pair measurement interface: 3 measurements in **a** pottery dataset, and **b** Louisiana dataset. Each measurement is marked in red line segment together with two endpoints, one in green and one in blue. Each pair of points in two images with the same label are matched feature points. Distance for each line segment is displayed on the right side

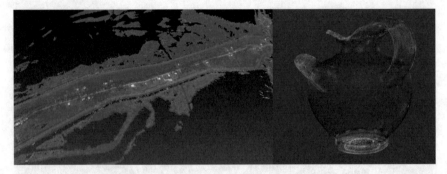

Fig. 10 3D reconstruction results for Louisiana dataset (left), and pottery dataset (right). BA4S [19] + PMVS [20] were applied on images together with precise metadata

in either imperial unit or metric unit. The user is given the freedom to switch each of the two images among the dataset because the target points might not be visible from certain angles. When occlusion occurs, user could switch any other image to perform the distance measurement.

4.4 3D Reconstruction Results Using Metadata

In Fig. 10, we showed three 3D reconstruction results for all three datasets: Albuquerque, Louisiana, and Elan using BA4S [19] + PMVS [20].

5 Automatic Feature Tracking, Camera Metadata Validation, and Error Measurement

Unlike what we have mentioned in Sect. 4.3, Euclidean epipolar error measurement, which is only able to show the epipolar error intuitively to users, now we are developing a new function for EpiX: automatic feature tracking and error measurement for camera parameters. This function allows users to track the same feature point along whole sequential images automatically using different feature detectors and feature descriptors and compute errors based on known ground truth for evaluation. Also it could be applied to check the accuracy of camera parameters before/after Bundle Adjustment for further use.

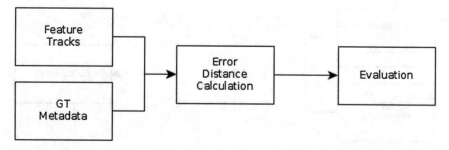

Fig. 11 Feature evaluation metrics

5.1 Automatic Feature Tracking and Evaluation

Many feature detectors and descriptors were exclusively designed for a specific application [21]. Their performances can be greatly affected by input data. It is most unlikely that one feature detector combined with one descriptor will outperform the others in all applications. Additionally, precise feature detection and matching are crucial for SfM and 3D reconstruction, so it is important to find a detector–descriptor combination that performs well for this application.

The on-developing function in EpiX could adopt different combinations of different feature detectors, such as Features from Accelerated Segment Test (FAST) [22], Scale-Invariant Feature Transform (SIFT) [23], Speeded Up Robust Features (SURF) [24], and Binary Robust Invariant Scalable Keypoints (BRISK) [25], and different feature descriptors, such as SIFT, SURF, and BRISK to evaluate and compare for SfM and bundle adjustment.

Workflow We use the pixel distance to measure errors in each correspondence (match pair) in the dataset (see Fig. 11) for features. The feature extraction methods were run on an aerial imagery dataset, WAMI, over Albuquerque downtown. After feature extraction, each extracted feature point was compared with corresponding known ground truth point and the pixel distance between two points were used as an error metric.

Evaluation Refer to our another paper [19], we were able to evaluate performance for different combinations of feature detectors and feature descriptors for further use.

5.2 Camera Metadata Validation and Error Measurement

Many image datasets were collected without useful camera metadata, and researchers have to apply SfM algorithm to roughly estimate it. Even some datasets came along with camera metadata, those metadata may be invalid or not accurate enough for 3D reconstruction or other purpose. Due to those reasons, we also apply another function in EpiX, which is camera metadata validation and error measurement.

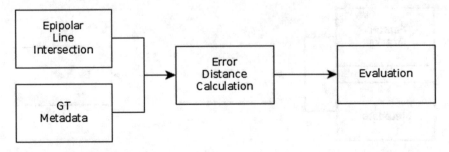

Fig. 12 Camera metadata validation

Workflow The workflow of this function is similar to automatic feature tracking and evaluation but with little difference (see Fig. 12). In this function, the feature point was selected at the beginning frame and middle frame in the sequence, then in each of the rest frames, the epipolar lines were calculated and the intersection point was computed. Then, the pixel distance between two points was used as an error metric.

This approach could be applied before Bundle Adjustment for camera metadata validation, and it could be used after Bundle Adjustment as well for evaluating the accuracy of results from SfM algorithm.

6   Conclusion and Future Work

EpiX is demonstrated to be a flexible annotation tool for exploratory analysis of cultural heritage dataset since it provides multiple effective and efficient functions for several specific tasks. Especially before applying 3D reconstruction for certain heritage, EpiX could quickly help users to obtain accurate metadata and useful length information. More concretely, the autofocusing function using epipolar geometry dramatically reduces the time needed for ground truth collection. The Euclidean epipolar error measurement function could intuitively indicate whether camera metadata is valid and accurate or not. The 3D length measurement function enables users to measure the height or length of certain heritage very precisely, even if the length they attempt to measure is not possible in practice. The fourth on-developing function already allows users to calculate the error for feature detecting, matching, and tracking. All the above functions could allow users to obtain useful information about certain heritage in a much shorted amount of time compared with current common techniques. Future improvements include full support for camera metadata validation and error measurement function, deploying SfM and Bundle Adjustment into EpiX, and applying more methods/algorithms for error measurement. A new use of EpiX would also support more useful tools for summarization and management of cultural heritage data.

Appendix

EpiX is not only a powerful and flexible annotation tool for cultural heritage dataset, but also every effective and efficient tool for large WAMI data. In appendix, we will demonstrate some of our results for WAMI dataset.

Figure 13 is one image example from Albuquerque dataset. A ground truth point is marked by a red circle.

Figure 14 demonstrates the autofocusing function on WAMI dataset.

Figure 15 shows the distance measurement interface on Albuquerque dataset.

Fig. 13 One image example from Albuquerque dataset

Fig. 14 Multiple epipolar lines intersect on Albuquerque image: target frame is the second frame in data sequence, computed epipolar lines from frame 1 and frame 108 are marked in blue, correspondence (intersection of two epipolar lines) is marked by a red circle

Fig. 15 Multi-pair measurement interface: 5 measurements in Albuquerque dataset. Each measurement is marked in red line segment together with two endpoints, one in green and one in blue. Each pair of points in two images with the same label is matched feature points. Distance for each line segment is displayed on the right side

References

1. Chetouani, A., Erdmann, R., Picard, D., Stanco, F.: Special section guest editorial: image processing for cultural heritage. J. Electron. Imaging **26**(1), 011001 (2017). https://doi.org/10.1117/1.JEI.26.1.011001
2. Younes, G., Asmar, D., Elhajj, I., Al-Harithy, H.: Pose tracking for augmented reality applications in outdoor archaeological sites. J. Electron. Imaging **26**(1), 011004 (2016). https://doi.org/10.1117/1.JEI.26.1.011004
3. Tabia, H., Riedinger, C., Jordan, M.: Automatic reconstruction of heritage monuments from old architecture documents. J. Electron. Imaging **26**(1), 011006 (2016). https://doi.org/10.1117/1.JEI.26.1.011006
4. Santagati, C., Turco, M.L.: From structure from motion to historical building information modeling: populating a semantic-aware library of architectural elements. J. Electron. Imaging **26**(1), 011007 (2016). https://doi.org/10.1117/1.JEI.26.1.011007
5. MacDonald, L., de Almeida, V.M., Hess, M.: Three-dimensional reconstruction of Roman coins from photometric image sets. J. Electron. Imaging **26**(1), 011017 (2017). https://doi.org/10.1117/1.JEI.26.1.011017
6. Detken, K.-O., Scheuermann, D., Hellmann, B.: Using extensible metadata definitions to create a vendor-independent SIEM system. In: International Conference in Swarm Intelligence. Springer International Publishing (2015)
7. Eren, M.T., Balcisoy, S.: A sensor based 3D annotation authoring tool for outdoor field applications. In: 2011 International Conference on Cyberworlds (CW). IEEE (2011)
8. Chaudhary, A., Blue, R., Payne, B., Woehlke, M.: VisGUI: A Visualization Framework for Video Analysis. Kitware Blog (2012)
9. Russell, B.C., et al.: LabelMe: a database and web-based tool for image annotation. Int. J. Comput. Vis. **77**(1–3), 157–173 (2008)
10. Hartley, R.I., Sturm, P.: Triangulation. Comput. Vis. Image Underst. **68**(2), 146–157 (1997)
11. Kanatani, K., Sugaya, Y., Kanazawa, Y.: Guide to 3D Vision Computation: Geometric Analysis and Implementation. Springer (2016)
12. Transparent Sky, LLC. http://www.transparentsky.net/
13. https://aha.missouri.edu/news/professor-marcello-mogetta
14. CNN, Sutter, J.D.: CNN Photographs by William Widmer/Redux for. "Each hour, a football field of land vanishes". CNN. Accessed 14 Apr 2017
15. Singh, R.K.: Web-based interactive editing and analytics for supervised segmentation of biomedical images. Master thesis, University of Missouri (2014)
16. AliAkbarpour, H., Palaniappan, K., Seetharaman, G.: Fast structure from motion for sequential and wide area motion imagery. In: Proceedings of the IEEE International Conference on Computer Vision Workshops (2015)
17. Aliakbarpour, H., Palaniappan, K., Seetharaman, G.: Robust camera pose refinement and rapid SfM for multiview aerial imagery without RANSAC. IEEE Geosc. Remote Sens. Lett. **12**(11), 2203–2207 (2015)
18. Stereo vision. http://vision.deis.unibo.it/smatt/Seminars/StereoVision.pdf. Accessed 15 Mar 2015
19. AliAkbarpour, H., Palaniappan, K., Seetharaman, G.: Fast structure from motion for sequential and wide area motion imagery. In: Proceedings of the IEEE International Conference on Computer Vision Workshops (2015)
20. Furukawa, Y., Ponce, J.: Accurate, dense, and robust multiview stereopsis. IEEE Trans. Pattern Anal. Mach. Intell. **32**(8), 1362–1376 (2010)
21. Guo, Y., Bennamoun, M., Sohel, F., Min, L., Wan, J., Kwok, N.M.: A comprehensive performance evaluation of 3D local feature descriptors. Int. J. Comput. Vis. **116**(1), 66–89 (2016)
22. Rosten, E., Drummond, T.: Machine learning for high-speed corner detection. In: European Conference on Computer Vision, pp. 430–443. Springer (2006)
23. David G.L.: Distinctive image features from scale-invariant keypoints. Int. J. Comput. Vis. **60**(2), 91–110 (2004)

24. Bay, H., Tuytelaars, T., Van Gool, L.: SURF: speeded up robust features. In: European Conference on Computer Vision, pp. 404–417. Springer (2006)
25. Leutenegger, S., Chli, M., Siegwart, R.Y.: BRISK: binary robust invariant scalable keypoints. In: 2011 International Conference on Computer Vision, pp. 2548–2555. IEEE (2011)

Digital Heritage Reconstruction Using Deep Learning-Based Super-Resolution

Prathmesh R. Madhu and Manjunath V. Joshi

1 Introduction

Heritage and archaeological sites across the world are a major source of information which acquaint us with our social history delineating the advancement of mankind. They are invaluable assets of cultural heritage. Such places serve as an excellent attraction for tourists which indirectly impacts the gross domestic product. This is one of the major reasons for government agencies globally for taking keen interest toward preserving these sites. Over a period of time, a number of natural calamities such as weathering, man-made hazards like pollution etc., have sabotaged these heritage sites. Fearing from any further damages to these sites by the tourists, access to many heritage sites is now restricted. One such example is the *mandapa with musical pillars* in Vithala temple at Hampi in India, where the visitors are not allowed to touch and experience the melodious sound from the musical pillars. A way to preserve the heritage sites is to physically renovate them. However, it requires a prolific amount of historical information in order to renovate them. It also poses a danger to the undamaged monuments and may fail to mimic the skill-full historical work.

One may overcome the above problems by using restoration in digital domain An image can be acquired by sampling a continuous scene using a camera and the restoration can be carried out by using in-painting and super-resolution methods. In this work, we restrict our degradation in spatial domain only and propose a super-resolution approach for spatial resolution enhancement. When the sampling rate of the acquired scene is less than the Nyquist rate which is often the case with mobile cameras used by the tourists, it results in aliasing effect leading to distortion in the captured image. In addition to this, sensor point spread function and the motion of the camera introduce the blur that degrades the quality of the image being captured. Image super-resolution is an algorithmic approach for increasing the spatial

P. R. Madhu (✉) · M. V. Joshi
Dhirubhai Ambani Institute of Information and Communication Technology,
Gandhinagar, India
e-mail: prmadhu@daiict.ac.in

M. V. Joshi
e-mail: mv_joshi@daiict.ac.in

© Springer Nature Singapore Pte Ltd. 2018
B. Chanda et al. (eds.), *Heritage Preservation*,
https://doi.org/10.1007/978-981-10-7221-5_4

resolution of an image from one or more LR observations. It aims at providing details finer than the sampling grid of a given imaging device by increasing the number of pixels per unit area in an image [18]. Alternatively, it aims at restoring the high-frequency components and removal of degradation which arise during the image acquisition process. Hence, a super-resolved image can be considered close to the true image captured using an HR camera.

SR methods can be broadly divided into three categories. They correspond to motion-based, motion-free, and single-frame SR techniques. Motion-based techniques use the relative motion between the observed LR images as a cue to estimate an HR image. On the contrary, motion-free techniques use cues such as blur, zoom, and defocus. Single-frame SR methods aim at reconstructing the HR image using a single degraded LR observation. However, in this case, a database of training images is required. Survey of different SR techniques is presented in the work by Park et al. [17].

The resolution enhancement of an image dates back to 1984 by Tsai and Huang [22], where they demonstrate the reconstruction of single enhanced resolution image using several downsampled noisy versions of it. One may find various approaches implemented in frequency domain in [2, 14, 19]. Irani and Peleg presented iterative back projection based method where a super-resolved image is estimated by computing the error between observed LR images and corresponding simulated LR images formed using current SR estimate. A unified approach of super-resolution and demosaicing using the bilateral regularization was proposed by Farsiu et al. [6]. They use L_1 norm minimization to make their method robust to data and modeling errors. Baker and Kanade [1], Lin and Shum [16] present the limitations of classical multi-image SR approaches. These limitations paved the way for example-based SR approach to achieve higher magnification factors. The first example-based approach was proposed by Freeman et al. [9], wherein they create an over-complete dictionary consisting of LR-HR patch pairs constructed using a large number of LR-HR training images. The dictionary generated is then used to restore the missing high-frequency details. Yang et al. [24] proposed a compressive sensing based approach by using sparsity constraint and over-complete dictionaries. New edge-preserving SR approaches are presented in [7, 8, 20]. Gajjar and Joshi [10] proposed a new wavelet-based learning process using the Inhomogenous Gaussian Markov Random Field (IGMRF) prior.

Recently, researchers have attempted to learn the mapping between the LR and HR images using machine learning techniques. Based on the work of Freeman et al. [9], Kim and Kwon proposed a regression-based approach for single-image SR [13]. Here, the authors use kernel ridge regression to estimate the high-frequency details of the underlying HR image. In [11], a hybrid of reconstruction and learning-based technique is implemented. With the efficient training scheme of deep neural networks proposed by Hinton et al. [12], deep learning has been applied in various applications such as classification and recognition in the field of computer vision as well as in speech processing, natural language processing, etc. Very recently, deep learning methods have been applied to image restoration. In [3], a multilayer perceptron (MLP) is used for natural image denoising and image deblurring. In [4], authors have combined the nonlocal self-similarity search with collaborative auto-encoders to super-resolve the LR test image. Convolutional neural networks (CNN) attempt to learn layered, hierarchical representations of higher dimensional data which are called features. Closely related to our work, CNN is applied for SR in [5], where the authors have proposed a CNN for SR.

In this chapter, we present a method for single image super-resolution based on deep learning. We eliminate the need for interpolation techniques as used in [5] during the training and reconstruction. To do this, we insert zeros in the alternate rows and columns of the LR training images and call them as zero-inserted LR (ZILR) training images. Note that we do not manipulate the training data by interpolation to get LR resized as done in [5]. In effect, we use the given training set of LR-HR pairs only and not the manipulated LR pixels. This is advantageous since the network directly learns the mapping between true LR and HR image pixels avoiding the use of manipulated (interpolated) pixels. For training the network, we use the ZILR and the corresponding original HR images as our input and the output of the network, respectively. Also, during training phase the backpropagation error is computed between the current pixel intensities of network output at those locations where zeros are inserted at the input and the corresponding intensities of true HR, thus manipulating only the pixel intensities of interest. This avoids manipulating already known HR values and it also reduces the training time. It also results in better learning of weights (parameters) of the network since the weights multiplied with the inserted zeros do not contribute while learning. Using the corresponding sub-images of ZILR and HR images, we first train our proposed CNN to find the direct mapping/transformation between LR and HR images. The trained network is then used to obtain the super-resolved output of test LR image. Another advantage of our approach is that once the network is trained for a magnification factor of 2, we need not train the network for obtaining SR for higher magnification factors. Once trained for a factor of 2, the same weights can be used in obtaining SR up to a factor of 8.

The outline of the chapter is as follows. Section 2 describes deep convolutional neural networks (CNNs) and learning of the CNN parameters. In Sect. 3, general description of the proposed method is presented. Implementation details are explained in Sect. 4, while the experimental results and the performance of the proposed approach are dealt in Sect. 5. Some concluding remarks are drawn in Sect. 6.

2 Convolutional Neural Networks

This section is a mini-tutorial on Convolutional neural networks in 2D. Readers may skip this section if they have a fair amount of knowledge in this field.

Convolutional neural networks (CNNs) are very useful in modeling a complex relationship between the input and the output data. They can be used in an unsupervised way to learn the features or in a supervised way for classification purpose. These networks are designed using three basic constituents: local receptive fields, shared weights, and pooling. Much of the earlier works on CNN was concentrated on classification. For this, the corresponding network architecture consists of three kinds of layers namely convolutional, pooling, and the fully connected layer, similar to multilayer perceptron (MLP). Every layer (except the pooling layer) is associated with the parameters or weights that correspond to a set of learnable filters. During the forward pass, we convolve each filter across the input volume, which results in a set of two-dimensional (2D) activation maps corresponding to that filter. Intuitively, the network learns filters that activate when there is a specific feature at different spatial positions in the input. A set of filter weights connects each neuron to a local region of the input volume making the connectivity as sparse. The spatial extent of this connectivity is called as the receptive field of a neuron. The filter weights are shared for the entire input image. Due to this weight-sharing property of CNN, there is a dramatic reduction in the number of weights to be learned when compared to conventional multilayer perceptron (MLP) [15]. Pooling layer is used for reducing the dimension and has a great significance while solving classification problem. In our work, since we are working on a reconstruction problem, we do not use the pooling layer. When a CNN has more than one hidden layer, then it is referred to as deep CNN (DCNN). These layers are added to learn hierarchical features between the input and the output.

The advantages of using CNN when compared to other neural networks are as follows:

- Sharing of weights, i.e., reduced number of network parameters to be learned.
- Self-learning of filters by the network that eliminates the need for prior knowledge.
- Input data is 2D, preserving the structure and spatial dependencies.
- Less memory requirement since the same filter is applied to the entire input image.

As seen in Fig. 1, a 3 hidden layered deep CNN used for super-resolution comprises of only convolutional layers. Layers such as pooling and fully connected layer are also used in the model while solving classification problem.

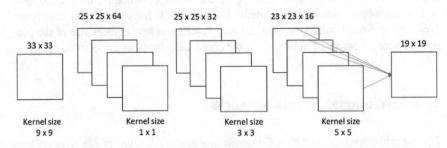

Fig. 1 General block diagram of CNN used for super-resolution

2.1 Training a CNN

In order to learn the parameters, one has to train the network by using a large amount of data (here images). The three steps involved in training a CNN correspond to forward propagation, backpropagation and updating weights. In what follows, we discuss each of these steps briefly.

2.1.1 Forward Propagation

Given an image of size $N \times N$ which is followed by our convolutional layer, if we use an $m \times m$ sized filter(s) denoted as ω, then the output of the convolutional layer will be of size $(N - m + 1) \times (N - m + 1)$. To get the convolved output at location (i, j) of an ℓth layer, i.e., $x^\ell(i, j)$, we need to sum up the contributions from previous layer cells i.e.,

$$x^\ell(i, j) = \sum_{c=0}^{m-1} \sum_{d=0}^{m-1} \omega(c, d) y^{\ell-1}(i + c, j + d). \tag{1}$$

Equation (1) represents convolving the filter and the receptive field at (i, j). Here, $y^{\ell-1}(i + c, j + d)$ represents the convolved output of $(\ell - 1)$th layer at location $(i + c, j + d)$. Carrying out the convolution over the entire image results in a convolved image or convolution layer map. Use of a number of filters gives us a number of images in the convolution layer. A nonlinearity applied on $x^\ell(i, j)$ for all i, j results in $y^\ell(i, j) = \sigma(x^\ell(i, j))$.

Here, σ represents a nonlinear function. Different kinds of nonlinear functions can be used. Since our work involves reconstruction, we use the rectified linear unit (ReLU) which thresholds negative values to zero and it can be mathematically represented as $\text{ReLU}(x) = max(0, x)$. It may be mentioned here that a sigmoid function is used while solving a classification problem.

2.1.2 Backward Propagation for Computing Error Derivatives with Respect to (w.r.t) Weights (Parameters)

Let us consider an error function E that corresponds to squared error between input (x) and the current output (y). Note that we consider the error corresponding to zero-inserted locations only while computing E. In order to perform a backward pass, we need to know the partial derivatives of error with respect to each neuron output $\left(\frac{\partial E}{\partial y^\ell(i,j)}\right)$. To do this, we first find the gradient of E with respect to (w.r.t) each weight for lth layer which is computed using the chain rule as,

$$\frac{\partial E}{\partial \omega(c,d)} = \sum_{i=0}^{N-m}\sum_{j=0}^{N-m} \frac{\partial E}{\partial x^\ell(i,j)} \frac{\partial x^\ell(i,j)}{\partial \omega(c,d)}$$

$$= \sum_{i=0}^{N-m}\sum_{j=0}^{N-m} \frac{\partial E}{\partial x^\ell(i,j)} y^{\ell-1}(i+c, j+d). \tag{2}$$

Note that, because of the weight-sharing property, $\omega(c,d)$ occurs in the sum of all $x^\ell(i,j)$ expressions. Also, from the forward propagation, we know that $\frac{\partial x^\ell(i,j)}{\partial \omega(c,d)} = y^{\ell-1}(i+c, j+d)$. Hence to compute the gradient, we need the values of $\frac{\partial E}{\partial x^\ell(i,j)}$, which are called deltas (errors). Once again, using the chain rule, one can calculate these deltas as

$$\frac{\partial E}{\partial x^\ell(i,j)} = \frac{\partial E}{\partial y^\ell(i,j)} \frac{\partial y^\ell(i,j)}{\partial x^\ell(i,j)}$$

$$= \frac{\partial E}{\partial y^\ell(i,j)} \frac{\partial}{\partial x^\ell(i,j)} \left(\sigma(x^\ell(i,j))\right) \tag{3}$$

$$= \frac{\partial E}{\partial y^\ell(i,j)} \sigma'(x^\ell(i,j)).$$

Note that σ' represents the derivative of σ.

Hence, it is simple to calculate the deltas $\frac{\partial E}{\partial x^\ell(i,j)}$ at the current layer by just using the derivative of the activation function $\sigma'(x)$ as we already know errors at current layer $\frac{\partial E}{\partial y^\ell(i,j)}$. Now the error needs to be backpropagated, where we again use the chain rule as

$$\frac{\partial E}{\partial y^{\ell-1}(i,j)} = \sum_{c=0}^{m-1}\sum_{d=0}^{m-1} \frac{\partial E}{\partial x^\ell(i-c)(j-d)} \frac{\partial x^\ell(i-c)(j-d)}{\partial y^{\ell-1}(i,j)}$$

$$= \sum_{c=0}^{m-1}\sum_{d=0}^{m-1} \frac{\partial E}{\partial x^\ell(i-c)(j-d)} \omega(c,d). \tag{4}$$

Note that we have used $\frac{\partial x^\ell(i-c)(j-d)}{\partial y^{\ell-1}(i,j)} = \omega(c,d)$ in Eq. (4) which can be obtained from Eq. (1).

2.1.3 Updating the Weights

In order to choose the optimum network parameters, we minimize the error function E. Stochastic gradient descent (SGD) method is an approximation of the gradient descent optimization method for minimizing an error function. SGD performs the update of weights and uses the gradient of the error function w.r.t weights of a single or a few training examples which are calculated using the backpropagation discussed in Sect. 2.1.2. Hence, the update equation for SGD is given as

$$w := w - \alpha \nabla_w E(w; x^{(i)}, y^{(i)}), \tag{5}$$

where w and $x^{(i)}$, $y^{(i)}$ represent the parameter vector and ith training example, respectively. Here, the term $\nabla_w E(w; x^{(i)}, y^{(i)})$ represents the gradient of the error function with respect to the network parameters, i.e., weights and α is the learning rate. The pseudo code for SGD is presented in Algorithm 1.

Algorithm 1: Pseudocode for SGD

---
for *every iteration:* **do**
    Randomly shuffle the input data;
    for *every example in the data:* **do**
        compute gradients with respect to weights using backpropagation;
        update weights as weights := weights - learning rate*gradient with respect to weights.
    end
end

---

3 Proposed Approach

The proposed technique of deep learning-based super-resolution is illustrated by the block diagram shown in Fig. 2. Given an LR test image and LR and HR training images, we first learn the mapping in terms of network parameters using a deep convolutional neural network (DCNN) for a magnification factor of 2. The only preprocessing we perform is the insertion of zeros into alternate rows and columns of the LR in order to enlarge it to the desired size. This is in contrast to the bicubic interpolation performed as a preprocessing step during the training phase in the method proposed by Dong et al. [5]. Inserting zeros avoids the creation of unwanted input data which is generated by the interpolation operation. In Fig. 2a, we show the block schematic of the training and the testing phase is shown in Fig. 2b. The expanded view of the proposed DCNN is shown in Fig. 3.

Note that in our approach, we propose a standard upsampling method by inserting zeros in alternate rows and columns of the LR images. This concept can be considered as an equivalent of denoising auto-encoder proposed by Vincent et al. [23], in which the image is corrupted with zeros. A denoising auto-encoder tries to encode the input mapping between the zero inserted input and the true output. It attempts to undo the effect of a corruption process by capturing the statistical dependencies between the corrupted input pixels. However, we model this as a super-resolution problem, where the missing values can be replaced by zeros and the DCNN learns the mapping

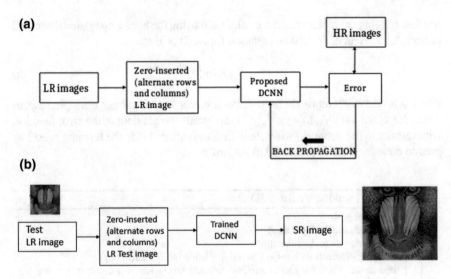

Fig. 2 Block Schematic of the proposed approach for image super-resolution. **a** Training phase; **b** Testing phase

between neighbors of ZILR pixels and the corresponding pixels in HR image. We train our proposed DCNN using sub-images (patches) of ZILR and HR images, details of which can be found in Sect. 4. The error at the output is calculated by the square of the difference between the network output and the cropped version of the HR sub-image corresponding to the output patch size where the values corresponding to ZILR only are considered in both the images. Weights are updated using standard error backpropagation and stochastic gradient descent method as discussed in Sect. 2.1. Once we obtain the learned network parameters, we use these in forward pass to obtain the SR for the test image.

4 Implementation Details

For a fair comparison with the traditional state-of-the-art methods in example-based learning, we use the same training sets, i.e., LR and HR images as used in [21]. There are 91 color images of different sizes. The Set5 consisting of five images is used to evaluate the performance for magnification factors of 2, 4, and 8.

As seen from Fig. 3, our input consists of the sub-images of size 33×33, and size of our filters f_1, f_2, f_3, f_4 are 9, 1, 3, 5, respectively. For all the 91 HR images, we first downsample them by removing alternate rows and columns, i.e., undersampling by a factor of 2 to generate the LR training images. We then insert zeros in alternate rows and columns of these LR training images and call them ZILR training images.

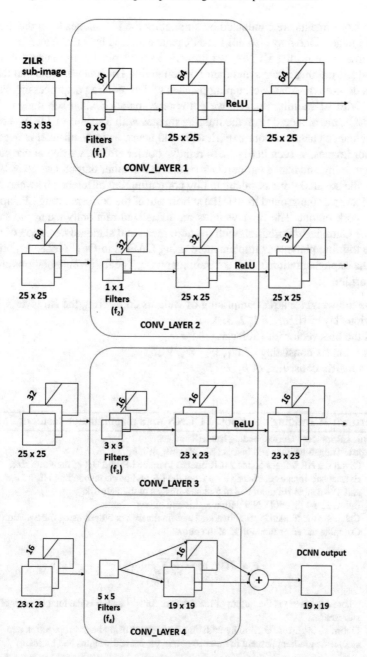

Fig. 3 Expanded view of the proposed DCNN architecture. Note that there are four convolutional layers. The output of each convolution layer is given as input to the next convolution layer

All our experiments are conducted by simulating the LR images from the available 91 HR images. One may also use LR-HR pairs acquired by a real camera.

In order to train the DCNN, we prepare 33×33 pixel sub-images from zero-inserted LR training images and their corresponding HR images. Note that the sub-images do not represent overlapping patches which require postprocessing as done in [5]. With 91 training images, we get approximately 35,000 sub-images. These sub-images are obtained from the training images with a stride[1] of 11. We consider the luminance channel in our experiments and hence a single channel is used from the color images, as seen in Fig. 3. To remove border effects, we do not use padding during training and hence our network results in a smaller output, i.e., 19×19. Due to this, the squared error is calculated by computing the difference between central 19×19 crop of the ground truth (HR) sub-image of the corresponding LR input and the network output. The filter weights are initialized randomly using the samples from the Gaussian distribution with the zero mean and standard deviation of 0.001.

The training phase was implemented using CAFFE in GPU mode. Algorithm 2 gives the implementation details for training phase. The following notations are used in Algorithm 2:

- W_i is the weight matrix comprising of weights connecting the ith layer with the previous layer. Here, i = 1, 2, 3, 4.
- b_i is the bias vector for ith layer.
- $\mathbf{W}$ is a matrix consisting of W_1, W_2, W_3, W_4
- $\mathbf{b}$ is a matrix consisting of b_1, b_2, b_3, b_4

Algorithm 2: Training of proposed DCNN for a magnification factor of 2.

Input: LR images , Corresponding true HR images.
Output: Trained weights and biases $(W_1, W_2, W_3, W_4, b_1, b_2, b_3, b_4)$.
1. Given the HR images create ZILR images to make LR and HR of the same size.
2. Extract sub-images of size 33 x 33 from the LR and its corresponding HR images. Let $x^{(i)}$ and $y^{(i)}$ denote ith input and output sub-images to the network.
3. Initialize a 4 layered CNN with weights and biases.
4. Calculate the hidden layer activations and final network output using the equation (1).
5. Compute the error function E at the output

$$E = J(\mathbf{W}, \mathbf{b}) = \frac{1}{m} \sum_{i=1}^{m} (\|h_{\mathbf{W},\mathbf{b}}(x^{(i)}) - y^{(i)}\|^2)$$

where $h_{W,b}(x^{(i)})$ is the output of the network for $x^{(i)}$ and m is the total number of training sub-images.
6. Optimize the error function by updating the weights using back-propagation and stochastic gradient descent in order to obtain the trained weights and biases.

---

[1]Stride—It is an arbitrary shift we use to obtain the next sub-image within the image.

5 Experimental Results

In this section, we discuss the efficacy of the proposed technique in the context of super-resolving an LR image using the learned deep convolutional neural network. We present the results on the luminance channel for the magnification factors of 2, 4 and 8. As already discussed in Sect. 4, the training data is the same in all experiments. The learning rate α during training was set to 0.0001. Given the test LR image and the already learned weights, we implement the forward pass in order to get SR for the test image.

To start with, we consider an experiment for a magnification factor of 2 on face image which is shown in Fig. 4. In order to obtain an LR image, we downsample the given test image by removing alternate rows and columns. Figure 4a shows an LR face image of a woman. The upsampled image for a factor of 2 with inserted zeros in

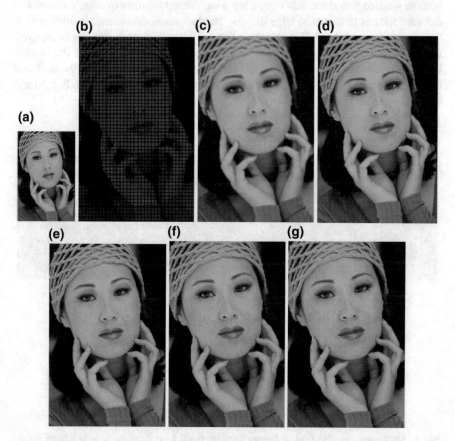

Fig. 4 SR Results for 2X: Woman. **a** Low-resolution; **b** ZILR; **c** Bicubically interpolated image; **d** Super-resolved image using Kim and Kwon [13] approach; **e** Super-resolved image using SRCNN [5] approach; **f** Super-resolved image using proposed method; **g** Ground truth image

alternate rows and columns is shown in Fig. 4b. The bicubically interpolated image is shown in Fig. 4c. Figure 4d, e display the super-resolved images by Kim and Kwon's [13] and Dong et al.'s [5] approaches, respectively. Super-resolved image using our approach is displayed in Fig. 4f, and the ground truth i.e., true HR image (available test image itself in this case) is shown in Fig. 4g. In comparison to the image shown in Fig. 4c, the super-resolved image in Fig. 4f shows clearer details. The features within the image such as texture in the cap, eyelashes, eyes, mouth etc. are hazy in the bicubic interpolated image shown in Fig. 4c while they are well preserved in Fig. 4f. One can see that the SR features in the image of the proposed approach are comparable to that of the ground truth displayed in Fig. 4g. The details are better preserved in the proposed approach when compared to Fig. 4c and the images shown in Fig. 4d, e.

To test our algorithm for images having high-frequency components, we now consider an image of a bird sitting on a tree branch. One may note that learning here is more challenging since this image has a significant number of edge features and the network has to learn the edge details. The low-resolution image is displayed in Fig. 5a, while our SR result is shown in Fig. 5f. We can observe that the beak, eyes, and the branches of the tree in the proposed approach look sharper than the bicubic interpolated image. It can also be seen from Fig. 5f that the texture near the beak and branches of the tree are better preserved when compared to the image in Fig. 5d and are similar to the image shown in Fig. 5e.

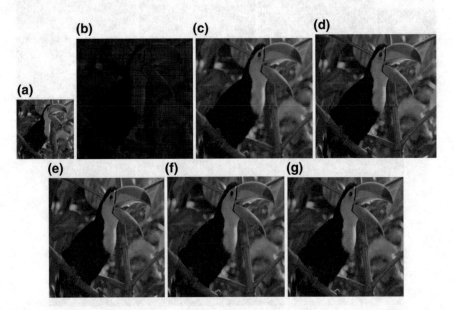

Fig. 5 SR Results for 2X: Bird. **a** Low-resolution; **b** ZILR; **c** Bicubically interpolated image; **d** Super-resolved image using Kim and Kwon [13] approach; **e** Super-resolved image using SRCNN [5] approach; **f** Super-resolved image using proposed method; **g** Ground truth image

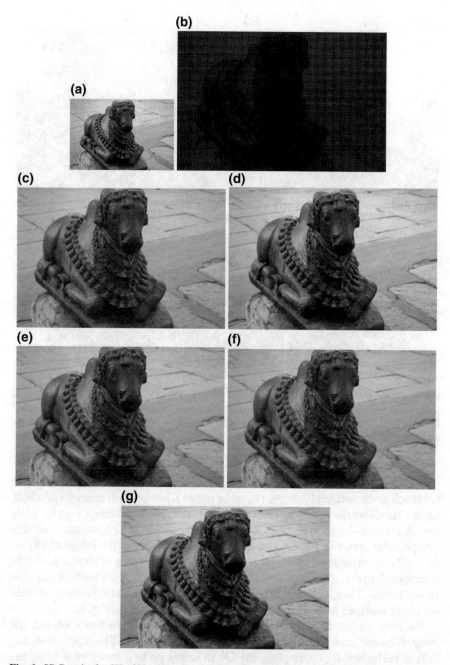

Fig. 6 SR Results for 2X of Nandi captured at Hampi temple. **a** Low-resolution; **b** ZILR; **c** Bicubically interpolated image; **d** Super-resolved image using Kim and Kwon [13] approach; **e** Super-resolved image using SRCNN [5] approach; **f** Super-resolved image using proposed method; **g** Ground truth image

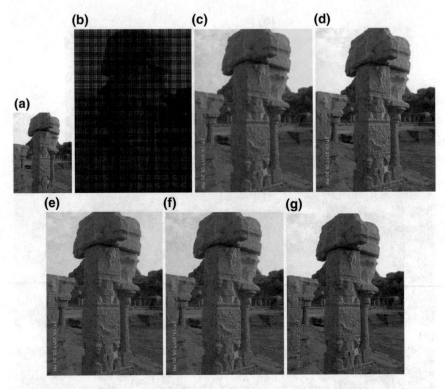

Fig. 7 SR Results for 2X: An art engraved on stone at one of the musical pillars at Hampi. **a** Low-resolution; **b** ZILR; **c** Bicubically interpolated image; **d** Super-resolved image using Kim and Kwon [13] approach; **e** Super-resolved image using SRCNN [5] approach; **f** Super-resolved image using proposed method; **g** Ground truth image

Next, we consider two test images from historical monument **Hampi temple** with reference to the cultural heritage. Figure 6a shows a low-resolution image of a bull, named Nandi which is said as Lord Shiva's chariot, taken at Hampi temple, while our SR result is shown in Fig. 6f. Observe the finer details in comparison to bicubic interpolation shown in Fig. 6c. Our SR result looks similar to the image of Fig. 6f. In Fig. 7, we show another result where the LR image which is shown in Fig. 7a corresponds to that of an engraved piece of art work on one of the musical pillars at Hampi temple. Here, we see that the finer texture of the stone and the edge transitions are nicely captured in the image of the proposed method shown Fig. 7f.

We now discuss results for a magnification factor of 4. In this case, the HR image is downsampled by a factor of 4 to obtain the LR image. The super-resolution is then performed by upsampling the LR in stages up to a factor of 4 using the following steps: (a) insert zeros in alternate rows and columns (b) super-resolve the resulting zero-inserted image to obtain SR for a magnification factor of 2 (c) insert zeros in alternate rows and columns in the resulting SR image (d) use the same network to super-resolve to obtain super-resolution for a factor of 4. Note

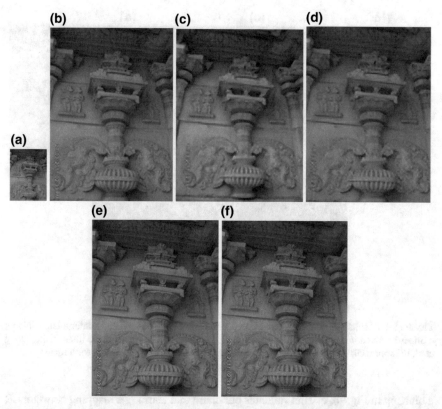

Fig. 8 SR Results for 4X: An art piece captured at Hampi temple. **a** Low-resolution; **b** Bicubic interpolation; **c** Super-resolved image using Kim and Kwon [13] approach; **d** Super-resolved image using SRCNN [5] approach; **e** Super-resolved image using proposed method; **f** Ground truth image

that no new model is trained here for a magnification factor of 4, instead, we make use of the already trained model that provides 2X magnification. This is possible since our input consists of patches of an image rather than the entire image itself. Once the network is trained, the same parameters can then be used in obtaining the upsampled patches for any magnification factor assuming that the result of the upsampled image is closer to the ground truth image. Figure 8a, f shows the LR image of the art piece engraved on the wall of Hampi temple and the ground truth image. Figure 8b, e corresponds to the bicubically interpolated image and the super-resolved image by our approach, respectively. Figure 8c, d corresponds to the SR image using Kim et al.'s [13] and SRCNN [5] approach, respectively. We observe that the high-frequency details have been preserved well in the image shown in Fig. 8e indicating that our method performs better for magnification factor 4 as well even when we do not train the network separately. One more result for a magnification factor of 4 wherein the experiment is conducted on the natural image is shown in Fig. 9. Here also, we observe sharper details in Fig. 9e, whereas one can clearly see

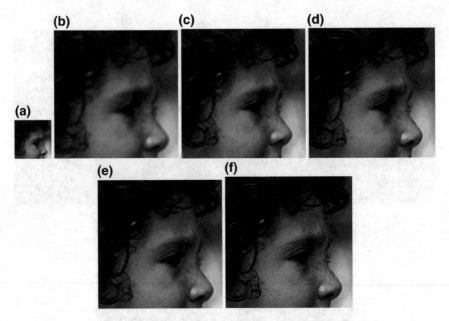

Fig. 9 SR Results for 4X: Head. **a** Low-resolution image; **b** Bicubically interpolated image; **c** Super-resolved image using Kim and Kwon [13] approach; **d** Super-resolved image using Dong et al. [5] approach; **e** Super-resolved image using proposed method; **f** Ground truth image

a blurring in Fig. 9b, c. This validates our claim that learning a mapping between LR and HR images using CNN does help in improving the spatial resolution. Looking at the perceptual quality, we observe that our method gives visually similar results as in [5]. However, our method has the advantage over [5] in the following ways: (1) elimination of bicubic interpolation during the training phase, (2) computationally more efficient since a single trained network for a factor of 2 is enough to reconstruct a super-resolved image for higher magnification factors, and (3) error computation for backpropagation is computationally less involved during training.

Finally, we show one result for a large magnification factor of 8 by considering another image from Hampi site. Similar to super-resolving by a factor of 4, here also the LR image is obtained by downsampling the HR image, but by a factor of 8 which is then super-resolved in stages. The LR and the ground truth image are shown in Fig. 10a, d, while the SR result using our approach is shown in Fig. 10c. Figure 10b displays the bicubically interpolated image of the LR in Fig. 10a. One can clearly see the difference between bicubic and our approach. The image interpolated bicubically appears blurred whereas the image super-resolved using our approach compares well with the ground truth.

To show the edge over the traditional interpolation techniques and existing learning-based methods, we show the quantitative comparison in terms of peak signal to noise ratio (PSNR) in Table 1. PSNR is computed as follows. Given a noise-free

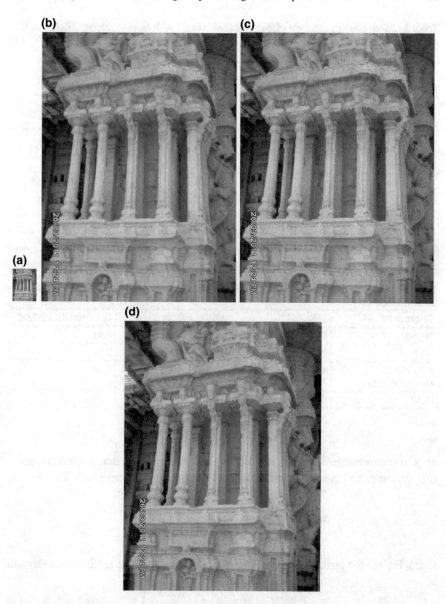

Fig. 10 SR Results for 8X: An image consisting of the musical pillars at Hampi temple. **a** Low-resolution image; **b** Bicubically interpolated image; **c** super-resolved image using proposed method; **d** Ground truth image

Table 1 PSNR (dB) comparison of our proposed method with bicubic interpolation (BI), Kim et al. [13] and SRCNN [5]. Here BI and MF represent bicubic interpolation and magnification factor respectively

Test images	MF	BI	[13]	[5]	Proposed
Woman	2	32.29	34.80	**35.02**	34.94
Bird	2	36.81	40.16	40.61	**40.81**
Nandi	2	35.79	36.35	37.62	**37.64**
Art engraved stone at Hampi temple	2	31.64	31.73	32.84	**32.89**
Art piece on walls of Hampi temple	4	29.5	29.74	30.54	**30.95**
Head	4	31.23	32.40	31.88	**32.88**
Pillars	8	33.03	–	–	34.36

Table 2 SSIM comparison. Here BI and MF represent bicubic interpolation and magnification factor respectively

Test images	MF	BI	Proposed SR method
Woman	2	0.87	0.91
Bird	2	0.93	0.94
Art piece on walls of Hampi temple	4	0.62	0.66
Head	4	0.42	0.46

$m \times n$ monochrome image I (true image) and its approximation K (reconstructed image), the mean squared error (MSE) between these two images is defined as

$$MSE = \frac{1}{mn} \sum_{i=0}^{m-1} \sum_{j=0}^{n-1} [I(i, j) - K(i, j)]^2. \tag{6}$$

Using Eq. (6) the peak signal to noise ratio (PSNR) measured in dB is then defined as

$$PSNR = 10 * log_{10} \left(\frac{MAX^2}{MSE} \right), \tag{7}$$

where MAX corresponds to the maximum value of the noise-free image I. We also compare our results with the bicubic interpolation using the structural similarity measure (SSIM) index as shown in Table 2. A higher value of SSIM indicates higher similarity of the SR image with the ground truth HR image. From Tables 1 and 2, we conclude that in addition to the perceptual betterment, we also see an improvement in PSNR and SSIM for the proposed approach indicating the usefulness of deep learning framework for super-resolution.

6 Conclusion

In this chapter, we addressed the problem of super-resolution from image processing and machine learning perspective. We have proposed a deep learning-based technique for super-resolution which aims at restoring details of a high-resolution image from the transformation learned by analyzing the spatial relationship during the training phase. We learn this transformation using a deep convolutional neural network. We have considered the limitations of classical multi-image SR and presented an approach showing results for higher magnification factors. The CNN filters and sub-image sizes play a major role in obtaining better results. The results obtained for the grayscale (luminance channel) show perceptual as well as quantifiable improvements over the digital zoom performed using bicubic interpolation.

Acknowledgements The authors would like to thank NVIDIA Corporation for providing the TITAN X GPU for the academic research. The authors are also immensely grateful to the reviewers of the book for their comments on the earlier versions of the manuscript. They are also thankful to their colleagues Dr. Milind G. Padalkar, Meet H. Soni, Ketul D. Parikh and Surabhi D. Sohoney for sharing their pearls of wisdom with them during the course of this research.

References

1. Baker, S., Kanade, T.: Limits on super-resolution and how to break them. IEEE Trans. Pattern Anal. Mach. Intell. **24**(9), 1167–1183 (2002)
2. Bose, N., Kim, H., Valenzuela, H.: Recursive implementation of total least squares algorithm for image reconstruction from noisy, undersampled multiframes. In: 1993 IEEE International Conference on Acoustics, Speech, and Signal Processing, 1993. ICASSP-93, vol. 5, pp. 269–272. IEEE (1993)
3. Burger, H.C., Schuler, C.J., Harmeling, S.: Image denoising with multi-layer perceptrons, part 1: comparison with existing algorithms and with bounds. arXiv:1211.1544 (2012)
4. Cui, Z., Chang, H., Shan, S., Zhong, B., Chen, X.: Deep network cascade for image super-resolution. In: Computer Vision–ECCV 2014, pp. 49–64. Springer (2014)
5. Dong, C., Loy, C.C., He, K., Tang, X.: Learning a deep convolutional network for image super-resolution. In: Computer Vision–ECCV 2014, pp. 184–199. Springer (2014)
6. Farsiu, S., Robinson, D., Elad, M., Milanfar, P.: Advances and challenges in super-resolution. Int. J. Imaging Syst. Technol. **14**(2), 47–57 (2004)
7. Fattal, R.: Image upsampling via imposed edge statistics. In: ACM Transactions on Graphics (TOG), vol. 26, p. 95. ACM (2007)
8. Freedman, G., Fattal, R.: Image and video upscaling from local self-examples. ACM Trans. Graph. (TOG) **30**(2), 12 (2011)
9. Freeman, W.T., Jones, T.R., Pasztor, E.C.: Example-based super-resolution. IEEE Comput. Graph. Appl. **22**(2), 56–65 (2002)

10. Gajjar, P.P., Joshi, M.V.: New learning based super-resolution: use of DWT and IGMRF prior. IEEE Trans. Image Process. **19**(5), 1201–1213 (2010)
11. Glasner, D., Bagon, S., Irani, M.: Super-resolution from a single image. In: 2009 IEEE 12th International Conference on Computer Vision, pp. 349–356. IEEE (2009)
12. Hinton, G.E., Osindero, S., Teh, Y.W.: A fast learning algorithm for deep belief nets. Neural Comput. **18**(7), 1527–1554 (2006)
13. Kim, K.I., Kwon, Y.: Example-based learning for single-image super-resolution. In: Pattern Recognition, pp. 456–465. Springer (2008)
14. Kim, S.P., Su, W.Y.: Recursive high-resolution reconstruction of blurred multiframe images. IEEE Trans. Image Process. **2**(4), 534–539 (1993)
15. Li, F.F., Karpathy, A., Johnson, J.: Cs231n: convolutional neural networks for visual recognition (2016). Accessed 28 June 2016
16. Lin, Z., Shum, H.Y.: Fundamental limits of reconstruction-based superresolution algorithms under local translation. IEEE Trans. Pattern Anal. Mach. Intell. **26**(1), 83–97 (2004)
17. Park, S.C., Park, M.K., Kang, M.G.: Super-resolution image reconstruction: a technical overview. IEEE Signal Process. Mag. **20**(3), 21–36 (2003)
18. Protter, M., Elad, M., Takeda, H., Milanfar, P.: Generalizing the nonlocal-means to super-resolution reconstruction. IEEE Trans. Image Process. **18**(1), 36–51 (2009)
19. Rhee, S., Kang, M.G.: Discrete cosine transform based regularized high-resolution image reconstruction algorithm. Opt. Eng. **38**(8), 1348–1356 (1999)
20. Sun, J., Sun, J., Xu, Z., Shum, H.Y.: Image super-resolution using gradient profile prior. In: IEEE Conference on Computer Vision and Pattern Recognition, 2008. CVPR 2008, pp. 1–8. IEEE (2008)
21. Timofte, R., De Smet, V., Van Gool, L.: Anchored neighborhood regression for fast example-based super-resolution. In: The IEEE International Conference on Computer Vision (ICCV) (2013)
22. Tsai, R., Huang, T.S.: Multiframe image restoration and registration. Adv. Comput. Vis. Image Process. **1**(2), 317–339 (1984)
23. Vincent, P., Larochelle, H., Bengio, Y., Manzagol, P.A.: Extracting and composing robust features with denoising autoencoders. In: Proceedings of the 25th International Conference on Machine Learning, pp. 1096–1103. ACM (2008)
24. Yang, J., Wright, J., Huang, T.S., Ma, Y.: Image super-resolution via sparse representation. IEEE Trans. Image Process. **19**(11), 2861–2873 (2010)

Restoration of Digital Images of Old Degraded Cave Paintings via Patch Size Adaptive Source-Constrained Inpainting

Veepin Kumar, Jayanta Mukherjee and Shyamal Kumar Das Mandal

1 Introduction

Cave paintings depict our glorious past and rich cultural heritage. In our country, places like Ajanta and Elora in the state of Maharashtra are famous for their cave paintings and sculptures. These paintings are getting degraded in various ways. They get covered with clay, soot, and dirt, over time. Deterioration due to moisture, insects, and fungus also takes place. Restoration of cave paintings is the process of improving visual quality of degraded images. Physical restoration of these paintings should be done with much care, and planning, as it may sometimes degrade the painting further. The digitization of these paintings opens up possibility of using image processing and computer graphics techniques to preserve this heritage for future generations. The task of this processing could be aimed at restoring the digital images of these old degraded paintings. This method is cheap and less time consuming. Further, they provide the cues for physical restoration of these paintings. In this chapter, we discuss digital restoration of cave paintings using exemplar-based *inpainting* techniques. To accomplish this task, we propose modifications over traditional exemplar-based *inpainting*. The *inpainting* technique is applied under a source-constrained framework.

Inpainting is the process of removal of an object from an image and filling the removed portion in such a way that an observer, unaware of the original image, should not be able to detect any artificial intrusion in the image. The region to

V. Kumar (✉) · J. Mukherjee · S. K. Das Mandal
Indian Institute of Technology Kharagpur, Kharagpur 721302, West Bengal, India
e-mail: veepinkmr@cet.iitkgp.ernet.in
URL: http://www.iitkgp.ac.in/

J. Mukherjee
e-mail: jay@cse.iitkgp.ernet.in

S. K. Das Mandal
e-mail: sdasmandal@cet.iitkgp.ernet.in

© Springer Nature Singapore Pte Ltd. 2018
B. Chanda et al. (eds.), *Heritage Preservation*,
https://doi.org/10.1007/978-981-10-7221-5_5

be removed is termed *target region*, and the rest of the image is termed *source region*. Various applications of image *inpainting* include restoration of photographs, removal of occluded objects, etc. The image *inpainting* techniques developed so far can broadly be classified into following three categories:

- Structure or geometric or Partial Differential Equation (PDE)-based techniques [4–6, 12, 32, 40, 41].
- Exemplar or texture-based techniques [9, 13, 14, 16, 18, 19, 27, 46, 49].
- Energy optimization-based techniques [2, 15, 23, 28, 31].

Structure-based methods fill the inpainted region by imitating a diffusion process, which is simulated by solving a *Partial Differential Equation*. These methods use information from the neighborhood of the missing region, and fill it and smoothly propagate to its neighbors in the target region. This processing is local in nature and not good for filling large missing regions. These techniques also produce some blur in the inpainted region. Exemplar-based methods are good at filling large missing regions, and do not cause blurring. They copy content from the known region of the image to the unknown region, either pixel wise or patch wise. They are global in nature, but are greedy as they do not check the visual consistency after filling a missing pixel or patch. They sometimes produce visually inconsistent results.

Energy optimization-based methods avoid the greedy nature by checking for visual consistency among neighboring patches in the unknown region. They consider image *inpainting* as a global energy optimization task. However, they do not generate good inpainted results in all cases, as determining a cost function, whose minimization leads to a good inpainted image, is a non-trivial task. Recent techniques proposed by the authors in [24, 25] check the quality of images during the process of *inpainting* so that the technique always proceeds toward producing good quality images.

Inpainting has been used in different ways to restore the digital images of old cave paintings. Some techniques are applied directly in conventional way as is done in *inpainting*. Some techniques involve user interaction, while some use a professional painter to create a sample restored image. A few of these techniques are discussed below.

In [20], the authors restore the digital images of old cave paintings of Dunhuang art. They decompose the RGB image into L, α, and β image components. $L - \alpha - \beta$ color space, introduced by Rederman [8], is based on human perception. In this color space, L corresponds to intensity, α to yellow-blue color value, and β to red-green color value. Then, these three gray channels are separated into texture and structure using Total Variation (TV) algorithm [10]. The texture image is inpainted using the technique reported in [13] and the structure image is inpainted by the technique reported in [11]. These texture and structure images are then integrated to get processed images for each channel (i.e., L, α, β). These are then converted back providing RGB space to the final *inpainting* image. In [21], computation of Curvature-Driven Diffusions (CDD) has been used to inpaint old cave paintings of Tibet. The technique recovers structural part of an image, but it performs poorly on its textured part.

In [22], the authors first get a painting restored from a conservator painter, and a traced drawing hypothesized by a specialist. To each segment, texture *inpainting* is applied based on texture information from the restored image. It provides good results. However, it is time consuming, laborious, and the method depends upon skill and knowledge of painters. In [3], first image is made more prominent through some image processing filters. Then, foreground and background are separated with a user's intervention. Background is repainted, based on the assumption that mostly background is smeared by inks, carbon soots, etc. Foreground may also be repainted, if required. Foreground and background are merged again. Finally, tonal and texture processings are applied to enhance the image. The technique gives good results for cases where background is corrupt, and foreground is in good condition. However, it sometimes suffers in cases, where foreground is also damaged, due to non availability of data to repaint it. In [34], the authors introduce a novel interactive technique, based on patch matching, to restore digital images of old cave paintings. First, a novel automatic fast coherent texture synthesis algorithm is used to restore texture. After this, a patch-based edge-enhancing anisotropic diffusion technique is applied to restore edges. This technique gives good inpainting results. However, the search space for source patches is the whole image like other traditional inpainting techniques, which requires more computational time and makes it vulnerable to the error in searching.

In digital image restoration, the goal is to automate image restoration process. In old cave paintings, the degraded regions are mostly small patches. So, exemplar-based *inpainting* has been used in this chapter as these methods produce visually good images for smaller target regions. Also, exemplar-based methods take less time to execute as compared to those involving energy optimization. The exemplar-based methods are highly sensitive to the patch size. Most of the exemplar techniques use a fixed patch size. This fixed patch size needs to be adjusted for each image. In this chapter, a modified exemplar-based technique, named PAMIT, is proposed, which uses patches of varying sizes. The technique automatically adjusts the patch size for different images. Moreover, it also adjusts the patch size as required within an image. This inpainting is applied in a source-constrained framework. The target regions are marked first. After this, source region is also marked. This reduces the search space for source patches. As a result, it requires less computation. The source-constrained framework also reduces the chances of getting wrong source patches for a target patch, resulting in better quality images. The results by the proposed technique have been found to be visually better than other exemplar-based techniques. Scores measuring image quality of these restored images have been computed by the BRISQUE technique proposed in [33]. Better quality scores confirm the superiority of PAMIT over other exemplar-based techniques in providing restored images.

In the next section, an overview of exemplar-based *inpainting* technique is provided. Section 3 briefly discusses the BRISQUE technique for measuring image quality. In this section, we also illustrate how this could be used in developing quality-aware techniques. In Sect. 4, modification to the traditional exemplar-based *inpainting* technique is described. Section 5 describes the source-constrained *inpainting*.

In Sect. 6, restoration of old degraded cave paintings through source-constrained exemplar-based *inpainting* is described. Section 6 discusses the results obtained by the proposed technique. In Sect. 7, a brief summary of this chapter is provided.

2 Exemplar-Based *inpainting*

In this section, Modified Exemplar-Based Inpainting (MEBI), as introduced in [26], is briefly described. In this work, this technique is extended to handle varying patch sizes. Consider an image I with a region to be inpainted, as shown in Fig. 1. The region to be inpainted is called *target region*, and is denoted by Ω. Rest of the image is called *source region*, and is denoted by $\phi = I - \Omega$. The technique fills target region patch by patch. For each pixel, at the boundary between source and target regions, a patch is formed by taking pixels from the neighborhood. This patch is called target patch. Then, the patch from the source region is found, which is most similar to this target patch. This patch is called source patch. The unknown content of target patch is filled by copying content from the corresponding locations of the source patch. The dissimilarity measure between two patches ψ_p and ψ_q is denoted by $d(\psi_p, \psi_q)$. It is given below:

$$d(\psi_p, \psi_q) = \sum_{i=1}^{m} \sum_{j=1}^{n} (\psi_p(i, j) - \psi_q(i, j))^2 , \tag{1}$$

where $(m \times n)$ is the size of the patches ψ_p and ψ_q.

Each target patch is filled according to its priority. Priority among candidate patches, centered at pixel p, in the target region is computed as given below:

$$P(p) = C(p)D(p)E(p) , \tag{2}$$

where $C(p)$ is called the confidence term, and $D(p)$ is called the data term. They are given by

$$C(p) = \frac{\sum\limits_{q \in \psi_p \cap (I-\Omega)} C(q)}{|\psi_p|}. \tag{3}$$

$$D(p) = \frac{|\nabla I_p^{\perp} \cdot n_p|}{\alpha}. \tag{4}$$

$$E(p) = \frac{\sum\limits_{q \in \psi_p \cap (I-\Omega)} \delta I(q)}{|\psi_p|}. \tag{5}$$

Fig. 1 Diagram showing the normal n_p and $\nabla I_p^{\perp}$ vectors

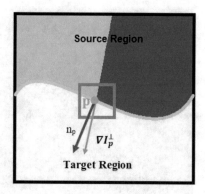

Here, ψ_p denotes the patch centered at pixel p, and $| \psi_p |$ is the area of the patch ψ_p, to be inpainted. Area of a patch is equal to the number of pixels in it. α is the normalization factor, n_p is an orthogonal unit vector to the fill front, $\perp$ denotes the orthogonal operator, and ∇ denotes the gradient operator. The product $| \nabla I_p^{\perp} \cdot n_p |$ gives a measure of the strength of an edge. ∇I_p is a vector in the gradient direction, and $\nabla I_p^{\perp}$ is a vector normal to this gradient direction, as shown in Fig. 1, where

$$\delta I(q) = | \delta I_x(q) | + | \delta I_y(q) | . \tag{6}$$

In the above equations, δI_x and δI_y are, respectively, intensity gradients in x and y directions. Color images are first converted to grayscale to calculate their *edge length* term. This "*edge length*" term gives a measure of number of pixels, which are part of an edge, and belongs to the known part of the candidate patch to be filled. Thus, it gives more priority to that edge whose length is more.

Target patch with maximum priority is filled first. As a result of this operation, the boundary between the source and target region changes, as shown in Fig. 2. With this, target patches at the boundary also change. So, priority is again determined for the target patches, and patch with the maximum priority is filled again. This procedure is repeated till whole target region is covered.

3 Image Quality Measure in the Context of *inpainting*

For judging the performance of an *inpainting* algorithm, it is often required to compare the visual quality of the processed images. In future, it can be extended to automate the inpainting process toward generating images with good quality measure. *Quality Assessment* (QA) is an active area of research in image and video processing. It plays a pivotal role in tuning many visual processing algorithms and systems [30, 42, 47, 48]. An image or video goes through different steps of processing, which may introduce some distortions [39]. Due to this, their quality may degrade. It is

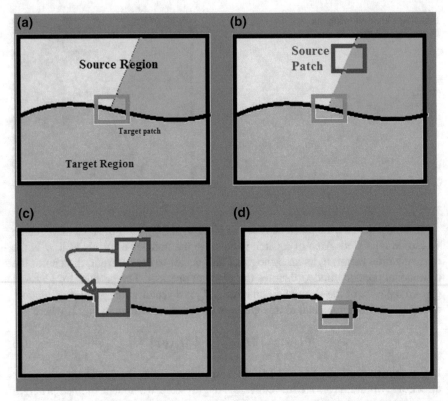

Fig. 2 **a** An image with target region and source region. **b** Image showing target patch and a candidate source patch. **c** Source patch copied to target patch. **d** Image with new boundary between source and target region

desired to get the amount of distortion, which is being added for various purposes, such as to evaluate the efficiency of capturing devices, display devices, processing algorithms, and obviously, to get a good image or video.

The image and video QA methods developed so far can be classified into following three categories:

- *Full Reference Quality Assessment* (FRQA) methods [37, 43, 45].
- *Reduced Reference Quality Assessment* (RRQA) methods [29, 35, 44].
- *No Reference Quality Assessment* (NRQA) methods [7, 17, 38].

In FRQA methods, original undistorted image is available as a reference. The quality is evaluated with respect to this reference image. Such methods can be used only for in-house experimentation. In RRQA methods, only partial information about the reference image is available. This partial information is used to evaluate the quality of the distorted image. In NRQA methods, no information about the reference image or video is available, and the algorithm estimates the quality without any prior knowledge of the reference image or video.

In particular, in the absence of any reference image, measurement of quality of an image is a difficult task and may not be always precise. Thus, in image *inpainting*, NRQA methods can be used to check the quality of the inpainted images. One such technique, named BRISQUE technique [33], used in [24, 25] and, in the present chapter, is discussed below.

3.1 The BRISQUE Technique

The BRISQUE technique, introduced in [33], is a no reference quality assessment technique. This technique is based on the observation that *Mean Subtracted Contrast Normalized* (MSCN) coefficients strongly tend toward a unit normal Gaussian characteristic for natural images [36]. The deviation of these coefficients from the unit normal Gaussian characteristic gives a measure of the distortion present in the image. The MSCN coefficients are given below:

$$MSCN = \frac{I(i, j) - \mu(i, j)}{\sigma(i, j) + C} . \tag{7}$$

Here, $i \in 1, 2, \ldots, M$ and $j \in 1, 2, \ldots, N$ are spatial indices. M and N are height and width of the image, respectively, and C (= 1) is a constant that prevents ill conditions in computation, when the denominator tends to zero (e.g., in the case of an image patch corresponding to the plain sky). $\mu(i, j)$, and $\sigma(i, j)$ are, respectively, the mean and standard deviation in a small Gaussian window.

These coefficients are used to derive the underlying features which are then fed to a *Support Vector Machine Regressor* (SVR) [1]. The SVR takes the feature vector as input, and gives the BRISQUE score as output. Mathematically, the operation is given by

$$f(x) = w^T \phi(x) + b . \tag{8}$$

Here, $f(x)$ corresponds to the BRISQUE score, $\phi(x)$ is the feature vector, and w, b are the parameters of the support vector machine regressor.

A block diagram of this technique is shown in Fig. 3. This technique gives a lower score to a good quality image. The details are available in [33].[1]

---

[1] A software release of the technique reported in [33] is available online: http://live.ece.utexas.edu/research/quality/BRISQUE_release.zip.

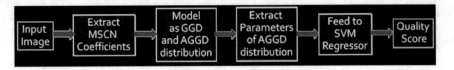

Fig. 3 Block diagram description of the BRISQUE technique

4 PAtch Modified Exemplar-Based InpainTing (PAMIT)

The patch size affects the *inpainting* result significantly. A smaller patch size increases computation and, hence, the execution time. It also increases the blockiness artifacts. The geometry inside a patch should be present in rest of the image for good reconstruction. If the patch size is large, the desired geometry may not be present in rest of the image. Ideally, the patch size should be such that the geometry contained in this patch should be present in rest of the image. However, determining this ideal patch size is a non-trivial problem. Many reported exemplar-based techniques take a patch size of 9×9, which gives good results in most cases. A typical example of effect of patch size on the inpainted images is shown in Fig. 4.

In Fig. 4, inpainted images obtained by techniques reported in [13, 50], MEBI [26], and LIMEP [24], with the patch size varying from 5 to 17, are shown. It can be observed that the results at smaller (5 and 7) and larger (15 and 17) patch sizes are not good. At middle patch sizes (9, 11, 13), the results appear better.

In the present work, patch size is first fixed to a high value, 17×17, corresponding to radius of the square window, $w = 8$. If the error between source and target patches is greater than a threshold, denoted by γ, patch size is reduced in steps decreasing the radius by 1 (i.e., $w = w - 1$), till the error becomes less than the threshold, else the algorithm proceeds with this patch size. The threshold value decides whether the most similar source patch is similar enough to be considered for filling the target patch. We consider in our work that the difference between source patch and target patch should be less than half the maximum difference value that can be obtained from candidate source patches. Mathematically, the threshold γ is given below:

$$\gamma_{\psi_p, \psi_q} = \frac{1}{2} \times max \left\{ d(\psi_p, \psi_q) \right\}. \tag{9}$$

Here, γ_{ψ_p, ψ_q} is the threshold value for the source patch ψ_p and target patch ψ_q. For fast approximation of γ, we adopted the following strategy. For a square patch size of $(2 \times w + 1) \times (2 \times w + 1)$ (corresponding to a radius of w of the square window), the maximum value of $d(\psi_p, \psi_q)$ occurs when source patch consists of all white pixels (of intensity value 255) and target patch of all black pixels (of intensity value 0). It is given below:

$$\gamma = \frac{1}{2} \times 3 \times (2 \times w + 1)^2 \times 255^2. \tag{10}$$

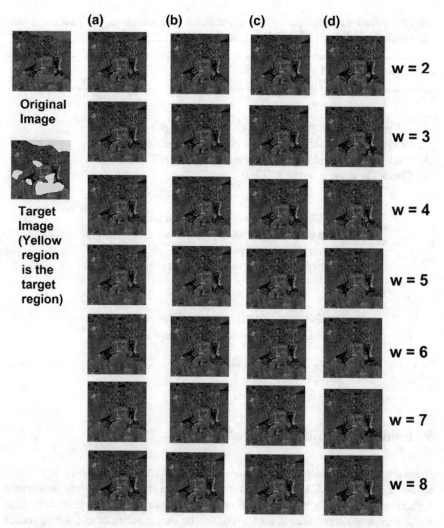

Fig. 4 Inpainted images (zoom for clarity in electronic version) obtained by following technique in **a** [13], **b** MEBI technique, **c** LIMEP technique, and **d** proposed PAMIT technique. Patch size = $(2 \times w + 1) \times (2 \times w + 1)$. At patch size of 9×9, $w = 4$, the four *inpainting* techniques produce best inpainted image

The computational steps are shown in Algorithm 1. This technique is named PAtch Modified InpainTing (PAMIT). The inpainted images obtained by PAMIT are also shown in Fig. 4. It is observed that there are dark patches around the shoulder and neck in the inpainted images given by techniques in [13, 24, 26], while the results obtained by proposed PAMIT technique do not suffer from this undesirable effect. In all the cases, the inpainted results look visually better than the other techniques under comparison. Thus, the limitations imposed by a fixed patch size have been overcome with the proposed technique. Also, as the patch size increases, the execution time decreases, even though the quality of image remains at par.

Algorithm 1: PAMIT

---

1. Set p to a high value, so that patch size $= 2 \times (p + 1)$.
2. Find target patch with maximum priority as given by Eq. 2.
3. Find the best matching source patch according to Eq. 1.
4. Check the value of error E (Eq. 1).
   If $E \leq \gamma$,

   ·   fill the unknown contents of this target patch with the known contents of source patch,
   ·   Move on to next target patch
   ·   Repeat steps 2 to 4, till whole target region is filled.

   else

   ·   Break this target patch into four smaller patches
   ·   For these four target patches repeat steps 2 to 4.

---

5 Source-Constrained *inpainting*

In source-constrained *inpainting*, source region is also marked manually, in addition to the target region. With a marked source region, the *inpainting* algorithm searches for source patches only in the marked region. This reduces the computational time, as the search space is reduced. It also reduces the chances of selecting wrong source patches for filling the target patches, as only the source region, which contains desired texture and structure, is marked.

Constraining the source is particularly useful in restoring the digital images of cave paintings, where high accuracy is desired. The cave paintings have many spots of degraded region. Manually marking the source region for these spots increases the accuracy of *inpainting*. A typical example is shown in Figs. 5, 6, and 7. In Fig. 5, an original image is shown along with marked source and target regions. In Fig. 6, results of *inpainting* algorithms are shown, and in Fig. 7 zoomed versions are shown. It can be observed that the proposed PAMIT algorithm provided images with best BRISQUE scores as compared to other techniques. Also, the techniques have been applied in a source-constrained way and corresponding *inpainting* results are shown in Fig. 6e–f. From Figs. 6 and 7, it can be observed that the techniques gave some

(a)   (b)   (c)

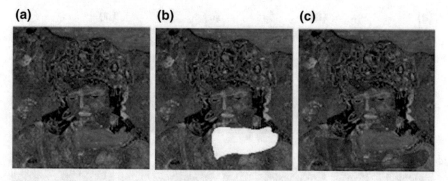

Fig. 5 **a** Original degraded image ($BS = 26.05$) ("Ajanta Padmapani" by Unknown—http://www.
national-geographic.ru/ngm/200801/article_168/gallery_1394/. Licensed under Public Domain via
Commons). **b** Image with marked target region. **c** Image with marked source region

dark patches in the target region when applied in a traditional way. On the other hand,
when applied in a source-constrained manner, the techniques gave better *inpainting*
results (complete absence of or presence of less number of dark patches) as compared
to their traditional counterparts. The execution times, denoted by ET, and BRISQUE
scores, denoted by BS (as determined by the technique reported in [33]), of different
inpainting techniques are also given in captions of figures. It can be observed that
the source-constrained counterparts of the techniques take less execution time, and
have less BRISQUE score, indicating better quality image. The proposed PAMIT
algorithm took the least execution time and gave the least BRISQUE score (indicating
the best quality of reconstruction) among all of them.

6 Results and Discussion

In this section, first the effectiveness of the proposed PAMIT technique is demonstrated for removing objects from images, in general. After this, results for restoration
of degraded images of old cave paintings are presented. The proposed technique is
compared to other *inpainting* techniques. BRISQUE scores of the inpainted images
(denoted as BS) are also calculated, and are shown in the legends of figures. All
experiments have been performed using MATLAB R2013a, dual-core i3 64-bit processor with 8 GB RAM.

6.1 Effectiveness of PAMIT

In this section, the proposed technique is applied to remove objects from images and
compared with some other *inpainting* techniques. In Fig. 8, typical results are shown.

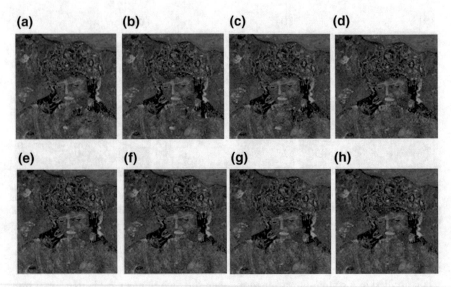

Fig. 6 Image inpainted by **a** Criminisi's technique ($ET = 78s$, $BS = 25.87$), **b** MEBI technique ($ET = 84s$, $BS = 25.67$), **c** LIMEP technique ($ET = 89s$, $BS = 25.52$), **d** PAMIT technique ($ET = 27s$, $BS = 25.41$), **e** Criminisi's technique applied in source-constrained manner ($ET = 47s$, $BS = 25.76$), **f** MEBI technique applied in source-constrained manner ($ET = 53s$, $BS = 25.45$), **g** LIMEP technique applied in source-constrained manner ($ET = 56s$, $BS = 25.32$), **h** PAMIT technique applied in source-constrained manner ($ET = 17s$, $BS = 25.19$)

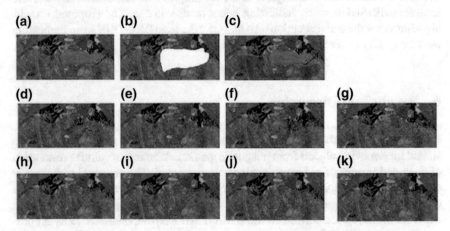

Fig. 7 **a–c** Zoomed versions of images in Fig. 5a–c, respectively, **d–k** Zoomed versions of images in Fig. 6a–h

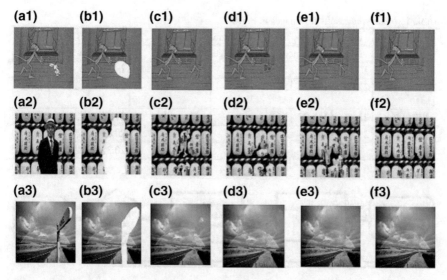

Fig. 8 **a** Original image. **b** Image with marked target region. Image inpainted by **c** Criminisi's technique, **d** MEBI technique, **e** LIMEP technique, **f** Proposed PAMIT technique

In the first row of images of Fig. 8, it can be observed that the techniques in [13, 24, 26] produce an unwanted lion portion, while the PAMIT technique does not suffer from this intrusion. In the second row of images, the techniques in [13, 24, 26] do not construct the box region properly, while the PAMIT technique provides a good reconstruction of the box. In the third row of images, the PAMIT technique demonstrates almost comparable results. However, the execution time of PAMIT is much less (refer to Table 1).

The execution time and number of patches are given in Table 1. It can be observed from Table 1 that the proposed PAMIT technique takes very less time as compared to other techniques under comparison. This is due to the fact that the numbers of patches required are less in PAMIT (refer to Table 1) as compared to other techniques. However, there is an overhead of determining an appropriate patch size for a target patch during inpainting. As the algorithm starts from larger patch size, this gets compensated on the average. Otherwise, if the patch size is always found to be around 9×9, PAMIT technique may suffer from this overhead computation. However, this situation rarely occurs, as we found, empirically, that most of the larger size source patches are sufficiently accurate to fill the target region. The frequency distribution of different patch sizes used in the inpainting is given in Table 2. In this table, ps_n denotes the number of patches of patch size $n \times n$. From the table, it can be observed that for PAMIT technique most of the target patches have higher sizes (i.e., 17×17, 15×15, 13×13), while the patch size is fixed at 9×9 for other techniques.

Table 1 *Inpainting* results for images in Fig. 8

Technique	Execution time (in s)			Number of patches			BRISQUE score		
	Image row number			Image row number			Image row number		
	1	2	3	1	2	3	1	2	3
Criminisi's [13]	22.08	104.37	51.48	88	447	212	21.34	23.23	22.12
MEBI [26]	23.97	113.97	55.31	88	447	212	21.10	23.18	21.98
LIMEP [24]	25.87	124.04	58.95	88	447	212	20.67	23.04	21.67
PAMIT	7.15	30.07	16.32	28	130	66	20.35	22.89	21.56

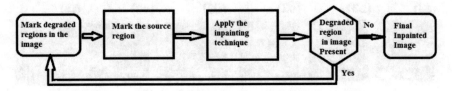

Fig. 9 Block diagram showing the manner of applying inpainting algorithm

6.2 Restoration of Images of Old Degraded Cave Paintings

In this section, we discuss restoration of degraded cave paintings using PAMIT. The *inpainting* techniques as reported in [24–26] are also applied under the source-constrained framework and compared with the proposed technique. Some typical results are shown in Figs. 10, 11, 12, 13, 14, 15, 16, 17, and 18. Execution times, denoted by ET, and the BRISQUE Score [33], denoted by BS, of the inpainted images are shown in captions of figures.

First, the degraded regions are marked in the image. Then, source regions are also marked. After this, the inpainting technique is applied. If the inpainted image contains degraded regions, it is inpainted again in the same way till no degraded regions are left. The overall procedure of applying the inpainting algorithm is given in block diagram in Fig. 9.

In Fig. 10, a degraded cave painting is shown. The marked target and source regions are also highlighted. Inpainted images as obtained by different techniques are shown. Some parts of these images are zoomed and shown in Fig. 11 for clarity. From Fig. 10, it can be observed that after *inpainting*, eye region is not reconstructed properly. In this case, the eye region gets filled, which is not desirable. To overcome this, the eye is marked in the next stage, for *inpainting*, and this time the source region is restricted to other eye only, for better reconstruction. Improved results are shown in Fig. 12.

Table 2 Frequency distribution of different patch sizes used in the inpainting

Patch size	Row number of image in Fig. 8											
	1				2				3			
	Criminisi's	MEBI	LIMEP	PAMIT	Criminisi's	MEBI	LIMEP	PAMIT	Criminisi's [13]	MEBI [26]	LIMEP [24]	PAMIT
ps_3	0	0	0	0	0	0	0	0	0	0	0	0
ps_5	0	0	0	0	0	0	0	0	0	0	0	0
ps_7	0	0	0	1	0	0	0	2	0	0	0	0
ps_9	88	88	88	1	447	447	447	2	212	212	212	0
ps_{11}	0	0	0	1	0	0	0	4	0	0	0	2
ps_{13}	0	0	0	3	0	0	0	12	0	0	0	4
ps_{15}	0	0	0	8	0	0	0	32	0	0	0	21
ps_{17}	0	0	0	14	0	0	0	78	0	0	0	39

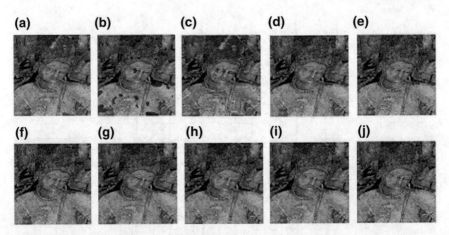

Fig. 10 **a** Original degraded image ($BS = 26.05$) ("Ajanta Padmapani" by Unknown—http://www.national-geographic.ru/ngm/200801/article_168/gallery_1394/. Licensed under Public Domain via Commons). **b** Image with marked target region. **c** Image with marked source region. Image inpainted by **d** Criminisi's technique ($BS = 25.98$, $ET = 79s$), **e** MEBI technique ($BS = 25.84$, $ET = 84s$), **f** LIMEP technique ($BS = 25.73$, $ET = 89s$), **g** MEBIPO technique ($BS = 25.23$, $ET = 947s$), **h** COMEP technique ($BS = 25.36$, $ET = 1047s$), **i** IIMI technique ($BS = 25.50$, $ET = 847s$). **j** PAMIT technique ($BS = 25.67$, $ET = 27s$)

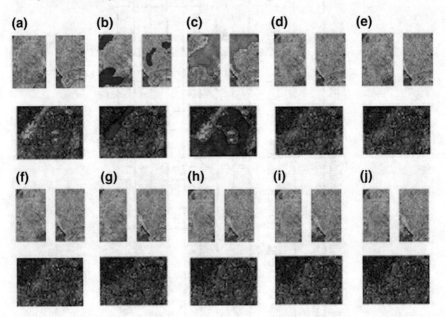

Fig. 11 Zoomed parts of images in Fig. 10

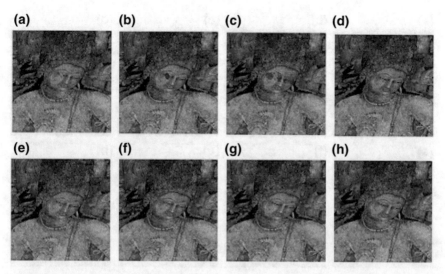

Fig. 12 **a** Original degraded image ($BS = 25.50$). **b** Image with marked target region. **c** Image with marked source region. Image inpainted by **d** Criminisi's technique ($BS = 25.98$, $ET = 49s$), **e** MEBI technique ($BS = 25.34$, $ET = 54s$), **f** LIMEP technique ($BS = 25.32$, $ET = 67s$), **g** MEBIPO technique ($BS = 25.13$, $ET = 848s$), **h** COMEP technique ($BS = 25.21$, $ET = 923s$), **i** IIMI ($BS = 25.24$, $ET = 785s$). **j** PAMIT technique ($BS = 25.35$, $ET = 18s$)

The degradations in images in Figs. 13 and 16 are such that no clear-cut source region can be marked. So, rest of the image, after marking the target region, is taken as the source region. The *inpainting* is again applied in two steps, and corresponding results for second steps are shown in Figs. 15 and 17. Some zoomed parts of images in Figs. 13, and 17 are shown in Figs. 14, and 18, for clarity. It can be observed that the degraded regions in these images have been restored to a visually pleasing quality. However, it is difficult to determine visually which technique provides the best restored image. From the BRISQUE scores, it can be observed that the proposed PAMIT technique yields better image quality scores, as compared to those obtained from Criminisi's [13], MEBI [26], and LIMEP [24] techniques.

It can be observed that the proposed technique generates better quality images compared to other exemplar-based techniques, while the quality is comparable when compared to energy optimization-based techniques. The execution time of the proposed technique is significantly less than those techniques under comparison.

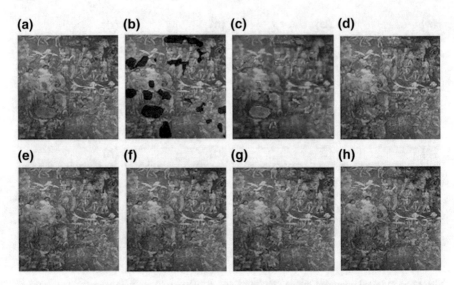

Fig. 13 a Original degraded image ($BS = 25.78$) ("Coming Of Sinhala (Mural At Ajanta In Cave No 17)" by Unknown—Scanned from "A Reign of Ten Kings" (1999-Book) By Nalini De Lanerolle—ISBN 955-9223-00-3, Page 8. Licensed under Public Domain via Commons). **b** Image with marked target region. **c** Image with marked source region. Image inpainted by **d** Criminisi's technique ($BS = 24.15$, $ET = 48s$), **e** MEBI technique ($BS = 23.97$, $ET = 54s$), **f** LIMEP technique ($BS = 23.96$, $ET = 64s$), **g** MEBIPO technique ($BS = 23.85$, $ET = 936s$), **h** COMEP technique ($BS = 23.74$, $ET = 957s$), **i** IIMI ($BS = 23.80$, $ET = 855s$), **j** PAMIT technique ($BS = 23.86$, $ET = 15s$)

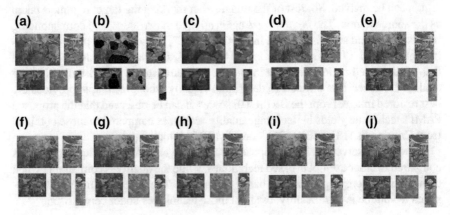

Fig. 14 Zoomed parts of images in Fig. 13

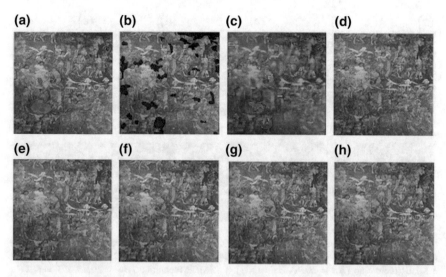

Fig. 15 **a** Original degraded image (BS = 23.80). **b** Image with marked target region. **c** Image with marked source region. Image inpainted by **d** Criminisi's technique ($BS = 23.89$, $ET = 59s$), **e** MEBI technique ($BS = 23.75$, $ET = 67s$), **f** LIMEP technique ($BS = 23.73$, $ET = 85s$), **g** MEBIPO technique ($BS = 23.32$, $ET = 986s$), **h** COMEP technique ($BS = 23.42$, $ET = 1043s$), **i** IIMI ($BS = 23.10$, $ET = 943s$), **j** PAMIT technique ($BS = 23.18$, $ET = 23s$)

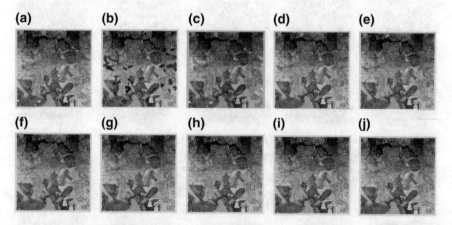

Fig. 16 **a** Original degraded image ($BS = 21.37$) ("Hamsa jtaka, Ajanta, India" by Unknown—From Le Muse absolu, Phaidon, 10-2012. Licensed under Public Domain via Commons). **b** Image with marked target region. **c** Image with marked source region. Image inpainted by **d** Criminisi's technique ($BS = 21.23$, $ET = 75s$), **e** MEBI technique ($BS = 20.97$, $ET = 83s$), **f** LIMEP technique ($BS = 20.96$, $ET = 85s$), **g** MEBIPO technique ($BS = 20.85$, $ET = 990s$), **h** COMEP technique ($BS = 20.66$, $ET = 1057s$), **i** IIMI ($BS = 20.93$, $ET = 968s$), **j** PAMIT technique ($BS = 20.98$, $ET = 29s$)

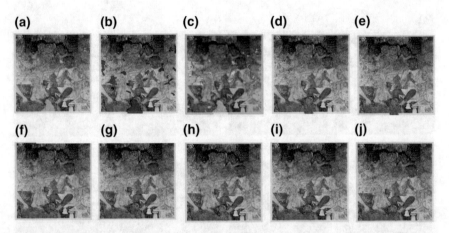

Fig. 17 **a** Original degraded image ($BS = 20.93$). **b** Image with marked target region. **c** Image with marked source region. Image inpainted by **d** Criminisi's technique ($BS = 20.83$, $ET = 51s$), **e** MEBI technique ($BS = 20.77$, $ET = 55s$), **f** LIMEP technique ($BS = 20.73$, $ET = 60s$), **g** MEBIPO technique ($BS = 20.34$, $ET = 723s$), **h** COMEP technique ($BS = 20.28$, $ET = 937s$), **i** IIMI ($BS = 20.42$, $ET = 672s$), **j** PAMIT technique ($BS = 20.53$, $ET = 16s$)

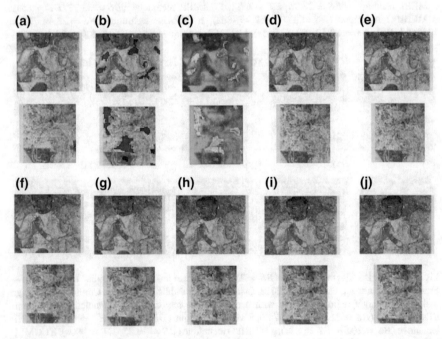

Fig. 18 Zoomed parts of images in Fig. 17

7 Summary

This chapter discusses a modified exemplar-based *inpainting* technique, called PAMIT. This technique has been applied under the source-constrained framework to restore the digital images of old degraded paintings. Other exemplar-based and energy optimization-based techniques are also applied under the same framework. The proposed technique generates better quality images compared to those techniques, while the execution time is comparable. The execution time of the proposed technique is less than that of the energy optimization-based techniques, while the quality is comparable. Quality of inpainted images has been observed both by visual inspection and from the BRISQUE score [33]. Future scope of the work lies in automating the selection of source and target regions for the task of source-constrained *inpainting*.

References

1. Abe, S.: Support Vector Machines for Pattern Classification, vol. 2. Springer (2005)
2. Arias, P., Caselles, V., Sapiro, G.: A variational framework for non-local image inpainting. In: Energy Minimization Methods in Computer Vision and Pattern Recognition, pp. 345–358. Springer (2009)
3. Aswatha, S.M., Mukherjee, J., Bhowmick, P.: An integrated repainting system for digital restoration of Vijayanagara murals. Int. J. Image Graph. **16**(01), 1650005 (2016)
4. Ballester, C., Bertalmio, M., Caselles, V., Sapiro, G., Verdera, J.: Filling-in by joint interpolation of vector fields and gray levels. IEEE Trans. Image Process. **10**(8), 1200–1211 (2001)
5. Bertalmio, M., Sapiro, G., Caselles, V., Ballester, C.: Image inpainting. In: Proceedings of the 27th Annual Conference on Computer Graphics and Interactive Techniques, pp. 417–424. ACM Press/Addison-Wesley Publishing Co. (2000)
6. Bornemann, F., März, T.: Fast image inpainting based on coherence transport. J. Math. Imaging Vis. **28**(3), 259–278 (2007)
7. Brandão, T.: No-reference image quality assessment based on DCT domain statistics. Signal Process. **88**(4), 822–833 (2008)
8. Buchsbaum, G., Gottschalk, A.: Trichromacy, opponent colours coding and optimum colour information transmission in the retina. Proc. R. Soc. Lond. B: Biol. Sci. **220**(1218), 89–113 (1983)
9. Buyssens, P., Daisy, M., Tschumperlé, D., Lézoray, O.: Exemplar-based inpainting: technical review and new heuristics for better geometric reconstructions. IEEE Trans. Image Process. **24**(6), 1809–1824 (2015)
10. Chambolle, A.: An algorithm for total variation minimization and applications. J. Math. Imaging Vis. **20**(1), 89–97 (2004)
11. Chan, T., Shen, J.: Mathematical models for local deterministic in-paintings. UCLA CAM TR 00–11 (2000)
12. Chan, T.F., Shen, J.: Nontexture inpainting by curvature-driven diffusions. J. Vis. Commun. Image Represent. **12**(4), 436–449 (2001)
13. Criminisi, A., Pérez, P., Toyama, K.: Region filling and object removal by exemplar-based image inpainting. IEEE Trans. Image Process. **13**(9), 1200–1212 (2004)
14. De Bonet, J.S.: Multiresolution sampling procedure for analysis and synthesis of texture images. In: Proceedings of the 24th Annual Conference on Computer Graphics and Interactive Techniques, pp. 361–368. ACM Press/Addison-Wesley Publishing Co. (1997)
15. Demanet, L., Song, B., Chan, T.: Image inpainting by correspondence maps: a deterministic approach. Appl. Comput. Math. **1100**(217–50), 99 (2003)

16. Efros, A.A., Leung, T.K.: Texture synthesis by non-parametric sampling. In: The Proceedings of the Seventh IEEE International Conference on Computer Vision, 1999, vol. 2, pp. 1033–1038. IEEE (1999)
17. Ferzli, R., Karam, L.J.: A no-reference objective image sharpness metric based on the notion of just noticeable blur (JNB). IEEE Trans. Image Process. 18(4), 717–728 (2009)
18. Ghorai, M., Chanda, B.: An image inpainting algorithm using higher order singular value decomposition. In: 2014 22nd International Conference on Pattern Recognition (ICPR), pp. 2867–2872. IEEE (2014)
19. Ghorai, M., Chanda, B.: An image inpainting method using plsa-based search space estimation. Mach. Vis. Appl. 26(1), 69–87 (2015)
20. Huang, W., Wang, S.W., Yang, X.P., Jia, J.F.: Dunhuang murals in-painting based on image decomposition. Shandong Daxue Xuebao (GongxueBan), 40(2), 24–27 (2010)
21. Jun, J., Wang, Z.: The research of Tibet mural digital images inpainting using CDD model. In: 2nd International Symposium on Instrumentation and Measurement, Sensor Network and Automation (IMSNA), 2013, pp. 805–807. IEEE (2013)
22. Kawanaka, H., Kosaka, S., Iwahori, Y., Sugiyama, S.: Image reproduction based on texture image extension with traced drawing for heavy damaged mural painting. Procedia Comput. Sci. 22, 968–975 (2013)
23. Komodakis, N., Tziritas, G.: Image completion using efficient belief propagation via priority scheduling and dynamic pruning. IEEE Trans. Image Process. 16(11), 2649–2661 (2007)
24. Kumar, V., Mukherjee, J., Das Mandal, S.K.: Combinatorial exemplar based image inpainting. In: Proceedings of International Workshop on Combinatorial Image Analysis, pp. 284–298. Springer (2015)
25. Kumar, V., Mukherjee, J., Das Mandal, S.K.: Image inpainting through metric labelling via guided patch mixing. IEEE Trans. Image Process. (2015)
26. Kumar, V., Mukhopadhyay, J., Das Mandal, S.K.: Modified exemplar-based image inpainting via primal-dual optimization. In: Proceedings of Pattern Recognition and Machine Intelligence. PReMI 2015, Warsaw, Poland, 30 June–3 July 2015, Proceedings, vol. 9124, pp. 116–125. Springer (2015)
27. Kwatra, V., Schödl, A., Essa, I., Turk, G., Bobick, A.: Graphcut textures: image and video synthesis using graph cuts. In: ACM Transactions on Graphics (ToG), ACM, 2003, vol. 22, pp. 277–286
28. Le Meur, O., Ebdelli, M., Guillemot, C.: Hierarchical super-resolution-based inpainting. IEEE Trans. Image Process. 22(10), 3779–3790 (2013)
29. Li, Q., Wang, Z.: Reduced-reference image quality assessment using divisive normalization-based image representation. IEEE J. Sel. Top. Signal Process. 3(2), 202–211 (2009)
30. Lin, W., Jay Kuo, C.-C.: Perceptual visual quality metrics: a survey. J. Vis. Commun. Image Represent. 22(4), 297–312 (2011)
31. Liu, Y., Caselles, V.: Exemplar-based image inpainting using multiscale graph cuts. IEEE Trans. Image Process. 22(5), 1699–1711 (2013)
32. Masnou, S.: Disocclusion: a variational approach using level lines. IEEE Trans. Image Process. 11(2), 68–76 (2002)
33. Mittal, A., Moorthy, A.K., Bovik, A.C.: No-reference image quality assessment in the spatial domain. IEEE Trans. Image Process. 21(12), 4695–4708 (2012)
34. Purkait, P., Chanda, B.: Digital restoration of damaged mural images. In: Proceedings of the Eighth Indian Conference on Computer Vision, Graphics and Image Processing, p. 49. ACM (2012)
35. Rehman, A., Wang, Z.: Reduced-reference image quality assessment by structural similarity estimation. IEEE Trans. Image Process. 21(8), 3378–3389 (2012)
36. Ruderman, D.L.: The statistics of natural images. Network: Comput. Neural Syst. 5(4), 517–548 (1994)
37. Sheikh, H.R., Bovik, A.C.: Image information and visual quality. IEEE Trans. Image Process. 15(2), 430–444 (2006)

38. Sheikh, H.R., Bovik, A.C., Cormack, L.: No-reference quality assessment using natural scene statistics: JPEG2000. IEEE Trans. Image Process. **14**(11), 1918–1927 (2005)
39. Sheikh, H.R., Bovik, A.C.: Information theoretic approaches to image quality assessment. In: Handbook of Image and Video Processing. Elsevier (2005)
40. Shen, J., Kang, S.H., Chan, T.F.: Euler's elastica and curvature-based inpainting. SIAM J. Appl. Math. **63**(2), 564–592 (2003)
41. Tschumperlé, D.: Fast anisotropic smoothing of multi-valued images using curvature-preserving PDE's. Int. J. Comput. Vis. **68**(1), 65–82 (2006)
42. Wang, Z., Bovik, A.C.: Modern Image Quality Assessment. Synthesis Lectures on Image, Video, and Multimedia Processing, vol. 2, no. 1, pp. 1–156 (2006)
43. Wang, Z., Bovik, A.C., Sheikh, H.R., Simoncelli, E.P.: Image quality assessment: from error visibility to structural similarity. IEEE Trans. Image Process. **13**(4), 600–612 (2004)
44. Wang, Z., Simoncelli, E.P.: Reduced-reference image quality assessment using a wavelet-domain natural image statistic model. In: Electronic Imaging 2005, pp. 149–159. International Society for Optics and Photonics (2005)
45. Wang, Z., Simoncelli, E.P., Bovik, A.C.: Multiscale structural similarity for image quality assessment. In: Conference Record of the Thirty-Seventh Asilomar Conference on Signals, Systems and Computers, 2004, vol. 2, pp. 1398–1402. IEEE (2003)
46. Wei, L.-Y., Levoy, M.: Fast texture synthesis using tree-structured vector quantization. In: Proceedings of the 27th Annual Conference on Computer Graphics and Interactive Techniques, pp. 479–488. ACM Press/Addison-Wesley Publishing Co. (2000)
47. Winkler, S.: Perceptual Video Quality Metrics—A Review (2005)
48. Winkler, S., Mohandas, P.: The evolution of video quality measurement: from PSNR to hybrid metrics. IEEE Trans. Broadcast. **54**(3), 660–668 (2008)
49. Qing, W., Yizhou, Y.: Feature matching and deformation for texture synthesis. ACM Trans. Graph. (TOG) **23**(3), 364–367 (2004)
50. Zhang, S., Zhou, X.: An improved scheme for Criminisi's inpainting algorithm. In: 2011 4th International Congress on Image and Signal Processing (CISP), vol. 4, pp. 2048–2051. IEEE (2011)

3D–2D Data Fusion in Cultural Heritage Applications

Robert Frohlich, Stefan Gubo, Attila Lévai and Zoltan Kato

1 Introduction

Recently, cultural heritage experts have a lot of options to choose from for document-ing architectures, excavation sites, caves [1], or other large-scale objects or scenes. Different devices working on different principles are available, each imposing a spe-cific workflow for the creation of a colorized 3D model. But unfortunately as it is well known for all experts working in this field, there is no one single solution that could be used for all types of case studies. Reviewing recent CH publications, we observed that based on the actual case's properties and the available budget, different groups used completely different approaches starting from the low-cost options like photogrammetry or relatively cheap, entry-level structured light scanners up to the more professional Lidar scanners and even expensive laboratory setups. As strict laboratory conditions can hardly be ensured on the field, and not all case studies require the highest possible precision of the results, usually some compromises are made as long as the lower quality results still meet the project's needs.

Multiple works are comparing all the different available techniques, [2] compared photogrammetry, laser scanning, and also their combined use. But most of the recent works rely on either laser or structured light-based 3D scanners or photogramme-try to obtain the 3D model of an object. Though the latter is widely used, a recent overview of multiple techniques is presented in [3], and its main disadvantages are well known: a large number of images have to be captured without any feedback, not being able to verify partial results on the go, and processed later on powerful

R. Frohlich
Institute of Informatics, University of Szeged, P.O. Box 652, 6701 Szeged, Hungary

S. Gubo · Z. Kato (✉)
Department of Mathematics and Informatics, J. Selye University, Komarno, Slovakia
e-mail: kato@inf.u-szeged.hu

A. Lévai
Reformed Theological Faculty, J. Selye University, Komarno, Slovakia

© Springer Nature Singapore Pte Ltd. 2018
B. Chanda et al. (eds.), *Heritage Preservation*,
https://doi.org/10.1007/978-981-10-7221-5_6

workstations that is also time consuming. The level of detail captured can only be verified after the final reconstruction is finished; if accidentally some parts were not captured from enough viewpoints, it can only be corrected by a new acquisition. In order to overcome this issue, the authors of [4] have experimented with a mathematical positioning procedure to reduce the required number of images captured and ensure a high level of detail over all regions. Others usually use various software solutions to do the 3D reconstruction using more images taken from arbitrary positions [5]. Since most commercial software relies on the detection of some key points, problems can occur with objects having no texture at all. In these cases, the best practice is placing external markers near or on the object if it is possible, visible on the captured images. A good example is presented in [6], where geotagged marker points were used for both photogrammetric and laser scanning techniques.

3D scanners on the other hand are generally more expensive devices than the DSLR cameras used for photogrammetry, but they are gaining popularity thanks to the entry level, easy to use, relatively cheap devices available, while serious professionals are indisputably relying on laser or structured light scanners for the best possible results. Considering only the Lidar scanners or even some structured light scanners that have a built-in RGB camera as well, we can say that these devices cannot produce data that has the necessary color detail for most of the cultural heritage applications, maybe except for visualization purposes in education. For others, a good quality, possibly color-calibrated, high-resolution RGB information has to be attached to the point cloud data. Lidar scanners that do not have an external camera attached will not capture RGB information in the same time with point cloud data, while structured light scanners that have a small sensor camera built in will only capture poor-quality color information. In both cases, the solution is the same, RGB images have to be captured with a separate device, and even a full-frame DSLR camera is quite commonly used for this task; and then fused with the point cloud.

Some recent works have shown that while the separate approaches may produce good partial results, the true potential is in combining multiple approaches. [7] used laser scanners and digital cameras for the documentation of desert palaces in the Jordan desert, while others also included CAD modeling in their work to complete the missing parts of the data [8]. An effective workflow using the combination of these three techniques was presented for 3D modeling of castles [9].

In archeological CH study, 3D modeling has become a very useful process to obtain indispensable data for 3D documentation and visualization. While the precise surveying and measurement of architecture, or excavation sites, is possible with total stations (e.g., manufactured by Leica Geosystems), the use of these devices and the creation of a precise model based on the measurements needs highly experienced professionals. Using a Lidar scanner instead, one can also produce a metric 3D model, with relatively high precision, that could be sufficient for most tasks, and could be used for completing different measurements later on the data itself, even special measurements impossible to perform in real world. As we found out it can also be indispensable for planning the renovation process of some cultural heritage buildings that were never measured properly before, the plans can only be designed once a complete model of the building's actual state is available. Also spatial and color features are important factors for specialists to analyze the ruins of some historical building, make hypothesis about the 3D models, and obtain a 3D view of the assumed original look of the structure, to use it then as an educational or research tool. For these reasons, we only focus on Lidar scanners, since they can produce a widely usable, precise metric 3D model. A possible solution to provide a colorized model is to fuse high-resolution, possibly color-calibrated RGB images with the 3D data. The main challenge of such a fusion is the estimation of the camera's relative pose to the reference 3D coordinate system. In the computer vision community, many solutions are available solving this problem based on finding point or line correspondences between the two domains [10], using mutual information [11], and large number of solutions relying on specific artificial landmarks or markers [12].

In this paper, we propose a complete pipeline to fuse individual Lidar scans and 2D camera images into a complete high-resolution color 3D model of large buildings. Commercial software provided by Lidar manufacturers is limited to the rigid setup of a laser scanner and a camera attached to it, for which they can produce correctly colorized models that are usable in many applications. Unfortunately, in cultural heritage applications, usually a higher level of detail is necessary, especially for some parts of the scene of major importance. For this reason, we have to separate the camera from the scanner and capture fine details from closer viewpoints using different tele lenses as well. Thus, the proposed workflow contains a specific step used to select an optimal camera image for each 3D region that has the best view of that surface based on different criteria. This way we can project images of arbitrary cameras onto the 3D data in an efficient way, wide-angle images providing a good general colorization for most parts, while close-up shots and tele images provide better resolution for selected parts. The efficiency and quality of the method have been demonstrated on two large case studies: the documentation of the reformed churches of Klížska Nemá (Kolozsnéma) and Šamorín (Somorja) in Slovakia.

2 Method

In this chapter, we will describe the steps of the proposed method. The processing workflow is shown in Fig. 1.

2.1 Data Acquisition

For 3D measurements, we used the Riegl VZ-400 Lidar scanner with a horizontal angle resolution of 0.01° and a vertical angle resolution of 0.06°. A complete scan with 100° vertical and 360° horizontal field of view takes about 15 min, and produces a dense point cloud of 100–200 million points, with a nominal depth precision of less than 5 mm at distances below 400 m. Since a single scan only captures the surfaces visible from the Lidar's point of view, the whole surface of a complete building has to

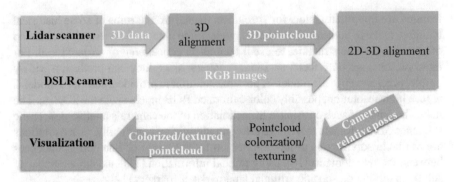

Fig. 1 Workflow of our processing pipeline. Light green shows the input data

be scanned from multiple viewpoints. Usually, interior scenes are more complex than exterior ones, so these require a higher number of scans. For a more complex interior, a preliminary planning of scan positions is needed to provide the best coverage of the scene.

For 2D imaging, a Canon EOS 5D Mark III DSLR camera has been used with various optics. Actually, many Lidar manufacturers provide a solution to place a wide field of view camera on a rigid frame over the scanner, and let the scanner control the 2D capturing process as well. While this technique provides a reliable way to match 2D–3D data in subsequent processing steps, the common viewpoint constraint yields limited resolution of the 2D imagery for distant surfaces. In a typical cultural heritage application, the archeological site is far more complex, which cannot be captured in high detail from such a limited number of positions using a wide-angle lens. Due to the fact that the Lidar scanner has a drastically higher range, being able to capture objects at up to 400 m with high resolution, it is not necessary to place the scanner closer to capture the small details, but with 2D imaging we can only produce high-resolution images of small details (e.g., frescos) if we move the camera closer and use longer focal lengths for better reach. In addition, a 2D camera produces only sharp images of 3D objects located within its *depth of field* range. Hence, for this reason, it is mandatory to separate the camera from the scanner and take additional images from different viewpoints capturing all the fine details of the scene.

Thus, the 3D–2D acquisition procedure typically consists of two stages: (1) acquisition of 3D Lidar scans together with a set of 2D images covering the complete 360° field of view from every scan position with a 24-mm-wide lens; (2) acquisition of 2D images of all the important details from optimal viewpoints, using various focal lengths in the 70–200 mm range. These high detail images would then be used to enhance the color and spatial resolutions of the textured point cloud obtained from the wide-angle images.

2.2 Point Cloud Alignment

The first step of 3D data processing is to register the Lidar scans into a common global coordinate frame. Let us consider a scanner that observes a 3D world point $\mathbf{X}$ from different positions. In the first position S_1, the scanner will record the position $\mathbf{X}'_1$ of the point $\mathbf{X}$ in the Lidar's coordinate system that has its origin in the projection center of S_1. Moving the device to another position S_2 will measure position $\mathbf{X}'_2$ for the same point $\mathbf{X}$ in the coordinate system of S_2. The points $\mathbf{X}'_1$ and $\mathbf{X}'_2$ are related by a rotation $\mathbf{R}$ and translation $\mathbf{t}$:

$$\mathbf{X}'_1 = \mathbf{R}\mathbf{X}'_2 + \mathbf{t} \tag{1}$$

Given a sufficient number of $(\mathbf{X}'_1, \mathbf{X}'_2)$ point pairs, one can easily compute the aligning rigid body transformation $(\mathbf{R}, \mathbf{t})$ between the scans S_1 and S_2. Actually, the calculated transformation brings the coordinate system of S_2 into S_1. If we choose S_1 the global coordinate system, then we can align each S_i scan in the same way, bringing all the data into the same coordinate system, hence merging the partial scans into one single point cloud. For this task, we used the standard marker-based automatic registration algorithm available in the Lidar's software. As an alternative solution for outdoor scans, the software can also use the recorded GPS data instead of markers. If no markers nor GPS data is available, we can still do a registration by manually selecting sufficiently many corresponding $\mathbf{X}'_i$ point pairs in the point clouds, but this will inherently be less precise.

2.3 Camera Pose Estimation

Next, we have to bring the 2D camera images into our world coordinate system established in the previous step. Suppose we have now a camera C_1 that sees a 3D scene point $\mathbf{X}$, expressed with homogeneous world coordinates $\mathbf{X} = (X_1, X_2, X_3, 1)^T$. It will get projected on the image plane as [13]

$$\mathbf{x} = \mathbf{P}\mathbf{X}, \tag{2}$$

where $\mathbf{P}$ is the 3×4 camera matrix composed of $\mathbf{P} = \mathbf{K}\mathbf{R}[\mathbf{I}|\mathbf{t}]$, $\mathbf{I}$ is the identity matrix, and $\mathbf{K}$ is the 3×3 upper triangular calibration matrix:

$$\mathbf{K} = \begin{pmatrix} f_x & & o_x \\ & f_y & o_y \\ & & 1 \end{pmatrix}, \tag{3}$$

containing the camera intrinsic parameters: the focal lengths (f_x, f_y) and the principal point (o_x, o_y) of the camera, while $\mathbf{R}$ and $\mathbf{t}$ are the rotation and translation aligning the camera frame with the world coordinate frame [13]. The internal parameters of the camera can be easily estimated prior to data acquisition using standard camera calibration algorithms. Herein, we used the *Caltech Calibration Toolbox* [14]. However, the relative pose has to be estimated for each image using, e.g., standard feature-based methods relying on correspondences between a set of X_i 3D points and x_i pixels [13]. In our experiments, we simply used the Lidar's software to compute relative pose from a given set of 2D–3D point pairs.

For a particular camera image, point correspondences can be obtained in a semi-automatic way using the markers detected in the point cloud and manually picking their corresponding pixel positions in the image. Images taken by wide-angle lenses are likely to contain such markers detected in the Lidar scans, and hence they can be reliably aligned this way. However, fine details are captured by telephoto lenses with a narrow field of view where markers may not be visible. Hence, the selection of the corresponding points will become a manual task in both domains. We solved this by following a two-step procedure: first, wide field of view images are processed in a semi-automatic way yielding a colorized point cloud. This data enables us then to manually select color-based feature points in the tele images and the point cloud. As a result, we will have the pose for all images that capture different views at different resolutions of the scene, giving us various possibilities for colorizing the point cloud.

2.4 Point Cloud Colorization

At this point, we have a complete metric 3D point cloud of the scene and a lot of different images taken from arbitrary viewpoints, but all registered with the global coordinate system. Since a particular 3D point X may be seen by several cameras, the question naturally arises: How can we project the color information from the images onto the 3D points? In order to produce a high-quality textured 3D model, several constraints have to be satisfied: the image used to colorize a point X should have a *sharp* image of X (i.e., it has to be within the camera's depth of field); the camera has to see the point X under an optimal angle (i.e., as close as possible to a perpendicular viewing angle) as well as the resolution around X should be as high as possible. Given a 3D point X and its projection in cameras $C_1 \ldots C_n$ as pixels $x_1 \ldots x_n$, we can write the projection of the 3D point X in camera C_i using (2):

$$x_i = K_i R_i [I|t_i] X, \tag{4}$$

where all the parameters are known by now. Thus, the RGB color of the point X can be transferred from a particular camera image by making use of the above equation.

The commercial software solutions provided with Lidar devices usually assume that the camera is used in a rigid setup with the scanner, having approximately the same viewpoint. In case of overlapping image regions, the colors are simply averaged out for the corresponding 3D points. This approach is correct for this constrained setup, but becomes unusable when we separate the camera from the scanner and place it in completely different positions, making the problem a more complex one. In this case, every camera will have a completely different relative pose that has to be estimated, while in the standard commercial setup this is also reduced to only a change in the rotation **R** of the camera, which is directly recorded by the rotating Lidar. The visibility of the points from the camera viewpoint also has to be verified to avoid problems caused by occlusion. Using the commercial software in this special case, the more images are used; the results can get more blurry because of the averaging of color information from cameras that had suboptimal view of a surface (e.g., camera at a bad angle, out of focus image region, and camera too far away).

Therefore, we propose a much more effective algorithm to tackle this problem, which will select for every 3D point one single camera that has the best view of it, i.e., it is not occluded, captured sharply, from the best angle and with the best resolution.

2.4.1 Visibility

First, we have to detect if a point $\mathbf{X}$ is visible from a camera or it is occluded. For this purpose, we have adopted the *Hidden Point Removal* operator [15]. It relies on the observation that extracting the points that reside on the convex hull of a spherically flipped point cloud with respect to a given viewpoint, we get the visible points from that viewpoint. Let us consider the point cloud PC and the camera position C_1 from which PC is observed. Considering a sphere with the origin in C_1 and radius r constrained to include all the points of PC, spherical flipping will reflect all the points $\mathbf{X} \in PC$ with respect to the sphere by applying the following equation:

$$\hat{\mathbf{X}}_i = \mathbf{X}_i + 2(r - \|\mathbf{X}_i\|)\frac{\mathbf{X}_i}{\|\mathbf{X}_i\|}. \tag{5}$$

Visible points from C_1 are those that will reside on the convex hull of $\hat{PC} \cup C_1$ where $\hat{PC}$ denotes the transformed point cloud of PC [15]. Repeating this step for each camera C_i will give us the set of cameras from which a particular 3D point $\mathbf{X}$ is visible.

2.4.2 Sharpness

Next step is to verify if a point has a sharp image in the camera, only points that fall inside the *depth of field* of a camera C_i should be colorized from that camera image. The real-world focus distance of the camera is not easily retrievable using only the image, but instead we can directly measure the upper and lower limits of the depth of field. Since for each image pixel we have the corresponding 3D point $\mathbf{X}$ and from the camera pose we can directly compute the camera-to-point distance, we only have to find the image regions that are in focus. For this purpose, we adopt the focus measure introduced by [16], which reflects the statistical properties of the wavelet transform coefficients in different high-frequency subbands. Considering a 2D discrete wavelet transformation, in a single-level transformation, we will have four coefficient blocks, each 1/4 of the size of the original image. The one noted with *LH* (Low High frequency) contains coefficients representing the vertical edges in the image, while the *HL* block shows horizontal edges, and the *HH* block containing high-frequency components both in horizontal and vertical direction will represent the diagonal edges in the image. Using a randomly positioned window w over the original image, its corresponding operator windows in the single-level wavelet transformation's *LH*, *HL*, and *HH* subbands are denoted by w_{LH}, w_{HL}, and w_{HH} respectively, while the wavelet transform images in the subbands are denoted by W_{LH}, W_{HL}, and W_{HH}. The focus measure operator is defined using the standard deviation of the wavelet coefficients as

$$
\begin{aligned}
M_{WT}^2 = \frac{1}{N_w}[&\sum_{(i,j)\in w_{LH}} (W_{LH}(i, j) - \mu_{LH})^2 + \\
&\sum_{(i,j)\in w_{HL}} (W_{HL}(i, j) - \mu_{HL})^2 + \\
&\sum_{(i,j)\in w_{HH}} (W_{HH}(i, j) - \mu_{HH})^2],
\end{aligned}
\tag{6}
$$

where N_w is the number of pixels in w and μ is the expectation of the wavelet coefficients in each subband denoted with the corresponding subscript. We selected the windows w_s that had the focus measure M_{WT}^2 above the experimentally determined threshold level of 1.1. We also experimentally determined an appropriate size for the window w, as a square window having 200px width, since on a full-frame camera's 24Mpx image this is roughly similar in size to the focus detection squares that the camera uses, while smaller windows tend to often miss the sharp details on homogeneous regions.

Since the absolute pose of the camera C_i is known, we can simply calculate the average distance between the camera and the 3D points visible in window w_s as the average of the Euclidean distances from point to camera. Having a physical metric distance value $dist(w_s)$ assigned to each sharp window, let us create a histogram of the different distance values, and take the 5 and 95% percentiles of the distribution of the values to filter out possible outliers. These values are an appropriate estimate for lowest and highest distance limits.

$$
\begin{aligned}
lowest\_dist &= hist(dist(w_s), @5\%) \\
highest\_dist &= hist(dist(w_s), @95\%)
\end{aligned}
\tag{7}
$$

Points in this distance domain projected in camera C_i will have a sharp image. We apply these limits to filter out the cameras that do not see a given point sharply.

2.4.3 Viewing Angle

At this point, we have for each 3D point $\mathbf{X}$ a set of cameras assigned in which it is visible and in focus. As a next step, we have to choose the one that sees the point from an optimal viewing angle and at highest resolution. Let us first calculate the angle between the surface normal $\mathbf{n_X}$ in $\mathbf{X}$ and the projection ray $\mathbf{o_{Xi}}$ pointing from $\mathbf{X}$ into the optical center of camera C_i. Since all the camera poses are known, the camera's projection center coordinates $\mathbf{c_i} = (x, y, z)^T$ are available. The surface normals in a point cloud can be calculated by different methods, like fitting local planes over a small neighborhood of the points [17], but these methods could have trouble detecting the correct orientation of the normals in case of large point clouds of complex scenes. Fortunately, most Lidar scanners already provide the raw scan data with the correct normals in it, so we used this instead. The angle of these two vectors can be simply calculated using

$$\theta = \arccos\left(\frac{\mathbf{n_X} \cdot \mathbf{o_{Xi}}}{\|\mathbf{n_X}\| \cdot \|\mathbf{o_{Xi}}\|}\right) \tag{8}$$

with $\mathbf{o_{Xi}} = \mathbf{X} - \mathbf{c_i}$ being the projection vector of point $\mathbf{X}$ into the ith camera. The angles $|\theta| \in (0 \ldots \pi/2)$ are the geometrically correct ones, as any other angle would mean that the camera is looking at the back side of the surface. Of course a mostly perpendicular view with small $|\theta|$ value is more favorable here.

2.4.4 Resolution

Next, we also check the projection resolution of the region, since a higher focal length camera can produce higher level of detail even from a larger distance, or a lower focal length camera from a closer position as well might have better resolution. We characterize the resolution of the projection of point $\mathbf{X_m}$ in the ith camera as $res_{mi} = f_i/D_{mi}$, where f_i is the focal length of the camera and D_{mi} is the distance of camera i from point $\mathbf{X_m}$.

2.4.5 Selection

Then, the final decision is taken by choosing the camera with the highest value of

$$dc_{mi} = res_{mi}/\theta', \tag{9}$$

where θ' is the scaled version of angle θ into $\theta' \in (0 \ldots 1)$ with 0 corresponding to the perpendicular view and 1 corresponding to the $\pi/2$ angle. dc_{mi} stands for the decision value of camera i with respect to the 3D point $\mathbf{X_m}$. The algorithmic overview of the method is summarized in Algorithm 1. Examples of the colorization with this vertex-based color assignment can be seen in Figs. 3, 7, and 9.

2.5   *Texture Mapping*

The above-presented algorithm provides a point cloud that has the best color assigned
to each vertex point. In many applications, it is desired to have good visual quality but
with reduced data size, suitable for online streaming, storing, or mobile applications.
This can be achieved using the triangular mesh that the scanner software provides us
instead of just the point cloud. This also allows us to simplify the model by reducing
the number of vertices defined and visualizing surfaces instead. This also brings the
benefit that we can map texture files to each triangle of the mesh, so instead of using
the points' assigned color blended over the triangle face, what most software do when
visualizing a colorized mesh, we can map a patch of the high-resolution texture on it.
This technique obviously will provide higher level of detail, and even on a reduced
size data the apparent quality is almost the same. The size of the 3D data itself can be
efficiently reduced by decimation algorithms [18] that will try to collapse multiple
neighboring triangles on the same smooth surface into one single bigger triangle,
reducing the necessary number of faces for smooth regions, while trying to keep a
higher vertex number in the parts that are geometrically more complex.

Applying this to our proposed workflow, we observe that for each point $\mathbf{X}$, we
only need to store the corresponding texture coordinate in each camera image instead
of the RGB value, so according to (4) we can extract the list of pixel coordinates
$\mathbf{x_i}$ for each camera C_i. After that, going through the camera selection steps, when
we already have a camera C^v assigned for each vertex v we can select for each face
$F_j = (v_a, v_b, v_c)$ the best camera, simply by selecting the one that was commonly
assigned to each vertex:

$$C^{F_j} = C^{v_a} \text{ iff } C^{v_a} = C^{v_b} = C^{v_c}.$$

But what happens if the three vertices do not have a common camera assigned?
This naive approach will cause issues on the edges of texture maps when it is the
edge of the texture image and also at the boundary line between two textures. As an
example for the latter, see Fig. 2, where on the left-hand side, we have a fresco that
got textured from two different cameras, and at the boundary line there is a string of
triangles (shown explicitly on the middle image) that did not get either of the cameras
assigned, since their vertices got assigned to different cameras.

Dealing with all these situations may be cumbersome, instead we adopted a new
approach that iterates over all the triangles F of the mesh instead of the points. This
way we are able to select different cameras for neighboring faces that have common
vertices, and we are not limited to one single camera assigned per vertex point.
The camera ranking steps presented in the previous section still remain valid and
necessary, we only have to adapt the final step of the algorithm, in this case iterating
over faces F of the mesh. For each face, we look at the three C^{v_k} camera ranking
lists assigned to each vertex that contains the previously defined dc decision values
for all C_i cameras:

Fig. 2 Issue with texture mapping on the boundary of different texture images (left and middle). Switching from vertex-based to face-based texture mapping the textures can join seamlessly (right)

$$C^{v_k} = dc_{ki}, \text{ where } k \in (a, b, c) \text{ and } i \in (1..n), \tag{10}$$

and select the camera C_i that got included in all three C^{v_k} lists and has the highest values of dc. Assign this to face F_j:

$$C^{F_j} \in (C^{v_a} \cap C^{v_b} \cap C^{v_c}) \text{ where } dc = \max dc_{ki}. \tag{11}$$

The single value assigned to c^{F_j} will be the camera index that was chosen for the triangle. The corresponding texture coordinates are already available for all three vertices of the triangle, since we prepared them in the previous step. The data structure prepared this way can easily be written out in an ASCII wavefront OBJ file based on its standard specifications [19]. The results obtained using the face-based approach can be seen in Fig. 2 on the right-hand side image, where different image textures are seamlessly connected. The algorithmic difference between the vertex-based colorization and the face-based texture mapping can be seen in Algorithm 1.

Algorithm 1 The proposed camera selection algorithm.

Input: A point cloud/triangular mesh and a set of images registered to it.
Output: A list with one camera assigned to every 3D point/face.
1: Considering a 3D point **X**, first filter the list of cameras by visibility using (5).
2: Then filter the list of cameras by their depth of field (7) domain and the camera to point distance, keeping only those that have a sharp image of the point **X**.
3: Using the remaining list of cameras, calculate for each the angle between the projection vector and the surface normal in point **X** using (8).
4: Also calculate each camera's projection resolution with respect to their distance from point **X** and the focal length.
5: Rank the cameras for each vertex v_k using (9), putting them in the list c^{v_k}.
6: Repeat steps 1–5 for all points of the point cloud.
7: **CASE** For vertex-based colorization select the best camera from c^v for each vertex and assign the color seen by that camera according to (4).
   CASE For texture mapping, iterate over all the faces $F_j = (v_a, v_b, v_c)$, and select the camera that is best ranked in all three vertices' camera list c^{v_k} according to (11).

---

3   Experimental Results

The efficiency of the proposed method has been demonstrated on two large case studies. First, the documentation of the Reformed church of Somorja (Šamorín), then the documentation of the Reformed church in Kolozsnéma (Klížska Nemá), both of them located in Slovakia.

3.1   Reformed Church of Somorja

Somorja (Samaria, Sommerein, Zenthmaria) is a sacred edifice of great importance to the Upper Great Rye Island region. It also ranks among the most significant monuments of Christianity in the whole Carpathian Basin and is standing proof of the high standard and prestige of medieval Hungarian Christian culture in Europe. A small chapel had stood on the site of the church sometime before the eleventh century. The chapel was later continually expanded from the eleventh through the twentieth centuries. By the fourteenth century, the building's construction was supported by the likes of King Saint Stephen, King Béla III, Emperor Sigismund, King Matthias, King Wladyslaw II, and King Ludwig the Great.

The building had great sacred significance starting in the early Middle Ages and contributed to a large degree the development of the municipality. Archeological finds have revealed that, by 1521, the church had undergone twelve separate phases of reconstruction. The building's oldest part is the foundation of the Romanesque altar, situated below the current apse, which experienced continual additions since the eleventh century. The tower has been standing in its current form since the thirteenth century. It is made entirely of brick, from its belowground sections to the cap on the very top. The main nave's vaulted ceiling was built at the end of the fifteenth century in Late Gothic style under King Wladyslaw II, in the style of the Prague castle.

The majority of the painted depictions of the main nave have not yet been revealed. Researchers have discovered that several ornate layers are still under the current plaster, the earliest of which dates back to the eleventh century.

During the Romanesque and Gothic era, i.e., in the eleventh–twelfth and fourteenth centuries, the interior was completely covered with paintings, similar to Europe's other significant churches. On the northern wall of the apse, the earliest mural paintings appeared in a horizontal band depicting King Saint Stephen, King Béla III, and Saint Adalbert the Bishop of Prague. To the right of these three portrayals, the painter depicted the most well-known scene from the life of Bishop Saint Martin when, as a Roman soldier, he dismounted his horse and handed half of his cloak to a shivering beggar. In a mural band under these images, the painter depicted the death of Mary. The imposing frescoes are an eloquent testimony to the significance of the town of Somorja in the thirteenth and fourteenth centuries. Few similar apse decorations have been preserved intact in Central and Western Europe.

Fig. 3 Two views of the model colorized with the proposed vertex-based method using a low number of images (24). The regions that were not sharply visible on any of the images are left white

The depiction's intellectual message and iconographic statement praise a scholar–theologian. According to the celestial vision of John the Apostle, these glorify the mysterious magnificence of the invisible God.

The pictures were covered by several layers of plaster for 600–700 years. What we see today is mostly the paintings' preparatory coating. The complete renovation of the exterior of the Reformed church in Somorja was supported by the Ministry of Human Resources of Hungary under Minister Zoltán Balog. Restoration work started in May 2014, and was completed in September 2015.

Fig. 4 Detail comparison of a wide and short telephoto image. On the left a crop of the 24 mm camera image, on the right the same region as viewed by the 70 mm camera

Fig. 5 A wide and short telephoto image used for texturing the mesh, viewed in a split way. The added detail of the tele image is clearly visible. White regions were not visible from any camera's point of view, therefore are not colorized

In Fig. 3, partial views are shown of the interior 3D model of the church in Šamorín. One of its invaluable heritages, the frescos on the sanctuary's ceiling, is visible in Fig. 3 on the first image. We used this fresco, depicting the coronation of Maria, to demonstrate the difference in resolution between an image taken with a telephoto lens, and a wide field of view image. In Fig. 4, we can see the region highlighted with red in Fig. 3 being cropped from a 70 mm focal length (short telephoto lens) image and from a 24 mm focal length camera image that captured a wide-angle overview of the whole sanctuary. In Fig. 5, we can see the comparative results if we use these images for texture mapping on the triangular mesh. Regions that were not visible from any of the cameras are white.

Nevertheless, as we have shown previously, we need both types of images, to produce a highly detailed model, since we can only do a complete colorization of the model using wide field of view images, and when these already provide a color information for the points, we can register the high-resolution images of the small details. As we can see in Fig. 5, this second registration step is also performed with good precision, since the two sides of the mesh are textured from the two

Fig. 6 Model textured with distant images, while a close-up image brings significant improvement in resolution, as seen on the bottom part of the pillar. Green line marks the texture boundary

images mentioned before, just for presentation purpose shown in a split way, and the transition between the regions is quite seamless. It is also noteworthy that just by being able to move the camera freely, we can get much higher resolution details even if using the same focal length lens by taking close-up images. Capturing such images may be more intuitive for the non-professionals and they can still provide an improvement to the 3D model's level of detail, as shown in Fig. 6, where the bottom of the pillar has been textured from a close-up image, taken by the same camera that provided the wide-angle images that textured the rest of the visible walls.

All the above-mentioned comparison images show that the registration of the data is correct. Since our main interest was in the geometric registration and the camera selection process for the colorization, we did not deal with color calibration in this work. Of course, the correct color representation in such a cultural heritage documentation application is also a key factor, but standard solutions are available [20]. So instead we intentionally left all the images uncorrected in the color and lighting sense, and this way the colorized model can give us a clue about which regions were colorized from different cameras, since these transitions are not blended in any way. It is well visible in Fig. 3 on the walls and on the floor that these kinds of visible errors are only caused by the constantly changing illumination of the scene, the shadows, and the inhomogeneous lighting in some regions. If we examine closely the transitions between the different colorizations on the ground, we can see the correct alignment of the cameras, since the edge lines of the bricks are well matched. In Fig. 7, we can observe what improvements can be achieved by attempting to correct the white balance and exposure of the images in post-processing, done by an unexperienced user. While the color tones are more similar between the different

Fig. 7 Overview of the colorized interior using the vertex-based method. Some white balance and exposure correction has been done on the camera images

images, the most visible issue caused by the constantly changing lights and shadows would only be avoidable by using a controlled lighting setup during the acquisition.

One interesting use of a 3D model, produced this way, is the possibility to illustrate historical stages of the buildings, for example, by removing completely the organ from the sanctuary (visible in Fig. 3) that was only added recently, we could visualize how the sanctuary could have looked like centuries ago. This kind of depiction is only possible on such 3D data. An example is shown in Fig. 8, it is noticeable how the windows, the walls, and the paintings behind the organ get visible on the second image.

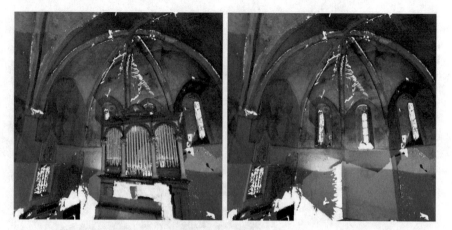

Fig. 8 Illustrating the sanctuary with and without the organ on a textured model

3.2 Reformed Church of Kolozsnéma

There are two separate theories related to the foundation of the reformed church located in the village of Kolozsnéma (Klížska Nemá). According to those theories, the church could have been a Turkish mosque or a Catholic chapel, however, most likely in the reality the church is a tower of a castle owned by the family Kolosfi, built approximately in 1375 at the age of Ludwig the Great. It can be assumed that after the devastation of the castle the church was built on its place and the crypt of Kolosfi's can be still found under the building keeping the possibility to perform an archeological excavation in that area. A dream of the people, living in Kolozsnéma, about the magnification of the church came true during the ministry of Ferenc Borza (1784–1794). The congregation has renovated their church in 1819 and during the construction work a small window has been structured in the western part of the building in order to make the indoor part brighter. Due to the fact that the place dedicated for the men was not big enough, they have built a gallery at the western part and in the same time two brand new windows have been constructed to keep the necessary level of the natural brightness inside. Unfortunately, a huge fire has destroyed all of the buildings belonging to the congregation at the time of Albert Kőváry who was the last pastor of the village living on site. In the fire, almost all of the assets have been damaged like the church, the school, the bowls of the Lords table as well as both of the bells. The congregation was depressed by the calamity; however, they did not give up. The damaged church has been corrected on the May 23, 1858 and later in 1928 and 1929 the church has been renovated by the people living in the village. The internal renovation of the church has been performed during the ministry of László Mikes at the second half of the twentieth century (1951–1952) and finally in the period of 2002 and 2004 the outer part of the building was renovated as well. In the same time, the roof was renewed and the slate used before has been replaced

Fig. 9 Exterior model of the
Kolozsnéma church. Point
cloud colorized from only 21
images using the
vertex-based method

by shingle respecting the strict rules regulating the renovation of the monuments. In
the same time period, the mechanism of the bells has been automatized, the star on
the top of the tower was renovated, the targeting was renovated as well as the doors
and the windows, and further the door located on the rotunda has been unfolded. In
the past 3 years as a part of the work to keep the consistency of the building, the
tower as well as the roof structure made from shingle has been repainted, the pulpit,
the Chair of Moses, the gallery as well as the benches have been renovated.

The exterior model of the church of Kolozsnéma is presented in Fig. 9. This example illustrates well how only a reduced number of images can be sufficient to colorize the complete model of such a building: we only used 21 images in this case with good results. Of course for a more complex structure more images will be needed to cover every part without occlusion, and if important details have to be documented in higher resolution then again the number of images will increase. In this scenario, we faced a similar issue as with the organ in the sanctuary of the other church. The tombstones around the church did not allow for capturing images of the walls without occlusion; so to be able to correctly colorize the building without projecting the image of the tombstones on it, we had to make sure that these objects are also included in the 3D scans, and we kept them in the 3D model while processing the data, simply to obstruct the parts that are not visible from a given camera's viewpoint. After the colorization is finished, these tombs can easily be removed if necessary from the model.

4 Conclusion

A workflow has been proposed for the 2D–3D visual data fusion. While most of the commercial solutions can give good results in the generic setup, we deal with a different, more complex case, when the camera is not attached to the scanner, this way being able to produce higher level of detail, that is necessary for the cultural heritage applications. We proposed a point cloud colorization method based a camera selection algorithm that chooses for every point the camera with the best view of that point based on different parameters. We also presented a texture mapping step that takes advantage of the full resolution of the captured images, and even enables us to create a reduced size model for online visualization. We have shown that the detail level of such a colorized 3D model can greatly be increased from what we might get with a camera mounted on the scanner, by capturing high-resolution images of the important details by moving the camera closer and using higher focal length lenses if necessary.

Acknowledgements This work was partially supported by the NKFI-6 fund through project K-120366; the Research & Development Operational Programme for the project "Modernization and Improvement of Technical Infrastructure for Research and Development of J. Selye University in the Fields of Nanotechnology and Intelligent Space", ITMS 26210120042, co-funded by the European Regional Development Fund. The authors would like to thank Istvan Bucsuhazy for his valuable help.

References

1. Rüther, H., Chazan, M., Schroeder, R., Neeser, R., Held, C., Walker, S.J., Matmon, A., Horwitz, L.K.: Laser scanning for conservation and research of african cultural heritage sites: the case

study of wonderwerk cave, south africa. J. Archaeol. Sci. **36**(9), 1847–1856 (2009). http://www.sciencedirect.com/science/article/pii/S0305440309001344

2. Kadobayashi, R., Kochi, N., Otani, H., Furukawa, R.: Comparison and evaluation of laser scanning and photogrammetry and their combined use for digital recording of cultural heritage. Int. Arch. Photogramm. Remote Sens. Spat. Inf. Sci. **35**(5), 401–406 (2004)

3. Santagati, C., Inzerillo, L., Paola, F.D.: Image-based modeling techniques for architectural heritage 3d digitalization: Limits and potentialities. Int. Arch. Photogramm. Remote Sens. Spat. Inf. Sci. XL-5(w2), 555–560 (2013). http://openarchive.icomos.org/1444/

4. Grosman, L., Smikt, O., Smilansky, U.: On the application of 3-d scanning technology for the documentation and typology of lithic artifacts. J. Archaeol. Sci. **35**(12), 3101–3110 (2008)

5. Koutsoudis, A., Vidmar, B., Arnaoutoglou, F.: Performance evaluation of a multi-image 3d reconstruction software on a low-feature artefact. J. Archaeol. Sci. **40**(12), 4450–4456 (2013)

6. Grussenmeyer, P., Landes, T., Voegtle, T., Ringle, K.: Comparison methods of terrestrial laser scanning, photogrammetry and tacheometry data for recording of cultural heritage buildings. Int. Arch. Photogramm. Remote Sens. Spat. Inf. Sci. **37**(B5), 213–218 (2008)

7. Al-kheder, S., Al-shawabkeh, Y., Haala, N.: Developing a documentation system for desert palaces in Jordan using 3d laser scanning and digital photogrammetry. J. Archaeol. Sci. **36**(2), 537–546 (2009). http://www.sciencedirect.com/science/article/pii/S0305440308002513

8. Agnello, F., Brutto, M.L.: Integrated surveying techniques in cultural heritage documentation. ISPRS Arch. **36**, 5 (2007)

9. El-Hakim, S., Gonzo, L., Voltolini, F., Girardi, S., Rizzi, A., Remondino, F., Whiting, E.: Detailed 3d modelling of castles. Int. J. Archit. Comput. IJAC **5**(2), 200–220 (2007)

10. Mastin, A., Kepner, J., III, J.W.F.: Automatic registration of lidar and optical images of urban scenes. In: Proceedings of International Conference on Computer Vision and Pattern Recognition, June, pp. 2639–2646. IEEE, Miami, Florida, USA (2009)

11. Viola, P., Wells III, W.M.: Alignment by maximization of mutual information. Int. J. Comput. Vis. **24**(2), 137–154 (1997)

12. Alismail, H.S., Baker, L.D., Browning, B.: Automatic calibration of a range sensor and camera system. In: Second Joint 3DIM/3DPVT Conference: 3D Imaging. Modeling, Processing, Visualization and Transmission, October, pp. 286–292. IEEE, Zurich, Switzerland (2012)

13. Hartley, R., Zisserman, A.: Multiple View Geometry in Computer Vision, 2nd edn. Cambridge University Press, New York, NY, USA (2003)

14. Bouguet, J.Y.: Caltech calibration toolbox. http://www.vision.caltech.edu/bouguetj/

15. Katz, S., Tal, A., Basri, R.: Direct visibility of point sets. In: ACM SIGGRAPH 2007 Papers. SIGGRAPH '07. ACM, New York, NY, USA (2007). http://doi.acm.org/10.1145/1275808.1276407

16. Yang, G., Nelson, B.J.: Wavelet based autofocusing and unsupervised segmentation of microscopic images. In: IEEE/RSJ International Conference on Intelligent Robots and Systems, IROS 2003, Las Vegas, Nevada, October, vol. 3, pp. 2143–2148. IEEE (2003)

17. OuYang, D., Feng, H.Y.: On the normal vector estimation for point cloud data from smooth surfaces. Computer Aided Design **37**(10), 1071–1079 (2005). http://dx.doi.org/10.1016/j.cad.2004.11.005

18. Garland, M., Heckbert, P.S.: Surface simplification using quadric error metrics. Proceedings of the 24th Annual Conference on Computer Graphics and Interactive Techniques—SIGGRAPH '97 pp. 209–216 (1997)

19. McHenry, K., Bajcsy, P.: An overview of 3D data content, file formats and viewers. Technical Report (2008). https://www.archives.gov/files/applied-research/ncsa/8-an-overview-of-3d-data-content-file-formats-and-viewers.pdf

20. Chang, Y.C., Reid, J.F.: RGB calibration for color image analysis in machine vision. IEEE Trans. Image Process. **5**(10), 1414–1422 (1996)

Haptic Rendering of Oriented Point Cloud of Heritage Objects Using Proxy Projection

K. G. Sreeni and Subhasis Chaudhuri

1 Introduction

Representation of an object by its bounding surface is commonly used in graphics and haptics as it is quite simple. Triangular patches are widely used to represent the surface because once the triangular mesh is given the succeeding process is straight-forward. Zilles and Salisbury [1] have proposed god-object rendering to properly render triangular patches. But the required number of triangles increases drastically with the increase in detail in the represented object. In such situations, point cloud itself can be effectively used instead of creating a triangular mesh. This is the reason why the point cloud model receives an increasing attention in graphics. It is also easier to resample the point cloud data when it is required to represent an object at different levels of detail [2].

However, there are very few methods to render a virtual object described with a point cloud [3–5]. Here, we propose a computationally efficient method for rendering a dense but not regularly spaced points without constructing a mesh structure. In the case of normal information not being given with the 3D positions, it can be estimated from the point cloud data [6–8].

The paper is organized in the following manner. An introduction to the literature relevant to haptic rendering is given in Sect. 2. Section 3 describes the proposed method of haptic rendering followed by results in Sect. 4. The new rendering method is physically evaluated in Sect. 5 by sampling the trajectory of the haptic device during collision with an object and we conclude the paper in Sect. 6.

K. G. Sreeni (✉)
Department of Electronics and Communication Engineering, College of Engineering,
Thiruvananthapuram, India
e-mail: sreenikg79@gmail.com

S. Chaudhuri
Department of Electrical Engineering, Indian Institute of Technology, Bombay, India
e-mail: sc@ee.iitb.ac.in

© Springer Nature Singapore Pte Ltd. 2018
B. Chanda et al. (eds.), *Heritage Preservation*,
https://doi.org/10.1007/978-981-10-7221-5_7

2   Related Work

There are mainly two different approaches in the haptic rendering literature: geometry-based rendering and rendering based on voxels. Some methods also use a combination of these two approaches [9]. Salisbury et al. [10] and Laycock et al. [11] have given a very good introduction to the rendering techniques used in haptics. The geometry-based haptic rendering is the traditional haptic rendering method which primarily uses triangular patches.

With mesh-based rendering, each time the HIP interacts and penetrates the object surface, the haptic rendering algorithm computes the nearest surface point on the polygonal mesh, and hence the corresponding penetration depth. If **d** denotes the penetration depth of HIP in the given model, the reaction force is determined as $\mathbf{f} = -k\mathbf{d}$, where k denotes the object stiffness constant. This method fails in deciding the appropriate force direction while rendering objects which are thin. Ruspini et al. and Zilles et al. independently introduced the proxy-based algorithm [12] and god-object rendering concept [1], respectively, to solve the difficulties associated with rendering thin objects.

In voxel-based rendering, the object is sampled on a grid of voxels. The simplest and the most basic form of representing a volumetric object is using an array of voxels with each discrete spatial location either showing the presence or absence of the material. The external bounding surface ∂O of a solid object O can be described by the implicit equation [13] as

$$\partial O = \{(x, y, z) \in \mathbb{R}^3 \mid \phi(x, y, z) = 0\}, \tag{1}$$

where ϕ is the implicit function (also called the potential function) and (x, y, z) is the coordinate of a point in 3D. In other words, the set of points for which the potential is zero defines the implicit surface.

In a distance function or a distance field-based method, each point within the field represents the distance from that point to the nearest point on the bounding surface ∂O. Usually, a negative sign is added to the function for inside part the object [14]. This has found applications in haptic rendering. Payne and Toga [15] have explained the basic approach to calculate the distance to triangular patches. The mesh sweeper algorithm is another hierarchical approach proposed by Guéziec [16]. We can use a bounding volume around each triangle and the distances at grid nodes inside the specified bounding volume can be calculated [17]. An algorithm has been proposed by Mauch (in the year 2000) in which he converted the features of a triangular mesh into a polyhedron [18]. For example, the feature vertex becomes a cone with a polygonal base, edge becomes a wedge and the face becomes a prism. The polyhedron containing points closer to the respective feature is then scan converted to compute the distances. A graphic hardware can be used to scan convert the characteristics for a faster implementation [19] as proposed by Sigg et al. The basic principle of distance transform lies in propagating the distance function to the remaining volume once the distance close to the boundary is computed. In Chamfer distance transform

(CDT), a distance template is used [20, 21] to compute the distance of a voxel from the distance values of its neighbouring voxels.

The accuracy of CDT reduces with an increase in distance from the surfaces. Similarly, a vector distance transform uses boundary conditions of voxels containing the vector to the closest point on the surface, and propagating these vectors according to a given vector template [22]. The fast Marching method proposed by Tsitsiklis [23] and Sethian [24] uses the Eikonal equation to compute the distance function. For a distance field-based representation, collision of the HIP and the objects and the corresponding depth of penetration can be easily calculated by computing the potential at the HIP.

With the advancement in scanning technology over the last decade, it has been quite easy to generate a dense point cloud data representing an object. Researchers have been trying to render point cloud bypassing the steps of distance transformation or mesh formation. Point cloud rendering technique proposed by Lee et al. defined a moving least square fitted surface with the given point set and computed the reaction force using the distance from HIP to the nearest point on the computed surface [25]. This technique also suffers from thin object problem.

El-Far et al. filled the voids in the point cloud with pre-computed axis-aligned bounding boxes and then used a god-object rendering technique for haptic interaction [3]. Here, a proxy-based rendering technique is developed to render the point cloud data on the fly without building a surface as is done in god-object rendering to make it computationally efficient. A locally computable implicit function method [4] has been used by Leeper et al. for rendering a dense point cloud data. In [5] and [26], a spherical volume proxy has been used instead of a point proxy, which tends to reduce the user experience as small surface undulations are not felt properly and a smaller choice of the radius of the sphere may lead to sinking of the proxy through the point cloud. In our work, we propose a point proxy-based method to render a dense, oriented point cloud with a proxy projection technique. Thompson et al. [27] used a tracing algorithm in conjunction with surface proximity testing to render the sculptured models to which our approach bears similarity. However, unlike their method, our approach is proxy based and retains all advantages of proxy-based rendering techniques.

3 Proposed Method

In proxy-based rendering techniques, the proxy point should follow the HIP point, in free space. During interaction, HIP penetrates the object and the proxy move over the object without penetrating it so that the distance between the HIP and the proxy can be minimized. Let X_p and X_h denote the current proxy point and the HIP point, respectively. Let $\phi(X)$ denote the distance function. In free space $\phi(X_p) > 0$, and therefore proxy is allowed to move with the HIP. During collision with the given object, i.e. when $\phi(X_p) < 0$. The bounding surface of the object can be expressed as the zero iso-surface of the distance function and is given in Eq. 1. Hence, the

Fig. 1 2D Illustration of finding the closest zero iso-surface point of the current proxy location

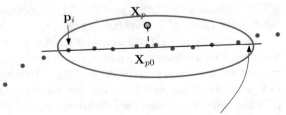

Tangent on which proxy is projected

objective function to be minimized can be rewritten as $\Psi = \frac{1}{2}|\mathbf{X}_p - \mathbf{X}_h|^2$, subject to $\phi(\mathbf{X}_p) = 0$. Distance function $\phi(\mathbf{X})$ for an arbitrary 3D object is generally stored at a finite number of samples and may not have a closed form. Hence, the function ϕ may be combined with the objective function Ψ as a regularization term to form a cost function for an unconstrained optimization. $\Psi = \frac{1}{2}|\mathbf{X}_p - \mathbf{X}_h|^2 + \frac{\lambda}{2}|\phi(\mathbf{X}_p)|^2$, where λ is a regularization parameter. So we can solve the problem iteratively by taking at the kth iteration a small positive step size $\gamma > 0$ such that $\mathbf{X}_p^{(k+1)} = \mathbf{X}_p^{(k)} - \gamma \nabla \Psi(\mathbf{X}_p^{(k)})$, where $\mathbf{X}_p^{(k)}$ and $\nabla \Psi(\mathbf{X}_p^{(k)})$ are the proxy position and the gradient of the objective function, respectively, in the current iteration and $\mathbf{X}_p^{(k+1)}$ is the proxy location for the next iteration and the resulting solution becomes

$$\mathbf{X}_p^{(k+1)} = \mathbf{X}_p^{(k)} - \gamma(\mathbf{X}_p - \mathbf{X}_h)^{(k)} - \beta\phi(\mathbf{X}_p^{(k)})\nabla\phi(\mathbf{X}_p^{(k)}), \tag{2}$$

where the constant $\beta = \gamma\lambda$.

Figure 1 illustrates a typical situation in which the proxy is nearing the boundary points of a point cloud data in 2D. The blue dots denote the boundary points of the object and $\mathbf{X}_p$ denotes the proxy point (shown with a green dot). The straight line in Fig. 1 shows the tangent (plane) to the local object surface. The red dot is the nearest point on the object from the proxy and it can be obtained by projecting the proxy on to the local tangent plane. This projection procedure when performed iteratively can effectively bring the proxy on to the zero iso-contour $\phi(\mathbf{X}) = 0$. In the case of a 3D object, the neighbourhood of the proxy is searched to find the closest surface point.

The bounding surface near the proxy point is approximated as a planar surface corresponding to the closest surface point, lying on this plane called the active surface point. However, the projected proxy on this plane need not lie on the given surface. Hence, this process must be repeated by iteratively projecting the proxy on the locally approximated plane. We use a projection operator to project the proxy point $\mathbf{X}_p$ on to the plane during collision. To find the projected point $\mathbf{X}_{p0}$, we can form the parametric representation (in terms of the parameter ρ) of a line which is normal to the plane, passing through the point $\mathbf{X}_p$ as $\mathbf{X}_p + \rho\mathbf{v}_n$. Here, $\mathbf{v}_n$ stands for the local surface normal and ρ is a scalar parameter which needs to be estimated. Since $\mathbf{X}_{p0}$ lies on the plane having equation of the form $ax + by + cz + d = 0$, we must have $[\mathbf{X}_p + \rho\mathbf{v}_n, 1]^T\boldsymbol{\theta} = 0$, $\rho \in \mathbb{R}$. With a known $\mathbf{X}_p$, $\mathbf{v}_n$ and $\boldsymbol{\theta} = [a, b, c, d]$, the solution

for ρ is $\rho_0 = -\dfrac{[\mathbf{X}_p, 1]^T \boldsymbol{\theta}}{|\mathbf{v}_n|}$ and the corresponding projected point is $\mathbf{X}_{p0} = \mathbf{X}_p + \rho_0\, \mathbf{v}_n$.
If the points are not dense, the direction of normal at the projected point can be approximated as an average of the sample normals, i.e. $\mathbf{v}_n = \dfrac{1}{k} \sum_{i=1}^{k} \mathbf{n}_i$, where k denotes the number of neighbourhood points and $\mathbf{n}_i$ denotes the normal vector associated with the ith neighbourhood point. In order to move the proxy on the surface, a tangent vector is computed from the HIP and proxy positions as $\mathbf{v}_t = \mathbf{v}_h - (\mathbf{v}_n \cdot \mathbf{v}_h)\mathbf{v}_n$, where $\mathbf{v}_h = \mathbf{X}_h - \mathbf{X}_p$. For the movement of proxy on the tangent plane, we use the following proxy update equation:

$$\mathbf{X}_p^{(k+1)} = \mathbf{X}_p^{(k)} + \delta \mathbf{v}_t^{(k)}. \tag{3}$$

The parameter $\delta < 1$ and to be chosen appropriately for a proper haptic experience.
There are two steps in haptic rendering:

1. detection of collision of the HIP with the object, and
2. force computation if a collision is detected.

We calculate the dot product $\mathbf{v}_n \cdot \mathbf{v}_h$ to determine the collision of HIP with the object. When $(\mathbf{v}_n \cdot \mathbf{v}_h) > 0$, the proxy is allowed to move freely with the HIP and hence force fed back to the device is zero. As the proxy collides the object, the quantity $\mathbf{v}_n \cdot \mathbf{v}_h$ becomes less than zero. The reaction force, $\mathbf{f}$ during collision, is given by

$$\mathbf{f} = -K\, \mathbf{d}_h, \tag{4}$$

where K is called the Hooke's constant and $\mathbf{d}_h$ denotes the depth of penetration, $\mathbf{d}_h = \mathbf{X}_h - \mathbf{X}_p$.

3.1 Surface Friction

The technique discussed so far does not take care of the surface properties like friction and hence create the feeling of a slippery surface. In order to get a more realistic feeling of touching the surface, effect of friction is also added to the model. Let the reaction force on the haptic device be denoted with $\mathbf{f}$ as illustrated in Fig. 2. $\mathbf{f}_n = |\mathbf{f}| \cos \beta\, \mathbf{u}_n$ denotes component of the applied force normal to the surface. Similarly, $\mathbf{f}_t = |\mathbf{f}| \sin \beta\, \mathbf{u}_t$ denotes the tangential component of the force on the surface. If the static friction parameter is denoted by μ_s, then the proxy is in static contact with the surface as long as $|\mathbf{f}_t| < \mu_s |\mathbf{f}_n|$.

During haptic interaction, dynamic friction exerts a retarding force on the proxy while moving on the surface of the object. If the coefficient of dynamic friction is denoted with μ_n, the magnitude of the retarding force on the proxy is given by $\mu_d |\mathbf{f}_n|$ and is directed opposite to $\mathbf{f}_t$. The resultant force, $\mathbf{f}_r$ on the proxy, is given by $\mathbf{f}_t - \mu_d \mathbf{f}_n$.

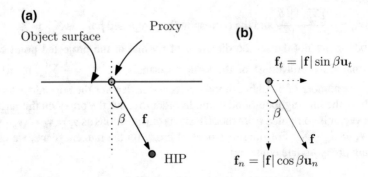

Fig. 2 Illustration of calculating the resultant vector for the proxy movement with the addition of surface friction

$$\mathbf{f}_r = \mathbf{f}_t \left(1 - \mu_d \cot \beta\right) \qquad if \qquad |\mathbf{f}_t| \geq \mu_d |\mathbf{f}_n| \tag{5}$$
$$= \mathbf{0} \qquad\qquad\qquad else.$$

Equation 5 provides a direct description of the frictional force. However, for haptic rendering, such an equation has to be used in slowing down the proxy movement. Comparing Eq. 5 with Eq. 3, we observe that $\mathbf{f}_r$ is found to be proportional to $\mathbf{v}_t$. Hence, we use a parameter δ with friction given by $\delta_f = \delta(1 - \mu_d \cot \beta)$. Equation 3 is modified as

$$\mathbf{X}_p^{(k+1)} = \mathbf{X}_p^{(k)} + \delta(1 - \mu_d \cot \beta^{(k)})\mathbf{v}_t^{(k)}. \tag{6}$$

4   Results and Discussion

In order to implement the proposed method, we used visual C++ in a windows XP platform with a CORE 2QUAD CPU @ 2.66 GHZ and with a RAM size of 2 GB. A 3-DOF haptic device from NOVINT has been used for haptic interaction. The haptic interaction space is partitioned with a regular 3D grid of voxels. A grid size of 300 × 300 × 300 has been selected for the experiment to divide the 10 cm cube interaction space, resulting in a spacing of 0.33 mm between adjacent grid nodes along all the three axes. A 1 kHz refresh rate was used for the haptic rendering algorithm which was run on a separate thread. The technique has been experimented with various point cloud data and results are discussed below.

A dense-oriented point cloud data of happy Buddha with 543,652 points is shown Fig. 3a. Proxy and HIP positions during haptic interaction with the object at a specific time instant are shown. The proxy position is shown with the green ball and the HIP position with the red ball. The red line connected between the HIP and the proxy denotes the penetration depth of HIP in the object for a particular haptic inter-

Fig. 3 Illustration of rendering dense point cloud data. **a** Happy (*Data courtesy* www.cc.gatech. edu/projects/large_models), **b** boy (*Data courtesy* http://model.3dcool.net/list/K/290/5.html)

action. As the points are dense in the data, a neighbourhood search radius of 0.5 mm (which is equivalent to a radius of 1.5 times the voxel length) is used and the average time for computation of the tangent vector is only 0.0159 ms around the shown proxy location. This evaluation time includes the time to find out the neighbourhood points of the current proxy position, time to compute the tangent plane and also the time required to move the proxy in the tangent direction after projecting it on to the surface. Figure 3b shows a point cloud data of a boy with 77,311 points. The algorithm took an average tangent computation time of 0.0137 ms with a search radius of 0.8 mm. The base cylindrical plate of the object could not be rendered with the above-mentioned search radius as the points are too sparse compared to the search volume near that region. It may be noted that the proxy can be initialized anywhere in the haptic space. In all our experiments, we have initialized at the periphery, namely top-left front corner.

Figure 4 shows a few other point cloud data rendered with our technique. Table 1 summarizes the computational requirement for various point cloud objects based

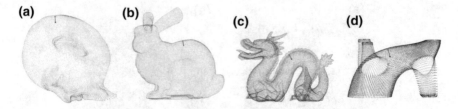

Fig. 4 Thumbnail representation of various other point cloud data. **a** Bonzew, **b** Bunny, **c** Dragon, **d** Magis (*Data courtesy* www.turbosquid.com for (**a**) and (**d**), and www.cc.gatech.edu/projects/large_models for (**b**) and (**c**))

Table 1 Summary of computational requirements for various point cloud objects during interaction with the haptic device

Object name	Number of points	Search radius (mm)	Avg. computation time (ms)		#Nbd points
			Single touch	Multi-touch	
Happy	543,652	0.50	0.0159	0.0174	10
Boy	77,311	0.80	0.0137	0.0150	9
Dragon	427,645	0.50	0.0152	0.0168	8
Bonzew	31,718	1.60	0.0187	0.0200	14
Bunny	35,947	0.90	0.0094	0.0103	7
Magis	28,190	1.40	0.0172	0.0182	9

on the number of points and the search radius. The search radius is more when the data is sparse. The table also suggests that for the worst-case computation time of 0.0187 ms, if needed one can perform up to 50 iterative steps of proxy updation for a typical interaction time of 1ms. However, we observe that typically 6–8 such iterations suffice for our application.

The magnitude of the haptic device position vector $(\mathbf{X}_h)$ and the rendered force without the effect of friction is plotted for a particular interaction with the point cloud data, and bunny is shown in Fig. 5. The haptic device position (magnitude in polar coordinate) during the interaction is plotted in Fig. 5a as a function of time. It is clear from Fig. 5b that the interaction force changes as we move the haptic device. After moving the device for a particular duration, the haptic device position is kept constant. The reaction force instantly attains a constant value indicating that the iteration converges very fast. Further, the fact that the nature of these curves is very different during the interaction suggests that the rendered force is not affected by the specifics of the proxy updation scheme. In order to test how the proposed system handles a thin object, we interacted with the object bunny (Fig. 4b) near the earlobe. We did not experience any pop through effect in any of our experiments.

We have also tried using two haptic devices for simultaneous interaction with the point cloud data. This allows a person to use both hands to feel the bounding surface of the object. Addition of one more haptic device needs creating one more

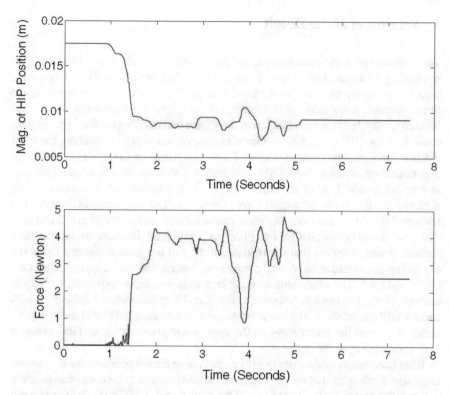

Fig. 5 Haptic device position and the rendered force versus time graph for a particular interaction with the point cloud model bunny. **a** Magnitude of the haptic device position, **b** magnitude of the rendered reaction force

thread for another tangent vector evaluation. It is found during the experiment that one additional thread does not affect the computation time significantly due to the selection of a quad-core computing machine. The increase in computation is very marginal when one more device is added for parallel operation. It may be noted that Ryden et al. [5] estimated the surface normal from the data points, which results in smoothing of the finer surface details. They used a fixed step size of 1 mm for the proxy movement, which results in a movement of the proxy point even after the convergence. Our technique uses a variable step size proportional to the projection of vector $\mathbf{v}_h$ on the tangent plane. This gives a stable proxy point on convergence as shown in Fig. 5b. This also helps in adding the effect of friction as discussed in Sect. 3.1. Also, our technique is developed for a full 3D object rather than for the depth map (Monge surface representation) of any particular side of the object.

5   Validation of the Result

The proposed rendering technique is validated using a specific point cloud data corresponding to a spherical object. Since the bounding surface $\phi(\mathbf{X})$ of a spherical object is precisely known, the rendered reaction force can be compared with the force computed using the implicit equation of the sphere. We used a spherical object for comparison because the equation of the sphere can readily give the depth of penetration of the HIP in the object. Once the penetration depth is obtained, the ideal reaction force may be computed using Eq. 4. The radius of the sphere used for our experiment was 40 mm. A 3-DOF haptic device is used for interaction with the surface of the sphere. During the interaction, the HIP position and the corresponding rendered reaction force are sampled from the device. The magnitude of the rendered force and the departure from the ideal reaction force (called error) are calculated. The experiment is repeated for two different point cloud densities on the spherical surface. It was observed that the rendered force and the force computed using the explicit sphere equation to be very close during interaction with a highly dense data (40,000 points). The magnitude of error increases further, as expected, with 2500 surface points. The error is, however, still within 3% of the rendered force even with sudden HIP movements, and the average error is less than 0.2%. All these experiments show that the proxy stays on the appropriate point on the surface, giving a very good feeling of the object.

It has been mentioned earlier that the computation time depends on the neighbourhood size. For a sphere of radius 40 mm and 90,000 surface points, we progressively reduced the search radius to 0.5 mm. This search took 0.0078 ms for the tangent vector evaluation (i.e. for one iteration to complete). Table 2 compares the tangent vector evaluation time with different values of search radius for the same object. The evaluation time increases with an increase in search radius. So a smaller choice of search radius is preferred depending on the density of the given point cloud data.

Table 2 Computational requirements for different values of the search radius during interaction with a spherical object

Search radius (mm)	Tangent computation time (ms)	Number of points
0.5	0.0078	4
1.0	0.0172	14
1.2	0.0235	20
1.4	0.0359	26
1.6	0.0375	37
1.8	0.0485	43
2.0	0.0510	57

6 Conclusions

This paper proposes a novel method for proxy-based haptic rendering of an object described by a dense, oriented point cloud data without a pre-computed polygonal mesh. Proxy position during collision with the object is easily found by projecting the proxy point on the best fit local planar surface. The tangent computation time increases with an increase in neighbourhood size as well as the density of points in the point cloud and is inversely related to the voxel length.

3D space is partitioned using a regular grid of voxels with $300 \times 300 \times 300$ grid nodes. The happy Buddha data (Fig. 3a) with the highest number of points in our experiment used a spherical search space of radius 0.5 mm. The neighbourhood search and the computation of tangent vector together took only 0.0159 ms which is very much less than the required haptic update time of 1 ms for the object. We validated our results using a spherical point cloud object, and the rendering technique was found to be working well even with sudden changes in hand movement. We also tested our technique with multiple haptic interaction points without incurring much additional computation time. As a future work, the search radius can be adaptively changed according to the density of points in the data, so that the tangent evaluation time can be maintained almost the same everywhere in a point cloud data.

References

1. Salisbury, K., Brock, D., Massie, T., Swarup, N., Zilles, C.: Haptic rendering: programming touch interaction with virtual objects. In: Proceedings of the 1995 Symposium on Interactive 3D Graphics, I3D '95, pp. 123–130. ACM, New York, NY, USA (1995)
2. Sreeni, K.G., Priyadarshini, K., Praseedha, A.K., Chaudhuri, S.: Haptic rendering of cultural heritage objects at different scales. In: Eurohaptics, pp. 12–15. Tampere, Finland, June 2012
3. El-Far, N.R., Georganas, N.D., El Saddik, A.: An algorithm for haptically rendering objects described by point clouds. In: Proceedings of the 21th Canadian Conference on Electrical and Computer Engineering, pp. 1443–1448. Niagara, ON, Canada (2008)
4. Leeper, A., Chan, S., Salisbury, K.: Constraint based 3-DOF haptic rendering of arbitrary point cloud data. In: RSS Workshop on RGB-D Cameras, University of Southern California (2011)
5. Ryden, F., Kosari, S.N., Chizeck, H.J.: Proxy method for fast haptic rendering from time varying point clouds. In: IROS, pp. 2614–2619. IEEE (2011)
6. Dey, T.K., Li, G., Sun, J.: Normal estimation for point clouds: a comparison study for a Voronoi based method. In: Proceedings Eurographics/IEEE VGTC Symposium Point-Based Graphics, pp. 39–46 (2005)
7. Jones, T.R., Durand, F., Zwicker, M.: Normal improvement for point rendering. IEEE Comput. Graph. Appl. **24**(4), 53–56 (2004)
8. Mitra, N.J., Nguyen, A., Guibas, L.: Estimating surface normals in noisy point cloud data. Special Issue Int. J. Comput. Geom. Appl. **14**, 261–276 (2004)
9. Kim, L., Sukhatme, G.S., Desbrun, M.: A haptic rendering technique based on hybrid surface representation. IEEE Comput. Graph. Appl. Special Issue Haptic Render. Beyond Visual Comput. **24**(2), 66–75 (2004)
10. Salisbury, K., Conti, F., Barbagli, F.: Haptic rendering: introductory concepts. IEEE Comput. Graph. Appl. **24**(2), 24–32 (2004)

11. Laycock, S.D., Day, A.M.: A survey of haptic rendering techniques. Comput. Graph. Forum **26**(1), 50–65 (2007)
12. Ruspini, D.C., Kolarov, K., Khatib, O.: The haptic display of complex graphical environments. In: Proceedings of ACM SIGGRAPH, pp. 345–352 (1997)
13. Kim, L., Kyrikou, A., Desbrun, M., Sukhatme, G.: An implicit-based haptic rendering technique. In: Proceeeedings of the IEEE/RSJ International Conference on Intelligent Robots, vol. 3, pp. 2942–2948 (2002)
14. Mark, W., Jones, J., Brentzen, A., Sramek, M.: 3D distance fields: a survey of techniques and applications. IEEE Trans. Visual. Comput. Graph. **12**(4), 581–599 (2006)
15. Payne, B.A., Toga, A.W.: Distance field manipulation of surface models. IEEE Comput. Graph. Appl. **12**, 65–71 (1992)
16. Guéziec, A.: 'Meshsweeper': dynamic point-to-polygonal-mesh distance and applications. IEEE Trans. Visual. Comput. Graph. **7**, 47–61 (2001)
17. Dachille, F., Kaufman, A.: Incremental triangle voxelization. In: Graphics, Interface, pp. 205–212 (2000)
18. Mauch, S.: A fast algorithm for computing the closest point and distance transform. Technical Report, California Institute of Technology (2000)
19. Sigg, C., Peikert, R., Gross, M.: Signed distance transform using graphics hardware. In: Proceedings of the 14th IEEE Visualization 2003 (VIS '03), pp. 83–90. IEEE Computer Society, Washington, DC, USA (2003)
20. Rhodes, F.: Discrete Euclidean metrics. Pattern Recogn. Lett. **13**, 623–628 (1992)
21. Rosenfeld, A., Pfaltz, J.L.: Sequential operations in digital picture processing. J. ACM **13**, 471–494 (1966)
22. Mullikin, J.C.: The vector distance transform in two and three dimensions. CVGIP Graph. Models Image Process. **54**, 526–535 (1992)
23. Tsitsiklis, J.N.: Efficient algorithms for globally optimal trajectories. IEEE Trans. Auto. Control **40**(9), 1528–1538 (1995)
24. Sethian, J.A.: A fast marching level set method for monotonically advancing fronts. Proc. Natl. Acad. Sci. United States Am. **93**(4), 1591–1595 (1996)
25. Lee, J.-K., Kim, Y.J.: Haptic rendering of point set surfaces. In: Proceedings of the Second Joint EuroHaptics Conference and Symposium on Haptic Interfaces for Virtual Environment and Teleoperator Systems, WHC '07, pp. 513–518. IEEE Computer Society, Washington, DC, USA (2007)
26. Sreeni, K.G., Chaudhuri, S.: Haptic rendering of dense 3D point cloud data. In: IEEE Haptic Symposium, pp. 333–339. Vancouver, BC, Canada, March 4–7, 2012
27. Thompson II, T.V., Johnson, D.E., Cohen, E.: Direct haptic rendering of sculptured models. In: Proceedings of the 1997 Symposium on Interactive 3D Graphics, I3D '97, pp. 167–176. ACM, New York, NY, USA (1997)

Ontology-Driven Content-Based Retrieval of Heritage Images

Dipannita Podder, Jit Mukherjee, Shashaank Mattur Aswatha, Jayanta Mukherjee and Shamik Sural

1 Introduction

The ancient artworks, in various forms, help us to decode the underlying history of civilization and its societal condition, human lifestyle, religion, culture, education, etc. of a particular region. The civilization in Indian subcontinent is a rich source of cultural heritage, in a variety of forms like monuments, sculpture, paintings, manuscripts, and mythological stories, performing arts such as music and dance [17]. Moreover, mythological stories are depicted in sculptures, paintings, etc., which reflect on social practices, and lifestyle of various sections of people of that period. Rich information on our cultural heritage needs to be preserved, to be disseminated to people for their increasing awareness and participation in the process. Digital format of the heritage data can play a key role in this regard. In this paper, we propose an archiving framework for the preservation of heritage images, which are captured from temples, palaces, and other historic monuments.

Image retrieval system is an information system for browsing, searching, and retrieving of images from a database of digital images. There are two major approaches followed in image retrieval, namely concept-based [3] and content-based retrieval [20]. In *concept-based retrieval* schemes, metadata of images such as captioning, keywords, or descriptions are used. On the other hand, *content-based image retrieval* (CBIR) systems analyze visual information of the image and then form a representation of the image, which is used while searching for similar images. Here, the content or information in an image is usually the visual attributes and cues like shape, color, texture, etc [2, 11, 13, 19]. The major advantage of a CBIR system is that the search results are not affected by subjective classification of images. A good CBIR system should use robust features that exploit rich content in images.

D. Podder (✉) · J. Mukherjee · S. M. Aswatha · J. Mukherjee · S. Sural
Visual Information Processing Laboratory, Department of Computer Science
and Engineering, Indian Institute of Technology Kharagpur, Kharagpur 721302, West Bengal,
India
e-mail: dipannitapodder@iitkgp.ac.in

© Springer Nature Singapore Pte Ltd. 2018
B. Chanda et al. (eds.), *Heritage Preservation*,
https://doi.org/10.1007/978-981-10-7221-5_8

The system should have unique and reproducible description of every image by its own set of features.

However, metadata of images are used to make the searches more focused and relevant to the need of users. But with mere annotations it may not be always possible to operate on a domain of interrelated facts. An ontology in an area of knowledge defining related concepts and their relations provide a platform for such operation. Even with a few annotations of images, it can form associated information using the ontology-based framework. Domain ontology is used to interpret these conceptual annotations in the context of a specific query. Thus, the ontology needs to be customized for different collections. The ontology and the metadata schemes are tightly coupled in these approaches. It is necessary to create a central metadata scheme for the entire collection to maintain the data integration with heritage image collections. Thus, a CBIR system operating in tandem with the ontology of the domain of images becomes more powerful in providing relevant information to users. It has the ability to model the semantics of what occurs in images such as objects, events, etc. It represents knowledge in a hierarchical structure, which is used to describe and organize a collection of images and reflect their relationships.

We propose a two-phase scheme to retrieve heritage images, which works with both context and content of images. In the first phase, the contextually similar images are fetched using the query word and its semantically related words. The irrelevant images are discarded for the final content-based image search phase. The CBIR system retrieves similar images from the reduced search space using the structural features of images. In this way, incorporation of ontology with CBIR system helps to retrieve semantically and structurally similar images fast. Many image retrieval systems use CBIR and ontology for different applications. Structure analysis of heritage images for retrieval of cultural heritage images like dance, music, painting, etc., has been focused previously. Our main objective is to develop a CBIR system exploiting the context of heritage images, which can help us to know the history and culture of people. In this work, we take Hindu mythological images as instances to define this context.

2 Related Work

In recent years, a few approaches are reported which use ontology to address the semantic gap in multimedia and digital library projects [1, 6, 22, 23, 29].

A technique for retrieving document images using ontology is presented in [9]. An automatic classification of archaeological pottery sherds is reported in [15]. It uses simple local features which focus on color properties of sherds. In this work, bag of words model has been effectively used. In [7], a new image retrieval system is discussed, which uses topological relations like connectivity, adjacency, membership, and orientation. Topological relations combined with low-level image features like color and texture are used for building a CBIR system, making it robust to spatial and intensity transformations. However, heritage images have many fine distinctive structural features. These images may have different scales, orientation, texture of same content, due to different styles of carving, material, etc. Thus, low-level features like shape and color of images are not enough for distinguishing them. So, low-level feature-based CBIR systems [6, 7] may not yield desired results in case of heritage images.

In [16], a system for building repository of intangible cultural heritage of Indian classical dance forms has been reported. The approach uses *multimedia web ontology language* (MOWL) to represent the domain ontology [18]. The ontological framework also includes a labeled set of training data. It is further used to automatically annotate new instances of digital heritage artifact. In [17], an Indian mural painting archival system is proposed, which simultaneously uses features and patterns of the paintings and ontology of narratives. A cross-modal, conceptual linkage between repository of semantically annotated Indian mural paintings and a collection of labeled text documents of their narratives is also provided by the framework. The system is also facilitated by a mural painting browsing interface, which is capable of handling semantic query. The work in [8] proposed an algorithmic approach to discover abstract patterns in Indian monument images. It augments a transfer learning-based approach with ontology to categorize images of tomb, fort, and mosque. The domain knowledge is transferred during training, and the images are categorized using convolutional neural network and ontology tree. In the following section, we discuss our proposed ontology and CBIR system for heritage images related to Hindu religion and mythology.

3   Content-Based Image Retrieval System

Our implementation of content-based image retrieval system is based on bag of visual words (BoVW) approach, which is a technique for image representation, inspired by the models used in natural language processing [21, 26]. The BoVW-based retrieval works in three phases. In the first phase, local features are computed over the images. These local features are clustered into predetermined labels of classes. Using this cluster information, an image signature is generated, which can be used to search content-wise similar images.

3.1   Feature Extraction

We use SURF features [2] for representing image attributes, which are invariant to scale and rotation. An interest point in SURF technique is computed by thresholding the local maxima of the determinant of the Hessian matrix. To handle the key

Fig. 1 Extracted local descriptors on a heritage image

points occurring at different scales, second-order Gaussian derivatives of the image are used to choose appropriate scale of each key point. A speedup in computation is achieved by using integral image representation. Haar wavelet responses at different directions are computed, and maximum direction of response is considered in assigning orientation to each SURF key point. Finally, each key point is described by a 64-dimensional vector. An example of feature extraction of heritage image is shown in Fig. 1.

3.2 Clustering

The extracted 64-dimensional SURF descriptors are then clustered to form the visual words. For this purpose, K-means clustering algorithm is employed to partition the features into a predefined number of vocabularies. The cluster centers generated at the end of clustering process are called *visual words,* and the number of clusters becomes the size of the visual vocabulary. When a user specifies a query image, features are extracted from it, and its BoVW representation is constructed. This vector is compared against already built set of indexes, and the images represented by similar vectors are gathered as the retrieved image set.

An appropriate vocabulary size has to be chosen to obtain a good performance over a dataset, which is usually determined experimentally. Vocabulary size in our approach is chosen to be 10000. The analysis will be discussed in Sect. 6.

3.3 Bag of Visual Words

Once visual words are generated from the local descriptors for each image in the database, the next step is to generate the bag of visual words for all the images by binning the occurrence of visual words in every image. With this, each image is represented as a histogram of visual words.

3.4 The Index Structure

Locality-sensitive hashing (LSH) has been used to build an index structure for the database. The LSH technique in our approach is implemented on the basis of p-stable distribution [4]. Each bag of words of images in the database is hashed, and the corresponding hash index is stored. We use the following function to hash the multidimensional data points onto a scalar line and generate a hash table:

$$h^{x,b}(v) = \lfloor \frac{x \cdot v + b}{w} \rfloor, \tag{1}$$

where $\lfloor . \rfloor$ indicates the floor operation, w is the width of each quantization bin, v is the high dimensional query point, x is a randomly selected vector, and b is a random variable uniformly distributed between 0 and w.

To reduce the impact of unlucky projection in one hash table, multiple hash tables are constructed so that the near-by points get hashed to the same bucket in at least one of the hash tables. When a user makes a query by an image, features are extracted from the image, and the bag of word is built using the same visual dictionary. Then, this bag of words is also hashed according to Eq. 1. Depending on the bucket index of the query, all the corresponding images are retrieved, and a linear search is performed among them to obtain the final result.

4 Ontology for Hindu Mythology

The images have extensive mythological associations, and they depict various historical and mythological events. These historical and mythological descriptions, which are related to image content, can only be represented by text. The textual semantics are included as the annotations of images. An ontology is developed for Hindu

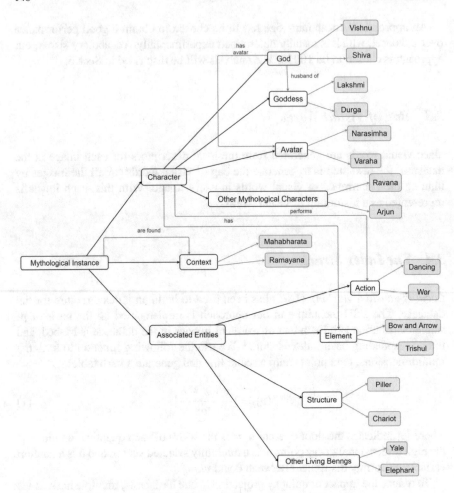

Fig. 2 Basic ontology structure for Hindu mythology

mythology using standard ontology markup language (OWL) on Protege framework [10]. The dataset contains images from some heritage sites of Karnataka,[1]
West Bengal,[2] and Andhra Pradesh.[3] The images are analyzed thoroughly and some
key semantic attributes have been identified. Correspondingly, various classes, individuals, and tangible properties have been created.

<hr/>

[1]http://asi.nic.in/asi_monu_alphalist_karnataka_bangalore.asp.

[2]http://asi.nic.in/asi_monu_alphalist_andhra.asp.

[3]http://asi.nic.in/asi_monu_alphalist_westbengal.asp.

4.1 Ontological Structure

A basic ontology for our domain is prepared using an ontology editing tool, Protege, by a group of domain experts. The ontology preparation focuses on properties and relations of domain concepts. In general, the concepts followed a domain-driven hierarchy. The details of ontology are given below:

- **Classes**: Classes are sets, collections, concepts, types of objects, or kinds of things related to the corresponding ontology. Three main classes are created, namely, *Context*, *Characters*, and *Associated Entities*. Further, these classes are divided into the following subclasses:

  1. Subclasses in *Characters* are *God*, *Goddess*, and *Other Mythological Characters*.
  2. Subclasses in *Associated Entities* are *Structure*, *Element*, *Other Living Beings*, and *Action*.

- **Individuals**: *Individual members* are instances or objects (the basic or *ground-level* objects) in the ontology. After creating classes, all the available individuals are created under them. Some of the individual members are as follows:

  1. *Bhagavata*, *Purana*, *Mahabharata*, *Ramayana*, etc. are included in class *Context*.
  2. *Rama*, *Krishna*, *Vishnu*, *Shiva*, *Ganesha*, *Brahma*, *Hanuman*, *Indra*, *Yaksha*, *Varaha*, *Karthikeya*, *Garuda*, *Surya*, etc. are included under subclass *God* in class *Characters*.
  3. *Durga*, *Parvati*, *Laxmi*, *Sita*, *Radha*, *Saraswati*, *Kali*, *Durga*, *Indrani*, etc. are included under subclass *Goddess* in class *Characters*.
  4. *Arjuna*, *Bhishma*, *Nandi*, *Prahlada*, *Ravana*, *Ghatotkacha*, *Duryodhana*, *Sudama*, and *Unknown deity* are included under subclass *Character* in class *Characters*.
  5. *Cow*, *Elephant*, *Fish*, *Snake*, *Monkey*, *Horse*, *Deer*, *Lion*, *Yale*, etc. are included under subclass *Other Living Beings* in class *Associated Entities*.
  6. *Bow and Arrow*, *Chakra*, *Damru*, *Flute*, *Veena*, *Sword*, *Gada*, *Trishula*, *Vajra*, *Dholak*, *Kalasha*, *Shankha*, etc. are included under subclass *Element* in class *Associated Entities*.
  7. *Dancing*, *Fighting*, *Praying*, *Hunting*, *Killing*, *Tandav*, *Playing Music*, *Traveling*, etc. are included under subclass *Action* of class *Associated Entities*.
  8. *Stone Wheel*, *Gopuram*, *Pushkarini*, *Mantapa*, *Pillars*, etc. are included under subclass *Structure* of class *Associated Entities*.

- **Object Properties**: Relationships among classes for supporting qualitative semantic issues are handled via object properties. Classes and individual members can be related to one another through these object properties. Object properties that are created in this ontology are

1. *Avatar Of*: Usage—Narasimha was *Avatar Of* Vishnu.
2. *Has element*: Usage—Krishna *Has element* Flute.
3. *Has Vahana*: Usage—Durga *Has Vahana* Lion.
4. *Has face Of*: Usage—Ganesha *Has face Of* an elephant.
5. *Wife Of*: Usage—Sita was *Wife Of* Ram.
6. *Has Disciple*: Usage—Bhishmapitamaha *Has Disciple* as Arjuna.
7. *Son Of*: Usage—Ganesha was *Son Of* Shiva.
8. *Parent Of*: Usage—Shiva and Parvati were *Parent Of* Ganesha and Karthikeya.
9. *Has appearance Of*: Usage—Durga *Has appearance Of* Kali.
10. *Context Of*: Usage—Ram belongs to *Context Of* Ramayana.
11. *Found On*: Usage—Ram *Found On* pillar.

The ontology is structured as classes to facilitate the ease of understanding of class hierarchy. For a compact and effective representation of the ontology graph in Fig. 2, a few subclasses and ground-level objects are shown in the figure. Ontology can be useful in addressing any query of a known attribute, where the related results and properties could be retrieved. The ontology has been designed in such a way that it can be extended with any new category and object. We should note that ontological facts may vary in different parts of India. We are presenting a typical case study here.

4.2 Ontological Similarity

In information retrieval system, ontological similarity is important for finding the semantics. Information in queries is mapped to ontology for retrieving the exact match. Different similarity metrics are reported in [27]. Any similarity measure must necessarily satisfy some basic properties which are described as follows.

- *Commonality Property*: Two nodes A and B are more similar, if they have more shared commonality.
- *Difference Property*: Two nodes A and B are less similar, if they have more differences.
- *Identity Property*: Two nodes A and B are similar, if they are identical, no matter how much commonality they share.
- *Symmetric Property*: $sim(A, B) = sim(B, A)$, where A, B are two nodes.

Most of the measures are based on computation of the length of the shortest path where lower distance indicates higher similarity. The objective of these measures is to keep the number of edges between two nodes minimal, i.e.,

$$dist(c_i, c_j) = minimal\ number\ of\ edges\ in\ a\ path\ from\ c_i\ to\ c_j \qquad (2)$$

where c_i and c_j are nodes of the ontology graph. The number of edges is referred to as distance between the concepts. *Weighted Shortest Path* also considers edges for similarity measure. For instance, in depth relative scaling approach [28] the weight attached to each relation ranges in $[min_r..max_r]$, where min_r and max_r represent the lower and upper values of an interval the real axis. The distance becomes nonuniform due to the weight of the edges. This edge-counting shortest path approach only considers the best path among the other paths. Sometimes, more number of paths between the concepts are required in computing the similarity measure. This multiple-path property has been achieved by considering shared nodes. Since similarity is dependent on the number of nodes between two concepts, larger the number of shared nodes higher is the similarity.

The other group of similarity measures incorporates corpus analysis as their basis with the same approach of computing the shortest path. This integration is performed by merging knowledge about concepts with corpus statistics. One approach for incorporating the corpus uses the measures based on Resniks information content [25].

We adopt the shortest path length approach for similarity measure between query and concept. We use *SPARQL protocol and RDF query language* SPARQL [24], a semantic query language for databases, to retrieve the data. Both query and concepts are individuals of the ontology. The individuals are related by properties of their classes. Considering query word as an individual, we retrieve the nearest individuals from it, depending on the threshold distance.

5 Retrieval of Visually Similar Images with Semantics

We develop an ontology in the context of Hindu mythology to guide the search of an image with related information and to overcome the semantic gap. A database of images is maintained, with their corresponding precomputed bag of visual words (BoVW) [12, 26]. For any query image, its BoVW vector is computed, which is searched against a pool of data for similar vectors (and hence, similar images). The search is performed by an engine, which is a fusion of ontology-based information system and CBIR-based retrieval system. The retrieval of images is performed in two stages: (1) pruning the search space to relevant set of data by seeking the information through ontology, and (2) content-based image retrieval on this pruned search space by bag of visual words technique. These two stages are shown in Fig. 3.

At first, the ontology has been searched with a query word which generates a pruned search space. An index structure is built in run time for this pruned search space using LSH. Each bag of words of images in the pruned search spaced is hashed according to Eq. 1 using the randomly selected vector, which is used to index the whole database. Then, the bag of visual words of the query image is also hashed to the newly built hash table. Depending on the bucket index of the query, all the corresponding images are retrieved, and a linear search is performed among them to obtain the final result.

5.1 Web-Based System

A web-based system [14] has been developed to disseminate the image retrieval framework, which can search images and related information with respect to a query image, that is uploaded by a user. It also allows the user to upload an image with

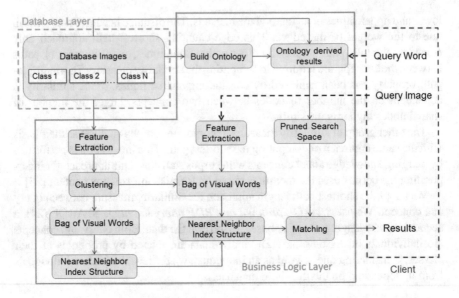

Fig. 3 Ontology-driven Bag of visual words-based Image Retrieval System

or without any related information into the existing database running on the server. The architecture of web-based system is shown in Fig. 4. On the client side, a user uploads a query image. Once the image is uploaded, it is saved in the system and the searching process is initiated. The image is fed to the inbuilt functions in *Business logic layer*. The query image is searched within the stored database for nearly similar images. Uploading of new images with proper information, which can be used as training set, is also facilitated in the proposed system. The retrieved results are shown to client.[4]

This system has been developed using Apache Jena and OpenCV libraries. MySQL database server is used in this architecture by connecting it through *JDBC* (*Java Database Connectivity*) driver, for archiving and retrieving data.

6 Results and Discussions

This system has been tested on heritage datasets. The system is hosted in an internal cloud environment (Meghamala of IIT Kharagpur[5]) with a VM configuration of 8GB RAM with 4 VCPUs. For training, the datasets have been considered with 2060 images.

---

[4]This system is hosted in https://viplab.iitkgp.ac.in/smarak/index.jsp.

[5]http://www.sit.iitkgp.ernet.in/Meghamala/.

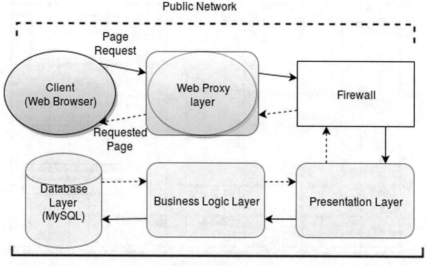

Fig. 4 Architecture of the web-based system

These images are obtained from various heritage sites in Karnataka (Hampi, Belur, Halebidu, Somnathpur, Ikkeri, Shivamogga Museum, Kaidala), West Bengal (Bishnupur, Baharampur), and Andhra Pradesh (Surabheswara Kona). Images are of size ranging from 5 MB to 15 MB. *Mean Average Precision* (MAP) defined in Sect. 6.1 is used as a performance measure to evaluate the system.

6.1 Calculation of MAP

The MAP is computed, as discussed below [5]. The precision, P_k, is obtained as

$$P_k = \frac{|n(Rt) \bigcap n(R)|}{n(Rt)}, \tag{3}$$

where P_k is the precision upto kth retrieved result, $n(Rt)$ is the number of retrieved results, and $n(R)$ is the number of relevant results upto kth retrieved result. The average precision value is given by

$$AP_i = \frac{\sum_{k=1}^{N_r} P_k}{N_r}, \tag{4}$$

where AP_i is the average precision for ith query, N_r is the number of retrieved images, and k varies from 1 to N_r. In our experiments, total number of retrieved results, N_r, is kept at 4, 6, 8, and 10. The MAP is given by

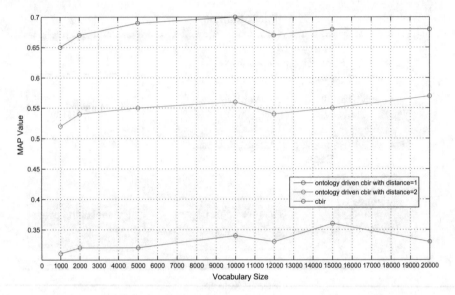

Fig. 5 MAP of CBIR System with different vocabulary sizes

$$MAP = \frac{\sum\limits_{i=1}^{N_t} AP_i}{N_t}, \tag{5}$$

where MAP is the mean average precision for complete dataset, N_t is the total number of query images, and i is ranging from 1 to N_t.

6.2 Parameter for Implementation

We have experimented with 21 different images in three different scenarios for choosing the parameter of the system. These are for, (i) CBIR system, (ii) Ontology-driven CBIR system with distance threshold 1, and (iii) Ontology-driven CBIR system with distance threshold 2. It is observed from Fig. 5 that *mean average precision (MAP)* value of the retrieval system is almost the best for a vocabulary size of 10000. Distance threshold is selected as 1 for this algorithm, because larger distance threshold in the ontology graph implies that more number of nodes are to be considered, which would make the search expensive. Also, from Fig. 5 it is observed that the algorithm performs better for distance threshold *1* than *2*.

Typical values of some of the parameters of the system using BoVW and LSH indexing used in our experimentation are shown in Table 1.

Table 1 Parameters used for implementation

Distance threshold	1
Vocabulary size	10000
Width of hash table (Bucket width)	10
Number of hash table	10
Number of projections	1
Success probability	0.98
Failure probability	0.02

Fig. 6 Examples of ontology-driven CBIR system

6.3 Search Results

The CBIR system considers the structural features of images. An ontological query extracts all the properties of existing classes, subclasses, and individuals, and delivers the results accordingly. Within this pruned set of images, visually similar images are searched by CBIR algorithm and the similar image set is retrieved.

Figure 6 shows search results for proposed ontology-driven CBIR system. The leftmost black-colored box contains the query word and query image, and others are

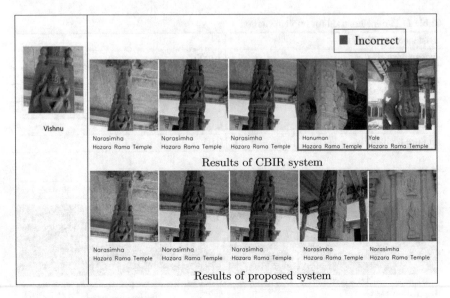

Fig. 7 Comparison of CBIR system with ontology-driven CBIR system with a query image taken from Hampi with the keyword *Vishnu*

retrieved images. The retrieved images are arranged from left to right in order of decreasing similarity, and some of the associated information is shown with each of retrieved results.

In Fig. 6a, an image of *Shiva* is given as query and the element *Trishula* is mentioned as the query word. Among the retrieved results all, but the fourth image, are different images of *Shiva* holding *Thrishula*. The fourth image, marked with red, is an image of *Durga*, who has element *Trishula*. In Fig. 6b, an image of *Narasimha* is given as query and the context *Vishnu* is mentioned as the query word. The first three images are of *Narasimha*. In Fig. 6c, an image of *Lion*, sculpted as pillar, is given as query and the same is mentioned as the query word. All the images are different instances of *Lion*.

6.4 Comparative Study

A few more search results are shown in Figs. 7, 8, 9, and 10. Ontology-driven CBIR system uses both query word and query image, whereas the plain CBIR system uses only the query image. Here, the irrelevant results are highlighted in red. In Fig. 7, the query is an image of *Narasimha*. The CBIR system retrieves only three similar images of *Narasimha*, whereas our proposed system is able to retrieve similar images of *Narasimha* with the corresponding textual query word. Next, an image of *War between Ram and Ravana with Bow and Arrow* is given as a query, and

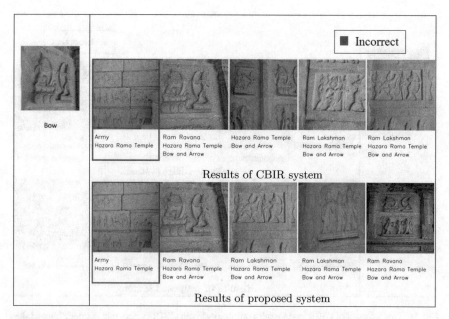

Fig. 8 Comparison of CBIR system with ontology-driven CBIR system with a query image taken from Hampi with the keyword *Bow*

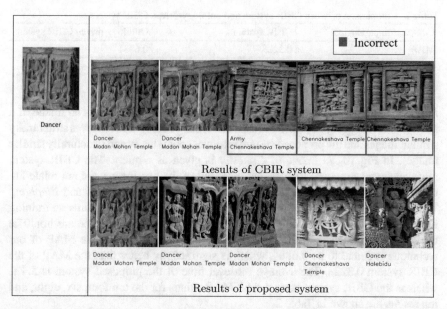

Fig. 9 Comparison of CBIR system with ontology-driven CBIR system with a query image taken from Bishnupur with the keyword *Dancer*

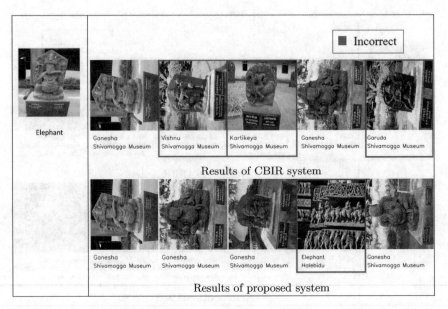

Fig. 10 Comparison of CBIR system with ontology-driven CBIR system with a query image taken from Shivamogga Museum with the keyword *Elephant*

Table 2 Comparison between CBIR system and ontology-driven CBIR system

Comparison parameters	CBIR system	Ontology-driven CBIR system
MAP	0.3228	0.6884
Average retrieval time (s)	4.8	3.4

Bow is mentioned as the query word in Fig. 8. In Fig. 9, the query is an image of a *Dancer* with the query keyword *Dancer*. Here, the CBIR system retrieves structurally similar images and the proposed system retrieves contextually and structurally similar images. In Fig. 10, an image of *Ganesha* is given as a query. The CBIR system retrieves many structural images, but three out of the five images are not related to *Ganesha*. Ontology-driven system retrieves the images of *Ganesha* and *Elephant*. The test image set consists of 50 images which have similar features as training images. Some of the test images are included in database and some are not. The testing is performed with the parameters, reported in Table 1. The MAP of our technique is found to be 0.6884, which is significantly better than the MAP of the CBIR system 0.3228. The average retrieval time of the proposed system is 3.4 s, whereas the CBIR system takes 4.8 s.[6] MAP values for the top four, six, eight, and ten results are shown in Table 2.

---

[6]System Configuration: 8GB RAM with 2.66 GHz.

7 Conclusions

An ontology-driven image retrieval system has been developed for retrieving heritage images of Hindu mythology. The CBIR system uses the BoVW model for image representation, and locality-sensitive hashing has been used for nearest neighbor index structure. An ontology of mythological objects is built over the stored information using an ontology markup language (OWL). This ontology is used to search the results with partial/detailed query information. Though this system is designed by considering the images from heritage sites, the framework developed here can be extended for any kind of image retrieval system, where the retrieved results are linked by a semantic relation between content and annotation. For efficient dissemination of data and demonstration of the proposed technique, a web-based system has been developed.

Acknowledgements This work is carried out under the sponsorship of Department of Science and Technology, Govt. of India through sanction number NRDMS/11/1586/2009.

References

1. Angelides, M.C.: Multimedia content modeling and personalization. In: Encyclopedia of Multimedia, pp. 510–515. Springer (2008)
2. Bay, H., Ess, A., Tuytelaars, T., Van Gool, L.: Speeded-up robust features (SURF). Comput. Vis. Image Underst. **110**(3), 346–359 (2008)
3. Chua, T.-S., Pung, H.-K., Lu, G.-J., Jong, H.-S.: A concept-based image retrieval system. In: Proceedings of the Twenty-Seventh Hawaii International Conference on System Sciences, 1994, vol. 3, pp. 590–598. IEEE (1994)
4. Datar, M., Immorlica, N., Indyk, P., Mirrokni, V.S.: Locality-sensitive hashing scheme based on p-stable distributions. In: Proceedings of the Twentieth Annual Symposium on Computational Geometry, pp. 253–262. ACM (2004)
5. Evaluation of ranked retrieval results. http://nlp.stanford.edu/IR-book/html/htmledition/evaluation-of-ranked-retrieval-results-1.html. Accessed 15 July 2016
6. Gowsikhaa, D., Abirami, S., Baskaran, R.: Construction of image ontology using low-level features for image retrieval. In: 2012 International Conference on Computer Communication and Informatics (ICCCI), pp. 1–7. IEEE (2012)
7. Gudewar, A.D., Ragha, L.R.: Ontology to improve CBIR system. Int. J. Comput. Appl. **52**(21), 23–30 (2012)
8. Gupta, U., Chaudhury, S.: Deep transfer learning with ontology for image classification. In: 2015 Fifth National Conference on Computer Vision, Pattern Recognition, Image Processing and Graphics (NCVPRIPG), pp. 1–4 (2015)
9. Harit, G., Chaudhury, S., Paranjpe, J.: Ontology guided access to document images. In: Proceedings of the Eighth International Conference on Document Analysis and Recognition, pp. 292–296. IEEE (2005)
10. Horridge, M.: A Practical Guide To Building OWL Ontologies Using The Protege-OWL Plugin and CO-ODE Tools Edition 1.0. The University Of Manchester (2004)
11. Jégou, H., Douze, M., Schmid, C.: Improving bag-of-features for large scale image search. Int. J. Comput. Vis. **87**(3), 316–336 (2010)
12. Liu, J.: Image retrieval based on bag-of-words model. CoRR. Arxiv:abs/1304.5168 (2013)

13. Lowe, D.G.: Distinctive image features from scale-invariant keypoints. Int. J. Comput. Vis. **60**(2), 91–110 (2004)
14. Maji, A.K., Mukhoty, A., Majumdar, A.K., Mukhopadhyay, J., Sural, S., Paul, S., Majumdar, B.: Security analysis and implementation of web-based telemedicine services with a four-tier architecture. In: Second International Conference on Pervasive Computing Technologies for Healthcare, 2008. PervasiveHealth 2008, pp. 46–54 (2008)
15. Makridis, M., Daras, P.: Automatic classification of archaeological pottery sherds. J. Comput. Cult. Herit. (JOCCH) **5**(4), 15 (2012)
16. Mallik, A., Chaudhury, S., Ghosh, H.: Nrityakosha: preserving the intangible heritage of Indian classical dance. J. Comput. Cult. Herit. (JOCCH) **4**(3), 11 (2011)
17. Mallik, A., Chaudhury, S., Madan, S., Dinesh, T., Chandru, U.V.: Archiving mural paintings using an ontology based approach. In: Asian Conference on Computer Vision, pp. 37–48 (2012)
18. Mallik, A., Ghosh, H., Chaudhury, S., Harit, G.: MOWL: an ontology representation language for web-based multimedia applications. ACM Trans. Multimed. Comput. Commun. Appl. (TOMM) **10**(1), 8:1–8:21 (2013)
19. Mishra, S., Mukherjee, J., Mondal, P., Aswatha, S.M., Mukherjee, J.: Real-time retrieval system for heritage images. In: Emerging Research in Electronics, Computer Science and Technology, pp. 245–253. Springer (2014)
20. Mukherjee, J., Aswatha, S.M., Mondal, P., Mukherjee, J., Mitra, P.: Duplication detection for image sharing systems. In: Proceedings of the 2014 Indian Conference on Computer Vision Graphics and Image Processing (ICVGIP), pp. 4:1–4:7 (2014)
21. Mukherjee, J., Mukhopadhyay, J., Mitra, P.: A survey on image retrieval performance of different bag of visual words indexing techniques. In: Proceedings of the IEEE Students' Technology Symposium (TechSym), pp. 99–104 (2014)
22. Popescu, A., Millet, C., Moëllic, P.-A.: Ontology driven content based image retrieval. In: Proceedings of the 6th ACM International Conference on Image and Video Retrieval, pp. 387–394. ACM (2007)
23. Popescu, A., Moëllic, P.-A., Millet, C.: SemRetriev: an ontology driven image retrieval system. In: Proceedings of the 6th ACM International Conference on Image and Video Retrieval, pp. 113–116. ACM (2007)
24. Prud, E., Seaborne, A., et al.: SPARQL query language for RDF (2006)
25. Resnik, P., et al.: Semantic similarity in a taxonomy: an information-based measure and its application to problems of ambiguity in natural language. J. Artif. Intell. Res. (JAIR) **11**, 95–130 (1999)
26. Sivic, J., Zisserman, A.: Video Google: efficient visual search of videos. In: Toward Category-Level Object Recognition, vol. 4170, pp. 127–144. Springer (2006)
27. Styltsvig, H.B.: Ontology-based information retrieval (2006)
28. Sussna, M.: Word sense disambiguation for free-text indexing using a massive semantic network. In: Proceedings of the Second International Conference on Information and Knowledge Management, pp. 67–74. ACM (1993)
29. Town, C., Sinclair, D.: Ontological query language for content based image retrieval. In: IEEE Workshop on Content-Based Access of Image and Video Libraries, 2001. (CBAIVL 2001), pp. 75–80. IEEE (2001)

On the Deep Structure of Ragas and Analytic Rating of Music Scores

Sudipa Mandal, Shilpi Chaudhuri, Antonio Anastasio Bruto da Costa, Gouri Karambelkar and Pallab Dasgupta

1 Introduction

Traditional music is the mirror of any society. Indian culture and heritage has always been rich in terms of art and music. Indian classical music evolved early on in the era of Vedas. Ragas in Indian classical music were traditionally taught via aural methods and, until the twentieth century, did not employ notations as the primary media of instruction, understanding or transmission. The rules of Indian classical music and compositions themselves are taught and passed on from a guru (teacher) to a sishya (student), in person. Various Indian music schools follow notations and classifications, for example the notation system created by Vishnu Narayan Bhatkhande. In spite of the introduction of notation systems and documentations of classical music only a few decades ago, several rules of Ragas are still incompletely documented.

One of the other defining features of Indian classical music is that, the musicians do not follow notations, composed previously, while presenting a rendition of a

S. Mandal (✉) · A. A. B. da Costa · P. Dasgupta
Department of Computer Science, Indian Institute of Technology Kharagpur,
Kharagpur, India
e-mail: contacttosudipamandal@gmail.com

A. A. B. da Costa
e-mail: antonio.cse.iitkgp@gmail.com

P. Dasgupta
e-mail: pallab@cse.iitkgp.ernet.in

S. Chaudhuri
Dhirubhai Ambani Institute of Information and Communication Technology,
Gandhinagar, Gujarat, India
e-mail: shilpimegha@gmail.com

G. Karambelkar
Department of Humanities and Social Sciences, Indian Institute of Technology Kharagpur,
Kharagpur, India
e-mail: gourikarambelkar@gmail.com

© Springer Nature Singapore Pte Ltd. 2018
B. Chanda et al. (eds.), *Heritage Preservation*,
https://doi.org/10.1007/978-981-10-7221-5_9

Raga. They develop the note sequences on the fly, obeying the rules and grammar of the Raga. The goodness of a rendition depends not only on the tonal quality of the music, but also on the ability of the musician to compose the phrases (note sequences described in a later section) that bring out the aesthetic value of the Raga. Hence, it is a nontrivial task to express the rules of a rendition in the form of a language. It is this fascinating feature of Indian classical music that makes it amenable to a language theoretic study of Indian Ragas.

An output of any structural model can be rated easily when the goodness of an output is dependent on a set of rules and the rules are equivalent for all outputs. The difficulty in rating a music score which has aesthetic value is that, the rating depends on the perspective and knowledge of the listener. A Raga rendition can sound amazing to a listener who is trained in classical music but the same rendition can sound dull to another listener who has a different taste in music. Similarly, a well-trained musician can find a Raga rendition poor because he/she belongs to a separate gharana (different music styles based on spatial distances in India). Capturing the aesthetic essence of a music score for different people is out of the scope of our present work. We, instead, have tried to rate a music score based on the universal structural rules of Ragas which are accepted consensually. In this article, we present the dynamic programming algorithm *RScore*, that rates renditions on the basis of the deeper structure of Ragas.

The structure of the paper is as follows. Related work is described in Sect. 2. A brief background study on Raga system has been discussed in Sect. 3. In Sect. 4, we have discussed how Raga can be described as a formal language. The methodology for rating a music score in described in Sect. 5. We have validated our methodology with results in Sect. 5.2. In Sect. 6, we have done extension to our previous methodology and shown the results. Finally, in Sect. 7 the impact of the context of phrases in a Raga rendition is discussed.

2   Related Work

Not much literature is available in language theoretic analysis of Indian classical music from the perspective of computer science. Nevertheless, a few relevant studies have been found which are of interest to this research. We discuss these below.

Pandit Bhatkhande classified Indian Ragas based on the Thaat system [1]. He classified more than 70 Ragas based on the notes used in the Raga. Though this classification has been criticized because of the lack of completeness of the classification, his contributions in documenting and classifying Ragas is enormous.

The contribution of Preeti Rao et al. in identification of a Raga from hummed music [2], Raga classification by pitch analysis [3], etc., are remarkable, however, dealing with signal processing, pitch analysis, etc.

Parag Chordia et al. have worked in Raga recognition using pitch class distributions [4]. Their work in analysis and representation of bandishes using humdrum syntax [5] has been used in our present work.

The work done by Gaurav Pandey et al. [6] in the field of Indian classical music, builds a system named 'TANSEN' that uses a Hidden Markov Model and string matching. Studies have also been carried out on note transcribers, which deal with strategies based on the pitch of sound to automatically identify Ragas from audio samples. However, their study uses solely Pakad matching and does not take advantage of any other information present in the rendition.

Kippen et al. worked in modelling music with grammars [7]. They developed a formal language representation for tabla drumming in the Bol Processor, a software system used in interactive fieldwork with expert musicians.

3 Raga System—A Background Study

The unifying factor in music from all parts of the world is the system of notes in an octave. Formally, an octave may be defined in the frequency spectrum as the region between any given frequency, f, and its double, 2f. For any octave, an upper octave (from 2f to 4f) and a lower octave (from f/2 to f) are defined.

A *Raga* in Indian classical music is defined over a subset of the 12 notes in an octave. When a specific Raga is rendered, the musician only uses the notes that are allowed in that Raga.

In Indian music there are seven basic tones or notes—Sa, Re, Ga, Ma, Pa, Dha, Ni which are equivalent to Do, Re, Mi, Fa, So, La, Ti, respectively, of the Western system. There is also a notion of semitone. The first and fifth notes, Sa and Pa are unalterable. The other five notes can be altered from their natural position. When Re, Ga, Dha, and Ni are lowered by a semitone, they are called *Komal*. A sharp Ma is called *tivra*. So, in total, there are 12 semitones.

The notations of these semitones are shown in Table 1.

A *Thaat* in Indian classical music is the set of notes allowed in a Raga. Only a subset of the 12 semitones are in the Thaat, examples of which are shown in Table 2.

The *Arohana–Avarohana* describe the legal movements in a Raga. *Arohana* is the pattern in which the Raga ascends the octave and *Avarohana* is the pattern in which the Raga descends the octave.

Table 1 Note system

All notes	S r R g G m M P d D n N
Sudha notes	S R G m P D N
Komal notes	r g d n
Tivra notes	M
Higher octave	$\bar{S}\,\bar{r}\,\bar{R}\,\bar{g}\,\bar{G}\,\bar{m}\,\bar{M}\,\bar{P}\,\bar{d}\,\bar{D}\,\bar{n}\,\bar{N}$
Lower octave	$\underline{S}\,\underline{r}\,\underline{R}\,\underline{g}\,\underline{G}\,\underline{m}\,\underline{M}\,\underline{P}\,\underline{d}\,\underline{D}\,\underline{n}\,\underline{N}$

Table 2 Thaat system

Raga	Thaat
Bilawal	S R G m P D N
Yaman	S R G M P D N
Bhopali	S R G P D

Table 3 Raganga Padhati

Raganga	Raga	Patterns
Bhairav	Bhairav, Kalingra, Bairagi, etc.	Ga Ma Dha Pa; Ga Ma Re Sa
Kalyan	Yaman, Sudha Kalyan, Hem Kalyan, etc.	Pa Re; Pa Dha Pa Pa Sa'
Todi	Miya-ki-Todi, Lakshmi Todi, etc.	Sa Re Ga Re Sa

The *Raganga Padhati* is a phrase based categorization of the Ragas. These phrases (a sequence of notes) give individual Ragas their personality, flavour and identity. They are learnt through the Guru–Sishya parampara or through the style of various gharanas (for example, the Varanasi gharana).These phrases are popularly known as 'Positive phrases' of the Raga. On the other hand, there are also phrases which obey the grammar of the Raga but do not characterize the Raga. These are called the Raga's 'Negative phrases'.

Based on the movement of the notes in an octave, the *Chalan*, the Ragas are classified into 32 categories. Each category defines a specific Chalan in the rendition. Each such Chalan follows the Thaat system for choosing the notes for the Raga. Each class/category contains several Ragas(examples of which are shown in Table 3). Ragas in a category may use different variations of notes (Sudha/Komal/Tivra), but they all adhere to similar patterns.

4 Ragas as Formal Languages

The connection between Ragas and formal languages is very intriguing. The subset of notes, used in a Raga, defines the alphabet of the Raga. A rendition of a Raga is a sequence of notes (of arbitrary length) that conforms with the grammar of the Raga, that is, the constraints imposed by the Thaat, Arohana–Avarohana and Raganga Padhati. An interesting aspect of the positive phrases in Raganga Padhati, is that, different schools of music (called Gharanas) have evolved rendition styles for the same Raga using different combinations of phrases, all of which conform to the grammar of the Raga but can impart widely varying experience to the listeners. Therefore in language theoretic terminology, note sequences that conform to the grammar of the Raga are the words of the language defined by the Raga, but since the essence of the Raga is brought out in various degrees by the different words, the membership of words in the language can be graded (fuzzy).

In mathematics, computer science and linguistics, a **formal language** is a set of strings of symbols that may be constrained by rules that are specific to it. The **alphabet** of a formal language is the set of symbols, letters or tokens from which the strings of the language may be formed. Finite sequence of symbols over an alphabet is called **string**. Language is nothing but a set of strings as mentioned above.

We can easily map the structure of a Raga with the structure of a formal language.

1. **Alphabet**: The 12 semitones (*S r R g G m M P d D n N*) in Indian classical music form the alphabet. In fact, any Raga rendition has movements between the lower octave and the higher octave via the middle octave. In such cases, the notes of the lower octave and the higher octave can also be appended to the alphabet.
2. **String**: For a particular Raga, there are several constraints implied by the *Thaat, Arohana-Avarohana, Raganga Padhati* and *Chalan*. A finite sequence of notes constrained by these rules form a string of the Raga.
3. **Language**: A set of strings forms the formal language. Similarly, a set of strings made by the specific notes constrained by Raga specific rules forms a rendition of a Raga.

In this manner, we observe that the Ragas obey structural rules of a formal language. As any string in a language is bound by the constraints or the rules of the grammar, a Raga rendition is also bound by rules at two levels as follows:

- **Rules for the string**: Any note sequence in the rendition follows the constraints of Thaat and Raganga Padhati. The Thaat maintains the notes used in the sequence and Raganga Padhati maintains the movements of notes/phrases in the (also known as Chalan) note sequence.
- **Rules for the rendition**: A rendition, as a whole, is also constrained by specific rules. The rendition typically starts with a slow elaboration of the Raga known as *Alaap*. In vocal music, the *Alaap* is followed by a *Bandish*, generally accompanied by the tabla, around which the Raga is improvised. In the case of instrumental music, the *Alaap* could be followed by a more rhythmic piece known as *Jod* in which the artist provides rhythm with no rhythmic cycle, and subsequently a piece in a fast tempo called *Jhala*. The counterpart of the *Bandish* in instrumental music is known as the *Gat*. The *Bandish* or *Gat* is initially sung or played in slow tempo known as *Vilambit Laya* to be followed by a medium tempo known as *Madhya Laya* which in turn may be followed by a composition in a fast tempo known as *Drut gat*.

5   Methodology

Aesthetic evaluation of a Raga rendition is not dependent on a single aspect. In fact, there is no specific rule for rating a Raga rendition. *Raganga Padhati* is one of the

Table 4 String Alignment Operations-1

String-1:	G	Q	T	A	–	N	B
String-2:	G	–	T	A	Y	M	B
Operation:	Match	Insertion	Match	Match	Deletion	Substitution	Match

closest characteristics of Ragas, which carries the essence of each Raga along with *Thaat* and *Arohana-Avarohana*. In this section, we present a methodology to score a Raga rendition based on a dynamic phrase matching algorithm. The phrases are provided by the *Raganga Padhati*.

The *Raganga Padhati* provides a set of positive phrases and occasionally a set of negative phrases. The proper use of positive phrases makes a rendition aesthetically beautiful; however, the use of the negative phrases is not soothing to the ear. Hence, rating a Raga rendition with the help of these positive and negative phrases, translates into a phrase matching algorithm where the count of positive phrases in the rendition is directly associated with the goodness of the rendition. But this direct phrase matching procedure is not sufficient for rating a Raga rendition for the following reasons:

- If we make a string of notes, concatenating the positive phrases repeatedly, we will get a string which will have the highest scoring with the positive phrase matching procedure but aesthetically, it will not sound appealing. That means, the presence of positive phrases is not sufficient; the orientation of these phrases in the rendition plays a greater role in scoring.
- The notion of exact matching of the positive phrases for scoring is a very strict constraint. For instance, in a Raga, according to the *Raganga Padhati*, 'Ga Pa Dha' is a positive phrase. But that particular Raga rendition uses 'Ga Ma Pa Dha' which does not match the positive phrase exactly but surely carries the essence of the phrase. Cases like this imply that exact matching of phrases does not suffice as the condition for scoring.

The scenarios indicate that using string alignment algorithms is more appropriate than string matching algorithms. String alignment algorithms do not match one string with the other. They align one string with the other string *optimally*. The term 'optimally' has been used because, in string alignment, the operations used have an associated cost (based on the nature of the problem). We say that an alignment is optimal, if the total cost of the operations, during the alignment, is maximum.

In the example in Table 4, we want to align String-2 with String-1. In the second column, to align String-2 with String-1, we need to insert 'Q' in String-2. The characters which matches are shown by the operation 'Match'. In the fifth column 'Y' has to be deleted from String-2 for optimal alignment. In sixth column the operation is 'Substitution', where 'M' is substituted by 'N'. This 'Substitution' operation could also be done by one insertion and one deletion operation as shown in Table 5 and thus resulting in two 'Insertion' and two 'Deletion' operations as a total.

Table 5 String Alignment Operations-2

String-1:	G	Q	T	A	–	N	–	B
String-2:	G	–	T	A	Y	–	M	B
Operation:	Match	Insertion	Match	Match	Deletion	Insertion	Deletion	Match

Table 6 String Alignment Operation Costs

Operation	Insertion	Deletion	Substitution	Match
Costs	−2	−2	−1	2

Since insertion and deletion operations change a string more than a substitution operation, the cost of insertion and deletion are higher than the cost of a substitution. The costs used for these operations are shown in Table 6.

According to the costs mentioned above the Alignment Cost for Table 4 will be:

$$(2 + (-2) + 2 + 2 + (-2) + (-1) + 2) = 3$$

Similarly the alignment cost for Table 5 will be:

$$(2 + (-2) + 2 + 2 + (-2) + (-2) + (-2) + 2) = 0$$

In the next subsection, we will describe the dynamic programming algorithm for string alignment for the purpose of rating raga renditions.

5.1 RScore: A Dynamic Programming Algorithm for Phrase Alignment

Rating of a rendition is dependent on many aspects such as, structural accuracy, audience response, aesthetic value, etc. Rating a Raga rendition is difficult because neither its structure nor its aesthetic value can be captured by a set of rules. Although challenging, here, we present a methodology that uses the structure of the Raga and the rendition for the purpose of rating the rendition. As stated earlier, Raganga Padhati provides us a set of positive phrases that bring out the essence of the Raga to a greater extent.

We propose an algorithm which finds the *best* alignment of positive phrases along the rendition string. Our strategy uses a bottom-up approach. Given the rendition string Q of length l, we first align positive phrases along sub-strings of Q. These sub-string matches act as solved sub-problems that are built upon to larger strings until the entire rendition string is scored.

The proposed algorithm uses the following variables:

Q The sequence of notes of the rendition. $|Q| = l$.

X The set of all positive phrases for the Raga, treated as a 2D character array.

α A positive phrase (a row) in X, denoted as $\alpha \in X$.

Q^k Suffix of Q starting at position k, $Q^k = Q[k, k+1, ..., l-1]$

α^k Suffix of α starting at position k, $\alpha^k = \alpha[k, k+1, ..., |\alpha|]$

There are two functions used in the algorithm to compute the score. They are as follows:

- **Match_Score(Q, start, end,** α**)** = Best cost match of $\alpha \in X$ with Q[start, start+1, ..., end] with the help of string alignment algorithm.
- **Cost(Q, X, $|X|$, start)** = Best cost for aligning all members of X (with repetition) with $Q[start, start+1, ..., l-1]$.

Algorithm 1 Match_Score Function

1: **procedure** MATCH_SCORE(Q, START, END, α)
2:     $len \leftarrow |Q|$
3:     $sublen \leftarrow |\alpha|$
4:     **if** ($sublen > len$ || $len == 0$ || $sublen == 0$) **then**
5:        **return** 0
6:     **else**
7:        $cost1 =$ MATCH_SCORE(Q, START+1, END, α) $+ c$(INSERTION)
8:        $cost2 =$ MATCH_SCORE(Q, START, END, α^1) $+ c$(DELETION)
9:        $cost3 =$ MATCH_SCORE(Q, START+1, END, α^1) $+ c$(MATCHING)
10:       $cost4 =$ MATCH_SCORE(Q, START+1, END, α^1) $+ c$(SUBSTITUTION)
11:       **return** $max(cost1, cost2, cost3, cost4)$

The function **Match_Score(Q, start, end,** α**)** recursively computes the score for the four possible string alignment operations described earlier, of α on the sub-string $s = Q[start, start+1, ..., end]$, and returns the maximum score from among applying the four operations. The applicability of each operation is as follows:

- A *Match* is applicable when the characters of α and s match.
- A *Substitution* is applicable when the first characters of α and s don't match, the mismatch is penalized, and the match of the rest of α and s is tested.
- An *Insertion* operation is applicable when the first character of α does not match the first character of s. The operation inserts the unmatched character into the phrase and the string alignment cost is computed on the leftover suffix of s.
- A *Deletion* operation is applicable when the second character of α matches the first character of s. The operation deletes the first character of α and s is matched with the rest of α.

This function is shown in Algorithm 1.

The function **Cost(Q, X, $|X|$)** (described in Algorithm 2), uses the function **Match_Score(Q, start, end,** α**)** to calculate the cost of aligning each $\alpha \in X$ with all suffixes of Q and returns the best (maximum scoring) cost of all alignments. The algorithm calculates optimal cost of alignments and save them in an array $c[l]$. The value of $c[j]$ indicates the optimal cost for the string alignment of $Q[j, j+1, ..., l-1]$. We also maintain a Boolean-valued array $update[l]$. A value of 0 at $update[j]$ signifies that $c[j]$ has not been calculated. The function **Subcost(Q, X, |X|, start)** (shown in Algorithm 3) is used to update the value of $c[j]$. A value of 1 at $update[j]$ signifies that $c[j]$ has already been computed. Memoization using the array c and $update$ greatly improves the algorithm computation time.

Algorithm 2 Cost Function

```
1: procedure COST(Q, X[], |X|)
2:     max2 ← −∞
3:     for k = l-1 to -1 do
4:         max1 ← −∞
5:         j ← (l-1)-k
6:         for i = 0 to |X| − 1 do
7:             α ← X[i]
8:             sublen ← |α|
9:             if (update[j]) then
10:                val ← c[j] + Match_Score(Q, start, k, α)
11:            else
12:                val ← subcost(Q, X, |X|, k + 1) + Match_Score(Q, start, k, α)
13:            if val > max1 then
14:                max1 ← val
15:        if max2 < max1 then
16:            max2 ← max1
       return max2
```

5.2 Results

The proposed methodology has been applied on several Raga renditions. The inputs of our algorithm are a rendition file and a phrase file. The rendition file is a text file, in which the notes of a rendition of a particular Raga is written in R-Notation (an in-house notation format inspired from [5]). The phrase file is also a text file containing all the phrases. The output of the methodology is the average cost, i.e. the total cost divided by the length of the rendition. We have applied our methodology on the renditions discussed in the case study that follows.

Case Study: Raga Behaag In this case study, we have taken several renditions of Raga Behaag. We have generated the phrase file with a set of positive phrases for Raga Behaag, obtained from a trained classical singer. In our case study, we have taken a set of 21 positive phrases. For each of the renditions, we have modified the rendition and then calculated the cost.

The versions on which the experiments have been performed are enlisted below:

Algorithm 3 Subcost Function

```
1: procedure SUBCOST(Q, X[], |X|, START)
2:     if start > |Q| then
3:         return 0
4:     len ← |Q[start...l]|
5:     max2 ← −∞
6:     for k = len-1 to 0 do
7:         j ← len − 1 − k
8:         max1 ← −∞
9:         for i = 0 to |X| − 1 do
10:            α ← X[i]
11:            sublen ← |α|
12:            val ← c[j] + Match_Score(Q, start, k + start, α)
13:            if val > max1 then
14:                max1 ← val
15:            if max2 < max1 then
16:                max2 ← max1
17:        c[j] ← max2
18:        update[j] ← 1
19:    return max2
```

Fig. 1 Result for Behaag
Rendition-1

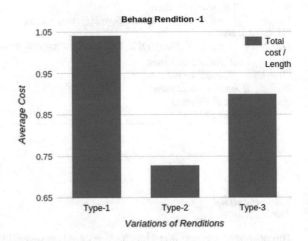

1. Type-1: The original rendition without any changes.
2. Type-2: Some of the sudha Ga (G) and sudha Re (R) are substituted by komal Ga(g) and komal Re (r).
3. Type-3: Forbidden phrases like 'PDN' and 'SRG' are injected. In Raga Behaag, R and D are never used in ascent, but always on the way down.

The results generated by the four such renditions for each of the mentioned 'Type' are shown in Fig. 1, Fig. 2, Fig. 3 and Fig. 4 respectively.

Regarding these four renditions of Raga Behaag, we make the following observations:

Fig. 2 Result for Behaag
Rendition-2

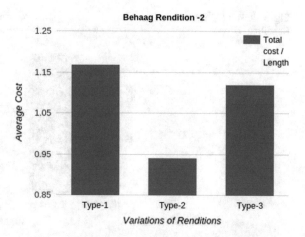

Fig. 3 Result for Behaag
Rendition-3

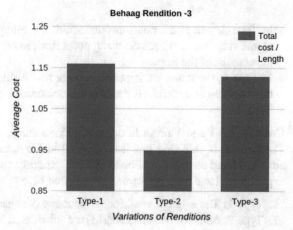

Fig. 4 Result for Behaag
Rendition-4

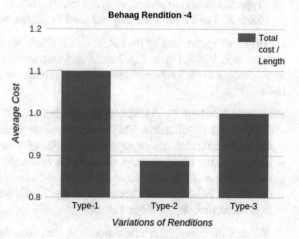

Fig. 5 Result for Yaman
Rendition-1

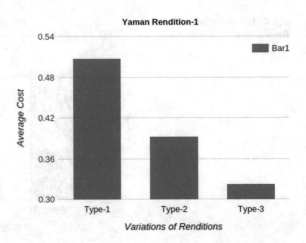

- In Type-2, where the notes are tampered, the rating has decreased. This result seems very intuitive because using notes that are not allowed in a Raga damages the essence of the Raga.
- In Type-3, the notes are kept intact but a few forbidden phrases are injected in the rendition and therefore, the cost has decreased but it is higher than the cost of Type-2.

Case Study: **Raga Yaman** In our second case study, we have taken Raga Yaman. The phrases in this case are also obtained in the same way. Eleven such phrases are considered as positive phrases in these experiments. The versions on which the experiments have been performed are enlisted below:

1. Type-1: The original rendition without any changes.
2. Type-2: Some of the Tivra Ma(M) are substituted by Sudha Ma(m).
3. Type-3: Forbidden phrases like 'N,SR', 'NS'R" and 'MPD' are injected. In Raga Yaman, S and P are generally not used in ascent, but always on the way down.

The results generated by the four such renditions for each of the mentioned 'Type' are shown in Fig. 5, Fig. 6, Fig. 7 and Fig. 8 respectively.

Regarding these four renditions of Raga Yaman, we make the following observations:

- In Type-2, where Sudha Ma(m) is used instead of Tivra Ma(M), the score has dropped off significantly. This result seems very intuitive because using Sudha Ma in the rendition has damaged the essence of Yaman.
- In Type-3, the notes are kept intact but a few forbidden phrases are injected in the rendition. The scores have been lessened notably in these scenarios because the all the 'N,RS' phrases are replaced by 'N,SR' and 'N,RS' is one of the most significant phrases for Raga Yaman.

We can, therefore, infer that using forbidden notes harms the goodness of a Raga substantially more than the use of forbidden phrases.

Fig. 6 Result for Yaman
Rendition-2

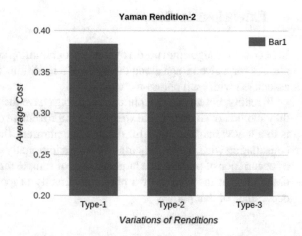

Fig. 7 Result for Yaman
Rendition-3

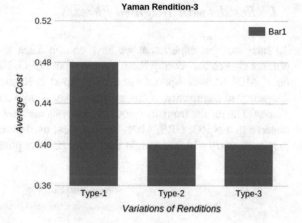

Fig. 8 Result for Yaman
Rendition-4

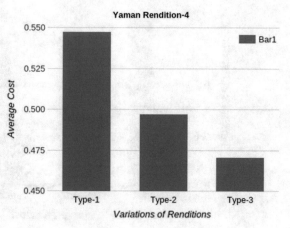

6 Extensions to *RScore*

In Sect. 5.1 the algorithm used a dynamic programming approach to align the positive
phrases for a given Raga along the notes of a rendition. Therein, equal weights were
associated with each phrase match.

In reality, not all positive phrases for a Raga have the same importance and hence
they should not all carry equal weight. An improvement of the work presented earlier
is to allow variable weights for the positive phrases. These weights are assigned in
consultation with musical experts. We have additionally also examined the frequency
of occurrence of phrases in a large number of sample renditions for the Raga. It was
observed that the weight of a phrase is directly proportional to the frequency of
occurrence of that phrase.

6.1 Results with Weighted Phrases

To carry out this experiment we have chosen Raga Yaman. Some of the positive
phrases chosen for scoring Raga Yaman were N,RG, NR'G', GRS, G'R'S', MDN,
NDP, MDNS', etc. Apart from taking expert opinions, we have also studied the
frequency of occurrence of these phrases over a large number of renditions of Raga
Yaman. The results from the frequency analysis matches with the expert opinion. We
observe that N,RG, GRS, MDN are the most used phrases in Raga Yaman. Hence
they must carry a higher weight than other positive phrases because the occurrence

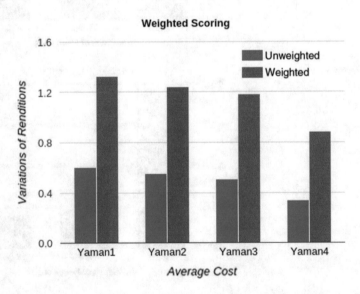

Fig. 9 *RScore*: Un-weighted versus weighted scoring of renditions of Raga Yaman

of phrases of higher weights has a greater impact on the goodness of the rendition. Based on the notion of variable weights, *RScore* was tuned and new experiments were conducted considering four renditions of Raga Yaman. The results of this study are shown in Fig. 9.

7 Effects of Phrase Ordering and Phrase Separation

The dynamic programming algorithm, *RScore*, was based on the best possible alignment of positive phrases along the Raga rendition. The context of these phrases, the effect of other phrases rendered before/after a phrase, was not taken into account. However, the goodness of a Raga rendition is dependent not only on the quantity and quality of positive phrases used but also on the artistic quality embedded in the ordering among the phrases, i.e. the sequence in which phrases are used in the rendition.

To observe phrase context and its impact on the analytical scoring of a rendition, we present a novel methodology. We divide the rendition into several sub-sequences and gaps as shown in Fig. 10. The sub-sequences are those parts of a rendition where one or more positive phrase/phrases has/have aligned. Gaps are those parts of a rendition where no phrase is aligned. A note count threshold is maintained to distinguish between gaps and sub-sequences. If the length of the sequence of notes in a gap is lesser than the threshold value, the gap is considered part of the sub-sequence preceding it, and the two sub-sequences around the perceived gap coalesce into a single sub-sequence.

Once sub-sequences are identified in the main rendition, the positive phrases contained in each of the sub-sequences are observed. In a sub-sequence, phrases occur locally. It is desirable that the note distance between consecutive phrases is small. Here, for two neighbouring phrases, the distance between the two phrases is defined as the distance from the last note of the first phrase to the first note of the second phrase. The average of all such distances between the phrases in a sub-sequence is called the *'Local Weight'* of the sub-sequence. In case of a rendition, the average of all Local Weights of all sub-sequences is calculated.

Fig. 10 Sub-sequence and gaps

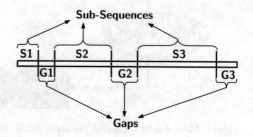

For example, assume that sub-sequence X contains three positive phrases, named S1, S2 and S3. To compute the Local Weight L_W of X, the distance between S1 and S2 is calculated and the distance between S2 and S3 is calculated. The average of these two distances is called the Local Weight of X. A lower value of a Local Weight indicates that the phrases used in a sub-sequence are close to each other.

In a rendition R, say, we have n sub-sequences, $X_1, X_2, ..., X_n$ with Local Weights $L_{W_1}, L_{W_2}, ..., L_{W_n}$. The Local Weight of the rendition L_{W_R} will be the average of all the Local Weights from L_{W_1}, L_{W_2} to L_{W_n}.

This is one of the characteristics of a Raga rendition that is indicative of its quality. Another characteristic of a Raga rendition has to do with the fact that the whole rendition should span all three octaves i.e. the rendition should not be restricted to notes within a single octave. It must have significant amount of upward 'Chalan'/movements and also significant amount of downward movements. This is one of the many requirements for a rendition to be considered *good*.

To measure the upward and downward movements of a rendition, we calculate the distance between the gaps. Each gap is surrounded by two sub-sequences. The distance of a gap is measured by calculating the distance from the last note of the previous sub-sequence to the first note of the next sub-sequence. The average of all the distances of all the gaps in a rendition are computed. We call this the *'Global Weight'*.

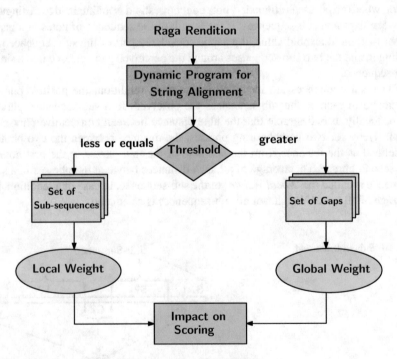

Fig. 11 Methodology for finding out Local and Global Weight

A higher value of the Global Weight depicts a significant amount of movement along the octaves in the rendition.

The methodology for finding out the average Local Weight and Global Weight is shown in Fig. 11.

A Raga rendition first passes through the *RScore* algorithm for string alignment. This algorithm provides the weighted scoring for the rendition. It also shows which parts of the rendition are aligned with positive phrases. The whole rendition is now seen as being divided into several aligned and non-aligned parts. A threshold value is then selected (we use five notes) to convert these aligned and non-aligned parts into sub-sequences and gaps. If the length of some non-aligned part is less than the threshold value, it will merge with the previous and next aligned parts and form a sub-sequence. Otherwise the non-aligned portion will be identified as a Gap.

This procedure divides the rendition into a set of sub-sequences and a set of gaps. The Local Weights are computed for all the sub-sequences and the average is calculated for the rendition. Similarly, the Global Weight is computed for the rendition. Both the weights together have an impact on the scoring of the rendition. This is further explained as part of the results in the section that follows.

7.1 Impact of Local and Global Weight on Scoring

As we have described previously, scoring a Raga rendition depends on several things. The alignment of positive phrases is necessary. The dynamic programming approach for string alignment gave us a score based on the best possible matching of the phrases with the Raga rendition. We enhanced our proposed algorithm by adding varying weights to the phrases based on their priority. This feature helped in making the score more realistic because the use of a phrase that is more representative of the essence of the Raga, must enhance the score assigned to the rendition.

We have also noted that the goodness of a rendition depends on the context of the phrases. In most cases, a phrase used in a rendition is close to the phrase preceding it. We capture this characteristic by computing the average Local Weight for a rendition. The lesser value of the Local Weight denotes that the rendition is good. So, the Local Weight of a rendition is inversely proportional to the goodness of the rendition.

The goodness of a Raga rendition also depends on the fact that the rendition moves along all the three octaves and does not confine itself only in one part of these three octaves. This characteristic is captured by computing the Global Weight for a rendition. The higher value of the Global Weight says that throughout the rendition, phrases are used from all three octaves and it contains a significant amount of upward and downward movements. Hence, the Global Weight of a rendition is directly proportional to the goodness of the rendition.

Based on these two kinds of weights, we have come up with a new measurement named, Local_Global_Weight_Impact which is computed as follows:

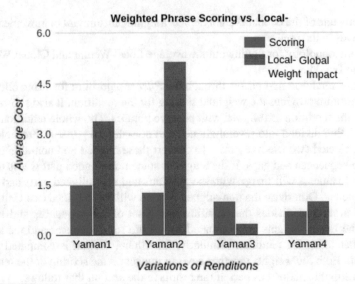

Fig. 12 Weighted scoring versus Local_Global_Weight_Impact

$$Local\_Global\_Weight\_Impact = \frac{GlobalWeight}{LocalWeight}.$$

To observe the relationship between the scoring of a Raga rendition and the Local_Global_Weight_Impact, we have computed both the measurements for four renditions of Raga Yaman. The results are shown in Fig. 12.

Here we observe that, Yaman1, Yaman2 have higher scores (denoted by the blue bar graph) and Yaman3, Yaman4 have lower scores. We also observe that the Local_Global_Weight_Impact (denoted by the red bar graph) of Yaman1 and Yaman2 have much higher values than those of Yaman3 and Yaman4. This measurement, therefore, confirms that the Local and Global Weight of a rendition is responsible for the goodness of the rendition. This shows a strong case for the inclusion of Local_Global_Weight_Impact in the extension of our existing scoring algorithm because the score is dependent on this measurement.

8 Conclusion

Music is an aesthetic and creative domain and hence, we cannot capture its essence by scoring it based on some rules. Nevertheless, our endeavour was to analyze the effect of deep structural aspects of a Raga on the goodness of its renditions. Through several experiments, we have observed that goodness of a Raga rendition depends on the usage of positive phrases characterizing that Raga. RScore, computed by the dynamic programming algorithm for phrase alignment, is the scoring that captures the alignment of the positive phrases along the Raga rendition. It has also been examined that the beauty of a rendition relies upon the context of the positive phrases, the effect of other phrases rendered before/after a phrase, etc. The Local_Global_Weight_Impact captures these characteristics of a Raga rendition. As a future work, we will explore and include more such aspects of Indian classical music in our model for analytical rating of Raga renditions.

References

1. Bhatkhande, V.N.: Hindustani Sangeet Paddhati, vol. 1 (1990)
2. Raju, M.A., Sundaram, B., Rao, P.: TANSEN: a query-by-humming based music retrieval system. In: Proceedings of the National Conference on Communications (NCC) (2003)
3. Belle, S., Joshi, R., Rao, P.: Raga identification by using swara intonation. J. ITC Sangeet Res. Acad. **23** (2009)
4. Chordia, P., Rae, A.: Raag recognition using pitch-class and pitch-class dyad distributions. In: ISMIR, pp. 431–436. Citeseer (2007)
5. Chordia, P.: A system for the analysis and representation of bandishes and gats using humdrum syntax. In: Proceedings of Frontiers of Research in Speech and Music Conference (2007)
6. Pandey, G., Mishra, C., Ipe, P.: TANSEN: a system for automatic raga identification. In: IICAI, pp. 1350–1363 (2003)
7. Bel, B., Kippen, J.: Modelling music with grammars: formal language representation in the Bol Processor. In: Computer Representations and Models in Music, pp. 207–238. Academic Press (1992)

Restoration of Archival Videos for Preserving Digital Heritage of India

Saumik Bhattacharya, K. S. Venkatesh and Sumana Gupta

Abbreviations

ADM	Alternating direction method
DCT	Discrete cosine transform
LRSD	Low rank-sparse decomposition technique
MM	Majorization-minimization
PCA	Partial color artifact
ROD	Rank-order difference
SAD	Sum of absolute distance
SALSA	Split-augmented Lagrangian shrinkage algorithm
TVD	Total variation-based decomposition

1 Introduction

Films form an important part of the culture of any country. The first Indian film was made more than a century ago; since then Indian films have spread their wings all over the world and today they can claim an important place in our national heritage. Films portray the traditions, history, lifestyle of people, in brief the evolution of a nation. They combine the power of literature, photography, and music into a language of their own. It is the most recent of the modern arts, born out of twentieth-century

S. Bhattacharya (✉) · K. S. Venkatesh · S. Gupta
Department Electrical Engineering, Indian Institute of Technology Kanpur,
Kanpur, India
e-mail: saumik@iitk.ac.in

K. S. Venkatesh
e-mail: venkats@iitk.ac.in

S. Gupta
e-mail: sumana@iitk.ac.in

© Springer Nature Singapore Pte Ltd. 2018
B. Chanda et al. (eds.), *Heritage Preservation*,
https://doi.org/10.1007/978-981-10-7221-5_10

technology and has been revolutionized by the development of digital technology. It is a national responsibility to restore the huge stock of archival motion pictures as they are the unique records of cultural, artistic, and historic developments of the country. Archived film and video sequences can be preserved by transferring them onto new digital media. However, there are numerous reasons why these sequences should be restored before storing them as digital media. First, restoration improves the visual quality of a video, and it thereby increases the commercial value of the video documents. Second, restoration generally reduces the bandwidth of the video data that increases the compression ratio without sacrificing the quality. Thus, we can achieve identical quality at lower bitrates. This enables the television companies to store and broadcast the data at lower cost as the cost of broadcasting/storage is directly proportional to the number of bits being broadcast/stored. There is a need for a unified platform for archival image and video restoration as manual restoration process is time consuming and laborious. Recent progress in research has brought this within our reach, in India and elsewhere. This contribution makes an attempt to put together this area of research, with focus on the contributions made by our research group.

Nature of Artifacts Present in Archival Films/Videos:
In Fig. 1, we show some of the artifacts that are common in archival videos. Figure 1a shows an artifact caused by chemicals or mechanical defects that damage the analog film locally. The artifact appears as a very bright/dark localized spot on the frame, and is known as 'blotch'. In Fig. 1b, another localized artifact, known as 'Digital dropout', is shown which is common in digital videotapes. We often observe random

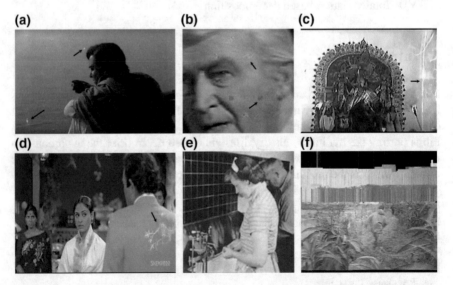

Fig. 1 Different artifacts in archival videos—**a** dirt and sparkle; **b** digital dropout; **c** scratches and tears; **d** emulsion melting; **e** color casting; **f** betacam dropout

scratches and tears in old movies that arise due to extensive use of the films or because of mechanical damage. Figure 1c shows a frame with random scratches. One major artifact in old analog film movies is 'Vinegar Syndrome' or 'Emulsion Melting' that affects a large portion of the frame and severely degrades the quality of one or more color channels. Due to aging of films, melting of its colors, and other chemical changes, we observe a global degradation in color quality of a frame. This is famously known as 'Color Casting' problem. In Fig. 1d, e, we show frames affected with vinegar syndrome and color casting effect respectively. Figure 1f shows an artifact that is known as 'Betacam Dropout'. This artifact results when missing information is wrongly interpolated by a codec. There are several other artifacts, e.g., intensity flicker, persistent scratches, vignette effect, etc., that one may encounter while restoring archival videos [22]. In most of cases, they are affected by more than one artifact. This makes the restoration process unique and challenging. There are several algorithms proposed in the literature to restore the artifacts individually but there is no unified approach to tackle this problem.

In this contribution, we attempt to provide a unified approach to handle this problem in a different manner. Our entire work on the restoration of archived videos is based on a novel parallelizable video decomposition algorithm that performs the following operations:

(1) Denoising of image sequences;
(2) Detection of artifacts by exploiting spatiotemporal sparsity of affected pixels;
(3) Restoration of artifacts by exploiting spatiotemporal redundancy to interpolate the affected pixels.

The work presented here is organized as follows. In Sect. 2, we describe in detail the parallelizable video decomposition scheme adopted here. This is followed by the discussion on denoising of videos in Sect. 3, based on the decomposition method. In Sects. 4 and 5, we describe the detection of different artifacts followed by their restoration. We summarize our efforts to preserve our digital heritage in Sect. 7.

2 Total Variation-Based Decomposition (TVD)

Before discussing the detection and restoration process of the artifacts, we briefly discuss the parallelizable video decomposition scheme that we have used in all restoration process. From an input video, the decomposition technique estimates one background video where the frames are visually similar and a residual video that has all the remaining information.

As the main objective of video decomposition is to decompose the input video, say $\mathbf{V}$ into background video $\mathbf{L}$ and feature video $\mathbf{S}$, we will first estimate the background video from the input video cube and then construct the feature video $\mathbf{S}$ using $\mathbf{V}$ and $\mathbf{L}$.

Let us assume that for a given video $\mathbf{V}$ with K number of frames and frame resolution $M \times N$, a particular pixel $\mathbf{p} = (x, y)$ belongs to the background of the video. If we observe the intensity at pixel location $\mathbf{p}$ for all frames, the intensity should not vary between two neighboring frames as $\mathbf{p}$ is located at the background. This reflects that if we consider a vector $\mathbf{x_p}$ of dimension $K \times 1$, such that x_p^i, ith element of the vector, represents the intensity at pixel location $\mathbf{p}$ in ith frame, then if we calculate a vector $\mathbf{v_p}$ such that

$$\mathbf{v_p} = [x_p^1 - x_p^2, x_p^2 - x_p^3, \dots, x_p^{K-1} - x_p^K]^t \tag{1}$$

the vector $\mathbf{v_p}$ will be a sparse vector as $\mathbf{p}$ is a background pixel. We can rearrange Eq. 1, as $\mathbf{v_p} = \mathbf{Tx_p}$, where $\mathbf{T}$ is the variation matrix, defined as

$$\mathbf{T} = \begin{bmatrix} 1 & -1 & 0 & \dots & 0 \\ 0 & 1 & -1 & \dots & 0 \\ & & & \ddots & \\ 0 & 0 & \dots & 1 & -1 \end{bmatrix}_{(K-1) \times K}$$

Generalizing this idea of background pixel, we first construct a vector $\mathbf{y_p}$ of dimension $K \times 1$, for any pixel location $\mathbf{p} \in M \times N$, such that y_p^i, the ith element of the vector, represents the intensity at pixel location $\mathbf{p}$ in ith frame. Then we estimate $\mathbf{x_p}$ from $\mathbf{y_p}$ such that $\mathbf{Tx_p}$ is a sparse vector. This estimation gives us the background intensity at pixel location $\mathbf{p}$ for all K frames. To solve for $\mathbf{x_p}$, we define the optimization problem as

$$\begin{aligned} \underset{\mathbf{x_p}}{\text{minimize}} \quad & \{\|\mathbf{y_p} - \mathbf{x_p}\|_2^2 + \lambda \|\mathbf{Tx_p}\|_0\} \\ \text{subject to} \quad & \lambda \geq 0 \end{aligned} \tag{2}$$

where $\|.\|_2$ and $\|.\|_0$ denote l_2 norm and l_0 norm of a vector respectively. The first term of the expression relates to stability of the estimation, the second term ensures that the estimated vector $\mathbf{x_p}$ must be smooth, and λ determines the level of smoothness of $\mathbf{x_p}$. As λ increases, estimated $\mathbf{x_p}$ becomes smoother, i.e., $\mathbf{Tx_p}$ becomes sparser.

Since Eq. 2 is nonconvex, estimation of optimal $\mathbf{x_p}$ is a NP-hard problem. As l_0 norm can be fairly approximated using l_1 norm [15], we modify the optimization problem of Eq. 2 as

$$\begin{aligned} \underset{\mathbf{x_p}}{\text{minimize}} \quad & \{\|\mathbf{y_p} - \mathbf{x_p}\|_2^2 + \lambda \|\mathbf{Tx_p}\|_1\} \\ \text{subject to} \quad & \lambda \geq 0 \end{aligned} \tag{3}$$

To solve for the minimization problem given by Eq. 3, we define the following cost function

$$C(\mathbf{x_p}) = \underset{\mathbf{x_p}}{\min} \{\|\mathbf{y_p} - \mathbf{x_p}\|_2^2 + \lambda \|\mathbf{Tx_p}\|_1\}. \tag{4}$$

It can be observed that l_1 norm is not differentiable. However, we can modify Eq. 4 as

$$C(\mathbf{x_p}) = \min_{\mathbf{x_p}} \{\|\mathbf{y_p} - \mathbf{x_p}\|_2^2 + \lambda \max_{-1 \leq \mathbf{r} \leq 1} \mathbf{r}'\mathbf{Tx_p}\}$$

$$= \min_{\mathbf{x_p}} \max_{-1 \leq \mathbf{r} \leq 1} \{\|\mathbf{y_p} - \mathbf{x_p}\|_2^2 + \lambda \mathbf{r}'\mathbf{Tx_p}\}. \tag{5}$$

where the inequality constraint of $\mathbf{r}$ is to be incorporated element wise. Using min-max theorem [36], we can represent Eq. 5 as

$$C(\mathbf{x_p}) = \max_{-1 \leq \mathbf{r} \leq 1} \min_{\mathbf{x_p}} f(\mathbf{x_p}, \mathbf{r}) \tag{6}$$

where

$$f(\mathbf{x_p}, \mathbf{r}) = \|\mathbf{y_p} - \mathbf{x_p}\|_2^2 + \lambda \mathbf{r}'\mathbf{Tx_p}. \tag{7}$$

To compute the minimization part of Eq. 6, we set $\frac{\partial}{\partial \mathbf{x_p}} f(\mathbf{x_p}, \mathbf{r}) = 0$ and obtain

$$\mathbf{x_p} = \mathbf{y_p} - \frac{\lambda}{2} \mathbf{T}'\mathbf{r} \tag{8}$$

Putting this value of $\mathbf{x_p}$ in Eq. 6, we obtain,

$$C(\mathbf{x_p}) = \min_{-1 \leq \mathbf{r} \leq 1} W(\mathbf{r}) \tag{9}$$

where $W(\mathbf{r}) = \mathbf{r}'\mathbf{TT}'\mathbf{r} - \frac{4}{\lambda}\mathbf{r}'\mathbf{Ty_p}$.

Equation 9 can be solved using majorization-minimization (MM) algorithm [9, 16] setting $\mathbf{r}^{(n)}$ as point of coincidence and defining a nonnegative majorizer of $W(\mathbf{r})$ as stated in [4]. Solving the MM algorithm, we get

$$\mathbf{r}^{(n+1)} = clip(\mathbf{r}^{(n)} + \frac{2}{\beta\lambda}\mathbf{Tx_p}^{(n+1)}, 1) \tag{10}$$

where clipping function, $clip(\mathbf{z}, Q)$ is an element-wise operation defined as

$$clip(\mathbf{z}, Q) = \begin{cases} z & |z| \leq Q \\ Qsign(z) & otherwise. \end{cases}$$

We execute Eqs. 8 and 10 iteratively to estimate $\mathbf{x_p}$. Finally, we construct the two videos $\mathbf{L}$ and $\mathbf{S}$ where video $\mathbf{L}$ contains the background information of the input video and $\mathbf{S}$ contains the residual feature part of the input video $\mathbf{V}$ defined as $\mathbf{S} = \mathbf{V} - \mathbf{L}$, the intensity values at pixel location $\mathbf{p}$ in the ith frame are x_p^i and s_p^i for videos $\mathbf{L}$ and $\mathbf{S}$ respectively, where x_p^i is the ith element of estimated vector $\mathbf{x_p}$.

3 Denoising of Videos

3.1 Motivation

The inherent thermal noise, present in all image sensors, affects a captured video. At low signal-to-noise ratio (SNR), the noise appears as random fluctuations that are annoying to a viewer. Denoising plays a crucial role not only to increase the visual quality of the video but also for any vision-based application, e.g., surveillance, telemedicine, robot maneuvering, machine vision, etc. There exist several methods to denoise an input video using the spatiotemporal information of the video cube. The existing denoising algorithms can be broadly classified into three classes—spatial denoising, temporal denoising, and spatiotemporal denoising. In recent times, spatiotemporal denoising gained popularity as its performance is better than spatial or temporal denoising alone. Depending upon the method used for exploiting the spatiotemporal information, each class can be subdivided into further subclasses. For example, in wavelet- based denoising, a wavelet function is used along with the statistical information of the scene to denoise a video [2, 21, 43]. In [6, 13, 19, 34], nonlocal spatial estimation is used for video denoising. The denoising problem has been formulated as matrix recovery problem in [19, 27]. Recently, low rank-sparse decomposition technique (LRSD) has gained importance in the field of denoising due to its accuracy and different solvable models [7, 8]. In this approach, the noisy video is decomposed into two videos namely, a low-rank video that contains visually similar frames and a sparse video containing the motion information and noise. The sparse part is further processed to remove the noise present. Finally, denoised sparse video volume is added with low rank video to attain the final denoised video. Though existing decomposition-based algorithm performs well, its high computational complexity makes denoising a time-consuming process.

Some Unique Features of Proposed Denoising Algorithm:

- The proposed algorithm uses TV decomposition that is fully parallelizable.
- Unlike some of the existing algorithms, the proposed algorithm does not assume any noise distribution. This makes the algorithm more suitable for real-world applications, where the distribution of the noise is unknown.
- The proposed algorithm is used to restore random scratches often observed in archived films/videos.

3.2 Proposed Approach

Video denoising process can be divided into two stages: decomposition of a noisy video to extract the noisy sparse video; and denoising of the noisy sparse features. In the first step, we decompose the input noisy video into noise-free background video and noisy feature video. As features cannot be extracted directly from the noisy video, we use a second stage of noise removal and use spatial information of a frame to remove the noise from the features present.

Consider a video $\mathbf{V}$ with K frames each of dimension $M \times N$. At first, we try to remove noise using the time- varying nature of the noisy pixels. At each pixel $\mathbf{p} \in M \times N$, as mentioned in Sect. 2, the intensity $\mathbf{x_p}$, which is not varying with time, can be modeled as

$$\underset{\mathbf{x_p}}{\text{minimize}} \ \{\|\mathbf{y_p} - \mathbf{x_p}\|_2^2 + \lambda \|\mathbf{Tx_p}\|_1\}$$
$$\text{subject to} \ \ \lambda \geq 0 \tag{11}$$

where $\mathbf{x_p}$ and $\mathbf{y_p}$ are estimated vectors of background intensities and observed intensities at location $\mathbf{p}$, λ and $\mathbf{T}$ are the regularization parameter and difference matrix as discussed in Sect. 2.

As we desire to remove all temporal fluctuations at the first stage, we select λ and number of iterations in a manner such that all the time-varying information is present in the feature video $\mathbf{S}$ for further processing. As discussed in [4], we select $\lambda = 200$, $\beta = 3$, and $n = 500$ so that the rank of the background video $\mathbf{L}$ becomes 1 and all time-varying information is captured by the feature video $\mathbf{S}$. Since noise is a time-varying component of the signal, it appears in the decomposed video $\mathbf{S}$ along with other the features. Hence, we need an additional step to remove the noise present in $\mathbf{S}$.

Denoising of the sparse video:
To denoise the sparse feature video, we exploit the fact that in a particular frame, the feature information have spatial correlation. But noise does not have any spatial correlation due to its random nature. Suppose, we want to decompose the sparse video $\mathbf{S}$ into denoised feature video $\mathbf{F}$ and video $\mathbf{N}$ containing only the noise part. As stated in [39], the decomposition problem can be formulated as

$$min\{\|\mathbf{F_M}\|_{STV} + \mu\|\mathbf{N_M}\|_1\}$$
$$s.t. \ \ \mathbf{F_M} + \mathbf{N_M} = \mathbf{S_M}, \tag{12}$$

where $\mathbf{F_M}$ and $\mathbf{N_M}$ represent the matrix forms of videos $\mathbf{F}$ and $\mathbf{N}$, respectively, such that, ith column of the matrix contains the ith frame of the video scanned in a lexicographic format, μ is a nonnegative constant and STV is the sum of the total variation norm defined as

$$\|\mathbf{W_M}\|_{STV} = \sum_{k=1}^{K} \|\mathbf{W}^k\|_{TV} \tag{13}$$

$$= \sum_{k=1}^{K}\sum_{i=1}^{M}\sum_{j=1}^{N} \sqrt{(w_{i,j}^k - w_{i-1,j}^k)^2 + (w_{i,j}^k - w_{i,j-1}^k)^2}, \tag{14}$$

where $\mathbf{W}^k$ is the kth frame of $\mathbf{W}$ and $w_{i,j}^k$ is the intensity value at pixel location (i, j) in the kth frame of video $\mathbf{W}$. The matrix l_1 norm for a 2D matrix is defined as

$$\|\mathbf{W_M}\|_1 = \sum_{k=1}^{K} \|\mathbf{W_M}^k\|_1, \tag{15}$$

where $\mathbf{W_M}^k$ is the kth column of the matrix $\mathbf{W_M}$ and $\|.\|_1$ denotes l_1 norm of a vector.

As STV norm and matrix l_1 norm are separable to the columns of $\mathbf{F_M}$ and $\mathbf{N_M}$, we can apply TV norm and l_1 norm to each column separately [39]. The augmented Lagrangian function in this case is

$$\mathcal{L}a(\mathbf{F_M}^i, \mathbf{N_M}^i) = \|\mathbf{F_M}^i\|_{TV} + \mu\|\mathbf{N_M}^i\|_1 - <\mathbf{p}(t), \mathbf{F_M}^i + \mathbf{N_M}^i - \mathbf{S_M}^i > \\ + \frac{c}{2}\|\mathbf{F_M}^i + \mathbf{N_M}^i - \mathbf{S_M}^i\|_F^2, \tag{16}$$

where $\mathbf{p}(t)$ is the Lagrange multiplier, $\mathbf{F_M}^i, \mathbf{N_M}^i, \mathbf{S_M}^i$ are the ith column of $\mathbf{F_M}, \mathbf{N_M}, \mathbf{S_M}$, respectively, and c is a positive constant. The alternating direction method (ADM) [3] minimizes the Lagrangian function in an iterative way to solve for $\mathbf{F_M}$ and $\mathbf{N_M}$ and updates $\mathbf{p}(t)$ at each iteration. The ADM solves Eq. 16 as follows:

$$\mathbf{F_M}^i(t + 1) = \underset{\mathbf{F_M}^i}{\operatorname{argmin}} \|\mathbf{F_M}^i\|_{TV} + \frac{c}{2}\|\mathbf{F_M}^i + \frac{\mathbf{p}(t)}{c} + \mathbf{N_M}^i(t) - \mathbf{S_M}^i\|_2^2$$

$$\mathbf{N_M}^i(t + 1) = \underset{\mathbf{N_M}^i}{\operatorname{argmin}} \mu\|\mathbf{N_M}^i\|_1 + \frac{c}{2}\|\mathbf{N_M}^i + \frac{\mathbf{p}(t)}{c} + \mathbf{F_M}^i(t + 1) - \mathbf{S_M}^i\|_2^2 \tag{17}$$

$$\mathbf{p}(t + 1) = \mathbf{p}(t) + c\{\mathbf{F_M}^i(t + 1) + \mathbf{N_M}^i(t + 1) - \mathbf{S_M}^i\}.$$

The subproblem for $\mathbf{F_M}^i(t + 1)$ can be solved using many efficient algorithms, e.g., split-augmented Lagrangian shrinkage algorithm (SALSA) [1] and the subproblem $\mathbf{N_M}^i(t + 1)$ can be solved using soft thresholding algorithm as mentioned in [39].

The parameters c and μ are crucial for this spatial decomposition and these parameters should be chosen appropriately to get the optimal restoration. As mentioned in [39], we select $\mu = 2$ and $c = 1$ for all the spatial decompositions.

Finally, we rearrange the matrix $\mathbf{F_M}$ to get the denoised feature video $\mathbf{S}_d$. The final denoised video $\mathbf{V}_d$ for the noisy input video $\mathbf{V}$ is constructed as

$$\mathbf{V}_d = \mathbf{L} + \mathbf{S}_d. \tag{18}$$

3.3   Experimental Results

We have tested the proposed denoising algorithm for different noise variances on several standard video datasets, like, *Bus*, *Flower*, *Akiyo*, *Mobile*, *Stefan*, *Car*, etc. In Table 1, we compare the proposed algorithm with the existing algorithms like ADF [10], TVM [11], SMWC [32], NLM [26], RMC [20], and VBM4D [28]. Figure 2 shows magnified portions of denoised videos of particular data for representation.

It is evident that in all the cases the proposed approach outperforms the existing algorithms. All the algorithms are executed in MATLAB 2013 on an Intel(R) core(TM) i7-4770 3.90 GHz PC with 8 GB RAM. In our proposed decomposition algorithm, we use 4 cores of the processor to generate all of the results. Though the proposed method is slower than some of the filtering-based algorithms, the restored video quality is far superior from the filtering- based algorithms as shown in Table 1. The videos are uploaded in the link given in the footnote.[1]

Removal of Random Scratches in Archived Videos:

As we use temporal decomposition followed by spatial decomposition to denoise a video, the proposed denoising algorithm not only restores pixel noise but can also detect and remove random scratches, as they are temporally random in nature and have very small spatial width to be recognized as an object in the spatial decomposition stage. We show the detection and restoration results of random scratches for different input videos in Fig. 3.

It is important to note that the existing decomposition algorithms like ADM [41]. GoDec [42], DRPCA [25] can be also used in the same way a video as the proposed algorithm, to denoise a video. However, due to the large execution time of these existing algorithms, the denoising process is computationally expensive. In comparison, the proposed denoising algorithm has greater practical utility since the video decomposition scheme is time efficient.

In summary, video denoising is a challenging task depending upon the amount and nature of the noise present in a video. Several authors have proposed different denoising algorithms that either distort the information present in a shot or have high execution times. In this section, we have proposed an algorithm which can denoise a noisy input video for different noise variances. The recovered videos in our algorithm appear visually superior to that achieved by the state-of-the-art methods.

---

[1] https://goo.gl/wcmE5Q.

Table 1 Comparison between different denoising methods

Dataset	Noise Type	Metrics	ADF [10]	TVM [11]	SMWC [32]	NLM [26]	RMC [20]	VBM4D [28]	Proposed
Bus	Uniform Speckle $\sigma^2 = 0.2, \mu = 0$	APSNR (dB)	19.42	18.91	19.83	22.54	25.91	26.77	**28.39**
		ASSIM	0.715	0.746	0.812	0.843	0.952	0.931	**0.968**
		Time (s)	63.1509	163.1436	89.2719	318.0914	1083.1173	273.5219	193.7814
Flower	Uniform Speckle $\sigma^2 = 0.2, \mu = 0$	APSNR (dB)	19.42	17.21	17.31	21.69	23.20	25.85	**27.44**
		ASSIM	0.588	0.620	0.641	0.766	0.873	0.941	**0.972**
		Time (s)	113.4673	264.762	168.2671	481.4328	2217.9037	416.1833	227.1741
Akiyo	Additive Gaussian $\sigma^2 = 0.15, \mu = 0$	APSNR (dB)	23.79	24.61	24.33	24.25	23.60	25.29	**27.31**
		ASSIM	0.749	0.767	0.794	0.902	0.885	0.953	**0.971**
		Time (s)	148.8172	373.5437	239.5507	578.1851	2681.6483	602.1741	248.3516
Mobile	Additive Gaussian $\sigma^2 = 0.15, \mu = 0$	APSNR (dB)	22.41	22.28	21.02	23.27	25.23	26.71	**28.25**
		ASSIM	0.761	0.758	0.647	0.764	0.923	0.914	**0.962**
		Time (s)	41.2162	87.5243	53.3266	136.8023	614.5963	61.6914	67.3816
Stefan	Locally varying Gaussian $\sigma^2 \in (0, 1), \mu = 0$	APSNR (dB)	22.10	21.84	21.74	21.41	26.76	28.49	**31.37**
		ASSIM	0.704	0.692	0.681	0.724	0.911	0.975	**0.981**
		Time (s)	46.5732	128.2096	82.9417	198.3171	917.3694	224.7618	137.3194
Car	Locally varying Gaussian $\sigma^2 \in (0, 1), \mu = 0$	APSNR (dB)	19.61	21.78	25.11	24.26	27.34	26.97	**28.23**
		ASSIM	0.703	0.729	0.715	0.742	0.887	0.912	**0.947**
		Time (s)	43.0517	82.9132	52.1711	142.1826	608.1783	63.1892	69.7623

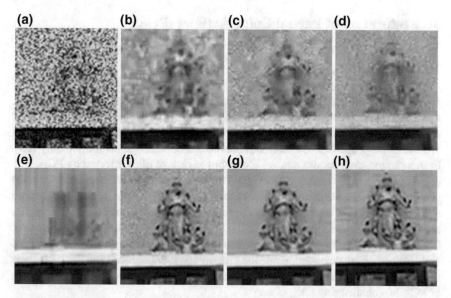

Fig. 2 **a** Portion of noisy RGB video frame at 400% zoom. The frame is affected with speckle noise with noise variance 0.2. Same portion of denoised frames at 400% zoom using **b** ADF [10]; **c** TVM [11]; **d** SMWC [32]; **e** NLM [26]; **f** RMC [20]; **g** VBM4D [28]; **h** proposed method

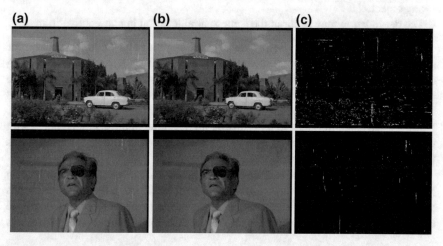

Fig. 3 **a** Input frames with random scratches; **b** restored frames using $\mu = 4$; **c** location of the scratches restored using the proposed approach

4 Restoration of Partial Color Artifact (PCA)

4.1 Motivation

Archival films are prone to degradation due to chemical changes, improper storage, and their extensive usage. Depending on the reason of occurrence, these degradations show different characteristics, in terms of their shape, appearance, intensity, size, etc. We use these properties to detect and restore the degraded areas individually [23]. In this section, we propose a novel algorithm to restore films affected by PCA. The partial color artifact occurs due to: (i) Vinegar Syndrome that happens when the gelatin layer in the negative film breaks down and (ii) Emulsion Melting that arises as a result of mixing of the colors in the film. This produces large degraded patches at a particular color plane of the frame. Hence, the word 'partial' is used in the name. Figure 4 shows a color frame of the video sequence affected by PCA, in which red and blue planes are degraded, while the green plane is undegraded and thus preserves the original structural information of the frame. Because of several factors restoration of PCA is a challenging task,

- Degraded regions can have arbitrary intensity value.
- In a particular frame, the size of the degraded area can be large enough to cover any object.
- The degradation may occur at the same spatial location in consecutive frames.

Rares et al. [33] have proposed a pixel-based restoration algorithm for partial color artifacts. The detection stage of the approach was based on hysteresis thresholding using two sets of threshold, which suffered from large false detection. The large number of false detections not only modified undegraded regions, but also increased the overall computation time. In [30], a block- based approach is used for restoration. However, the detection step contains histogram matching of the degraded plane with the undegraded plane followed by hysteresis thresholding, which again produces large amount of false detection.

Although partial color artifacts are common in old color videos, not much attention has been paid to develop robust restoration algorithm. Though the problem sounds simple as the color planes are partially degraded, but restoration of *PCA* can be challenging because of their large sizes. The restoration of partial color artifacts is

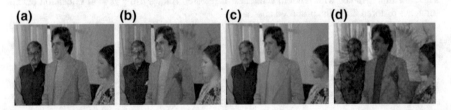

Fig. 4 Partial color artifacts: **a** RGB frame; **b** R plane; **c** G plane; **d** B plane

analogous to the video completion problem, where a degraded region in the frames need to be interpolated using the neighboring information. Video inpainting [31] can provide good results using the spatiotemporal information around a degraded patch. However the disadvantage is that it is a semiautomatic approach, i.e., the inpainting mask, indicating the locations of the regions to completed, has to be manually created. This approach can be used in the early stage when only some of the frames are affected by *PCA*.

The rest of the section is organized as follows. In Sect. 4.2, we formulate the detection as a decomposition problem. We also introduce a false alarm removal stage to reduce the outliers from the detected artifact mask. At the end of the section, we discuss interpolation of degraded regions using spatiotemporal information from the neighboring frames. Section 4.3 gives the experimental results of the proposed method tested on different degraded videos to prove the effectiveness of the proposed method.

4.2 Proposed Approach

Before restoring *PCA*, the input video is denoised using an adaptive median filter to remove impulsive noise [18]. If the noise density is high, we apply the denoising algorithm mentioned in Sect. 3 to improve the quality of the restored video.

Detection stage:
As any frame in a input video shot is highly correlated with its neighboring frames, most of the spatiotemporal artifact detection algorithms performs the detection on a degraded frame with respect to its nearest neighbors. But by doing so, they fail to exploit the fact that the degraded frame may have correlation with other nonconsecutive frames of the same shot that are further apart in time. Processing on the entire shot allows us to characterize degraded pixels as sparse elements in the entire video cube. The detection stage in the proposed algorithm consists of two steps (i) generation of the artifact mask and (ii) removal of false alarm.

After partitioning the input video into shots, we perform the video decomposition algorithm on each plane. For K color frames in a video shot $\mathbf{M}$, where each frame is of dimension $M \times N \times 3$, let us denote the obtained videos for the three color planes as $\mathbf{M_R}, \mathbf{M_G}$, and $\mathbf{M_B}$ respectively. As mentioned before, in a particular video shot, assuming the total number of degraded pixels are very few compared to the actual video volume, the artifact pixels can be considered to be sparse elements and will come in the feature video if we perform video decomposition algorithm on a particular shot. Let us assume that in a shot, R plane is degraded and G plane is intact. If B plane is degraded, it can be treated similarly as the R plane. We select the video $\mathbf{M_R}$ and decompose it into low-rank video ($\mathbf{L_R}$) and sparse video ($\mathbf{S_R}$) using TVD decomposition algorithm proposed in Sect. 2. We select $\lambda = 200$, $\beta = 3$ and $n = 500$ for the decomposition process so that all time- varying information of R plane is captured in $\mathbf{S_R}$. To generate the artifact mask in the ith frame, which indicates

the location of the degraded pixels in the R plane of the particular frame, we binarize
the ith frame of $\mathbf{S_R}$ as

$$\mathbf{U_R^i}(\mathbf{p}) = \begin{cases} 1, & \mathbf{S_R^i}(\mathbf{p}) \neq 0 \\ 0, & \text{otherwise} \end{cases} \tag{19}$$

where $\mathbf{S_R^i}$ is the ith frame of $\mathbf{S_R}$, and $\mathbf{U_R^i}$ is the i^h frame of the initial mask video $\mathbf{U_R}$,
$\mathbf{p}$ is the position vector. This will give us the binary mask $\mathbf{U_R^i}$ in R plane sequence
consisting of all the moving features and the degraded pixels. Because of the presence
of moving objects along with the degraded pixels, the number of false detection is
high in $\mathbf{U_R}$ and we require further refinement of the mask video $\mathbf{U_R}$ to get the actual
artifact mask video.

To improve the detection accuracy, we apply a false alarm removal (FAR) step
to remove the outliers present in $\mathbf{U_R}$. The step uses intra-frame information, i.e., the
information corresponding to the three color planes of any given frame, to remove
the outliers. To do this, first we generate $\mathbf{U_G^i}$ for undegraded G plane as we obtained
$\mathbf{U_R^i}$ in R plane mentioned in Eq. 19. In a particular frame, as the three color planes
posses the same structural information with different intensity information, the pixels
arising in the masks $\mathbf{U_R^i}$ and $\mathbf{U_G^i}$ due to a particular moving object will be at same
spatial locations in both the masks.

To remove the pixels, which come in the masks purely because of motion, we
compare the structural information present in sparse part of undegraded plane with
that of the structural information of sparse part of degraded plane. We traverse both
the masks $\mathbf{U_R^i}$ and $\mathbf{U_G^i}$ in lexicographic manner and at every nonzero pixel $\mathbf{p}$ in $\mathbf{U_R^i}$ of
R plane we consider a patch $\Psi_R(\mathbf{p})$ around it, and another patch $\Psi_G(\mathbf{p})$ at the same
spatial location in $\mathbf{U_G^i}$. If the patches have different number of nonzero elements then
we retain the value of $\mathbf{U_R^i}(\mathbf{p})$ as 1, otherwise it is made equal to zero. Thus, the final
artifact mask $\mathbf{F_R^i}(\mathbf{p})$ is generated as

$$\mathbf{F_R^i}(\mathbf{p}) = \begin{cases} 1 & \text{if } \|\Psi^R(\mathbf{p})\|_0 \neq \|\Psi^G(\mathbf{p})\|_0 \\ 0 & \text{otherwise} \end{cases} \tag{20}$$

where $\|.\|_0$ denotes an operator counts the number of nonzero elements in a matrix.

Restoration stage:
The restoration process is carried out sequentially starting from the first frame. For
any ith degraded frame, i.e., if, for any pixel $\mathbf{p} \in M \times N$, $\mathbf{F_R^i}(\mathbf{p}) = 1$, then we consider a patch $\Theta_G^i(\mathbf{p})$ centered at $\mathbf{p}$ in undegraded G plane and search for a patch
in the undegraded planes of the backward restored frames and the forward frame,
using minimum sum of absolute distance (SAD) criterion. In case of the first frame
and the last frame of a shot, we search only in neighboring forward frame and backward frame respectively. Though, we can faithfully pick a patch from backward
frame as it is already restored in the sequential restoration process, however, when
the patch is picked from forward frame there is a possibility that the patch itself
contains artifact. To handle this problem, we restrict the selection of patch from

forward frame only when it is not degraded itself. Mathematically, if $\Theta_G^j(\mathbf{p})$ is the patch with minimum SAD distance with $\Theta_G^i(\mathbf{p})$, it involves checking the condition $\mathbf{F_R^{i+1}}(\mathbf{p}) \neq 1$, $\forall \mathbf{p} \in \Theta_G^j(\mathbf{p})$. If this condition is not satisfied, we select the next patch with minimum SAD distance as suitable candidate patch. To reduce the complexity of the searching algorithm, we search for patches only in a particular search window. The location of the search window is decided by the optical flow vectors computed using the information present in the undegraded plane.

Direct transfer of this patch at the degraded location can lead to poor reconstruction as the structural information of the candidate patch may not match with the patch to be replaced. If $\Theta_G^j(\mathbf{p})$ is the patch which has minimum SAD distance with $\Theta_G^i(\mathbf{p})$ and $\Theta_R^i(\mathbf{p})$ is the degraded patch to be restored and $\Theta_R^j(\mathbf{p})$ is the undegraded patch in R plane which has the same location as $\Theta_G^j(\mathbf{p})$, $\Theta_R^j(\mathbf{p})$ may have a different structural information than $\Theta_G^i(\mathbf{p})$ and a direct substitution of $\Theta_R^j(\mathbf{p})$ to $\Theta_R^i(\mathbf{p})$ may produce visual distortion. Therefore, we first perform histogram matching before transferring the patch to make the patches structurally similar. Because of the large spatiotemporal redundancy in a video cube, we can assume that if $\Theta_G^i(\mathbf{p})$ and $\Theta_G^j(\mathbf{p})$ have similar intensity information, $\Theta_R^i(\mathbf{p})$ and $\Theta_R^j(\mathbf{p})$ should also have similar intensity information. Thus, we match the histogram of $\Theta_G^i(\mathbf{p})$ with $\Theta_R^j(\mathbf{p})$ to preserve the structural information with corresponding intensity information. If $\Theta^i(\mathbf{p})$ is the final patch after histogram matching, then

$$\Theta^i(\mathbf{p}) = \mathcal{H}(\Theta_G^i(\mathbf{p}), \Theta_R^j(\mathbf{p})) \tag{21}$$

$\mathcal{H}(\mathbf{h}_1, \mathbf{h}_2)$ is a histogram matching operation after which patch $\mathbf{h}_1$ will have the histogram of patch $\mathbf{h}_2$.

Finally we restore the pixel location $\mathbf{p}$ in the ith frame of R plane as

$$\mathbf{M_R^i}(\mathbf{p}) = \theta_p^i \tag{22}$$

where $\mathbf{M_R}^i(\mathbf{p})$ is the intensity at pixel location $\mathbf{p}$ in the ith frame of video $\mathbf{M_R}$ and θ_p^i is the intensity at the center pixel of the patch $\Theta^i(\mathbf{p})$. It is important to note that the patch matching is done in the undegraded plane, while the reconstruction is done only in degraded plane.

4.3   Experimental Results

The proposed approach is tested on several degraded video dataset and compared with state-of-the-art algorithm perceptually as well as quantitatively. We set the search

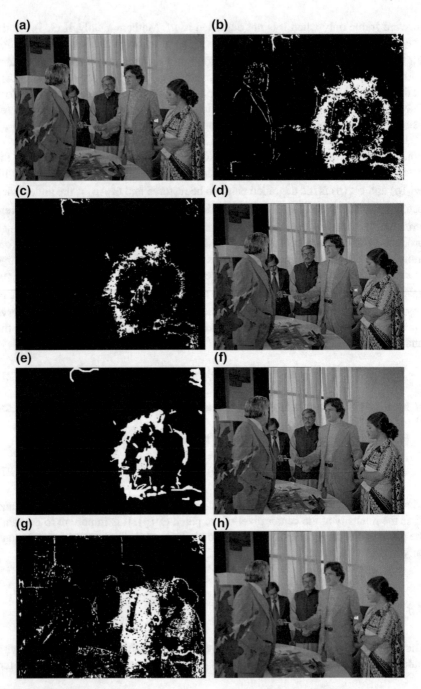

Fig. 5 Original degradation (Video#1): **a** degraded RGB frame; **b** artifact mask before FAR (Eq. 19); **c** mask after FAR (Eq. 20); **d** recovered frame; **e** manually selected Mask; **f** video inpainting [31]; **g** rares mask [33]; **h** rares recovered frame

window for temporal matching as 30×30, and patch size as 5×5. Pyramidal Lucas–Kanade tracking algorithm [5] is used to decide the search window region.

Two naturally degraded videos are used to evaluate the performance of the proposed algorithm. The quality of the restoration is compared with Rares [33], and the Video Inpainting [31] methods. Figure 5a shows a degraded frame in which R and B planes are degraded and G plane is intact. Fig. 5c, e, g show the artifact mask for the three restoration algorithms. It is clear from Fig. 5c, g that proposed method locates the degraded pixels more accurately. The mask obtained by the proposed algorithm is almost identical to the manually selected mask Fig. 5e. An accurate detection of degraded region does not distort undegraded pixels of the original video at the restoration step and reduces execution time. The results of video inpainting are comparable to the proposed approach, proving that its also an alternative option for restoring partial color artifact degraded videos providing the location of the degradation is known.

All the videos used in this work, are available at the link given below.[2]

Though the proposed algorithm restores degradation at a particular location when the degradation occurs in up to two color planes, but often it is observed that the information at a particular pixel is damaged in all three color planes. In that case, restoration of *PCA* is not sufficient and we need an algorithm to restore artifacts where the information is missing in all three color planes.

5 Detection and Restoration of Blotches

5.1 Motivation

As most of the archival videos are recorded using analog technologies, several artifacts are generated while storing or digitizing them. The most common artifact present in archival media is blotch. Blotches appear as patches of arbitrary shape where the gray values of all pixels are closely similar. These patches are spatiotemporally uncorrelated with the pixels in their neighborhood. Depending upon the genesis, blotch can be either semitransparent or opaque depending on whether the three color planes are partially or completely degraded at certain locations. Depending upon the reason of occurrence, opaque blotches are generally white or black in color.

Different algorithms are proposed by different authors to restore blotches. Crawford et al. proposed a wavelet decomposition-based algorithm to restore semitransparent blotches [12]. Hoshi et al. [17] proposed a probabilistic model based on first-order derivative of each pixel to detect the location of blotches and a spatiotemporal fuzzy filter to restore them. Saito et al. [35] developed a restoration method using nonlinear anisotropic smoothing filter. Tenze et al. proposed a morphological method to detect the blotches and used multilevel median filter to replace the

---

[2]https://goo.gl/zn4ClZ.

pixels affected with blotch [37]. A detection method based on rank-order difference (ROD) was proposed by Gullu et al. and affected pixels were restored using the spatiotemporal correlation of the neighborhood [37].

In this section, we discuss a video decomposition-based approach to detect blotches using their temporal discontinuity and restore the affected pixels using optimization. Because of the high sensitivity of video decomposition algorithm, the detection step is highly accurate which ensures removal of blotches irrespective of their size and shape. The proposed restoration method estimates the affected pixels accurately from the unaffected pixels and results in distortion free reconstruction.

In Sect. 5.2, we discuss the proposed approach to detect and restore blotches.

5.2   Proposed Approach

Detection of Blotches:
As in the case of the *PCA*, we first decompose an input video $\mathbf{V}$ into background video $\mathbf{L}$ and feature video $\mathbf{S}$ using the proposed TVD approach. But unlike *PCA*, in blotch the color information in all the three planes are lost due to chemical reaction or mechanical damage. But blotches generally do not occur at the same position in the consecutive frames and they have significantly high or low intensity [24]. For detecting blotches, we first define the initial mask $\mathbf{Z}'$ for blotches as

$$Z_i'(\mathbf{p}) = \begin{cases} 1, & I_i^S(\mathbf{p}) = max(I_i^S) \\ 1, & I_i^S(\mathbf{p}) = min(I_i^S) \\ 0, & \text{otherwise} \end{cases} \tag{23}$$

where $I_i^S(\mathbf{p})$ is the intensity value at $\mathbf{p}$ in S_i (ith frame of $\mathbf{S}$). In critical cases, $\mathbf{Z}'$ might contain moving object with very high or low intensity. To remove this false alarm at frame i, we compare the frame V_i to its motion-compensated frame V_i' generated using V_{i-1} and V_{i+1} to detect the final mask $\mathbf{Z}$ for blotches as

$$Z_i(\mathbf{p}) = \begin{cases} 0, & V_i(\mathbf{p}) = V_i'(\mathbf{p}) \\ Z_i'(\mathbf{p}), & \text{otherwise} \end{cases} \tag{24}$$

where V_i is the ith frame of $\mathbf{V}$ and V_i' is the respective motion- compensated frame.

Restoration of Blotches:
For restoring a pixel $\mathbf{p_j}$ affected by blotch, i.e., $Z_i(\mathbf{p}_j) \neq 0$, we first consider a patch Ψ of size $m_i \times n_i$ and create a column vector ψ from that using lexicographic representation. If we take a mapping $T : \mathbb{R}^{m_i n_i} \mapsto \mathbb{R}^{m_i n_i}$ such that the linear operator T mimics the action of 2D DCT of input on Ψ and represents the DCT coefficients in column form, then, $\mathbf{x} = T\psi$ is a compressible vector. We estimate the desaturated vector ψ^* using the optimization equation:

$$\psi^* = T^{-1}(\arg\min_{\mathbf{y}}||\mathbf{y}||_1 : U_{nb}T^{-1}\mathbf{y} = U_{nb}\psi, U_bT^{-1}\mathbf{y} \geq t_{blotch}) \qquad (25)$$

where U_{nb} and U_b are restriction matrices as defined in [29] and t_{blotch} is obtained by taking the average values of non-blotch pixels in ψ. If there are r number of undegraded pixels present in ψ, then matrix $U_{nb} \in \mathbb{R}^{r \times m_i n_i}$ selects the un-blotch pixels and the matrix $U_b \in \mathbb{R}^{(m_i n_i - r) \times m_i n_i}$ selects the blotch pixels from a vector. The constraint $U_bT^{-1}\mathbf{y} \geq t_{blotch}$ is important so that the reconstructed pixel should have similarities with surrounding pixels and constraint $U_{nb}T^{-1}\mathbf{y} = U_{nb}\psi$ ensures that the undegraded pixels remain unaltered. Here, the inequality in the constraint is meant to be understood element wise.

After estimating ψ^*, we rearrange it to a patch Ψ^* of size $m_i \times n_i$ and restor the video $\mathbf{V}$ as

$$\mathbf{V}^i_{p_j} = \Psi^*_c \qquad (26)$$

where $\mathbf{V}^i_{p_j}$ is the intensity at location at pixel $\mathbf{p_j}$ and Ψ^*_c is the intensity at the center pixel of patch Ψ^*.

5.3 Experimental Results

We test the proposed algorithm on several archival films affected naturally with blotches. In Fig. 6a, we show frames from old movies affected with blotches. The blotches vary from small spots to large areas in the videos which make the detection process challenging. In Fig. 6b, the corresponding frames from the restored videos are shown. Irrespective of the size and position of a blotch, the proposed method restores it faithfully. Figure 6c shows the mask of the regions where blotches are detected.

In Fig. 10a we show frames from old movies whose frames are affected with blotches and *PCAs*. Figure 10b shows the corresponding frames after restoration of *PCA* and blotch using proposed algorithms. It can be observed that serial execution of the restoration processes does not introduce any visible distortion in the restored video.

Though the methods discussed till now restore most of the artifacts which are temporally random irrespective of their sizes and shapes, it is evident that these methods can not be used for correcting contrast of old films. Moreover any artifact which is temporally persistent, will be treated as a static object in the background and consequently will not be part of the restoration process. Thus, to handle artifacts which affect the contrast of a video or which are temporally static require separate detection and restoration process. In the next section, we will discuss detection and restoration of flicker and persistent scratches, where the former is an artifact which decreases the contrast of certain frames in a video to cause temporal flickers and the latter is an artifact which is temporally persistent.

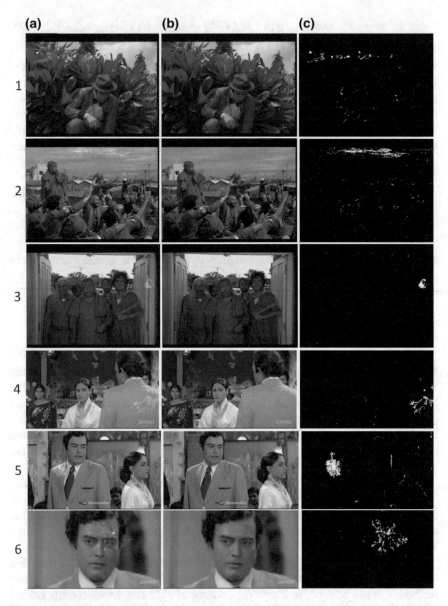

Fig. 6 **a** Original frames with blotches; **b** respective restored frames; **c** respective masks for restoration

6 Restoration of Intensity Flicker and Persistent Scratches

The removal of intensity flicker is broadly divided into two parts—detection of the frames affected by intensity flicker and restoration of the affected frames. Unnecessary processing of undegraded planes not only increases execution time of restoration but also decreases the overall quality of the restored video. Thus, accurate detection is an important step in the restoration process.

Detection of Intensity Flicker:
Let us consider that the input video $\mathbf{V}$ has intensity flicker and the video has K number of frames with frame dimension $M \times N$ each. Assuming the ambient illumination as global parameter, flickering frames can be detected by decomposing the input video. Using the proposed IRND algorithm discussed in Sect. 2, we decompose the input video into temporally smooth low- rank video $\mathbf{L}$ and a video $\mathbf{S}$ with residual information as $\mathbf{S} = \mathbf{V} - \mathbf{L}$. As flicker changes the temporal information abruptly, by analysing the video $\mathbf{S}$, we can detect the scene flicker easily.

To detect the flicker, we first define a vector $\mathbf{r}$ as

$$r_i = |\mathbf{S}_i|_0 \tag{27}$$

where r_i is the ith element of $\mathbf{r}$, $|.|_0$ denotes the l_0 norm of a matrix, $\mathbf{S}_i$ denotes the ith frame of the video $\mathbf{S}$. We define a vector $\mathbf{f}$ as

$$f_i = \begin{cases} 1 & |a_i| \geq \tau_0 \\ 0 & otherwise \end{cases} \tag{28}$$

where a_i is the ith element of the vector $\nabla \mathbf{r}$, where ∇ is the gradient operator and $\tau_0 = \mu_0 + \sigma_0$ where μ_0 and σ_0 are the mean and standard deviation of $\nabla \mathbf{r}$ respectively. As discussed in the previous section, if there is any camera motion or large moving object in the input video, then the residual video will have large number of nonzero elements and direct thresholding on $\mathbf{r}$ will result in large number of false detection. The use of gradient results into more robust detection as it detects the local incoherence in the vector $\mathbf{r}$. The nonzero elements of the vector $\mathbf{f}$ denote the position of the intensity flicker in the input video.

Restoration:
Restoration of a video frame which contains an illumination flicker can be often viewed as global enhancement problem [14, 38]. To keep the color information intact, instead of RGB color space, we use HSV color space because in this color space the color planes are uncorrelated. As V plane contains the overall intensity information of a given frame, we modify the V plane to remove the intensity flicker.

Let us assume that ith frame of the video $\mathbf{V}$ contains intensity flicker. We first find the singular values of the V plane of $\mathbf{V}_i$ such that

$$\mathbf{X_i} \Sigma_\mathbf{i} \mathbf{Y_i}^T = \mathbf{I_i} \tag{29}$$

(a)   (b)   (c)   (d)   (e)   (f)

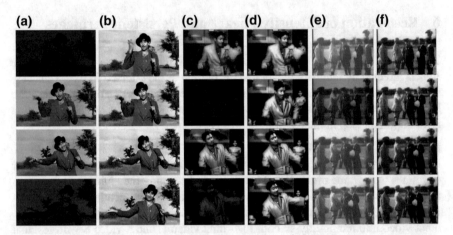

Fig. 7 **a**, **c** and **e** frames from videos having intensity flicker; **b**, **d**, and **f** frames of the respective videos after restoration

where $\mathbf{X_i}$ and $\mathbf{Y_i}$ are unitary matrices, Σ_i is a diagonal matrix containing the singular values and $\mathbf{I_i}$ is the V plane of the ith frame. As singular values denotes the distribution of the power in the space, we scale Σ_i and construct a new V plane $\mathbf{I}_i^m$ which is defined as

$$\mathbf{I}_i^m = \mathbf{X_i} \Sigma_i^m \mathbf{Y_i}^T \tag{30}$$

where $\Sigma_i^m = k\Sigma_i$. Clearly for restoration of intensity flicker where the artifact reduces the illumination, we should choose $k > 1$ and for artifact which increases the brightness of a frame, we should choose $0 < k < 1$. To select the optimal value of k, we select the value of $k \in (0, 255]$ with an interval of 0.2 such that the histogram of $\mathbf{V}_i^m$ has minimum Euclidean distance with the histogram of $\mathbf{V}_{(i-1)}^m$, where $\mathbf{V}^m$ is the restored video, $\mathbf{V}_i^m$ is the ith frame of $\mathbf{V}^m$ on which restoration operation is taking place and $\mathbf{V}_{(i-1)}^m$ is previous $(i-1)$th restored/undegraded frame.

After restoring the individual frames, we stretch the contrast of each frame individual using linear contrast stretching. This particularly has two advantages—it ensures maximum contrast in the final restored video and it also ensures that the entire video has the same contrast level which is desirable to a viewer.

If the degradation is severe and there is no information present in the affected frame, then the degraded frame is replaced using motion- compensated frame estimated from undegraded forward frame and backward frame [40]. In Fig. 7a, c, e selective frames of a monochrome video with intensity flicker are shown and in Fig. 7b, d, f respective frames after restoration using proposed algorithm are shown. It is important to note that, the proposed algorithm does not change the luminance information of the frames which are not affected by the artifact. This is possible as the proposed algorithm contains the detection step to localize the restoration process only within the affected frames.

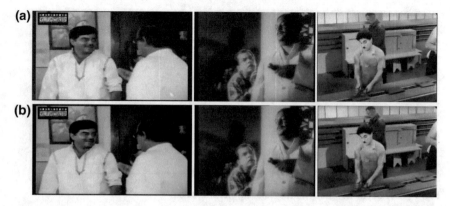

Fig. 8 **a** Original video frames with persistent scratch; respective frames after **b** inpainting

Restoration of Persistent Scratch:
The restoration of persistent scratch can be performed in two steps—detection of the scratch and restoration of the scratch using the information present in the neighboring pixels. As persistent scratch creates a sudden change in intensity which is limited to width of a few pixels, if we look at a video from appropriate orthogonal direction of the scratch, we will observe flicker at the locations of the persistent scratches due to the sudden change in intensity. A flicker, while observing along X-direction indicates a vertical scratch and a flicker, while observing along Y-direction indicates horizontal scratch. Thus, the detection is done by decomposing an input video along X-direction and Y-direction and applying the same flicker detection algorithm discussed before. However, as the persistent scratches are usually generated when analog films are played on projector in presence of particle or uneven surface on projector head, most of the persistent scratches in archival movies are long and vertical. After detecting the location of the scratch, we generate a mask and apply video inpainting as discussed in [31] to restore the persistent scratches. In Fig. 8 we show video frames with persistent scratches and the results after restoration steps. It is evident that the proposed approach restores most of persistent scratches with good visual quality. The shortcoming of the algorithm is that if there is a small persistent scratch present in a video that will affect the illumination locally when viewed from orthogonal direction and thus will neither be detected nor be restored by the proposed method.

7 Conclusion

Restoration of archival films is a necessary, yet complicated process due to the large varieties of the artifacts. In this contribution, we discussed some of the most common artifacts seen in archival films, their detection and restoration techniques. Though we have discussed each artifact individually, it is often observed that a single frame may

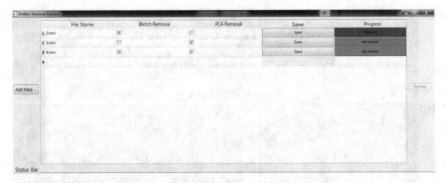

Fig. 9 User-interactive platform for restoring archival videos

Fig. 10 **a** Naturally degraded frames with *PCA* and blotches; **b** respective restored frames after restoration of *PCA* and blotches

contain more than one artifact due to several dependent or independent events. In that scenario, we restore it serially. For example, to restore a video affected with noise, *PCA*, and blotches, usually we first denoise the video to remove the effects of dust then restore the *PCA* and finally, we restore the blotches. The order of processing depends on the nature of the artifacts present in a video. We process that artifact first which can be restored with maximum confidence so that the propagation of error in the successive restoration processes is minimum.

With the financial support of ZEE Networks, we have also developed a graphical user interface based on OpenCV that restores archival movies affected with noise, scratches, blotches, and partial color artifacts using a GPU-based system. The interface allows an user to select the nature of the artifact that the user wants to restore. In case of partial color artifact restoration, the user can interactively select the degraded and undegraded color planes. Figure 9 shows a snapshot of the interface (Fig. 10).

An accurate detection of artifacts is a crucial step in any restoration process as it minimizes the distortion as well as the run time by limiting the restoration process in the affected area. As discussed in this chapter, video decomposition can be used as an effective tool in detection and restoration processes. The key advantage of video decomposition is that it separates out the region with probable artifact location to localize the processing. Its parallelizable nature makes it feasible to handle large video shots.

References

1. Afonso, M.V., Bioucas-Dias, J.M., Figueiredo, M.A.: Fast image recovery using variable splitting and constrained optimization. IEEE Trans. Image Process. **19**(9), 2345–2356 (2010)
2. Balster, E.J., Zheng, Y.F., Ewing, R.L.: Combined spatial and temporal domain wavelet shrinkage algorithm for video denoising. IEEE Trans. Circuits Syst. Video Technol. **16**(2), 220–230 (2006)
3. Bertsekas, D.P., Tsitsiklis, J.N.: Parallel and Distributed Computation: Numerical Methods, vol. 23. Prentice Hall, Englewood Cliffs, NJ (1989)
4. Bhattacharya, S., Venkatsh, K., Gupta, S.: Background estimation and motion saliency detection using total variation-based video decomposition. Signal, Image Video Process. **11**(1), 113–121 (2017)
5. Bouguet, J.Y.: Pyramidal implementation of the affine lucas kanade feature tracker description of the algorithm. Intel Corp. **5**(1–10), 4 (2001)
6. Buades, A., Coll, B., Morel, J.M.: Denoising image sequences does not require motion estimation. In: IEEE Conference on Advanced Video and Signal Based Surveillance, 2005. AVSS 2005, pp. 70–74. IEEE (2005)
7. Candès, E.J., Li, X., Ma, Y., Wright, J.: Robust principal component analysis? J. ACM (JACM) **58**(3), 11 (2011)
8. Candès, E.J., Recht, B.: Exact matrix completion via convex optimization. Found. Comput. Math. **9**(6), 717–772 (2009)
9. Chambolle, A.: Total variation minimization and a class of binary MRF models. In: Energy Minimization Methods in Computer Vision and Pattern Recognition. Lecture Notes in Computer Sciences, vol. 3757, pp. 136–152. Springer (2005)
10. Chan, T.W., Au, O.C., Chong, T.S., Chau, W.S.: A novel content-adaptive video denoising filter. In: Proceedings.(ICASSP'05). IEEE International Conference on Acoustics, Speech, and Signal Processing, 2005, vol. 2, pp. ii–649. IEEE (2005)
11. Chen, G., Zhang, J., Li, D., Chen, H.: Robust kronecker product video denoising based on fractional-order total variation model. Signal Process. **119**, 1–20 (2016)
12. Crawford, A.J., Bruni, V., Kokaram, A.C., Vitulano, D.: Multi-scale semi-transparent blotch removal on archived photographs using Bayesian matting techniques and visibility laws. In: 2007 IEEE International Conference on Image Processing, vol. 1, pp. I–561. IEEE (2007)
13. Dabov, K., Foi, A., Katkovnik, V., Egiazarian, K.: Image denoising by sparse 3-D transform-domain collaborative filtering. IEEE Trans. Image Process. **16**(8), 2080–2095 (2007)
14. Delon, J.: Movie and video scale-time equalization application to flicker reduction. IEEE Trans. Image Process. **15**(1), 241–248 (2006)
15. Donoho, D.L.: Compressed sensing. IEEE Trans. Inf. Theory **52**(4), 1289–1306 (2006)
16. Figueiredo, M.A., Bioucas-Dias, J.M., Nowak, R.D.: Majorization-minimization algorithms for wavelet-based image restoration. IEEE Trans. Image Process. **16**(12), 2980–2991 (2007)
17. Hoshi, T., Komatsu, T., Saito, T.: Film blotch removal with a spatiotemporal fuzzy filter based on local image analysis of anisotropic continuity. In: 1998 International Conference on Image Processing, 1998. ICIP 98. Proceedings, vol. 2, pp. 478–482. IEEE (1998)
18. Hwang, H., Haddad, R.A.: Adaptive median filters: new algorithms and results. IEEE Trans. Image Process. **4**(4), 499–502 (1995)
19. Ji, H., Huang, S., Shen, Z., Xu, Y.: Robust video restoration by joint sparse and low rank matrix approximation. SIAM J. Imaging Sci. **4**(4), 1122–1142 (2011)

20. Ji, H., Liu, C., Shen, Z., Xu, Y.: Robust video denoising using low rank matrix completion. In: CVPR, pp. 1791–1798. Citeseer (2010)
21. Jin, F., Fieguth, P., Winger, L.: Wavelet video denoising with regularized multiresolution motion estimation. EURASIP J. Appl. Signal Process. **2006**, 109–109 (2006)
22. Kokaram, A.C.: On missing data treatment for degraded video and film archives: a survey and a new Bayesian approach. IEEE Trans. Image Process. **13**(3), 397–415 (2004)
23. Kokaram, A.C.: On missing data treatment for degraded video and film archives: a survey and a new Bayesian approach. IEEE Trans. Image Process. **13**(3), 397–415 (2004)
24. Li, H., Lu, Z., Wang, Z., Ling, Q., Li, W.: Detection of blotch and scratch in video based on video decomposition. IEEE Trans. Circuits Syst. Video Technol. **23**(11), 1887–1900 (2013)
25. Lin, Z., Ganesh, A., Wright, J., Wu, L., Chen, M., Ma, Y.: Fast convex optimization algorithms for exact recovery of a corrupted low-rank matrix. In: Computational Advances in Multi-Sensor Adaptive Processing (CAMSAP), vol. 61 (2009)
26. Liu, Y.L., Wang, J., Chen, X., Guo, Y.W., Peng, Q.S.: A robust and fast non-local means algorithm for image denoising. J. Comput. Sci. Technol. **23**(2), 270–279 (2008)
27. Lu, Q., Lu, Z., Tao, X., Li, H.: A new non-local video denoising scheme using low-rank representation and total variation regularization. In: 2014 IEEE International Symposium on Circuits and Systems (ISCAS), pp. 2724–2727. IEEE (2014)
28. Maggioni, M., Boracchi, G., Foi, A., Egiazarian, K.: Video denoising, deblocking, and enhancement through separable 4-D nonlocal spatiotemporal transforms. IEEE Trans. Image Process. **21**(9), 3952–3966 (2012)
29. Mansour, H., Saab, R., Nasiopoulos, P., Ward, R.: Color image desaturation using sparse reconstruction. In: 2010 IEEE International Conference on Acoustics Speech and Signal Processing (ICASSP), pp. 778–781. IEEE (2010)
30. Narendra, V., Gupta, S.: Restoration of partial color artifact and blotches using histogram matching and sparse technique. In: 2013 Fourth National Conference on Computer Vision, Pattern Recognition, Image Processing and Graphics (NCVPRIPG), pp. 1–4. IEEE (2013)
31. Newson, A., Almansa, A., Fradet, M., Gousseau, Y., Pérez, P.: Video inpainting of complex scenes. arXiv:1503.05528 (2015)
32. Rahman, S.M., Ahmad, M.O., Swamy, M.: Video denoising based on inter-frame statistical modeling of wavelet coefficients. IEEE Trans. Circuits Syst. Video Technol. **17**(2), 187–198 (2007)
33. Rares, A., Reinders, M.J.T., Biemond, J.: Restoration of films affected by partial color artefacts. In: Proceedings of EUSIPCO, vol. 1, pp. 609–612 (2002)
34. Rudin, L.I., Osher, S., Fatemi, E.: Nonlinear total variation based noise removal algorithms. Phys. D: Nonlinear Phenom. **60**(1), 259–268 (1992)
35. Saito, T., Komatsu, T., Ohuchi, T., Hoshi, T.: Practical nonlinear filtering for removal of blotches from old film. In: 1999 International Conference on Image Processing, 1999. ICIP 99. Proceedings, vol. 3, pp. 164–168. IEEE (1999)
36. Selesnick, I.W., Bayram, I.: Total variation filtering. http://citeseerx.ist.psu.edu/viewdoc/download (2009)
37. Tenze, L., Ramponi, G., Carrato, S.: Blotches correction and contrast enhancement for old film pictures. In: 2000 International Conference on Image Processing, 2000. Proceedings, vol. 2, pp. 660–663. IEEE (2000)
38. Vlachos, T.: Flicker correction for archived film sequences using a nonlinear model. IEEE Trans. Circuits Syst. Video Technol. **14**(4), 508–516 (2004)
39. Wang, Z., Li, H., Ling, Q., Li, W.: Robust temporal-spatial decomposition and its applications in video processing. IEEE Trans. Circuits Syst. Video Technol. **23**(3), 387–400 (2013)
40. Wong, K., Das, A., Chong, M.: Improved flicker removal through motion vectors compensation. In: Third International Conference on Image and Graphics (ICIG'04), pp. 552–555. IEEE (2004)
41. Yuan, X., Yang, J.: Sparse and low rank matrix decomposition via alternating direction method. http://www.optimization-online.org/DB_FILE/2009/11/2447.pdf (2009)

42. Zhou, T., Tao, D.: GoDec: randomized low-rank & sparse matrix decomposition in noisy case. In: International Conference on Machine Learning (2011)
43. Zlokolica, V., Pižurica, A., Philips, W.: Wavelet-domain video denoising based on reliability measures. IEEE Trans. Circuits Syst. Video Technol. **16**(8), 993–1007 (2006)

Nrityamanthan: Unravelling the Intent of the Dancer Using Deep Learning

Aparna Mohanty, Kankana Roy and Rajiv R. Sahay

1 Introduction

India has a rich cultural heritage which can be dated back to the ancient Indus valley and Mohenjo-daro/Harappa civilizations of 3000 B.C. Sculptures depicting intricate details of ICD can still be found on the walls of temples in Hampi and Chidambaram of southern India. There are various forms of ICD such as *Bharatanatyam, Odissi, Kuchipudi, Kathakali*, etc. Practitioners of ICD have used elements of dance to convey semantic concepts such as short stories from epics or poems. An ancient treatise *Natya Sastra* has outlined the grammar and rules governing these dance forms. There has been a gradual evolution in rules and grammar of *Natya Sastra* too over the years. In this paper, first, we focus on understanding the meaning associated with both static and dynamic hand gestures in short video sequences depicting ICD (*Bharatanatyam*). Bharatanatyam [1] has 28 *Asamyukta hasta mudras*, i.e single hand gestures and 24 *Samyukta hasta mudras* (double hand gestures). The work also focuses on recognizing typical dynamic patterns in ICD known as an *Adavu* which comprises of positioning of legs (*Sthanakam*), standing posture (*Mandalam*), walking movement (*Chari*) and hand gestures (*Nritta hastas*). These four activities performed in synchronization with rhythm or *Tala* constitute an *Adavu*. Each *Adavu* consists of certain number of steps and has a *Bol* or *Sollukattu* (which is a set of audio syllables) associated with itself. Since, *Adavus* are the basic rhythmic units of dance within a specific

A. Mohanty (✉) · K. Roy · R. R. Sahay
Computational Vision Laboratory, Department of Electrical Engineering,
Indian Institute of Technology, Kharagpur, India
e-mail: aparnamhnty@gmail.com

K. Roy
e-mail: kankana.kankana.roy@gmail.com

R. R. Sahay
e-mail: rajivsahay@gmail.com

© Springer Nature Singapore Pte Ltd. 2018
B. Chanda et al. (eds.), *Heritage Preservation*,
https://doi.org/10.1007/978-981-10-7221-5_11

tempo and time structure, hence our work also attempts to understand the meaning associated with ICD videos by recognizing them.

Due to the unavailability of publicly available datasets for Indian Classical Dance, we propose multiple datasets comprising of both single hand and double hand gestures captured under constrained laboratory settings and in real-world unconstrained scenarios. The set of static single hand and double hand gestures captured in constrained environment are named as the Computational Vision Lab Single Hand (CVLSH) and Computational Vision Lab Double Hand (CVLDH) dataset, respectively. The set of static single and double hand gestures obtained from YouTube are named as YouTube Single Hand gestures (YSH) and YouTube Double Hand gestures (YDH), respectively. Background clutter has always remained a challenge in recognition of hand gestures. In ICD, costume, make-up, backdrop, jewellery, etc., increase the complexity of the task of recognizing hand gestures. Hence, a dataset of hand gestures captured in cluttered environment is proposed and named as the Cluttered Hand Data (CHD). Apart from static hand gestures, practitioners of various forms of ICD also use several dynamic hand gestures. Hence, we propose a dataset for dynamic hand gestures captured under controlled laboratory settings, called as the Dynamic Hand Data (DHD).

Adavus are the basic building blocks of *Bharatanatyam*. Hence, we propose a dataset of *Adavus* for recognition of the same. Unlike the prior work which focuses on the recognition of hand gestures only, in ICD, [2] the work here addresses the task of recognition of the *Adavus* also. The proposed work here differs from prior works [2, 3] in two ways. The first being the use of skin detector for reduction in false positives obtained during hand localization and the second being the recognition of *Adavus*.

In this work, initially a video is broken down into frames and we manually segregate images containing static and dynamic gestures. In the first proposed approach, static hand gestures in the video frames are localized using AdaBoost [4] with the histogram of oriented gradients as features. We also locate the spatial position of static hand gestures in the images using R-CNN [5]. A reduction in number of false positives is obtained with the use of a skin detector based on Convolutional Neural Network (CNN). The frames containing dynamic hand gestures after being manually separated are either used in sequence to generate a Motion History Image (MHI) or fed to a 3D CNN for direct video classification.

The ancient Indian text of *Natya Sastra* [6] details the intricate nuances associated with dance focusing on various body parts including head, hand, neck, eye movements, etc. More details about dance in general, and specifically with regard to Odissi dance can be obtained from [7].

The contributions of our work can be summarized as

- We propose a dataset of both static as well as dynamic hand gestures for ICD captured under constrained settings and also in real-world scenarios. A hand gesture dataset captured in cluttered environment is also proposed.
- As described above *Adavus* are the basic rhythmic units of *Bharatanatyam*. Hence we propose to create a new dataset containing instances of 6 different classes of

Adavus. We seek to propose deep learning algorithms for classification of these *Adavus*.

- We propose an algorithm for automatic hand localization in frames extracted from a video containing static hand gestures, using AdaBoost [4] and R-CNN [5] as opposed to manual hand region localization in [3].
- We propose a deep learning-based skin segmentation approach, for recognizing skin pixels to improve the performance of the localization of static hand detector.
- Unlike prior works using CNN [8] for static hand gesture recognition, we use motion history images (MHIs) and 3D CNN to identify dynamic hand gestures.
- Finally, we demonstrate the possibility of semantically interpreting short video sequences from ICD by identifying static and dynamic hand gestures as well as *Adavus*.

2 Prior Work

Hand Gesture Recognition (HGR) has remained an area of interest among the computer vision research community since a long time. But prior works have not focused on the semantic understanding of the hand gestures specifically related to ICD which has a direct relationship with cultural heritage. The area of HGR has remained a challenge because of the articulated nature of hands. Although few prior works [9, 10] have addressed the problem of hand detection, but not much work exists for hand localization in cluttered environments as in ICD.

For static hand gesture recognition, a general classifier or template matching is used. When labelled data is available, supervised learning is used and in absence of the same, prior works have resorted to unsupervised learning. Semi-supervised (i.e. mix of labelled and unlabelled data), reinforcement learning are among the other learning mechanisms adapted by researchers in the past. Works on dynamic hand gestures have generally used external devices such as depth sensors [11]. But the use of depth sensor might not be feasible in all environments such as during a live dance concert. Moreover, the usage of wearable hardware might be a reason for discomfort for the users [12]. Hand tracking in real-time was attempted using a Kinect in [13], but it did not address the task of semantic interpretation of the gestures. Researchers have addressed the problem of hand tracking using convolutional neural network [14] and detection-guided optimization [15] approaches but have not focused on the semantic meaning associated with them. Prior works on dynamic hand gesture classification, have generally used a sequence of hand gesture images [16] as input to a Hidden Markov Model (HMM) [17], time delay neural networks [18], or finite-state machines [19].

Skeleton structure of fingers were considered using the position of the joints or the rotation angles at joints as the visual feature in [20]. But the approach of [20] suffered from the problem of occlusion. Depth-based segmentation accompanied by skin colour-based segmentation was attempted by Bergh et al. in [21]. Earlier, hand regions were extracted using thresholding [22], region growing [23], etc. After hand segmentation, silhouettes were extracted as shape descriptor in [23].

Skin detection too has remained an active area of research in the computer vision community because of the complexities associated with it. Human skin detection in images finds applications in detection of face [24], hand [9], hand gesture tracking [25], human–computer interaction, pornographic image detection and blocking [26], human motion recognition [27], video surveillance [28], etc. Skin segmentation has remained a challenge due to the associated complexity in terms of skin tone variation, ambiguous foreground–background separation, occlusion, illumination, and lighting conditions [29]. Prior works have either relied on pixel or region-based classification approach for skin segmentation. The pixel-based approaches classify each pixel as skin or non-skin, whereas the region- based approach classifies a patch.

In this work, we seek to understand short video sequences of ICD such as *Bharatanatyam* by classifying static/dynamic hand gestures and *Adavus*. Our work is different from most related works in the literature since we aim to semantically understand video sequences of ICD. This is possible specifically in ICD since the dancer conveys semantic ideas using hand gestures, facial expressions and *Adavus*.

Initially, we split an input video into frames. The frames are then manually scanned for locating the images containing static and dynamic hand gestures. Then either AdaBoost [4] or a region-based convolutional neural network (R-CNN) [5] is used to localize the hands in the frames extracted from the video. False positives resulting from the use of AdaBoost [4] or R-CNN [5] are further reduced using our skin segmentation algorithm. The skin identification algorithm used in our work employs a CNN to classify a pixel as skin or non-skin. The sequence of frames corresponding to dynamic hand gestures in the video, are recognized by obtaining MHIs and then feeding them to a 2D CNN. *Adavus* are spatiotemporal patterns and constitute the core of pure dance in a performance of ICD. Alternatively, directly take the chunks of videos corresponding to *Adavus* and also use a 3D CNN to classify them.

3   Proposed Hand Gesture Datasets

ICD is comprised of single and double hand gestures. A snapshot of the proposed CVLSH dataset captured in constrained laboratory settings is shown in the first row of Fig. 1. The second row of Fig. 1, represents a snapshot of the single hand gesture images collected in unconstrained real-world scenario. Similarly, the first two rows of Fig. 2 represent a snapshot of the CVLDH dataset captured in a constrained environment, whereas the third row denotes a snapshot of the double hand gestures captured from real world.

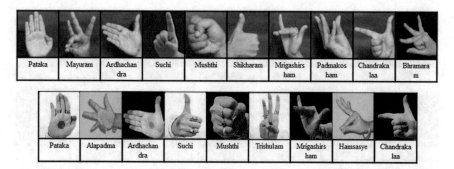

Fig. 1 First row represents samples depicting 10 single hand gestures used in our CVLSH dataset. The second row denotes sample images of nine single hand gestures for the dataset obtained using YouTube videos

3.1 Static Hand Gestures

Natya Sastra has outlined in *Bharatanatyam*, a set of 28 *Asamyukta Hasta Mudra* or static hand gestures and 24 *Samyukta Hasta Mudra* or double hand gestures. A detailed description of the hand gesture datasets used in this work is given below:

Single hand gestures (*Asamyukta Hasta Mudra*) CVLSH data:
Under constrained laboratory settings, a subset of 10 hand gestures of *Asamyukta Hasta Mudra* each performed 10 times by 14 different persons for a total of 1400 images is collected. The CVLSH dataset proposed comprises of *Pataka, Mayura, Ardhachandra, Suchi, Mushthi, Shikhara, Bhramara, Padmakosha, Mrigashirsha* and *Chandrakalaa*. A snapshot of the 10 *mudras* is shown in the first row of Fig. 1.

YouTube single hand gestures dataset (YSH):
For creating the real-world dataset, a total of 972 images are obtained corresponding to 9 single hand gestures collected from 10 YouTube videos. A snapshot of the nine *Asamyukta Hasta mudras* namely,*Pataka, Ardhachandra, Mushthi, Suchi, Mrigashirsham, Chandrakalaa, Trishula, Alapadma and Hamsasya*, is given in the second row of Fig. 1.

Double hand gestures (Samyukta Hasta Mudra) CVLDH data:
Out of the total set of 24 *Samyukta Hastah Mudra* used in *Bharatanatyam*, we propose to create a dataset using a subset of 14 double hand gestures captured from 6 individuals.

Every gesture is performed by each individual 10 times resulting in a total of 840 observations. A snapshot of all the 14 *mudras*, namely, *Anjali, Swastikam, Kapotam, Karkatam, Shivalingam, Pushpaputam, Shankha, Shakatam, Kurma, Chakram, Pasha, Garuda, Bherunda* and *Matsya* is shown in the first two rows of Fig. 2.

YouTube Double Hand Gestures dataset (YDH):
A total of 630 images of double hand gestures were collected from several YouTube videos, comprising of 7 double hand gestures performed by 9 different dancers

Fig. 2 Row 1 and 2 depict images of 14 double hand gestures used in our CVLDH dataset. The third row shows images of seven double hand gestures for the dataset obtained using YouTube videos

enacting each *mudra* 10 times. Sample images of the hand gestures, belonging to the categories *Anjali, Karkatam, Swastikam, Pushpaputam, Shivalingam, Chakram and Matsya* are shown in third row of Fig. 2.

3.2 Cluttered Hand Gesture Data (CHD)

In real-world concerts of ICD, the background of the dancer can be cluttered due to presence of different objects or dresses/body parts of accompanying performers. To demonstrate the robustness of the proposed deep learning approach in real-world scenarios, we propose to collect a novel dataset of hand gesture images with clutter in the background.

Such hand gestures data was collected from dancers performing against various cluttered environments. A total of 7 cluttered hand gestures were captured constituting a total of 1843 images. Two sample images depicting each of the 7 cluttered hand gestures are shown in Fig. 3. Note in Fig. 3, the presence of jewellery, colour on fingers of the hand and costume in the backdrop results in variation in the appearance of the hand gestures as a consequence affecting the performance of classifier.

3.3 Dynamic Hand Gestures Dataset (DHD)

The proposed Dynamic Hand Gesture Data (DHD) is captured under controlled laboratory conditions. We collect images of 8 different dynamic hand gestures from

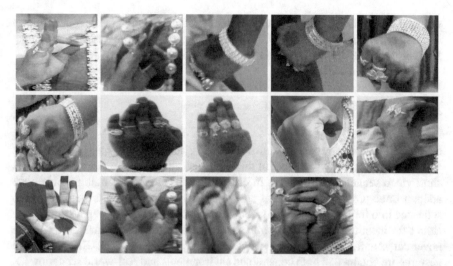

Fig. 3 Sample images depicting seven different hand gestures juxtaposed against cluttered backgrounds in our proposed dataset. Note that two consecutive images belong to a particular hand gesture category

Fig. 4 Few images from the videos of the proposed dataset of 8 dynamic hand gestures shown in each row. MHIs extracted from the corresponding videos are shown in the last column for each dynamic gesture

5 different persons with each individual enacting a particular gesture 10 times. A snapshot of the proposed DHD is shown in Fig. 4.

3.4 Adavu Dataset

Adavus are the basic building blocks of pure dance (*Nritta*) in *Bharatanatyam*. Choreographers of ICD interweave Adavus in a dance routine to convey semantic concepts as well as to enhance aesthetic appeal of the performance. We propose a dataset of *Adavus* which is created using videos collected from YouTube and also in constrained settings. A total of 305 videos are collected belonging to 6 classes, namely, *Kutitu Metadavu, Kuthadavu, Mandi Adavu, Nattadavu, Paraval Adavu and Tattu Adavu*. A snapshot of the *Adavus* collected for various classes is provided in Fig. 5.

4   Proposed Methodology

Several ICD dance forms are a blend of static and dynamic gestures, facial expressions and sequences of body postures. In this work, we attempt to semantically interpret short video sequences from ICD. In order to address this challenging problem we adopt a three-pronged approach as shown in Fig. 6. First, we split the input video sequence into frames and localize static hand gestures. We build deep learning algorithms for identification of both static single and double hand gestures. We propose novel datasets for single and double static hand gestures of ICD. The static hand gestures are obtained in both constrained environments and real-world scenarios, i.e. from YouTube videos. A dataset of static hand gestures is also captured in cluttered environments. Note that the static hand gestures are firstly detected and localized using AdaBoost [4] and R-CNN [5], and recognized using the proposed deep learning approach. The false positives at the output of the hand localizer are reduced with the skin segmentation cue. For this purpose, we build a CNN to classify each pixel in the input image as skin or non-skin. Those hand localization proposals which contain fewer skin pixels than a suitably selected threshold are discarded. Secondly, the MHIs of the manually segregated dynamic hand gestures are fed to the proposed 2D CNN architecture for recognition. The dynamic hand gestures are also fed to the proposed 3D CNN for classification as shown in Fig. 6. Thirdly, a direct video classification approach using 3D CNN is reported for the recognition of *Adavus* in the work.

For the static hand and dynamic hand gestures, we compare the performance of hand-crafted features using an end-to-end trained CNN. We also demonstrate the utility of pre-trained CNN models over a random initialization of the proposed network. Note that we manually segregate the frames of the video being analyzed to separate the static from the dynamic gestures.

4.1   Hand Localization

We split the input video into frames and look for static hand gestures in the individual images. For this purpose, the hands of the dancer have to be robustly localized in the images prior to using the proposed CNN to classify these static hand gestures.

In order to detect hand regions, we use an adaptive boosting algorithm [4] and R-CNN [5] on the frames extracted from the video. Note that false positives can occur while detecting hand regions using an automated algorithm in the individual frames. We seek to identify skin pixels as a post-processing step. For this purpose, a CNN,

Fig. 5 Sample frames from videos depicting the *Kutitu Metadavu*, *Kuthadavu*, *Mandi Adavu*, *Nattadavu*, *Paraval Adavu* and *Tattu Adavu* obtained from YouTube

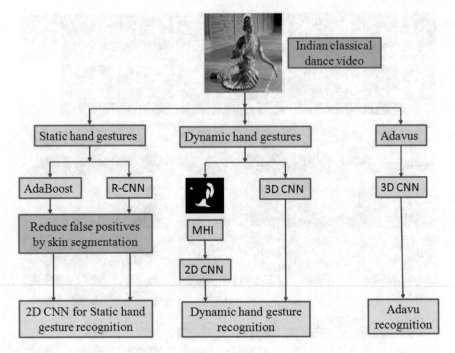

Fig. 6 Details of the proposed approach

shown in Fig. 7, comprising of two convolutional layers, is built to differentiate skin and non-skin pixels in the input image patch by taking an appropriate decision at the center pixel. To recognize a pixel or non-skin pixel, a model is created using training data comprising of positive and negative skin patch regions. The trained CNN model is used to evaluate each pixel of the new test image as skin or non-skin pixel. To create a robust model which can detect skin and non-skin regions efficiently, the training data consists of patches from different races, ethnicity, colour, illumination, image quality, etc. For this purpose, we used images from the ImageNet dataset [30], which are manually cropped to obtain patches of size 5×5 pixels of both skin and non-skin regions. The skin patches constitute the positive dataset while the non-skin patches comprise the negative dataset. Note that to improve robustness of the model, while creating the negative dataset, as in Fig. 8b, we deliberately collected non-skin patches which had some similarity in appearance with the skin patches such as patches corresponding to sand, fire, brown textures, etc. A total of 54, 375 positive patches of size 5×5 pixels and 47, 505 negative patches of the same size were obtained. A snapshot of the skin and non-skin patches used for training the model for semantic segmentation is shown in Fig. 8a, b, respectively.

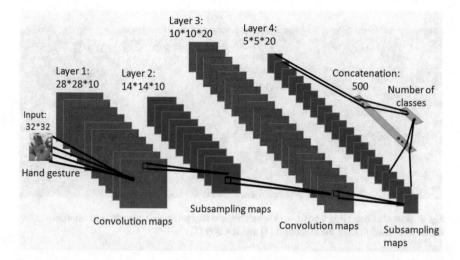

Fig. 7 The proposed 2D convolutional neural network for classification of static hand gestures and MHIs of dynamic hand gestures

4.1.1 Hand Localization Using R-CNN [5]

R-CNN is a state-of-the-art visual object detection system that combines bottom-up region proposals with rich features computed by a convolutional neural network. For the hand detection experiment, a training set was created comprising of data from PASCAL VOC 2012 [31] human layout training dataset, Flickr, Pinterest, DeviantArt which were annotated manually. For training the R-CNN, a positive set comprising of 1181 images with annotated hands were used. The weights of the model were randomly initialized. The false positives were reduced by using skin segmentation. Note that those bounding boxes were rejected in which number of skin pixels were less than 40% of the total number of pixels or a face was found.

4.1.2 Skin Segmentation

The proposed CNN architecture used for skin segmentation is similar to the architecture shown in Fig. 7, comprising of two convolutional and pooling layers. A dataset consisting of 54, 375 positive patches and 47, 505 negative patches of size 5×5 pixels were used to train the CNN. All patches were resized to 32×32 while being fed as input to the architecture. The input image patch is convolved with 10 different filter kernels of size 5×5 pixels to obtain 10 output maps in layer 1. These feature maps were cross-normalized and max-pooled to yield 10 output maps in layer 2. The output maps of layer 2 are convolved with 20 kernels each of size 5×5 pixels to produce 20 maps. The output maps are further downsampled, after cross normalization, by a factor of 2 using max-pooling to produce 20 output maps in layer

(a)   **(b)**

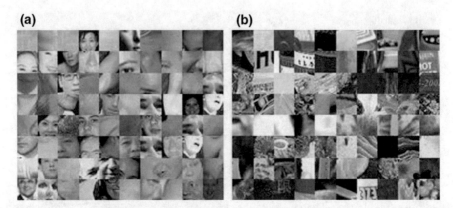

Fig. 8 Snapshot depicting **a** positive skin patches and **b** negative skin patches, i.e non-skin patches, which were used to train the Adaboost [4] and R-CNN [5]

4. These output maps are then concatenated to form a single vector of length 500 while training which is then fed to the next layer. The number of neurons in the final layer depends upon the number of classes in the database, i.e two here. Note that there is full connectivity between the final and penultimate layer. Rectified linear unit (ReLU) activation functions are used in the response of output neurons to produce a resultant score for each class. During the testing phase, a sliding window protocol was used to detect skin pixels in the input image over patches of size 5×5 pixels with a stride of one pixel.

4.2 Convolutional Neural Network (CNN)

In the proposed work, CNNs are used for classification of hand gestures (static/ dynamic) and *Adavus* of ICD to comprehend the associated meaning. CNNs have shown a remarkable improvement in accuracy for various machine learning problems as in [32–34]. We use 2D CNNs to classify static patterns and 3D CNN for recognizing dynamic spatiotemporal patterns such as *Adavus*. The proposed 2D convolutional neural network is shown in Fig. 7. A nonlinear activation function such as Rectified Linear Unit (ReLU) layer, $f(x) = max(0, x)$, follows the convolutional layer. Overfitting is avoided using a dropout layer [35]. The dropout layers are placed after the pooling layers in the proposed architecture of Fig. 7.

4.2.1 Architecture

The detailed architecture of the proposed 5-layer 2D CNN architecture is shown in Fig. 7. The architecture comprises of two convolutional and pooling layers. The manually extracted frames from a video containing static hand gestures are fed to an AdaBoost and R-CNN to get the localized hand regions which are then fed as input to the CNN. For the dynamic hand gestures, MHIs are estimated which are fed as input to the proposed CNN architecture. As shown in Fig. 7, the input image is convolved with 10 kernels of size 5×5 pixels to produce 10 output maps in layer 1. These feature maps are then downsampled with a 2×2 pixels max-pooling to yield 10 output maps in layer 2. The output maps of layer 2 are convolved with 20 kernels each of size 5×5 pixels to obtain 20 maps. The output maps are further downsampled by a factor of 2 using max-pooling to produce 20 output maps in layer 4. These output maps are then concatenated to form a single vector of length 500 while training and is fed to the next layer. The number of neurons in the ultimate layer depends upon the number of classes in the database. There is full connectivity between the final and penultimate layer. Nonlinear activation functions, ReLU, are used in the response of output neurons to produce a resultant score for each class.

Initially, the proposed static and cluttered hand datasets were fed separately as input to the 5-layer CNN architecture of Fig. 7 with random weight initialization to obtain a model for recognizing the detected hand gestures. The performance of this model was also analyzed using the weights of an already pre-trained model for initialization of the network. The pre-trained models used for weight initialization are obtained by training the model in Fig. 7 on CIFAR-10 [36] and MNIST [32] datasets.

4.3 Transfer Learning

We train the proposed CNN shown in Fig. 7 from random weight initialization using CIFAR-10 [36] and MNIST [32] datasets until convergence. The converged weights of the CNN are used for its initialization when the input dataset is taken as static/dynamic hand gestures. This is known as transfer learning. Similarly, we use a pre-trained AlexNet [33] architecture comprising of eight layer as shown in Fig. 9 which has been trained using the ImageNet [30] dataset. The CVLSH, CVLDH, single and double hand gestures collected from YouTube videos, cluttered hand gesture data, and MHIs obtained from dynamic hand gesture data were fed as input to the eight layer pre-trained model of Fig. 9. The feature vector of length 4096, at the fully connected layer is fed to a Support Vector Machine (SVM) for classification.

4.4 MHIs for Dynamic Gesture Classification

For classification of dynamic gestures, the proposed work uses Motion History Images (MHIs) in each pixel which is a function of motion density at that location such that newer movements appear brighter. The MHI is generated by difference of t_{th} frame $I(x, y, t)$ with difference distance Δ as

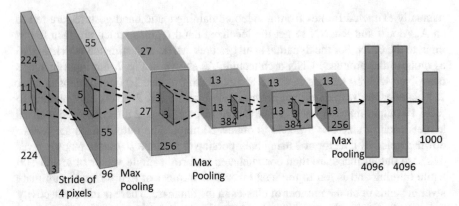

Fig. 9 Block diagram of the AlexNet [33] architecture for classification of ImageNet dataset [30]. We use this network as a pre-trained model

$$D(x, y, t) = |I(x, y, t) - I(x, y, t + \Lambda)|. \tag{1}$$

By considering a threshold ξ which is the minimal intensity difference between two images for change detection, the difference frame is binarized as

$$\psi(x, y, t) = 1 \quad if \quad D(x, y, t) > \xi \quad else \quad 0 \tag{2}$$

The MHI $H_\tau(x, y, t)$ can be obtained as

$$H_\tau(x, y, t) = \begin{cases} \tau, & if \ \psi = 1 \\ max(0, H_\tau(x, y, t-1) - 1), & \text{otherwise} \end{cases} \tag{3}$$

where τ denotes the temporal duration of the MHI.

4.5   3D CNN

To overcome the manual intervention while extracting the MHIs from the videos followed by recognition of the same, we propose to use 3D CNN for direct classification of videos. We also use the 3D CNN to directly classify the videos of dynamic hand gestures data and *Adavus*. The proposed 3D CNN model consists of two convolutional layers and two dropout layers to combat over-fitting. The architecture used for classification of dynamic hand gestures data consists of a convolutional layer followed by 80 kernels of size $5 \times 5 \times 5$ pixels and a max-pool layer with stride 2 in each direction. The pooling layer is followed by another convolutional layer, consisting of 80 kernels of size $3 \times 3 \times 3$ pixels. The convolved output obtained from the kernels are input to a fully connected layer having 128 nodes with a dropout factor

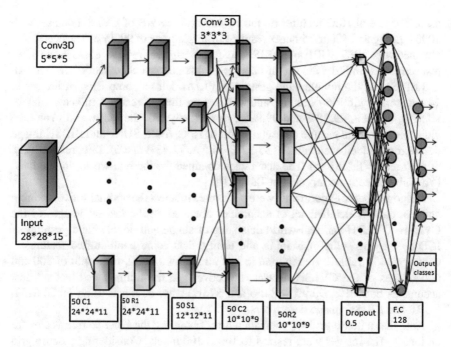

Fig. 10 Proposed 3D convolutional neural network architecture used for classification of dynamic hand gestures and *Adavus*

of 0.5. The fully connected layer is then followed by a dropout of 0.5 to the final classifier layer wherein the number of nodes is identical to the number of classes in the dataset. A similar architecture is proposed for the classification of the *Adavus* which differs only in the number of kernels in the two convolution layers. The 3D CNN architecture used for the classification of *Adavus* has 50 kernels each in both the convolutional layer instead of 80 as used in the architecture for dynamic hand gestures data classification. A detailed architecture of the 3D CNN used for dynamic hand gestures/*Adavu* classification is shown in Fig. 10.

5 Experimental Results

5.1 Hand-Crafted Features + SVM Classifier

Initially, hand-crafted features such as Histogram of Gradients (HoG), Scale-Invariant Feature Transform (SIFT), Speeded Up Robust Features (SURF) and Binary Robust Invariant Scalable Keypoints (BRISK) are extracted from the input images. For recognition of hand gestures, an SVM classifier with a linear kernel is used. The use of HoG features on the 10 different *mudras* of CVLSH dataset with 1000 training and 400 test images resulted in an accuracy of 99.75%. The accuracies obtained with SIFT, SURF and BRISK image descriptors are 91%, 85.75% and 87%, respectively. Similarly, the use of hand-crafted features such as HoG, SIFT, SURF and BRISK on the double hand gestures CVLDH dataset comprising of images in 14 categories with 560 training and 280 testing images resulted in accuracies of 98.57%, 96.78%, 99.98% and 99.92%, respectively. For the real-world (YouTube videos) single hand gesture dataset, the use of HoG, SIFT, SURF and BRISK image descriptors yielded accuracies of 95.37%, 84.5%, 71.43% and 61.23%, respectively, as reported in Table 1 (a). The accuracies obtained for the real-world double hand (YouTube videos) are reported in Table 1 (b).

A rigorous set of experiments were performed to select the optimal split of training and test data. A detailed set of accuracies obtained on the test set images of the CVLSH, CVLDH and real-world databases of single and double hand gestures of ICD by varying splits of training and testing data using hand-crafted features is enumerated in Table 2. As reported in second row of Table 2, for a split of 800 and 600 images of the CVLSH dataset respectively, in the training and test set, test accuracies of 99.1%, 90.9%, 88.0% and 87.0% were obtained using HoG, SIFT, SURF and BRISK image descriptors.

Note that a dense grid was considered for obtaining the HoG feature vector for an image. The images were resized to 100×100 pixels. Considering a dense grid with 9-bin histogram of gradients over the cells of 8×8 pixels and blocks of 2×2 cells, a feature vector of length 4356 was obtained. In contrast, key points-based feature vectors were obtained for the SIFT, SURF and BRISK descriptors. A 128-dimensional descriptor was defined for each key point for a SIFT descriptor while a 64-dimensional descriptor was defined for each key point of the SURF and BRISK features.

Supervised learning such as CNN is data- intensive approaches. Hence, to overcome the constraint of limited annotated data, we use the idea of transfer learning. As described in Sect. 4.3, we use pre-trained CNNs which were initially trained using MNIST [32] and CIFAR-10 [36] datasets. We also use a deeper CNN, namely, AlexNet [33] which is pre-trained on the Imagenet [30] data. The detailed architecture of the pre-trained AlexNet [33] model is shown in Fig. 9.

5.2   CNN Model: Indian Classical Dance Hand Gestures

The performance of the proposed CNN on the CVLSH, CVLDH, real-world, cluttered hand gesture data as well as DHD, is reported in Tables 3, 5 and 7, respectively. Table 3 reports the accuracy values using [37] with ReLU activation function and random weight initialization of CNN. The results are comparable to the '*shallow*' learning approach using hand-crafted features with a linear kernel SVM classifier. Note that the impact of using the weights of pre-trained model of MNIST [32] and CIFAR-10 [36] datasets, as the weight initialization for the proposed network is

Table 1 Results obtained by using an SVM classifier with hand-crafted features on YouTube video dataset of (a) Single hand gestures—*Asamyukta Hasta Mudra* and (b) Double hand gestures—*Samyukta Hasta Mudra*

(a)

No. of classes	Training set	Test set	Feature vector	Accuracy (%)
9	756	216	HoG + SVM	95.37
			SIFT	84.5
			SURF	71.43
			BRISK	61.23

(b)

No. of classes	Training set	Test set	Feature vector	Accuracy
7	490	140	HoG + SVM	100
			SIFT	77.65
			SURF	80.71
			BRISK	72.86

Table 2 Variation in classification performance of hand-crafted features on the proposed CVLSH, CVLDH and real-world databases of single and double hand gestures of ICD obtained by changing the number of images in the training and testing datasets

Data	No. of classes	Training set	Test set	HoG + SVM (%)	SIFT (%)	SURF (%)	BRISK (%)
CVLSH	10	1120	280	99.0	90.8	87.3	86.8
		800	600	99.1	90.9	88.0	87.0
CVLDH	14	672	168	98.3	96.3	99.7	99.8
		490	350	98.5	95.4	99.4	99.1
Single hand YouTube	9	1050	210	95.8	83.8	70.8	61.0
		980	280	95.5	84.0	71.2	61.1
Double hand YouTube	7	1134	756	99.8	78.1	79.9	71.8
		945	945	99.7	77.7	80.0	72.0

reported in columns 9 through 11 of Table 3 using [37]. Note there is an improvement in test accuracy obtained with reduced number of epochs by the use of pre-trained CNN model with CIFAR-10 [36] dataset as opposed to the use of the pre-trained model obtained using MNIST [32] data.

The proposed split of training and testing data was chosen for the cases on CVLSH, CVLDH and real-world databases of single and double hand gestures of ICD after rigorous experimentation. Details of several experiments in which the ratios of training and testing data were varied are given in Table 4.

The accuracies obtained using the proposed CNN (Fig. 7) as shown in on the cluttered hand dataset, collected from real-world concerts, for increasing number of

Table 3 The performance of the proposed CNN (with random initialization of weights) using ReLU activation function in MatConvNet [37] is depicted in columns 1 through 8. Columns 9 through 11 show the performance of the proposed CNN pre-trained using MNIST [32] and CIFAR-10 [36] data, respectively, on CVLSH, CVLDH and real-world databases of single and double hand gestures of ICD. Note that pre-training with CIFAR-10 [36] results in superior initialization as compared to the CNN pre-trained on MNIST [32] dataset

Data	α	Batch size	Epochs	No. of Classes	Training set	Testing set	Accuracy on testing set (%)	Epochs for pre-training	Pre-training with MNIST [32] (%)	Pre-training with CIFAR-10 [36] (%)
Single hand (CVLSH)	5×10^{-6}	10	200	10	1120	280	99.6	20	98.2	100.0
Double hand (CVLDH)	5×10^{-6}	10	500	14	672	168	98.8	50	97.6	100.0
Single hand (YouTube)	5×10^{-6}	10	100	9	1155	105	100	50	100.0	100.0
Double hand (YouTube)	5×10^{-6}	10	100	7	1323	567	100	40	99.6	100

Table 4 The performance of the proposed CNN (Fig. 7) for varying splits of training and test data (with random initialization of weights) using ReLU activation function in MatConvNet [37] is depicted in columns 6 through 9 and 9 through 11 on CVLSH, CVLDH and real-world databases of single and double hand gestures of ICD

Data	No. of classes	α	Batch size	Epochs	Training set	Testing set	Accuracy on testing set (%)	Training set	Testing set	Accuracy on testing set (%)
Single hand (CVLSH)	10	5×10^{-6}	10	200	1000	400	100.0	800	600	99.1
Double hand (CVLDH)	14	5×10^{-6}	10	500	560	280	98.2	490	350	98.5
Single hand (YouTube)	9	5×10^{-6}	10	100	1050	210	100	980	280	100.0
Double hand (YouTube)	7	5×10^{-6}	10	100	1134	756	100	945	945	99.8

Table 5 Column 1 through 8 represents the performance of the proposed CNN (with random initialization of weights) using ReLU activation function in MatConvNet [37] on the cluttered hand dataset (CHD). Columns 9 through 11 represents the performance of the proposed CNN pre-trained using MNIST [32] and CIFAR-10 [36] on cluttered hand dataset for varying number of classes. The final column represents the accuracy obtained using AlexNet pre-trained on ImageNet [30] dataset followed by an SVM classifier

Data	Training set	Test set	No. of classes	α	Batch size	Epochs	Accuracy on testing set	Epochs for pre-training	Pre-training with MNIST [32]	Pre-training with CIFAR-10 [36]	CNN-SVM
CHD 3 class	714	99	3	1×10^{-6}	10	4000	90.91	2000	72.0	93.94	100.0
CHD 5 class	1250	173	5	1×10^{-6}	10	4000	77.46	3000	49.71	78.61	100.0
CHD 7 class	1619	224	7	1×10^{-6}	10	5000	66.96	2000	62.0	73.66	100.0

Table 6 Result obtained using hand-crafted features on the MHIs of the proposed dynamic hand gestures dataset

No. of classes	Training set	Test set	Feature vector	Accuracy (%)
8	320	80	HoG + SVM	96.25
			SIFT	77.5
			SURF	88.75
			BRISK	46.25

classes containing 3, 5 and 7 categories are reported in Table 5. It is observed that with increased number of classes, the accuracy of the network is decreased. The impact of weight initialization using pre-trained networks trained on MNIST [32] and CIFAR-10 [36] datasets is also reported along with the result obtained using the pre-trained AlexNet [33] model which has been initially trained on ImageNet [30] dataset. Note that the deeper pre-trained AlexNet architecture is used as a feature extractor and is coupled to an SVM classifier to yield the CNN-SVM model. This model is seen to yield superior performance as compared to smaller pre-trained models obtained using MNIST and CIFAR-10 datasets.

The accuracies obtained using hand-crafted features and the proposed architecture of convolutional neural network (Fig. 7) on the dynamic hand gestures dataset are reported in Tables 6 and 7, respectively. The results obtained using hand-crafted features are reported on images of size 64×64. As explained in Sect. 4.4, MHIs were obtained for dynamic hand gesture data by collapsing the temporal information into a single image template wherein the intensity is dependent on the recency of motion.

5.3   Transfer Learning

The CNN toolbox of [37] was used to analyse the impact of transfer learning with CIFAR-10 [36] database. Column 9 through 11 of Table 3, denotes the accuracies obtained on the CVLSH, CVLDH and real-world data. Note that three dropout layers were used to avoid over-fitting along with a ReLU activation function for faster convergence. The 10th column of Table 3, denotes the impact of transfer learning using a model pre-trained with MNIST [32] data obtained for 100 epochs with batch size 10 and learning parameter $\alpha = 5 \times 10^{-6}$ using ReLU activation function and 3 dropout layers.

Similarly, the impact of using pre-trained models using MNIST [32] and CIFAR-10 [36] datasets with toolbox of [37] is reported in the last two columns of Table 7, for the MHIs obtained from DHD. For the dynamic hand gestures data (DHD), with a learning rate of 5×10^{-6} and batch size 10 we obtained an accuracy of 88.5% after 2000 epochs for the CNN trained from random weights. An accuracy of 93.6% for a learning rate of 5×10^{-6}, batch size 10 in 200 epochs was obtained with a

Table 7 Column 1 through 9 denotes the performance of the proposed CNN model using dropout on the proposed dynamic hand dataset using ReLU as the activation function. The accuracy obtained using pre-trained MNIST [32] and CIFAR-10 [36] model as the initialized weights, respectively (Column 10 through 11)

Size	Classes	Training set	Testing set	α	Batch size	Epochs	Training accuracy (%)	Testing accuracy (%)	MNIST [32] pre-training accuracy (%)	CIFAR [36] pre-training accuracy (%)
32×32	8	320	80	5×10^{-6}	10	2000	99.2	88.5	89.5	93.6

CNN model pre-trained with CIFAR-10 [36] data as shown in Table 7. As shown in Table 7, the pre-trained model derived using MNIST [32] data resulted in an accuracy of 89.5% for the same set of parameters as used for the pre-trained CIFAR-10 [36] model. The AlexNet [33] architecture pre-trained using the ImageNet [30] dataset was used on the MHIs obtained from DHD for feature extraction and was followed by an SVM for classification. The detailed architecture of the network, as shown in Fig. 9, resulted in a test accuracy of 94.70% and a training accuracy of 100%.

5.4 Results Obtained Using 3D CNN

The major advantage of the proposed 3D CNN is the capability of the proposed architecture to directly work upon videos, instead of working with MHIs of the dynamic hand gestures data as reported in Table 7. The proposed 3D CNN on the dynamic hand gestures data comprising of 320 training videos and 80 test videos obtained a test accuracy of 95% and a training accuracy of 99.58%. The proposed 3D CNN is also applied on the *Adavu* data. The proposed *Adavu* dataset consists of 305 videos collected under six categories and is split using a 70–30 ratio into training and test set. The accuracy obtained from the test data is 86.95% and a training accuracy of 99.48% is achieved.

6 Understanding a *Shloka*

Semantic understanding of short video sequences of ICD is a challenge due to problems such as automatic detection and labelling of static and dynamic gestures, clutter in the background, human clutter due to multiple dancers in the scene, poor illumination, etc. Here, we demonstrate the possibility of understanding a video in which a *Shloka* is enacted using the *Bharatanatyam* dance form. The *Shloka Ardhanariswara Stotram* considered here consists of static hand gestures, dynamic hand gestures and *Adavus*. Some static gestures in the video are shown in Fig. 11. Note that in this work manual segregation of static and dynamic gestures is performed prior to classification. Two different dynamic gestures are shown by the frames in each row of Fig. 12. The last column of Fig. 12 represents the corresponding MHIs extracted for each dynamic gesture. Some frames corresponding to the *Adavus* present in the *Shloka* are depicted in Fig. 13. Note that for classification of the static, dynamic hand gestures and *Adavus*, the frames of the video were manually cropped to retain only one dancer.

Fig. 11 Sample images depicting static hand gestures used in the *Shloka: Ardhanariswara Stotra* obtained from YouTube

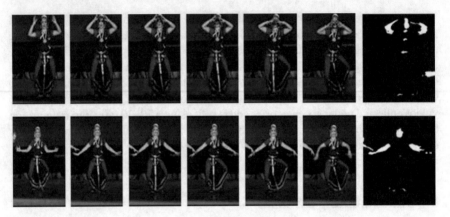

Fig. 12 Few images from the video of *Shloka: Ardhanariswara Stotra* depicting two different dynamic hand gestures. Note each row depicts a different dynamic hand gesture. The image in the final column represents the corresponding MHI for each dynamic gesture

Shloka: Ardhanariswara Stotram

Champeya gowrardha sareera kayai, Karpoora gourardha sareera kaya, Dhamilli kayai cha jatadaraya, **Namah shivaya cha namah shivaya**. *Kasthurika kumkuma* **charchithayai**, *Chitha rajah punja* **vicharchithaya**, *Kruthasmarayai Vikrutha smaraya,* **Namah shivayai cha namah shivaya**. *Chalath kanath kankana noopurayai, Padabja rajatphani noopuraya, Hemangadhayai bhujagangadhaya,* **Namah shivayai cha namah shivaya**. *Visala neelothphala lochanayai, Vikasi pankeruha lochanaya, Samekshanayai vishamekshanaya,* **Namah shivayai cha namah shivaya**. *Mandara mala kali* **thalakayai**, *Kapalamalnkitha kandharaya, Divyambarayai cha Digambaraya,* **Namah shivayai cha namah shivaya**. *Ambhodara syamala kunthalayai, Thadithprabha thamra* **jata dharaya**, **Gireeswarayai nikhileeswaraya**, **Namah shivayai cha namah shivaya**. *Prapancha srushtiyun mukha lasyakayai, Samastha samharaka* **thandavaya**, *Jagath jananyai jagadeka pithre,* **Namah shivayai cha namah shivaya**. *Pradeeptha rathnojjwala kundalaayai, Sphuran maha pannaga*

Fig. 13 Few images from the video of *Shloka: Ardhanariswara Stotra* corresponding to the *Paraval Adavu* are shown in the first two rows. The next two rows denote few images corresponding to the *Nattadavu* of the proposed *Adavu* dataset

bhooshanaya, Shivanvithayai cha shivanvithaya, **Namah shivayai cha namah shivaya**.

Meaning:

My salutations to both Parvathi and Shiva, To Her whose body shines as bright as molten gold, To Him whose body shines as brilliant as camphor, To Her who has well made up hair, And to Him who has the matted locks. My salutations to both Parvathi and Shiva, To Her whose body is smeared with musk and saffron, To Him whose body is smeared with ashes of a crematorium, To Her who radiates love through her beauty, And to Him who destroyed the God of love (Manmadha). My salutations to both Parvathi and Shiva, To Her who has pretty tinkling anklets, To Him who has the king of snakes (Adiseshu) as anklet, To Her who shines with golden bracelets, And to Him who has snakes as bracelets. My salutations to both Parvathi and Shiva, To Her who has eyes as wide as the blue lotus, To Him who has eyes as wide as the petals of fully blossomed lotus, To Her who has symmetrical eyes, And to Him whose eyes are asymmetrical. (Her both eyes always look at the same things together. His third eye will not be always open as his other two eyes, when it is opened, it results in apocalypse). My salutations to both Parvathi and Shiva, To Her whose hair

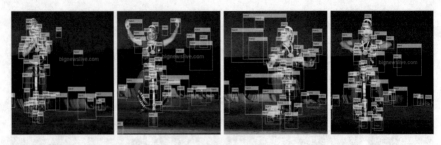

Fig. 14 Results of hand gestures localization in the *Shloka: Ardhanariswara Stotra* obtained using AdaBoost [4]

is decorated with sweet smelling divine flowers, To Him who wears a garland of skulls, To Her who dresses in great silks, And to Him wearing the eight directions. (*Digambara—Dig* means direction, *Ambara* means Cloth.) My salutations to both Parvathi and Shiva, To Her who has black hair like fresh rain cloud, To Him who has copper matted locks which resemble the colour of lightning, To Her who is the supreme goddess of the mountains, And to Him who is the Lord of the universe. My salutations to both Parvathi and Shiva, To Her whose dance marks the creation of the world, To Him whose dance indicates destruction of everything, To Her who is the mother of the universe, And to Him who is the father of the universe. My salutations to both Parvathi and Shiva, To Her with glittering ear rings of gems, To Him who wears a great serpent as an ornament, To Her who is divinely united with Shiva, And to Him who is divinely united with Parvathi.

The *Ardhanariswara Stotram* is a combination of static and dynamic hand gestures as well as *Adavus*. The static gestures comprising the *Ardhanariswara Stotram* Shloka are manually separated. The hand regions are localized using AdaBoost and R-CNN, followed by skin segmentation to reduce false positives. The output is then fed to a trained CNN network for classification of the hand gestures. It was observed that the hand gestures were properly identified by the model (Fig. 7). A snapshot of a few of the static hand gestures extracted from the *Shloka* is shown in Fig. 11. The result of hand localization, obtained on the extracted frames, with the use of AdaBoost [4] is shown in Fig. 14. Figure 15 denotes the localized hand regions obtained with the use of R-CNN [5] on the extracted frames. One can observe the reduction in false positives obtained during detection of hand regions using R-CNN [5] in Fig. 15. False positives for hand localization were reduced by intersection of the results obtained using R-CNN and skin segmentation while the face regions were eliminated from the false detections using the Viola– Jones face detector [38]. In Fig. 16, we show the results of skin pixel detection using the proposed CNN described in Sect. 4.1.

Note that the dynamic gestures in the *Shloka* are marked in bold font. A snapshot of the dynamic hand gestures is shown in Fig. 12. Since the video depicts two dancers enacting the *Shloka* in identical fashion, we cropped the frames of the video to retain the portion containing only one performer. The MHIs were then estimated from these cropped frames and fed to our trained CNN model (Fig. 7). The MHIs contain

Fig. 15 Static hand gestures localized using R-CNN [5] in a few sample frames of the video of the *Shloka*

Fig. 16 Results of the proposed deep learning algorithm for skin segmentation on the frames of the video corresponding to the *Shloka*. Note that black pixels represent the skin region

temporal motion information collapsed into a single image template. The intensity of the MHI is a function of the history of motion at that location. Brighter the intensity, more recent is the motion. The *Shloka* was observed to contain two distinct dynamic hand gestures used for training our CNN model. The trained model was successfully tested on the dynamic hand gestures present in the *Shloka*. Among the dynamic gestures which are boldfaced in the *Shloka*, *jata dharaya* and *Namah shivayai cha namah shivaya* are represented in first and second row of Fig. 12 respectively. The *Sholka* also consists of two *Adavus*, namely, the *Paraval Adavu* and *Nattadavu*, which were successfully identified by our trained 3D CNN model (Fig. 10).

7 Failure Cases and Discussions

In the proposed approach, there were instances where the hand detection module failed to perform well due to improper training of the AdaBoost [4] and R-CNN [5] for localizing hands, as well as due to false positives of the proposed skin segmentation CNN. A snapshot of the failure cases obtained with the use of AdaBoost [4] and R-CNN [5] are given in Fig. 17a through d. Further, the failure in obtaining proper MHIs of the dynamic hand gestures are shown in Fig. 17e, f. Cases where the hands were complex in articulation resulted in wrong localization by the proposed AdaBoost [4]

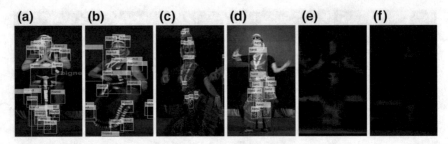

Fig. 17 Failure cases of the proposed approach in the *Shloka: Ardhanariswara Stotra*. **a** and **b** show the failure of AdaBoost [4] to localize hands in the dance video considered. **c** and **d** denote the failures of R-CNN [5] in a few sample frames of the video of the *Shloka*. **e** and **f** denote erroneously estimated motion history images using a few sample frames of the video of the *Shloka*

Fig. 18 Snapshots of failure cases of the proposed approach in the *Shloka: Ardhanariswara Stotra*. **a** and **c** show the images over which the proposed skin segmentation algorithm fails due to illumination variations and ambiguity between colour of costume and skin-tone. **b** and **d** depict the skin segmentation results

and R-CNN [5]. Instances where the skin detector failed are shown in Fig. 18. Note that poor illumination and costumes similar in colour to the human skin tone resulted in misclassification of the skin pixels.

8   Conclusion

The ambitious problem of understanding a short video sequence from ICD such as a *Shloka* enacted by a dancer is addressed in this work. We adopt a three-pronged approach by proposing deep learning algorithms for identification of static and dynamic hand gestures and *Adavus*. Since, availability of dataset of ICD is a constraint in developing machine learning algorithms for analyzing videos of dance, we propose datasets for static single and double hand gestures captured under constrained laboratory settings, real-world scenario and cluttered environment. Datasets of dynamic gestures and *Adavus* are also presented in this work. Note that the scope of our work does not include automated segregation of static and dynamic gestures. After manual separation of static hand gestures from the frames extracted from video, adaptive boosting [4] and R-CNN [5] are implemented for localizing hand regions in the images. Reduction in false positives is obtained after the hand localization step using the proposed skin segmentation algorithm. For the recognition of dynamic gestures, we propose two approaches. The first approach involves the use of 2D CNN after extraction of MHIs from the dynamic gestures. The second method involves the use of 3D CNN for direct video classification. As part of future work, we are investigating algorithms for automatic separation of static and dynamic gestures. The extension of dynamic hand gesture dataset along with *Adavu* dataset too is part of our future endeavours for understanding of *Shlokas* in ICD.

References

1. Meduri, A.: Bharatha natyam-what are you? Asian Theatre J. **5**(1), 1–22 (1988)
2. Mohanty, A., Duttagupta, A., Sahay, R.R.: Hand gesture recognition to understand indian classical dance videos. In: Accepted in Proceedings of Indian Conference on Computer Vision, Graphics and Image Processing (2016)
3. Mohanty, A., Vaishnavi, P., Jana, P., Majumdar, A., Ahmed, A., Goswami, T., Sahay, R.R.: Nrityabodha: towards understanding Indian classical dance using a deep learning approach. Signal Process.: Image Commun. **47**, 529–548 (2016)
4. Schapire, R.E., Singer, Y.: Improved boosting algorithms using confidence-rated predictions. Mach. Learn. **37**(3), 297–336 (1999)
5. Girshick, R., Donahue, J., Darrell, T., Malik, J.: Rich feature hierarchies for accurate object detection and semantic segmentation. In: Proceedings of the IEEE conference on Computer Vision and Pattern Recognition, pp. 580–587 (2014)
6. Gupt, B.: Dramatic Concepts Greek and Indian: A Study of the Poetics and the Natyasastra. DK Printworld (1994)
7. Raut, M.: Odissi, What, Why and How–: Evolution, Revival and Technique. BR Rhythms (2007)
8. Mohanty, A., Rambhatla, S.S., Sahay, R.R.: Deep gesture: static hand gesture recognition using CNN. In: Proceedings of International Conference on Computer Vision and Image Processing, pp. 449–461 (2017)
9. Mittal, A., Zisserman, A., Torr, P.H.: Hand detection using multiple proposals. In: Proceedings of British Machine Vision Conference, pp. 1–11 (2011)
10. Pisharady, P.K., Vadakkepat, P., Loh, A.P.: Attention based detection and recognition of hand postures against complex backgrounds. Int. J. Comput. Vis. **101**(3), 403–419 (2013)
11. Kurakin, A., Zhang, Z., Liu, Z.: A real time system for dynamic hand gesture recognition with a depth sensor. In: Proceedings of the 20th IEEE European Signal Processing Conference, pp. 1975–1979 (2012)
12. Shin, S., Sung, W.: Dynamic hand gesture recognition for wearable devices with low complexity recurrent neural networks. In: IEEE International Symposium on Circuits and Systems, pp. 2274–2277 (2016)
13. Oikonomidis, I., Kyriazis, N., Argyros, A.A.: Efficient model-based 3D tracking of hand articulations using kinect. In: Proceedings of British Machine Vision Conference, vol. 1, p. 3 (2011)
14. Tompson, J., Stein, M., Lecun, Y., Perlin, K.: Real-time continuous pose recovery of human hands using convolutional networks. ACM Trans. Graph. **33**(5), 169 (2014)

15. Sridhar, S., Mueller, F., Oulasvirta, A., Theobalt, C.: Fast and robust hand tracking using detection-guided optimization. In: Proceedings of the IEEE Conference on Computer Vision and Pattern Recognition, pp. 3213–3221 (2015)
16. Yamato, J., Ohya, J., Ishii, K.: Recognizing human action in time-sequential images using hidden Markov model. In: IEEE Conference on Computer Vision and Pattern Recognition, pp. 379–385 (1992)
17. Rabiner, L.R.: A tutorial on hidden Markov models and selected applications in speech recognition. Proc. IEEE **77**(2), 257–286 (1989)
18. Yang, M.H., Ahuja, N.: Recognizing hand gestures using motion trajectories. In: Proceedings of Face Detection and Gesture Recognition for Human-Computer Interaction, pp. 53–81 (2001)
19. Hong, P., Turk, M., Huang, T.S.: Gesture modeling and recognition using finite state machines. In: Proceedings of Fourth IEEE International Conference on Automatic Face and Gesture Recognition, pp. 410–415 (2000)
20. Henia, O.B., Bouakaz, S.: A new depth-based function for 3D hand motion tracking. In: International Conference on Computer Vision Theory and Applications, pp. 653–658 (2011)
21. Van den Bergh, M., Van Gool, L.: Combining RGB and ToF cameras for real-time 3D hand gesture interaction. In: IEEE Workshop on Applications of Computer Vision, pp. 66–72 (2011)
22. Suryanarayan, P., Subramanian, A., Mandalapu, D.: Dynamic hand pose recognition using depth data. In: Proceedings of 20th IEEE International Conference on Pattern Recognition, pp. 3105–3108 (2010)
23. Kollorz, E., Penne, J., Hornegger, J., Barke, A.: Gesture recognition with a time-of-flight camera. Int. J. Intell. Syst. Technol. Appl. **5**(3–4), 334–343 (2008)
24. Erdem, C., Ulukaya, S., Karaali, A., Erdem, A.T.: Combining Haar feature and skin color based classifiers for face detection. In: Proceedings of IEEE International Conference on Acoustics, Speech and Signal Processing, pp. 1497–1500 (2011)
25. Nalepa, J., Grzejszczak, T., Kawulok, M.: Wrist localization in color images for hand gesture recognition. In: Man-Machine Interactions 3, pp. 79–86. Springer International Publishing (2014)
26. Stöttinger, J., Hanbury, A., Liensberger, C., Khan, R.: Skin paths for contextual flagging adult videos. In: Proceedings Part II of 5th International Symposium on Advances in Visual Computing, pp. 303–314. Springer (2009)
27. Chan, C.S., Liu, H., Brown, D.J.: Recognition of human motion from qualitative normalised templates. J. Intell. Robot. Syst. **48**(1), 79–95 (2007)
28. Zhang, Z., Gunes, H., Piccardi, M.: Head detection for video surveillance based on categorical hair and skin colour models. In: 16th IEEE International Conference on Image Processing, pp. 1137–1140 (2009)
29. Vezhnevets, V., Sazonov, V., Andreeva, A.: A survey on pixel-based skin color detection techniques. In: Proceeding Graphicon, vol. 3, pp. 85–92 (2003)
30. Deng, J., Dong, W., Socher, R., Li, L.J., Li, K., Fei-Fei, L.: Imagenet: a large-scale hierarchical image database. In: IEEE Conference on Computer Vision and Pattern Recognition, pp. 248–255 (2009)
31. Everingham, M., Van Gool, L., Williams, C.K.I., Winn, J., Zisserman, A.: The PASCAL Visual Object Classes Challenge 2012 (VOC2012) Results. http://www.pascal-network.org/challenges/VOC/voc2012/workshop/index.html
32. LeCun, Y., Bottou, L., Bengio, Y., Haffner, P.: Gradient-based learning applied to document recognition. Proc. IEEE **86**(11), 2278–2324 (1998)
33. Krizhevsky, A., Sutskever, I., Hinton, G.E.: Imagenet classification with deep convolutional neural networks. In: Advances in Neural Information Processing Systems, pp. 1097–1105 (2012)
34. LeCun, Y., Huang, F.J., Bottou, L.: Learning methods for generic object recognition with invariance to pose and lighting. In: Proceedings of the IEEE Conference on Computer Vision and Pattern Recognition, vol. 2, pp. 97–104 (2004)
35. Srivastava, N., Hinton, G.E., Krizhevsky, A., Sutskever, I., Salakhutdinov, R.: Dropout: a simple way to prevent neural networks from overfitting. J. Mach. Learn. Res. **15**(1), 1929–1958 (2014)

36. Krizhevsky, A., Hinton, G.: Learning multiple layers of features from tiny images (2009)
37. Vedaldi, A., Lenc, K.: MatConvNet: convolutional neural networks for MATLAB. In: Proceedings of the 23rd ACM International Conference on Multimedia, pp. 689–692 (2015)
38. Viola, P., Jones, M.J.: Robust real-time face detection. Int. J. Comput. Vis. **57**(2), 137–154 (2004)

Characterization, Detection, and Synchronization of Audio-Video Events in *Bharatanatyam Adavus*

Tanwi Mallick, Partha Pratim Das and Arun Kumar Majumdar

1 Introduction

Bharatanatyam is a very popular form of Indian Classical Dance. *Adavu*s are basic choreographic units of a dance sequence in *Bharatanatyam*. In an *Adavu*, choreographic movements are accompanied by percussion instruments (*Tatta Palahai* (wooden stick)—*Tatta Kozhi* (wooden block), *Mridangam*, or *Tabla*) and rhythmic vocal sound (utterances). Optionally, vocal music, various woodwind (*Nagaswaram*, flute), or string (violin, or *veena*) instruments also accompany *Adavu*s. Hence, a performance of the *Adavu* is recorded as a multimedia stream comprising audio and video streams (based on the sensor there may be other streams as well). This is, therefore, a combination of video events that are either postures or movements synchronized with audio events that are rhythmic pattern of beats or Taals. The rhythmic patterns (meter) used for *Adavu*s are called *Sollukattu*s. Every *Adavu* is performed in sync with a *Sollukattu*. There are[1] 50 *Adavu*s each performed with one of the 23 *Sollukattus*.

In this paper, we first present an in-depth characterization of *Bharatanatyam* performances for representation and processing of its audio as well as video streams. We characterize the *Sollukattu*s (audio stream) in terms of audio events comprising beats (and half-beats), inter-beat silence, and their periodic structure. *Adavu*s (video stream) are characterized in terms of Key Postures and their transitions, and

---

[1]Depending on the school of *Bharatanatyam*, the exact set of *Adavu*s and *Sollukattu*s may vary.

T. Mallick · P. P. Das (✉) · A. K. Majumdar
Department of Computer Science and Engineering, Indian Institute of Technology,
Kharagpur 721302, India
e-mail: ppd@cse.iitkgp.ac.in

T. Mallick
e-mail: tanwimallick@gmail.com

A. K. Majumdar
e-mail: akmj@cse.iitkgp.ac.in

© Springer Nature Singapore Pte Ltd. 2018
B. Chanda et al. (eds.), *Heritage Preservation*,
https://doi.org/10.1007/978-981-10-7221-5_12

241

movements together defining video events. Finally, we characterize the synchronization between audio and video events and the associated issues in synchronization to understand the multimedia form of *Bharatanatyam* dance. These characterizations are severally used later to formulate algorithms, design tests and validations, and create the basis for solving various choreographic problems.

Computationally, we first present an algorithm to detect the beats of *Sollukattu*s. These provide major clues to the audio events. Several works on beat detection, tempo estimation, and beat tracking have been reported in [2–4]. These algorithms rely on a common scheme where the system extracts the onset locations from a time–frequency or sub-band analysis of the signal, traditionally using a filter bank or the discrete Fourier transform. Then, a periodicity estimation algorithm finds the rate at which these events occur.

Problem of estimating the meter of a musical piece has been addressed in [6–8, 13]. The work by [6, 12, 13] is based on *Indian Hindustani and Carnatic Music*. Gulati et al. [6] extended the two-stage comb filter-based approach (originally proposed for double/triple meter estimation) to septuple meter (such as 7/8 time signature) and evaluated its performance on a sizable Indian music database. In [12], Sridhar et al. propose a new algorithm to segment the instrumental and the vocal signals. The frequency components of the signal are determined on the voice signal, and then, these are mapped onto the *swara* sequence. Srinivasamurthy et al. [13] present an algorithm that uses a beat similarity matrix and inter-onset interval histogram to automatically extract the sub-beat structure and the long-term periodicity of a musical piece. On a manually annotated *Carnatic* music data set, the recognition accuracy of the algorithm is shown to be 79.3%.

Here, we develop a simple yet effective onset based [4] algorithm to detect the beats for the polyphonic music signal of *Bharatanatyam Adavu*. The algorithm achieves over 94% accuracy for beat detection for the 23 *Sollukattu*s for a set of annotated audio streams.

Next, we analyze the video for the extent of motion between its sequences of consecutive frames to detect Key Frames (containing Key Postures), Transition Frames, and Movements. These provide significant clues to video events. We achieve nearly 84% accuracy for key posture detection for the 50 *Adavu*s for a set of annotated video streams.

Finally, to explore the synchronization aspects, we correlate the audio events from *Sollukattu*s with the video events from *Adavu*s. There has been variety of work in this area including audio-based video event detection [11], dance synthesis based on visual analysis of human motion and audio analysis of music tempo [9], detection of dance motion structure using motion capture and musical information [10], and audio and video tempo analysis for dance detection [5]. However, there has been no attempt to analyze synchronization in Indian Classical Dance forms. Here, we work on synchronization between beats (audio events) and key frames (video events) for the *Adavu*s and achieve 72% accuracy of sync.

There has been no systematic research on multimedia streams of *Bharatanatyam Adavu*s. Hence, there is no comprehensive and annotated data set for it. So we also create an annotated repository of *Sollukattu*s and *Adavu*s for research. The data set is created using Kinect XBox (Kinect 1.0). Hence, it has depth and skeleton data streams synchronized with RGB stream that can be further used for analysis of specific postures and movements. The data set is captured for all 23 *Sollukattu*s performed independently by four trained music accomplices of dancers. All 50 *Adavu*s are also recorded using seven different professionally trained dancers. A part of the data has been annotated by *Bharatanatyam* experts. These have been used for validation of our algorithms and comparison with others in some cases. A selective subset of the data has been published[2] for public use.

There are several applications of the characterization and beat detection including music/music video segmentation, synchronization of the postures with the beats, automatic tagging of rhythm metadata, etc. Characterization, beat detection, synchronization, segmentation, or repository of *Bharatanatyam Adavu*s have not been attempted before.

The paper makes three major contributions: characterization of audio and video of *Adavu*s; algorithms for detection of audio events, video events, and their synchronization; and creation of an annotated repository of *Bharatanatyam* data.

The paper is organized as follows. We characterize the multimodal structure of *Bharatanatyam Adavu*s in terms of audio, video, and sync events in Sect. 2. Audio event (beat) detection is presented in Sect. 3 where we first outline the preprocessing, followed by onset detection and subsequent pruning, and beat detection. Video event (motion) detection is presented in Sect. 4. Estimation of sync is then discussed in Sect. 5. We conclude in Sect. 6.

2 Characterization of *Bharatanatyam Adavu*s

A *Bharatanatyam Adavu* consists of the following:

1. **Audio Stream**: *Sollukattu* or rhythmic music as generated by percussion instrument and vocal sound (utterances).
2. **Video Stream**: Stream of frames each capturing the combination of (a) position of the legs (*Sthanakam*), (b) posture of standing (*Mandalam*), (c) walking movement (*Chari*), and (d) hand gestures (*Nritta Hastas*) as assumed by the dancer.
3. **Synchronization**: Position, posture, movement, and gesture of an *Adavu* are performed in synchronization among themselves and in synchronization with the rhythm of the music.

To characterize the above and represent an *Adavu* in a succinct manner, we define a set of events.

---

[2]Data Repository: http://hci.cse.iitkgp.ac.in/.

2.1 *Events of* Adavus

An *Event* denotes the occurrence of an activity (called *Causal Activity*) in the audio
or the video stream of an *Adavu*. Further, synchronization (sync) events are defined
between multiple events based on temporal constraints. Sync events may be defined
jointly between audio and video streams. An event is described by:

1. *Category*: The nature of the event based on its origin (source) is called Category.
   It can be *audio*, *video*, or *sync*.
2. *Type*: Type relates to the causal activity of an event in a given category. Event
   types are listed in Table 1 with a brief description of respective causal activities.
3. *Time-stamp/range*: The time of occurrence of the causal activity of the event. This
   is elapsed time from the beginning of the stream and is marked by a function
   $\tau(.)$. Often a causal activity may spread over an interval $[\tau_s, \tau_e]$ which will
   be associated with the event. Time-stamp and time range are interchangeably
   denoted by the τ function of the event.

   For video events, we use a range of video frame numbers $[\eta_s, \eta_e]$ as the temporal
   interval. The Kinect video has a fixed rate of 30 fps. Hence, for any event, we
   interchangeably use τ or η as is appropriate in a context.
4. *Label*: One or more optional labels may be attached to an event annotating details
   for the causal activity.
5. *ID*: Every instance of an event in a stream is distinguishable. These are sequentially numbered (within a specific type of an event) in the temporal order of their
   occurrence.

2.2 *Characterization of Audio*

The musical *meter*[3] of an *Adavu* is called a *Sollukattu*. Traditionally, a *Tatta Palahai*
(wooden stick) is periodically struck on a *Tatta Kozhi* (wooden block) in the rhythmic
pattern of *Adi* or *Rupak Taals*[4] to produce the periodic beats (or α^{fb} events). Usually,
beats repeat in a *bar*[5] of $\lambda = 6$ or 8. The *tempo* of a meter is measured by beats
per minute (*bpm*). We use Period $T = (60/bpm)$ or the time interval between two
consecutive beats in secs as the temporal measure for a meter.

Consider two consecutive beats α_i^{fb} and α_{i+1}^{fb} in a bar of λ, where i denotes the
ith $(1 \leq i < \lambda)$ period. The time-stamps of the respective events are then related as
$\tau(\alpha_{i+1}^{fb}) - \tau(\alpha_i^{fb}) \approx T$. Further the bar repeats after an equal time interval of T. That
is, $\tau(\alpha_{\lambda*i+1}^{fb}) - \tau(\alpha_{\lambda*i}^{fb}) \approx T$, $i \geq 1$. We refer to such beats as *full beats* and hence

---

[3]The *meter* of music is its rhythmic structure.

[4]*Taal* is the Indian system for organizing and playing metrical music.

[5]A *bar* (or *measure*) is a segment of time corresponding to a specific λ number of beats. *Sollukattus*
also use longer bars (12, 16, 24, or 32).

Table 1 List of events in *Bharatanatyam Adavu*s

Event category	Event type	Event description	Event label
Audio	α^{fb}	Full beat with *bol*	*bol*[a], downbeat[b], upbeat[c]
Audio	α^{hb}	Half-beat with *bol*	*bol*
Audio	α^{fn}	Full beat having no *bol*	upbeat
Audio	α^{hn}	Half-beat having no *bol*	
Audio	α^{qn}	Quarter[d] beat having no *bol*	
Audio	α^{sl}	Silence—No beat or *bol*	upbeat
Audio	α^{f}	$\alpha^{fb} \mid \alpha^{fn}$	*bol*[a], downbeat[b], upbeat[c]
Audio	α^{h}	$\alpha^{hb} \mid \alpha^{hn}$	*bol*
Audio	α	$\alpha^{f} \mid \alpha^{h} \mid \alpha^{qn} \mid \alpha^{sl}$	
Video	ν^{nm}	No-motion[e]	Range of Frames[f], Key Posture[g]
Video	ν^{tr}	Transition Motion[h]	Range of Frames
Video	ν^{tj}	Trajectory Motion[i]	Range of Frames, Trajectory
Video	ν^{t}	$\nu^{tr} \mid \nu^{tj}$	Range of Frames, Trajectory
Video	ν	$\nu^{t} \mid \nu^{nm}$	
Sync	ψ^{fb}	No-motion @ Full beat[j]	Key Posture
Sync	ψ^{hb}	No-motion @ Half-beat	Key Posture
Sync	ψ	$\psi^{fb} \mid \psi^{hb}$	

[a] Vocalized *bol*s accompany some beats

[b] The first beat of a bar

[c] The last beat in the previous bar which immediately precedes, and hence anticipates, the downbeat

[d] *Sollukattu*s do not use quarter beats to define a meter. However, often the beat player would produce one that needs to be ignored

[e] Frames over which the dancer does not move (assumes a Key Posture)

[f] Sequence of consecutive frames over which the events spreads

[g] A Key Posture is a well-defined and stationery posture

[h] Transitory motion to change from one Key Posture to the next. This has no well-defined trajectory of movement for limbs

[i] Motion that follows a well-defined trajectory of movement for limbs

[j] α^{fb} and ν^{nm} in sync. That is, $\tau(\alpha^{fb}) \cap \tau(\nu^{nm}) \neq \phi$

Table 2 Pattern of *Kuditta Mettu Sollukattu* (Fig. 1a) annotated with time-stamps τ_i (start time of the full beat event α^{fb}). $Gap_i = \tau_i - \tau_{i-1}$ is computed from consecutive time-stamps and provides the distribution for tempo period T

Event	Time (τ_i)	Gap ($\tau_i - \tau_{i-1}$)	Event	Time (τ_i)	Gap ($\tau_i - \tau_{i-1}$)
α_1^{fb} (tei)	2.681		α_9^{fb} (tei)	12.271	1.207
α_2^{fb} (hat)	3.912	1.231	α_{10}^{fb} (hat)	13.386	1.115
α_3^{fb} (tei)	5.108	1.196	α_{11}^{fb} (tei)	14.512	1.126
α_4^{fb} (hi)	6.269	1.161	α_{12}^{fb} (hi)	15.603	1.091
α_5^{fb} (tei)	7.523	1.254	α_{13}^{fb} (tei)	16.764	1.161
α_6^{fb} (hat)	8.742	1.219	α_{14}^{fb} (hat)	17.902	1.138
α_7^{fb} (tei)	9.891	1.149	α_{15}^{fb} (tei)	19.028	1.126
α_8^{fb} (hi)	11.064	1.173	α_{16}^{fb} (hi)	20.178	1.150

the superscript *fb* in α^{fb} events. The first beat α_1^{fb} (last beat α_λ^{fb}) of a bar is referred to as a *downbeat* (*upbeat*). We mark these on the events as labels.

In many *Sollukattus*, beating is also performed at the middle of a period. These are called *half-beats* and produce the α_i^{hb} events in the *i*th period. Naturally, $\tau(\alpha_i^{hb}) - \tau(\alpha_i^{fb}) \approx \tau(\alpha_{i+1}^{fb}) - \tau(\alpha_i^{hb}) \approx T/2$.

A *Sollukattu* uses one of the three different speeds or *Tempo (Laya)*—*Vilambit Laya* (Slow), *Madhya Laya* (Medium), and *Drut Laya* (High). The *Period* (T) depends on the *Tempo* (shorter for faster tempo) and remains more or less uniform across *Sollukattus*.

Often in a *Sollukattu* an accomplice of the dancer also speaks out a distinct vocalization of rhythm with words like *tat*, *tei*, *ta*, etc., called *Bols*. These are done in sync with a full beat or a half-beat. We represent *bols* as labels of the respective α^{fb} or α^{hb} events. A *bol* is optional for an event.

There are 23 *Sollukattus*. We illustrate a few here to understand various meters. All *Sollukattus* are shown in *Vilambit Laya*.

1. *Kuditta Mettu* ($T \approx 1.2$ s, $\lambda = 8$): We show two meters of it in Table 2 and Fig. 1a. Note that it has only α^{fb} events.
2. *Tatta_C Sollukattu* ($T \approx 1.6$ s, $\lambda = 8$): It has α^{fb} as well as α^{hb} events (Table 3 and Fig. 1b).
3. *Kuditta Nattal_A & Tatta_E* ($T \approx 1.0$ s, $\lambda = 8$): In addition to α^{fb}, α^{fn} and α^{hn} events are also found (Table 4) where there is only beating and no *bol*.
4. *Joining_B* ($T \approx 1.5$ s, $\lambda = 8$): As such, it uses only α^{fb}'s (Table 4). But the fourth and eighth beats are silent (α^{sl}) with neither any *bol* nor any beating. So the upbeat in this case is guessed from T.

Table 3 Pattern of *Tatta_C Sollukattu* (Fig. 1b) annotated with time-stamps τ_i (start time of the full beat event α^{fb}). $Gap_i = \tau_i - \tau_{i-1}$ is computed from consecutive time-stamps and provides the distribution for tempo period T. Half-beat offsets happen roughly at $T/2$

Event	Time (τ_i)	Gap ($\tau_i - \tau_{i-1}$)	1/2–Beat offset	Event	Time (τ_i)	Gap ($\tau_i - \tau_{i-1}$)	1/2–Beat offset
α_1^{fb} (tei)	6.571			α_5^{fb} (tei)	13.003	1.64	
α_1^{hb} (ya)	7.395		0.82	α_5^{hb} (ya)	13.815		0.81
α_2^{fb} (tei)	8.185	1.61		α_6^{fb} (tei)	14.628	1.63	
α_2^{hb} (ya)	8.962		0.78	α_6^{hb} (ya)	15.441		0.81
α_3^{fb} (tei)	9.752	1.57		α_7^{fb} (tei)	16.184	1.56	
α_3^{hb} (ya)	10.565		0.81	α_7^{hb} (ya)	17.031		0.85
α_4^{fb} (tei)	11.366	1.61		α_8^{fb} (tei)	17.809	1.63	

Table 4 Variations in the patterns of *Sollukattu*s with *Adavu*s

Sollukattu	Description of Bol/Adavus
Kuditta Mettu	α_1^{fb} (tei) α_2^{fb} (hat) α_3^{fb} (tei) α_4^{fb} (hi) α_5^{fb} (tei) α_6^{fb} (hat) α_7^{fb} (tei) α_8^{fb} (hi)
	Adavu: Kuditta_Mettu 1, 2, 3, 4
Kuditta Nattal A	α_1^{fb} (tat) α_2^{fb} (tei) α_2^{hn} α_3^{fb} (tam) α_4^{fn} α_4^{hn} α_5^{fb} (dhit) α_6^{fb} (tei) α_6^{hn} α_7^{fb} (tam) α_8^{fn} α_8^{hn}
	Adavu: Kuditta_Nattal 1, 2, 3, 6
Tatta E	α_1^{fb} (tei) α_2^{fb} (tei) α_3^{fb} (tam) α_4^{fn} α_4^{hn} α_5^{fb} (tei) α_6^{fb} (tei) α_7^{fb} (tam) α_8^{fn} α_8^{hn}
	Adavu: Tatta 6
Joining B	α_1^{fb} (dhit) α_2^{fb} (dhit) α_3^{fb} (tei) α_4^{sl} α_5^{fb} (dhit) α_6^{fb} (dhit) α_7^{fb} (tei) α_8^{sl}
	Adavu: Joining 2

2.3 Characterization of Video

While performing an *Adavu*, the dancer closely follows the beats of the accompanying[6] *Sollukattu* and synchronizes her movements with the beats. At a beat, the dancer assumes a *Key Posture*[7] and holds it for a little while before quickly changing to the next *Key Posture* at the next beat. Consequently, while the dancer holds the key posture, she stays almost stationary and there is no or very slow motion in the video. This leads to ν^{nm} (no-motion) events. Further, while the dancer changes to the next key posture, we observe the ν^{tr} (transition) or ν^{tj} (trajectory) motion events.

---

[6]Every *Adavu* is performed with a specific *Sollukattu*. In this paper, we use 50 *Adavu*s each performed with one of 23 *Sollukattu*s.

[7]A *Key Posture* is defined in terms of Position of the legs (*Sthanakam*) and Posture of standing (*Mandalam*). Some are laterally symmetric ((c)–(h) in Fig. 2), while rest have *left-* and *right-*sided variants ((a)–(b)).

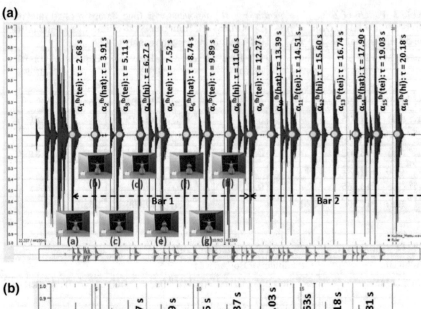

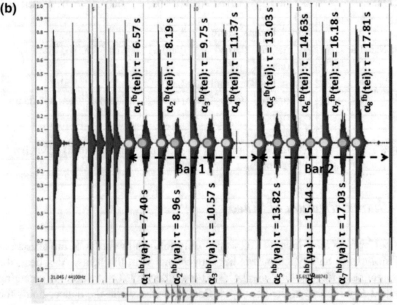

Fig. 1 Marking of beats and annotations of *bols* for 2 bars and $\lambda = 8$. Full beat (α^{fb}) and half-beat (α^{hb}) event positions are highlighted, and corresponding *bols* and time-stamps are shown (Tables 2 and 3). Note that several α^{hn} and α^{qn} events are visible in the signals. These are rather incidental and not intended in the *Sollukattu*. Also, the beatings before the downbeat (α_1^{fb}) are ignored. **a** *Kuditta Mettu Sollukattu* ($T = 1.16$ s). Right-sided *Key Postures* (Fig. 2) are also shown for the first eight beats. Left-sided *Key Postures* are performed for the next eight beats. **b** *Tatta_C Sollukattu* ($T = 1.56$ s)

(a) ν_1^{nm}, α_1^{fb}(tei)   (b) ν_2^{nm}, α_2^{fb}(hat)   (c) ν_3^{nm}, α_3^{fb}(tei)   (d) ν_4^{nm}, α_4^{fb}(hi)

(e) ν_5^{nm}, α_5^{fb}(tei)   (f) ν_6^{nm}, α_6^{fb}(hat)   (g) ν_7^{nm}, α_7^{fb}(tei)   (h) ν_8^{nm}, α_8^{fb}(hi)

Fig. 2 Right-sided Key Postures of *Kuditta Mettu Adavu* (Variant = 2, *Sollukattu = Kuditta Mettu*) with *Bols* for Bar 1. From **a** *tei* to the next *hat* or *hi*, the dancer sharply lowers her raised feet. Further, eight left-sided Key Postures are performed for the next eight beats in Bar 2

Since a frame is an atomic observable unit in a video, we can classify the frames of the video of an *Adavu* into two classes.

1. ***K-frames* or Key Frames**: These frames contain key postures where the dancer *holds* the Posture. Evidently, a ν^{nm} has the sequence of *K-frames* as labels. All *K-frames* of an ν^{nm} contain the same key posture.
2. ***T-frames* of Transition Frame**: These are transition frames between two *K-frames* while the dancer is rapidly changing posture to assume the next key posture from the previous one. A ν^{tr} or ν^{tj} event has a sequence of *T-frames* as labels.

   For an *Aadvu*, the transition can either be performed according to a well-defined trajectory[8] for the hands and legs or may just be undefined and arbitrary. Former is defined as ν^{tj} events and the latter is marked as ν^{tr} event. In this paper, we do not deal with trajectory-based motion and hence do not distinguish between ν^{tj} and ν^{tr} events.

In Fig. 2, we show the key postures of *Kuditta Mettu Adavu* at every beat of the first bar of *Kuditta Mettu Sollukattu*. The corresponding video and audio events are marked in Table 5 with *K-/T-Frames*. These are also marked on the *Sollukattu* in Fig. 1(a). Note that only the right-sided half of the postures are shown.

---

[8]In *Bharatanatyam*, these could be various forms of *Nritta (rhythmical and repetitive elements)* like *Chari*, *Karana*, *Angahara*, or *Mandala*.

Table 5 Patterns of *Kuditta Mettu Adavu* (Fig. 2)

Events	K-/T-Frames		Events	K-/T-Frames	
	Range	# of		Range	# of
ν_1^{nm} [α_1^{fb} (tei)]	70–99	30	ν_9^{nm} [α_9^{fb} (tei)]	359–386	28
ν_1^{tr}	100–103	4	ν_9^{tr}	387–390	4
ν_2^{nm} [α_2^{fb} (hat)]	104–124	21	ν_{10}^{nm} [α_{10}^{fb} (hat)]	391–410	20
ν_2^{tr}	125–145	21	ν_{10}^{tr}	411–429	19
ν_3^{nm} [α_3^{fb} (tei)]	146–172	27	ν_{11}^{nm} [α_{11}^{fb} (tei)]	430–451	22
ν_3^{tr}	173–176	4	ν_{11}^{tr}	452–455	4
ν_4^{nm} [α_4^{fb} (hi)]	177–191	15	ν_{12}^{nm} [α_{12}^{fb} (hi)]	456–470	15
ν_4^{tr}	192–214	23	ν_{12}^{tr}	471–492	22
ν_5^{nm} [α_5^{fb} (tei)]	215–245	31	ν_{13}^{nm} [α_{13}^{fb} (tei)]	493–521	29
ν_5^{tr}	246–249	4	ν_{13}^{tr}	522–525	4
ν_6^{nm} [α_6^{fb} (hat)]	250–262	13	ν_{14}^{nm} [α_{14}^{fb} (hat)]	526–542	17
ν_6^{tr}	263–287	25	ν_{14}^{tr}	543–564	22
ν_7^{nm} [α_7^{fb} (tei)]	288–314	27	ν_{15}^{nm} [α_{15}^{fb} (tei)]	565–587	23
ν_7^{tr}	315–317	3	ν_{15}^{tr}	588–590	3
ν_8^{nm} [α_8^{fb} (hi)]	318–345	28	ν_{16}^{nm} [α_{16}^{fb} (hi)]	591–620	30
ν_8^{tr}	346–358	13	ν_{16}^{tr}	621–	–

2.4 Characterization of Synchronization

A *Bharatanatyam* dancer intends to perform the key postures of an *Adavu* in synchronization with the beats. Hence, audio events like α^{fb} and corresponding video events like ν^{nm} should be in sync. Every *Adavu* has a well-defined set of rules that specifies this synchronization based on its associated *Sollukattu*. For example, in Fig. 2, we show how different key postures should be assumed in the *Kuditta Mettu Avadu* at every beat of the *Kuditta Mettu Sollukattu*. That is, how the α^{fb}'s of a bar in the audio should sync with the ν^{nm}'s of the video. Other *Adavus* require several other forms of synchronization between the audio-video events including sync between beats and trajectory-based body movements ν^{tj}.

We assert a sync event ψ^{fb} if a key posture (ν^{nm}) sync with a corresponding (full) beat (α^{fb}). In simple terms, a ψ^{fb} occurs if the time intervals of α^{fb} and ν^{nm} events overlap. That is, $\tau(\psi^{fb}) = \tau(\alpha^{fb}) \cap \tau(\nu^{nm}) \neq \phi$. Similar sync events may be defined between other audio and video events according to the rules of *Adavus*.

Perfect synchronization is always intended and desirable for a performance. However, we often observe the lack of it due to various reasons. The beating instrument, vocal *bols*, and body postures each has a different latency. If a posture is assumed *after hearing* the beat, ν^{nm} will lag α^{fb}. If the dancer assumes the posture in *anticipation*, ν^{nm} may lead α^{fb}. Lack of sync may also arise due to imperfect performance of the dancer, the beater, the vocalist, or a combination of them. Hence, analysis and estimation of sync are critical for processing *Adavu*.

While sync between the audio and video streams is fundamental to the choreography, there are a variety of other synchronization issues that need to be explored. These include sync between beats of beating (instrumental) and (vocalized) *bols*, uniformity of time gap between consecutive beats, sync between different body limbs while changing from one key posture to the next, and so on.

Based on the characterizations, we next present algorithms for detection of select audio, video, and sync events. In the rest of the paper, we focus only on α^{fb}, ν^{nm}, ν^{tr}, and ψ^{fb} events.

3 Audio Event Detection

We detect the beats in *Sollukattu*s in four steps as follows.

3.1 Preprocessing of the Audio Signal Sollukattu

A *Sollukattu* is a mixture of two sources of sound—percussion and vocal—that are synchronized by generation. It has dominant frequencies and is periodic. But it is cluttered with a lot of harmonics. So to eliminate the harmonics and noise to estimate the periodicity, we analyze it in the frequency domain.

Considering N samples in the signal $S(t)$, we compute its FFT as $S^*(f)$. The frequency components in $S^*(f)$ ranges from 0 to 8 kHz with up to 800 Hz contributing to vocal sound (*Bols*) and 1–2.6 kHz to percussion sound (beating stick). Rest are harmonics.

Hence, we filter $S^*(f)$ restricting between 1 Hz and 2.6 kHz to eliminate the vocal sound and the harmonics and get $S^*_{filt}(f)$. Inverse FFT of $S^*_{filt}(f)$ gives $S_{filt}(t)$. Usually, the beats have high amplitude. So we discard the low amplitude components in $S_{filt}(t)$ by a threshold $Th = 0.5$ to get $S_{Th}(t)$. This is used for onset detection.

3.2 Detection of Onsets

From $S_{Th}(t)$, we compute the *Onset Strength Envelope* using [4]. $S_{Th}(t)$ is resampled at 8 kHz, and STFT[9] (spectrogram) is calculated using 32 ms windows and 4 ms advance between frames. It is first mapped to *40 Mel bands* via a weighted sum of the spectrogram values and then the Mel spectrogram is converted to dB. The first-order difference along time is calculated in each band. Negative values are set

---

[9]Short-Time Fourier Transform.

to zero (half-wave rectification), and positive differences are summed up across all frequency bands. Finally, the signal is passed through a high-pass filter with a cutoff around 0.4 Hz to make it locally zero-mean, and then is smoothed by convolving with a Gaussian envelope of about 20 ms width. The output is the *OSE* as a function of time that responds to proportional increase in energy summed across approximately auditory frequency bands. The algorithm also outputs the onset time in the audio stream.

3.3   Detection of Local Maxima

Naturally, every beat has an onset in the OSE, but every onset in OSE is not necessarily a beat. An onset is associated with a beat only if it is a local maximum in the OSE. To model the locality, we use a window of time interval T_w, slide it over the OSE, and compute the set of local maxima L_{max} at every time position in OSE. This is given in Algorithm 1. L_{max} may have more than one local maxima in a window.

Algorithm 1 : Local Maxima Detection

1: **Inputs:**
2:   O_t = Vector of detected onset times, $nOnset = length(O_t)$;
3:   Val_t = Strength of onsets in O_t;
4:   T_w = Window of time interval for local maxima, a threshold parameter;
5: **Output:**
6:   L_{max} = Vector containing the indices of the locally maximal onsets
7: **for** $i = 1 : nOnset$ **do**
8:       $L_{max}(i) = 0$;
9: **end for**
10: **for** $i = 1 : nOnset$ **do**
11:       $max = i$;
12:       **for do** $j = i + 1 : nOnset$
13:             **if** $O_t(i) - O_t(j) < T_w$ **then**
14:                   **if** $Val_t(j) > Val_t(max)$ **then**
15:                         $max = j$;
16:                   **end if**
17:             **else**
18:                   break;
19:             **end if**
20:       **end for**
21:       $L_{max}(max) = 1$;
22: **end for**

So in Algorithm 2, we prune the set of onsets in L_{max} to ensure that only one onset can be present in a window T_w. Pruned L_{max} contains the candidates for detected beats.

3.4 Beat Detection

Using L_{max} and the periodicity of the *Sollukattu*s we detect and mark the beats in Algorithm 3. The first candidate beat is detected as the downbeat.[10] For every detected beat $beat_d$, we search for the next beat from L_{max} that lie within $period_{low}$ and $period_{high}$ from $beat_d$, where $period_{low}$ and $period_{high}$ are global bounds on the tempo period of the *Sollukattu* at given speed (*laya*) and are considered invariant. We also use a threshold period $period_{th}$ which is slightly more than $period_{high}$. If no beat is found in L_{max} within $period_{high}$ of $beat_d$ then the next beat in L_{max} that is away by $period_{th}$ or more is detected. This is done to avoid missing a beat.

Algorithm 2 : Prunning of Local Maxima

1: **Inputs:** O_t, Val_t, T_w, L_{max} = Vector containing the indices of the locally maximal onsets
2: **Output:**
3: L_{max} = Vector containing the pruned indices of the locally maximal onsets
4: **for** $i = 1 : length(L_{max}) - 1$ **do**
5:     **if** $L_{max}(i) == 1$ **then**
6:         **for** $j = i + 1 : length(L_{max})$ **do**
7:             **if** $L_{max}(j) == 1$ **then**
8:                 **if** $O_t(i) - O_t(j) < T_w$ **then**
9:                     **if** $Val_t(i) > Val_t(j)$ **then**
10:                         $L_{max}(j) = 0;$
11:                     **else**
12:                         $L_{max}(i) = 0;$
13:                     **end if**
14:                 **end if**
15:             **end if**
16:         **end for**
17:     **end if**
18: **end for**

We illustrate the working of the algorithm in Table 6 for *Kuditta Mettu* by striking out onsets in successive stages.

---

[10]The first beat of the *Sollukattu*.

Algorithm 3 : Beat Detection

1: **Inputs:**
2: L_{max} = Vector containing the pruned indices of the locally maximal onsets
3: $period_{max}$ = Maximum tempo period for any *Sollukattu*
4: $period_{min}$ = Minimum tempo period for any *Sollukattu*
5: $period_{th}$ = Threshold tempo period, $period_{th} > period_{max}$. Typically $period_{th} = 2$.
6: **Output:**
7: $Beats$ = Vector containing the indices of the detected beats
8: $Beats(1) = L_{max}(1)$;
9: $i = 1$;
10: **for** $ind = 2 : length(L_{max})$ **do**
11:     **if** $L_{max}(ind) - Beats(i) > period_{min}$ **then**
12:         **if** $L_{max}(ind) - Beats(i) < period_{max}$ **then**
13:             $i = i + 1$;
14:             $Beats(i) = L_{max}(ind)$;
15:         **else** $L_{max}(ind) - Beats(i) > period_{th}$
16:             $i = i + 1$;
17:             $Beats(i) = L_{max}(ind)$;
18:         **end if**
19:     **end if**
20: **end for**

3.5   Results of Audio Event Detection

Now, we present the beat detection results and compare our algorithm with the well-known algorithm of Ellis [4] using our recorded data set.

Audio Data Set: Recorded audio data of *Sollukattus* are not available for research. Hence, we have created a benchmark data set with the help of performers from a dance school.[11]

Sollukattus have been recorded by *Zoom H2n Portable Handy Recorder*. For each of the 23 *Sollukattus*, we have recorded six sets performed by four (three female and one male) accomplices. Of these, two sets have so far been annotated (sample annotations are shown in Tables 2, 3, 6 and 8) by experts by marking every beat in the audio file as a range of time-stamp of its occurrence. The accompanying *bol* for every beat is also annotated. One of the annotated sets[12] is taken as the golden audio and used for the recording of the videos.

Result Analysis: We now present the results of beat detection in Table 7 for all *Sollukattus* using the annotated set. For the ith annotated beat event[13] α_a^i in *Sollukattu* s, let the time range be $[\tau_b(\alpha_a^i), \tau_e(\alpha_a^i)]$ and let the corresponding detected beat be α_d^i with time-stamp $\tau(\alpha_d^i)$. The error in detected time is defined as $\epsilon_i = \tau(\alpha_d^i) - \tau_b(\alpha_a^i)$. The *Absolute Error* is defined as $E_{abs}^i = |\epsilon_i|$ and the *Relative Error* is defined as

---

[11]Natanam Kalakshetra, Kolkata, India.
[12]This data set is available at http://hci.cse.iitkgp.ac.in/.
[13]We consider only $\alpha^f \mid \alpha^h$.

$E^i_{rel} = E^i_{abs}/T$, where T is the tempo period of s. If s has n beats in its bar, then we define the following error metrics for accuracy:

1. $Max(s) = \max_{i=1}^{n} E_i$.
2. $85_{ptl}(s) = 85 \text{ } percentile \text{ } in \text{ } E_i, 1 \leq i \leq n$. That is, 85% of the errors are less than $85_{ptl}(s)$.
3. $Median(s) = \text{median}_{i=1}^{n} E_i$. That is, half of the errors are less than $Median(s)$.

where $E_i = E^i_{abs}$ or E^i_{rel}.

We compute the above error metrics for E_{abs} and E_{rel} in Table 7. Using 0.25 s, 0.15 s, and 0.10 s as cutoffs, respectively, for Max, 85_{ptl}, and $Median$, we have marked outlier measures in the table with underline. On the detected beats, also we have computed the outliers for these values and summarized their number under the *Remarks* column. There are 21 outliers in detection of 377 beats in total. Hence, 356 beats are detected correctly. So we achieve an accuracy of 94%.

It may be noted that 13 of the 21 outliers come from *Tatta D* and *Tatta G*. This is due to higher variation of inter-beat time in these cases. As expected, more outliers are observed when the inter-beat times vary more widely.

Next, we compare the accuracy of our results against the algorithm by Ellis [4].

Comparison with Ellis' [4] Algorithm: In Table 8, we compare the results of beat detection for *Pakka Sollukattu* by our method against [4] by computing the recall and precision in each case. Ellis' method achieves 100% recall at only 25% precision, while our method achieves 97% recall at 97% precision. However, this comparison is not exactly apple-to-apple because Ellis' method estimates the tempo period from the signal (during the dynamic programming stage) while we use a preset range of tempo periods and a tempo threshold (Algorithm 3).

So in Table 9, we study the accuracy of the estimation of tempo period that Ellis' method performs internally. The method makes two guesses for *Slower* and *Faster* tempo (in terms of *bpm*) and uses a *Strength* parameter for the final choice. If $Strength < 0.5$, it chooses the *Faster* tempo, else it chooses the *Slower*. Out of 23 cases, it gets the tempo period right in only five cases, and hence, the beat detection results degrade.

Finally, we tweak the algorithm of Ellis by inputting the correct tempo period for detecting the beats. We then compare the recall and precision of Ellis' method (with estimated as well as given tempo period) and our method (given a global range of tempo periods) in Table 10. We find that given the tempo period, the precision of Ellis' method improves (or remains same) in 22 cases (96%) while the recall degrades in 15 cases (65%). Our method has a better (or equal) precision in 18 cases (78%) and a better (or equal) recall in 19 cases (83%). Overall we achieve more than 80% precision for over 80% recall in 19 cases (83%). So we do better in terms of our pruning and detection strategies (Algorithms 2 and 3). We use the beats detected by our method in the synchronization with key video frames.

Next, we discuss the video event detection and event synchronization.

Table 6 Illustration of steps for beat detection in *Kuditta Mettu Sollukattu*. We use $T_w = 0.6$ s, $period_{max} = 1.6$ s, $period_{min} = 1.2$ s, $period_{th} = 2.0$ s. T_{anno} shows the set of time-stamps in annotation. These are used as reference for validation

Bol	tei	hat	tei	hi	tei	hat	tei	hi	tei	hat	tei	hi	tei	hat	tei	hi
T_{anno}	2.68	3.91	5.11	6.27	7.52	8.74	9.89	11.06	12.27	13.39	14.51	15.60	16.76	17.90	19.03	20.18
OSE	2.69	4.00	5.15	6.28	7.53	8.75	9.90	11.08	12.34	13.49	14.52	15.62	16.77	17.99	19.03	20.19
	2.76	4.80		~~6.35~~		~~8.83~~		~~11.15~~		13.95		~~15.69~~		18.47	19.09	~~20.26~~
				6.88		9.60		11.68		14.22		16.17		~~18.75~~		
				~~7.21~~				11.98								
L_{max}	2.69	4.00	5.15	6.28	7.53	8.75	9.90	11.08	12.34	13.49	14.52	15.62	16.77	17.99	19.03	20.19
	2.76	4.80		6.88		9.60		11.68		13.95		16.17		18.47	19.09	
								~~11.98~~		14.22						
L_{max} (pruned)	2.69	4.00	5.15	6.28	7.53	8.75	9.90	11.08	12.34	13.49	14.52	15.62	16.77	17.99	19.03	20.19
	~~2.76~~	~~4.80~~		~~6.88~~		~~9.60~~		~~11.68~~		~~13.95~~		~~16.17~~		~~18.47~~	~~19.09~~	
$Beats$	2.69	4.00	5.15	6.28	7.53	8.75	9.90	11.08	12.34	13.49	14.52	15.62	16.77	17.99	19.03	20.19

Table 7 Result of beat detection for all *Sollukattu*s using $T_w = 0.6$ s, $period_{max} = 1.6$ s, $period_{min} = 1.2$ s, $period_{th} = 2.0$ s. We compute several statistics for E_{abs} and E_{rel} for analysis. The absolute error E_{abs} as the difference between the annotated and detected time of a beat. Relative error E_{rel} is computed as a percentage of the period of the *Sollukattu*

Sr. No	Sollukattu	Tempo period	E_{abs}			E_{rel}			Remarks
			Max	85_{ptl}	Median	Max	85_{ptl}	Median	
1	Joining A	1.18	0.13	0.11	0.02	11	9	2	
2	Joining B	1.52	0.12	0.11	0.01	8	7	1	
3	Joining C	1.17	0.12	0.01	0.01	10	1	1	
4	Kartari Utsanga	1.07	0.15	0.11	0.05	14	10	5	
5	Kuditta Mettu	1.16	0.11	0.08	0.01	9	7	1	
6	Kuditta Nattal A	0.99	**0.28**	0.06	0.01	**29**	6	1	2 outliers
7	Kuditta Nattal B	1.30	0.08	0.07	0.05	6	5	4	
8	Kuditta Tattal	1.21	0.22	0.05	0.01	18	4	1	
9	Natta	1.39	0.08	0.07	0.01	6	5	1	
10	Paikkal	1.58	0.12	0.10	0.07	8	6	4	
11	Pakka	1.21	**0.50**	0.13	**0.10**	**41**	11	8	1 outlier
12	Sarika	0.93	0.15	0.05	0.03	16	6	3	
13	Tatta A	1.51	**0.39**	**0.38**	0.10	**26**	**25**	6	2 outliers
14	Tatta B	1.36	0.06	0.05	0.03	5	4	2	
15	Tatta C	1.56	0.13	0.13	0.07	9	8	4	
16	Tatta D	1.35	0.16	0.14	**0.11**	12	10	8	7 outliers
17	Tatta E	1.17	**0.53**	0.14	0.04	**45**	12	3	1 outlier
18	Tatta F	1.21	0.15	0.13	0.05	13	10	4	
19	Tatta G	1.32	0.24	**0.20**	**0.13**	18	**15**	10	6 outliers
20	Tei Tei Dhatta	1.41	0.12	0.11	0.06	8	8	4	
21	Tirmana A	1.23	0.04	0.04	0.01	4	3	1	
22	Tirmana B	1.22	0.10	0.09	0.04	8	8	3	
23	Tirmana C	1.46	**0.41**	**0.33**	0.02	**28**	**22**	1	2 outliers

Table 8 Comparison of beat detection results between Ellis' method [4] and our method for *Pakka Sollukattu* (data file = Pakka_14_HB1). For every *beat/bol* (col. 1), the range of estimated time as manually marked is shown under *Annotated Beat Range* (cols. 2–3). While Ellis' method detects all beats correctly (col. 4), it spuriously detects almost 100% (col. 5) and 200% (cols. 6–8) beats, respectively, within and outside the annotated time range. Hence, it achieves 100% recall at 25% precision (127 beats detected for 32 correct beats). In contrast, our method detects 31 out of 32 beats correctly (col. 9) for 97% recall but detects only one spurious beat (col. 10) for 97% precision

Beat	Bol	Annotated beast range		Ellis' method					Our method	
				Within range		Outside range			Within range	
				Correct beat	Spurious beat	Spurious beat			Correct beat	Spurious beat
(0)	(1)	(2)	(3)	(4)	(5)	(6)	(7)	(8)	(9)	(10)
1	ta	2.160	2.642	2.182	2.490	2.798	3.082	3.366	2.180	
2	tei	3.481	4.088	3.654	3.938	4.226	4.558		3.634	
3	tei	4.855	5.426	4.894	5.226	5.558	5.906		4.988	
4	tat	6.194	6.747	6.242	6.578	6.910	7.234		6.312	
5	dhit	7.479	8.032	7.554	7.870	8.190	8.514		7.541	
6	tei	8.764	9.336	8.822	9.138	9.450	9.778		8.808	
7	tei	10.067	10.639	10.114	10.434	10.750	11.086		10.199	
8	tat	11.353	11.817	11.390	11.706	12.022	12.346		11.455	
9	ta	12.602	13.155	12.670	12.982	13.298	13.602		12.785	
10	tei	13.905	14.423	13.926	14.230	14.534	14.842		14.037	
11	tei	15.101	15.619	15.154	15.466	15.778	16.082		15.260	
12	tat	16.351	16.886	16.390	16.690	16.986	17.298		16.483	
13	dhit	17.564	18.100	17.610	17.898	18.186	18.490		17.669	
14	tei	18.760	19.296	18.790	19.102	19.410	19.734		18.778	
15	tei	19.974	20.545	20.030	20.326	20.622	20.918		20.149	
16	tat	21.170	21.670	21.218	21.506	21.798	22.102		21.208	
17	ta	22.312	22.884	22.402	22.686	22.974	23.278		22.499	
18	tei	23.562	24.097	23.610	23.906	24.206	24.506		23.602	
19	tei	24.740	25.347	24.806	25.106	25.410	25.718		24.868	
20	tat	25.990	26.507	26.018	26.318	26.614	26.906		26.110	
21	dhit	27.114	27.632	27.202	27.498	27.794	28.082		27.268	
22	tei	28.364	28.917	28.402	28.694	28.990	29.294		28.391	
23	tei	29.524	30.095	29.594	29.882	30.170	30.478		29.654	
24	tat	30.773	31.345	30.814	31.106	31.402	31.706		30.804	
25	ta	31.934	32.523	32.010	32.298	32.590	32.894		32.099	
26	tei	33.165	33.683	33.194	33.482	33.770	34.066		33.271	
27	tei	34.343	34.843	34.366	34.658	34.946	35.238		34.352	35.514
28	tat	35.521	36.021	35.526	35.814	36.102	36.390			
29	dhit	36.610	37.128	36.678	36.958	37.242	37.534		36.743	
30	tei	37.806	38.324	37.834	38.118	38.406	38.698		37.945	
31	tei	38.966	39.466	38.998	39.282	39.570	39.866		39.112	
32	tat	40.145	40.644	40.190	40.510				40.263	

All times are in sec

Table 9 Estimation of tempo period by Ellis' method [4]

Sollukattu	Actual tempo period	Slower estimate		Faster estimate		Strength	Estimated tempo period	Remarks
		bpm	Period	bpm	Period			
(0)	(1)	(2)	(3)	(4)	(5)	(6)	(7)	(8)
Joining A	1.18	55.147	1.09	110.294	0.54	0.05	0.54	Wrong
Joining B	1.52	32.189	1.86	64.378	0.93	0.08	0.93	Right
Joining C	1.17	52.083	1.15	104.167	0.58	0.63	1.15	Wrong
Kartari Utsanga	1.07	59.055	1.02	118.110	0.51	0.41	0.51	Wrong
Kuditta Mettu	1.16	100.000	0.60	200.000	0.30	0.65	0.60	Wrong
Kuditta Nattal A	0.99	63.559	0.94	127.119	0.47	0.16	0.47	Wrong
Kuditta Nattal B	1.30	46.296	1.30	92.593	0.65	0.22	0.65	Wrong
Kuditta Tattal	1.21	101.351	0.59	202.703	0.30	0.74	0.59	Wrong
Natta	1.39	43.860	1.37	87.719	0.68	0.28	0.68	Wrong
Paikkal	1.58	38.660	1.55	77.320	0.78	0.11	0.78	Wrong
Pakka	1.21	100.000	0.60	200.000	0.30	0.66	0.60	Wrong
Sarika	0.93	61.983	0.97	123.967	0.48	0.68	0.97	Right
Tatta A	1.51	41.899	1.43	83.799	0.72	0.14	0.72	Wrong
Tatta B	1.36	22.189	2.70	44.379	1.35	0.01	1.35	Right
Tatta C	1.56	39.063	1.54	78.125	0.77	0.31	0.77	Wrong
Tatta D	1.35	45.455	1.32	90.909	0.66	0.19	0.66	Wrong
Tatta E	1.17	36.765	1.63	110.294	0.54	0.14	0.54	Wrong
Tatta F	1.21	48.387	1.24	96.774	0.62	0.65	1.24	Right
Tatta G	1.32	45.455	1.32	90.909	0.66	0.51	1.32	Right
Tei Tei Dhatta	1.41	66.964	0.90	133.929	0.45	0.32	0.45	Wrong
Tirmana A	1.23	47.468	1.26	94.937	0.63	0.06	0.63	Wrong
Tirmana B	1.22	50.000	1.20	100.000	0.60	0.13	0.60	Wrong
Tirmana C	1.46	90.361	0.66	180.723	0.33	0.87	0.66	Wrong

All times are in sec
bpm ≡ beats per minute. Period = 60/bpm

Table 10 Comparison of precision and recall between Ellis' [4] and our methods

Sollukattu	Ellis' method using				Our method using	
	Estimated[a] tempo period		Given[b] tempo period		Given ranges of[c] tempo period	
	Precision	Recall	Precision	Recall	Precision	Recall
Joining A	38	83	71	83	86	100
Joining B	73	92	54	58	100	100
Joining C	63	95	100	70	100	100
Kartari Utsanga	96	98	100	52	100	100
Kuditta Mettu	25	100	50	100	81	81
Kuditta Nattal A	37	96	40	25	71	92
Kuditta Nattal B	74	96	93	58	100	100
Kuditta Tattal	25	94	48	63	88	88
Natta	50	100	100	94	81	81
Paikkal	100	75	100	75	100	100
Pakka	25	100	97	97	97	97
Sarika	50	100	97	94	97	97
Tatta A	39	100	88	58	100	75
Tatta B	48	92	100	83	100	100
Tatta C	68	100	86	57	75	100
Tatta D	65	100	100	75	94	100
Tatta E	18	100	75	100	65	92
Tatta F	22	100	88	100	88	100
Tatta G	30	100	91	71	100	100
Tei Tei Dhatta	65	100	96	72	100	100
Tirmana A	68	100	68	100	91	82
Tirmana B	87	98	87	98	100	100
Tirmana C	41	100	100	58	95	75

[a]Original dynamic programming method of Ellis
[b]Ellis' method where the actual tempo period has been set for each Sollukattu
[c]Our method where a common range of tempo periods are set for all

4 Video Event Detection

We primarily detect no-motion[14] (ν^{nm} events) in the video. Given that ν^{nm} and ν^{tr} must alternate in the video, we then deduce the ν^{tr} events. We detect no-motion from the co-occurrence of the no-motion in the RGB and skeleton data of Kinect by (1) frame differences in RGB data and (2) velocity–acceleration of skeleton joints.

4.1 Frame Differences in RGB Stream

Frame difference or image sequence difference method refers to a very small time intervals of the two images before and after the pixel based on the time difference, and then using a threshold to extract the image regions of the movement. The image is then binarized based on motion (marked as 1) and no-motion (marked as 0). We sum the nonzero pixels (having motion) present in the image and then label it as motion or no-motion frame based on a threshold.

4.2 Velocity–Acceleration in Skeleton Stream

We compute the velocity and acceleration for four joint points (wrist, elbow, knee, and ankle) of the Kinect skeleton corresponding to every RGB frame. If the *Start Point* is (x_1, y_1, z_1) and the *End Point* is (x_2, y_2, z_2) then the instantaneous velocity is $v = (v_x, v_y, v_z) = velocity(x_2 - x_1, y_2 - y_1, z_2 - z_1)$ and the instantaneous acceleration is $a = (a_x, a_y, a_z) = acceleration(v_{x_2} - v_{x_1}, v_{y_2} - v_{y_1}, v_{z_2} - v_{z_1})$. If acceleration $|a|$ is less than a threshold then no-motion is inferred.

Finally, a frame is marked with no-motion (ν^{nm}) if it does not show symptoms of motion from frame difference as well as velocity–acceleration. The range of consecutive no-motion frames forms $\eta_{est}(\nu^{nm})$ (the frames preceding and following this range must have motion).

4.3 Results of Video Event Detection

Now, we present the results for video event detection using our data set.

Video Data Set: *Adavu*s are captured at 30 fps by *Microsoft Kinect XBox (Kinect 1.0)* using a special purpose capture software *nui Capture* [1]. Every recorded file comprises RGB, depth, skeleton, and audio streams. For each of 50 variants of 15 *Adavu*s, we have recorded over 20 sessions each as performed by seven dancers

---

[14]Actually, slow or low motion in the video as cutoff by a threshold.

Table 11 Results of video event detection

Sr.	Adavu	Precision	Recall	Remarks	Sr.	Adavu	Precision	Recall	Remarks
1	Tatta 1	100.00	100.00	Good	26	Kuditta Nattal 6	57.14	100.00	Moderate
2	Tatta 2	88.89	100.00	Good	27	Kuditta Tattal 1	85.00	35.42	Poor
3	Tatta 3	80.00	100.00	Good	28	Paikkal 1	50.00	75.00	Moderate
4	Tatta 4	94.12	100.00	Good	29	Paikkal 2	80.00	100.00	Good
5	Tatta 5	90.48	95.00	Good	30	Paikkal 3	70.00	87.50	Moderate
6	Tatta 6	81.82	75.00	Good	31	Tei Tei Dhatta 1	71.43	62.50	Moderate
7	Tatta 7	100.00	92.86	Good	32	Tei Tei Dhatta 2	50.00	87.50	Moderate
8	Tatta 8	100.00	100.00	Good	33	Tei Tei Dhatta 3	50.00	12.50	Poor
9	Natta 1	77.78	87.50	Good	34	Katti or Kartari 1	61.54	100.00	Moderate
10	Natta 2	80.00	100.00	Good	35	Utsanga 1	100.00	75.00	Good
11	Natta 3	94.12	100.00	Good	36	Mandi 1	51.11	71.88	Moderate
12	Natta 4	37.84	87.50	Poor	37	Mandi 2	86.36	59.38	Moderate
13	Natta 5	82.35	87.50	Good	38	Sarrikkal 1	60.53	71.88	Moderate
14	Natta 6	93.75	93.75	Good	39	Sarrikkal 2	80.00	66.67	Moderate
15	Natta 7	100.00	50.00	Moderate	40	Sarrikkal 3	54.55	56.25	Moderate
16	Natta 8	100.00	58.33	Moderate	41	Tirmana 1	62.50	50.00	Moderate
17	Pakka 1	77.78	87.50	Good	42	Tirmana 2	47.37	50.00	Poor
18	Kuditta Mettu 1	80.00	50.00	Moderate	43	Tirmana 3	72.22	72.22	Moderate
19	Kuditta Mettu 2	100.00	50.00	Moderate	44	Sarika 1	90.91	62.50	Moderate
20	Kuditta Mettu 3	87.50	82.35	Good	45	Sarika 2	92.31	75.00	Good
21	Kuditta Nattal 1	85.71	75.00	Good	46	Sarika 3	100.00	100.00	Good
22	Kuditta Nattal 2	91.67	78.57	Good	47	Sarika 4	57.14	50.00	Moderate
23	Kuditta Nattal 3	72.73	66.67	Moderate	48	Joining 1	75.00	100.00	Good
24	Kuditta Nattal 4	50.00	36.36	Poor	49	Joining 2	33.33	33.33	Poor
25	Kuditta Nattal 5	80.00	28.57	Poor	50	Joining 3	33.33	40.00	Poor

(four female and three male) giving over 1000 performance videos to analyze. 10% of the data has so far been annotated[15] by experts at frame level. An example for annotated audiovisual data of *Kuditta Mettu Adavu* is shown in Table 12.

Result Analysis: We compare the video events by using the above algorithms with the manually annotated video events. First, we get a sequence of no-motion frame ranges from the detection algorithm (as in the manual video annotation given in Table 5). Next, we determine the number of overlapped ranges between detected video (DV) and annotated video (AV) events and compute precision and recall of the detection as

$$Precision = \frac{Number\ of\ overlapped\ ranges\ between\ DV\ and\ AV}{Number\ of\ DV\ events} * 100$$

$$Recall = \frac{Number\ of\ overlapped\ ranges\ between\ DV\ and\ AV}{Number\ of\ AV\ events} * 100$$

The results are given Table 11. If the precision and recall both are $\geq 75\%$ then we mark it as *Good*, if their minimum is within 74–50% then we mark it as *Moderate*, otherwise mark the result as *Poor*. We achieve 84% accuracy for *Good* and *Moderate* quality detection of video events.

As expected, we achieve *Good* results where the distinction between key postures and transitions is clear in the dance sequence. In a few *Adavu*s like *Kuditta Nattal 1*, *Kuditta Nattal 5*, and *Kuditta Tattal 1*, the dancer holds the key postures in over only a few of frames (generally it is 15–20 frames, but in these cases, it is down to 2–3 frames). Such key postures are missed out in detection especially because the estimated skeletons are not stable and well formed. Thus, the detection performance goes down from *Good* to *Poor* depending on the clarity of the key posture in the sequence itself.

5   Estimation of Event Synchronization

For a detected beat α^{fp}, we have the estimated time-stamp $\tau(\alpha^{fp})$ from Sect. 3.4. We convert this to frame number $\eta(\alpha^{fp})$ of the video (using 30 fps). We use a buffer threshold of ± 5 frames to get the frame interval $\eta_{est}(\alpha^{fp})$ of α^{fp} as $[\eta(\alpha^{fp}) - 5, \eta(\alpha^{fp}) + 5]$. Similarly, for a detected no-motion event ν^{nm}, we have the estimated frame range as $\eta_{est}(\nu^{nm})$ from Sect. 4.

Finally, the sync event ψ^{fb} is inferred as

$$\eta_{est}(\alpha^{fb}) \cap \eta_{est}(\nu^{nm}) \neq \phi$$

Synchronization in annotated audio and video events are shown in Table 12.

---

[15]Part of this data set is available at http://hci.cse.iitkgp.ac.in/.

Table 12 Annotation of audiovisual data of *Kuditta Mettu Adavu*

Events	Audio annotation				Video annotation (in frame #)	
	(In time (Sec))		(In frame #)			
	Start	End	Start	End	Start	End
ν_1^{nm} [α_1^{fb} (tei)]	2.681	3.218	80	97	70	99
ν_2^{nm} [α_2^{fb} (hat)]	3.912	4.247	117	127	104	124
ν_3^{nm} [α_3^{fb} (tei)]	5.108	5.541	153	166	146	172
ν_4^{nm} [α_4^{fb} (hi)]	6.269	6.681	188	200	177	191
ν_5^{nm} [α_5^{fb} (tei)]	7.523	7.975	226	239	215	245
ν_6^{nm} [α_6^{fb} (hat)]	8.742	9.125	262	274	250	262
ν_7^{nm} [α_7^{fb} (tei)]	9.891	10.375	297	311	288	314
ν_8^{nm} [α_8^{fb} (hi)]	11.064	11.563	332	347	318	345
ν_9^{nm} [α_9^{fb} (tei)]	12.271	12.698	368	381	359	386
ν_{10}^{nm} [α_{10}^{fb} (hat)]	13.386	13.819	402	415	391	410
ν_{11}^{nm} [α_{11}^{fb} (tei)]	14.512	14.969	435	449	430	451
ν_{12}^{nm} [α_{12}^{fb} (hi)]	15.603	16.109	468	483	456	470
ν_{13}^{nm} [α_{13}^{fb} (tei)]	16.764	17.201	503	516	493	520
ν_{14}^{nm} [α_{14}^{fb} (hat)]	17.902	18.302	537	549	526	542
ν_{15}^{nm} [α_{15}^{fb} (tei)]	19.028	19.476	571	584	565	587
ν_{16}^{nm} [α_{16}^{fb} (hi)]	20.178	20.630	605	619	591	620

5.1 Results of Event Synchronization

After audio and video event detection, we get time-stamp of beats from the audio signal and range of Key Posture from the video stream. Next, we compute the quality of the match using the following measures:

Matching detected video (DV) events against annotated audio (AA) events:

$$Measure\ of\ Match\ (DV - AA) = \frac{Number\ of\ matched\ DV\ and\ AA\ events}{Number\ of\ AA\ Events} * 100$$

Matching detected video (DV) events against detected audio (DA) events:

$$Measure\ of\ Match\ (DV - DA) = \frac{Number\ of\ matched\ DV\ and\ DA\ events}{Number\ of\ DA\ Events} * 100$$

Detected audio and video events of *Kuditta Mettu 3 Adavu* are shown in Table 13. In 2 out of the 16 events, there is no overlap. Hence, we achieve 87.5% sync between the DA and DV events.

Table 13 Detected audio and video events of *Kuditta Mettu*

Events	Detected beats	Audio time to Video frame	Video frames	
			Start	End
ν_1^{nm} [α_1^{fb} (tei)]	2.742	82	78	83
ν_2^{nm} [α_2^{fb} (hat)]	3.964	119	95	119
ν_3^{nm} [α_3^{fb} (tei)]	4.798	144	143	150
ν_4^{nm} [α_4^{fb} (hi)]	6.280	188	157	198
ν_5^{nm} [α_5^{fb} (tei)]	7.215	216	215	247
ν_6^{nm} [α_6^{fb} (hat)]	8.753	263	252	265
ν_7^{nm} [α_7^{fb} (tei)]	9.600	288	289	299
ν_8^{nm} [α_8^{fb} (hi)]	11.156	**335**	**303**	**330**
ν_9^{nm} [α_9^{fb} (tei)]	12.333	370	364	389
ν_{10}^{nm} [α_{10}^{fb} (hat)]	13.485	405	392	405
ν_{11}^{nm} [α_{11}^{fb} (tei)]	14.566	437	428	437
ν_{12}^{nm} [α_{12}^{fb} (hi)]	15.624	469	442	481
ν_{13}^{nm} [α_{13}^{fb} (tei)]	16.776	503	500	539
ν_{14}^{nm} [α_{14}^{fb} (hat)]	17.973	**539**		
ν_{15}^{nm} [α_{15}^{fb} (tei)]	19.030	571	565	572
ν_{16}^{nm} [α_{16}^{fb} (hi)]	20.189	606	575	621

Result Analysis: In Table 14, we present the summary of sync results and analyze the quality of sync. We also achieve 72% accuracy of *Good* (DV-DA > 75%) or *Moderate* (50% < DV-DA < 75%) synchronization. We explain the reasons behind the poor results below:

1. We detect motion or no-motion of a frame from the change in the current frame with respect to the previous frame. If the change in the consecutive frames is very low, then very slow motion gets falsely detected as no-motion. Hence, the number of detected Key Posture is become more than number of annotated key postures. This is happening in *Paikkal 3*.

2. In some *Adavu*s like *Kuditta Nattal 4*, *Tei Tei Dhatta 3*, *Kuditta Nattal 5*, *Natta 7*, and *Natta 8*, the dancer holds the key posture for very small span of time. Hence, the Key Posture detection fails for the reasons explained in Sect. 4.3, and less Key Postures are detected than the actual annotated.

Table 14 Results of sync events in percentage of match

Sr.	Adavu	DV-AA	DV-DA	Remark	Sr.	Adavu	DV-AA	DV-DA	Remark
1	Tatta 1	100.00	100.00	Good	26	Kuditta Nattal 6	100.00	41.94	Poor
2	Tatta 2	100.00	100.00	Good	27	Kuditta Tattal 1	35.42	31.25	Poor
3	Tatta 3	100.00	100.00	Good	28	Paikkal 1	75.00	56.25	Moderate
4	Tatta 4	100.00	100.00	Good	29	Paikkal 2	56.25	56.25	Moderate
5	Tatta 5	93.75	94.12	Good	30	Paikkal 3	31.25	56.25	Moderate
6	Tatta 6	75.00	58.82	Moderate	31	Tei Tei Dhatta 1	62.50	62.50	Moderate
7	Tatta 7	92.86	81.25	Good	32	Tei Tei Dhatta 2	87.50	68.75	Moderate
8	Tatta 8	100.00	100.00	Good	33	Tei Tei Dhatta 3	12.50	12.50	Poor
9	Natta 1	87.50	81.25	Good	34	Katti or Kartari 1	100.00	54.17	Moderate
10	Natta 2	100.00	100.00	Good	35	Utsanga 1	50.00	29.17	Poor
11	Natta 3	100.00	93.75	Good	36	Mandi 1	64.58	87.23	Good
12	Natta 4	90.63	81.25	Good	37	Mandi 2	39.58	40.43	Poor
13	Natta 5	87.50	75.00	Good	38	Sarrikkal 1	52.08	68.09	Moderate
14	Natta 6	93.75	87.50	Good	39	Sarrikkal 2	37.00	38.31	Poor
15	Natta 7	50.00	50.00	Moderate	40	Sarrikkal 3	56.25	65.96	Moderate
16	Natta 8	58.33	43.75	Poor	41	Tirmana 1	50.00	72.73	Moderate
17	Pakka 1	50.00	65.63	Moderate	42	Tirmana 2	45.83	62.50	Moderate
18	Kuditta Mettu 1	50.00	56.25	Moderate	43	Tirmana 3	58.33	59.09	Moderate
19	Kuditta Mettu 2	81.25	50.00	Moderate	44	Sarika 1	62.50	68.75	Moderate
20	Kuditta Mettu 3	75.00	87.50	Good	45	Sarika 2	75.00	37.50	Poor
21	Kuditta Nattal 1	54.55	45.16	Poor	46	Sarika 3	53.13	56.25	Moderate
22	Kuditta Nattal 2	55.00	38.71	Poor	47	Sarika 4	50.00	28.13	Poor
23	Kuditta Nattal 3	50.00	41.94	Poor	48	Joining 1	100.00	85.71	Good
24	Kuditta Nattal 4	26.67	31.25	Poor	49	Joining 2	100.00	87.50	Good
25	Kuditta Nattal 5	26.67	18.75	Poor	50	Joining 3	37.50	56.25	Moderate

6   Conclusions

This paper is the maiden approach to characterize the *Bharatanatyam* dance form and attempt multimedia analytics for Kinect data of *Bharatanatyam Adavus*. In the process, we make the following contributions:

1. We characterize the events of *Bharatanatyam Adavus* for automated analysis. First, we analyze and document the structure of its music—understanding the pattern of beats and *bols* in depth. Next, we outline the characterization of its video in terms of key postures. Finally, we identify core synchronization issues in an *Adavu*.
2. We present a simple yet effective algorithm to detect beats in *Sollukattus*. We validate the results against annotated data. Overall, we achieve 94% accuracy. We compare our results against the Ellis' algorithm [4]. Under similar conditions, our algorithm performs better. We show that the correct estimation of tempo period is crucial for accurate beat detection and the same remains elusive for now.
3. We present algorithms to detect no-motion video events and achieve 84% accuracy for it.
4. In terms of audio-video sync, we achieve 72% accuracy.
5. No annotated data of *Sollukattus* and *Adavus* is available for research. We have recorded 6 six sets of all 23 *Sollukattus* and 20 sessions of all 50 variants of 15 *Adavus*. 30% of audio and 10% of video data have already been annotated by experts.

The paper also raises several questions including the following:

1. *Beat Detection and Marking*: From the characterization, we know that most beats are accompanied by a *bol*. Since the current approach is based on onsets, it ignores the *bols*. We can create a vocab of *bols*, detect these as utterances, and correspond with the onsets to achieve near 100% accuracy. Once *bols* are known, the same can be marked on the stream. Half-beats also need to be detected.
   Information of *bols* can also be used to estimate the tempo period accurately which, as discussed, is a critical factor in beat detection.
   Estimating lead/lag between instrumental and vocal sound and the uniformity of beat-to-beat time gaps would be key problems for a *Sollukattu*.
2. *Detection of Key Frames and Audio-guided Segmentation of Adavu*: The paper presents an important characterization of the video of *Adavu* in terms of *K*– and *T–Frames*. These can be further characterized in terms of motion parameters. Based on the marked beats and *bols*, the video may be segmented at approximate *K–Frames* and then refined with motion estimates.
3. *Synchronization Issues*: Based on the solution of the above problems, several synchronization issues as discussed in Sect. 2.4 may be attempted.

It may be reiterated that the characterization of *Adavus* and detection of beats in *Sollukattus* have several applications including music segmentation, music video segmentation, estimating the synchronization of the postures with the musical beats, automatic tagging of rhythm metadata of music, synchronization correction, and the like. These can be attempted in future.

References

1. Cadavid Concepts: nuiCapture Analyze. http://nuicapture.com/ (2014). Accessed 15 Oct 2016
2. Davies, M.E.P., Plumbley, M.D.: Context-dependent beat tracking of musical audio. IEEE Trans. Audio Speech Lang. Process. **15**(3), 1009–1020 (2007)
3. Dixon, S.: Evaluation of the audio beat tracking system BeatRoot. J. New Music Res. **36**(1), 39–50 (2007)
4. Ellis, D.P.W.: Beat tracking by dynamic programming. J. New Music Res. **36**(1), 51–60 (2007)
5. Faircloth, R.M.: Combining Audio and Video Tempo Analysis for Dance Detection. Ph.D. thesis, University of Central Florida Orlando, Florida (2008)
6. Gulati, S., Rao, V., Rao, P.: Meter detection from audio for Indian music. In: Speech, Sound and Music Processing: Embracing Research in India, pp. 34–43. Springer (2012)
7. Klapuri, A., et al.: Musical meter estimation and music transcription. In: Cambridge Music Processing Colloquium, pp. 40–45. Citeseer (2003)
8. Klapuri, A.P., Eronen, A.J., Astola, J.T.: Analysis of the meter of acoustic musical signals. IEEE Trans. Audio Speech Lang. Process. **14**(1), 342–355 (2006)
9. Panagiotakis, C., Holzapfel, A., Michel, D., Argyros, A.A.: Beat synchronous dance animation based on visual analysis of human motion and audio analysis of music tempo. In: International Symposium on Visual Computing, pp. 118–127. Springer (2013)
10. Shiratori, T., Nakazawa, A., Ikeuchi, K.: Detecting dance motion structure through music analysis. In: Sixth IEEE International Conference on Automatic Face and Gesture Recognition, 2004. Proceedings, pp. 857–862. IEEE (2004)
11. Shiratori, T., Nakazawa, A., Ikeuchi, K.: Detecting dance motion structure using motion capture and musical information. In: Proceedings of the International Conference on Virtual Systems and Multimedia (VSMM), vol. 3 (2004)
12. Sridhar, R., Geetha, T.V.: Raga identification of Carnatic music for music information retrieval. Int. J. Recent Trends Eng. **1**(1) (2009)
13. Srinivasamurthy, A., Subramanian, S., Tronel, G., Chordia, P.: A beat tracking approach to complete description of rhythm in Indian classical music. In: Proceedings of the 2nd CompMusic Workshop, pp. 72–78. Citeseer (2012)

An Image Dataset of Bishnupur Terracotta Temples for Digital Heritage Research

Mrinmoy Ghorai, Sanchayan Santra, Soumitra Samanta, Pulak Purkait
and Bhabatosh Chanda

1 Introduction

One of the basic units of the modern scientific research is a dataset, which is a collection of fields that collectively represent a single record of information. In the domain of image processing and computer vision, a dataset constitutes a collection of images/videos for a specific application. In recent years, a number of computer vision algorithms have been successfully presented by standing on the shoulder of large datasets, for example, Deep Learning [26, 39] on Imagenet,[1] Multiview geometry [20, 22] on YFCC100M.[2] Here we present an image dataset to promote and boost the research on different applications of digital heritage.

One of the most popular applications of computer vision techniques in the domain of digital heritage preservation is 3D reconstruction of the ruins as well as monuments/buildings/artifacts. Such works are facilitated by availability of 3D scanned data or range data. Levoy et al. [27] and Remondino [33] have provided such digital heritage 3D datasets of several archaeological artifacts and interiors of heritage buildings. These data are easy to manipulate and makes 3D reconstruction of model simpler. But at the same time, equipment and logistics of acquiring these data are costly as well as cumbersome. On the other hand, the data we provide here are acquired by simple camera, so are cheap. However, creating a 3D experience from these data requires in-depth knowledge and sophisticated techniques of computer

---

[1] http://www.image-net.org/.
[2] http://yfcc100m.appspot.com/.

M. Ghorai (✉) · S. Santra · B. Chanda
Indian Statistical Institute, Kolkata, India
e-mail: mgre04@gmail.com

S. Samanta
University of Liverpool, Liverpool, UK

P. Purkait
Toshiba Research Europe Ltd., Cambridge, UK

© Springer Nature Singapore Pte Ltd. 2018
B. Chanda et al. (eds.), *Heritage Preservation*,
https://doi.org/10.1007/978-981-10-7221-5_13

vision paradigm. So this approach may strongly influence in developing computer vision-based methods and create interest in digital heritage. The Bishnupur Heritage Image Datasets developed by us consist of the following sets of images (with purpose):

- For 3D reconstruction and 3D restoration: 4233 images of seven different temples,
- For image inpainting and missing texture completion: 127 images along with the image mask of the damaged portion,
- For texture classification: 2008 images in 16 different groups, and
- For sub-image spotting and image retrieval: 1101 small images and 66 large images.

We have used four different cameras to capture these images from different heritage temple sites of Bishnupur.

Brief History of Bishnupur: There are many sites of historical interest in India as well as in West Bengal. Some sites have additional attraction of beauty and craftsmanship. Bishnupur is one of them which is known for terracotta temples. This municipal town of West Bengal, India, is a prospective candidate for recognition as *World Heritage site* [1] by UNESCO. The history of Bishnupur is very old and reference to this region is found in the documents written during the reign of Samudragupta (c.335–380 AD). This region was the capital of Mallabhum kingdom which spread over four present districts of West Bengal: Murshidabad (a part only) in the east, Medinipur in the south, Barddhaman in the north, and the entire Bankura. Bishnupur was made the capital by Malla King Jagat Malla aka Jagannath (c.994–1007 AD) and it continued to be the capital for almost one thousand years till the end of this dynasty. Before that, the capital of Malla dynasty started by King Adi Malla aka Raghunath (c.694–710 AD) was at Pradyumnapur. One of the most important kings of this dynasty was Hambir Malla Dev aka Veer Hambir (c.1565–1620 AD), who defeated Pathan Sardar Dayud Khan in a battle. Bishnupur flourished and attained its highest glory during his reign. He later submitted to Lord Vishnu and became the disciple of Thakur Srinibas Acharya, who was the disciple of Jeev Goswamin, a great vaishnavite teacher. His successor Malla kings followed the same religious path and belief, and many Bishnu and Krishna temples were built in and around Bishnupur during seventeenth and eighteenth centuries [2].

The terracotta temples of Bishnupur, though made of primarily laterite stones, are the finest examples of hut type architecture of Bengal. There are predominantly two types of temple architectures in Bengal: "Chala" type and "Ratna" type based on the roof of the temples. Temples of Bishnupur mostly follow the second type of architecture, which have towers or "Sikhara" on the roof of the main temple resembling spires with faceted sides. "Eka-Ratna" (one spire), "Pancha-Ratna" (five spires), or "Nava-Ratna" (nine spires), as the names suggest, reveal the number of "Sikharas" on the top of the roof. Terracotta panels containing floral and geometric patterns, and also figures depicting contemporary life and, more commonly, mythological stories from "Puranas" [3, 18] are used to decorate the temple walls.

Rest of this chapter is organized as follows. Description of cameras and data acquisition is briefly presented in Sect. 2. Section 3 describes the details of the datasets. To establish the usefulness of our dataset, the state-of-the-art methods are evaluated on the dataset, and the results are presented in Sects. 4–7. The concluding remarks are summarized in Sect. 8.

2 Data Acquisition

A team of five members with reasonable knowledge in photography visited the heritage site of Bishnupur in the month of April for 5 days: Monday to Friday. They chose three bright sunny days for photography and the image acquisition time was mainly midday. The weekdays and timing were chosen to have adequate natural light and also to avoid other visitors as the place is a popular tourist spot.

Four cameras of different model and make were used to capture the images and those were set to auto contrast, auto focus mode and no tripod or any other camera stand was used. This was done with an aim that the algorithms developed using these images can be applied to crowdsourced images of other sites. The details of the cameras used are as follows:

- Camera I: Sony Cyber-shot DSC-HX200V Digital Camera with Carl Zeiss F/2.8 IS Lens.
- Camera II: Nikon D7200 Digital SLR Camera with Tamron SP 24-70mm F/2.8 Telephoto Lens.
- Camera III: Nikon D3300 with AF-S DX NIKKOR 18-55mm F/3.5-5.6G VR II Lens.
- Camera IV: Sony Cyber-shot DSC-WX60 16.2 Mega-pixel Digital camera with Carl Zeiss Lens.

Unfortunately, the team could not take images of temple roof as they did not have the suitable resources and permission for that task. The captured images were inspected manually by the team members, and only the clean, sharp, and sufficiently good quality images are included in the dataset based on majority voting. We have used different camera parameters to capture the images to encourage the development of parameter invariant algorithms. However, we provide the camera parameters for the users.

3 Dataset Composition

To make the dataset user-friendly and to widen its usage, we have categorized the images manually by partitioning the entire collection of images into application-specific groups. We envisage a few potential applications where our datasets can be employed extensively as enumerated below:

- 3D reconstruction of buildings (temples),
- image inpainting and texture synthesis for restoration of damaged region,
- texture feature extraction and classification, and
- content-specific figure spotting and image retrieval.

It is needless to explain the importance of these applications. Many other pattern recognition and machine learning algorithms may also be tested using these data.

Reconstruction of 3D model of an object is an excellent way for general viewing from different positions as well as for architectural study. Especially for historical monuments and artifacts, 3D reconstruction of objects is extremely important for preserving architectural history and cultural heritage. This also helpful for mass education and spreading awareness. Common people may view the objects of interest (the temples, in this case) from different angles with a feeling of augmented reality.

Acquisition and storage of good quality images of heritage artifacts is a simple way of archiving the different views of historical monuments. However, in many cases, the objects, while images are being archived, may have suffered from physical damages. It may not be easy or feasible to restore such damages in reality due to various reasons. It would be interesting and useful to restore these defects in the corresponding images using computer vision techniques, so that the viewer can get an impression of pre-damaged look (as close as possible) of the object. Image inpainting by texture synthesis is a computer vision-based method for doing this task. This image dataset provides a very good test bed because, as a result of long negligence and poor maintenance, these temples are badly affected due to aging, weathering, and hooliganism.

Various floral and geometric patterns can be found on terracotta panels on the temple walls. Sub-images extracted from such panels provide very rich texture data for various kinds of experiments and evaluation of different machine learning and pattern recognition systems. Texture feature extraction and texture classification may be considered as a pure academic problem rather than a specific heritage preservation issue. However, as a possible utilization, classification of temple wall textures may categorize the decoration style and period. To generate a useful texture dataset, we have utilized the close view of the temple wall(s) to capture delicate and fine ornamentation. We have also presented the results of some baseline methods to evaluate its usefulness.

We have already mentioned that the walls of the Bishnupur temples are mostly decorated with terracotta panels depicting, in addition to floral and geometric patterns, various scenes and glimpses from "Puranas", including "Ramayana" and "Mahabharata", especially the life of Lord Krishna (as the patrons were mainly vaishnavites). It is a very challenging as well as useful task to search and retrieve images automatically from the temple walls that contain panel(s) depicting an event specified by a similar panel image. This may be achieved by a computer vision-based technique called *content-specific figure spotting* and *content-based image retrieval*. This method may also be useful in analyzing the content of the temple wall images from cultural heritage point of view.

4 3D Reconstruction

The statistics of the presented dataset for 3D reconstruction of different temples is shown in Table 1. Our goal was to capture all possible views of each of the temples; however, the roof of the temples is not covered by the dataset as suitable infrastructure was not available. We also provide the intrinsic camera parameters, e.g., focal lengths, radial distortions (available in EXIF header). The principle points can be assumed at the center of the images. Moreover, the images are captured in the same lighting condition and are large enough to facilitate the dense reconstruction. A few examples of dense reconstructions on our datasets are displayed in Fig. 2.

Note that no ground-truth of the extrinsic camera parameters (absolute pose of the cameras) and the 3D map of the temples are available. The GPS informations are not accurate enough to infer geometry, thus, not helpful. However, a structure-from-motion reconstruction (pose and map) using a publicly available toolbox (VisualSFM) can be provided upon request. Hope this would encourage more research in this area.

Table 1 Image statistics for different temples of 3D reconstruction datasets

Temples	Camera I	Camera II	Camera III	Camera IV	Total
Jor Bangla	–	317	118	137	572
Kalachand	78	275	47	–	400
Madan Mohan	51	277	49	–	377
Nanda Lal	40	190	83	23	336
Radha Madhav	22	648	40	67	777
Rasmancha	91	497	145	412	1145
Shyamrai	48	334	118	126	626
Total	330	2538	600	765	4233

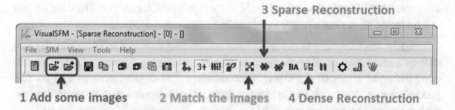

Fig. 1 Different steps of the pipeline of a 3D reconstruction process using the VisualSFM

4.1 Baseline Method

One of the classical and well-researched areas in computer vision is 3D reconstruction of the objects using structure from motion (sfm) [20, 41]. A GUI application for structure from motion—VisualSFM[3] is used here to build the 3D reconstruction [46, 47]. Since the dataset contains a large variety of images captured from different viewpoints of the temples, we consider a large baseline case in our application. The other settings, i.e., small baseline case, would be reconstructing a world scene from a sequence of images/video frames. However, the large baseline case provides more information for structure from motion. Here, we briefly describe the way of computing the structure from motion by the following steps.

Feature Detection and Matching: The VisualSFM toolbox provides us a GPU-based SIFT [28] binary for feature detection. It performs efficiently by exploiting multicore parallel processing for feature detection and feature matching. Different tools of VisualSFM are shown in Fig. 1.[4]

In Sect. 2, we present the details of the intrinsic camera parameters used to build the dataset. Some of these parameters (e.g., focal length) are very useful for 3D reconstruction. The baseline approach provided by the toolbox detects the sparse SIFT features from the images and matches those features across all the other images in the dataset. In the matching process, it determines the relative poses using projective transformation comprising rotation, translation, and scaling across different pairs of images along with the inlier point correspondences that agree with the pose. The following files are generated by the VisualSFM:

- .sift: This file stores the pixel coordinate, scale, rotation and the SIFT feature descriptor at the detected corner points of the corresponding images.
- .mat: It stores the pairwise matching information of each input image with the rest of the images. Note that here we exploit exhaustive pairwise matching. However, a more efficient nearest neighbor search based on a bag of feature descriptors for potential match could be employed to improve the runtime efficiency. We employed exhaustive matching to get a more accurate 3D map.
- .nvm: This file stores output of the N-view match which can be utilized for further refinement of the camera pose and the 3D map.

Usually, the matching is the most time-consuming step and to reduce it, the tool utilizes a multi-threading implementation and parallelizing through a GPU. Considering different views of a temple, approximately 250–500 number of images is a good choice to work with on a typical desktop system. However, in our experiments, we have considered only a subset of the dataset. The number of images for different temples used for this application is as follows: Jor Bangla (86), Kalachand (141), Madan Mohan (126), Radha Madhav (145), Rasmancha (167), Shyamrai (152) and Nanda Lal (148). For further inclusion of more images, subsampling of the images

---

[3]http://ccwu.me/vsfm/doc.html.
[4]The image is copied from http://ccwu.me/vsfm/.

and re-estimation of camera parameters are necessary [49]. We usually downsize the images with the resolution factor s and reduce the focal lengths with the same factor s. If one wants to keep the original high-resolution images, a more sophisticated hardware system is required for 3D reconstruction and a better 3D map could be generated.

As this exhaustive pairwise match can be expensive, it could take a long time to process. In contrast, recent methods, e.g., [22], incorporate a preselection of the potential matches using the co-occurrence of the SIFT features. Then, the method matches potential image pairs only. However, in our dataset, the number of images is 300–1000 for which CUDA-enabled VisualSFM takes only 30–300 min for this task. Note that preselection of potential matching could be useful for city-level reconstruction. However, in the case of our building-level dataset exhaustive matching is a more sensible approach.

Sparse Reconstruction: After the feature detection and matching, the very next step is reconstruction. For this, we first take a pair of images to obtain the 3D points of the object by triangulating the inlier points. Then, we add more images in the process to generate more object points. However, the algorithm discards the outliers, i.e., the 3D points which are observed in less than three images. Note that this incremental method may produce different results based on the initial choice of the image pair. In some scenario, it could not find enough matches during the iterative bundle adjustment and ends up with generating multiple point clouds, which can be merged during the postprocessing of the 3D map. There are some direct global methods available [7, 45], unlike the incremental method utilized here, which are not very efficient for large-scale datasets and possibly one of the potential future research directions that could be exploited with our datasets. Our sparse reconstruction example for the Jor Bangla and Nandalal temple datasets are shown in Fig. 2 along with the camera positions. The 3D points are colored by the average intensities of the pixels in the observed images and the camera poses are represented by the randomly chosen colors. From the figure, it is clear that our dataset has enough variety of poses to correctly reconstruct the object with sparse point cloud. This incremental sparse reconstruction takes only 15–60 min for each of our datasets. This step could be expensive for a large-scale 3D reconstruction.

Bundle Adjustment: In this step, the initial camera parameters and the 3D points are refined to rectify the poses of the images. For this purpose, we perform a nonlinear optimization that minimizes the error of the re-projection of the 3D points to the image plane. The idea is to minimize the discrepancy between the observed pixel location and projected pixel locations. With the said camera settings and the number of images, the estimation of the initial parameters is quite accurate. Also, Bundle Adjustment technique finds an appropriate solution. Throughout the experiments, we have used the binaries of Bundle Adjustment [40] from Noah Snevely's web page.[5] This step rectifies all the drifts of the estimated poses of the images that may have occurred during the incremental reconstruction process. It takes only a few minutes

---

[5]https://github.com/snavely/bundler_sfm.

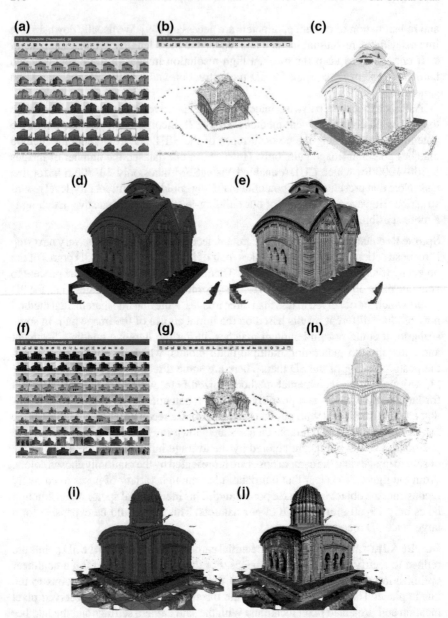

Fig. 2 3D reconstruction of JorBangla and NandaLal datasets. **a, f** Screenshot of sample images used for reconstruction displayed in VisualSFM toolbox [47]; **b, g** estimated camera poses and the sparse point clouds; **c, h** dense point clouds estimated by CMVS/PMVS [14]; **d, i** corresponding line meshes; and **e, j** 3D object of the texture maps. The reconstructions are near perfect and of high quality

to run the Bundle Adjustment on the datasets with the initialization of the 3D point cloud and the camera parameters obtained by the previous step.

Dense Reconstruction and Rendering: We finally come to the last step which consists of the dense reconstruction and rendering. These processes are performed immediately after the generation of sparse point cloud. For dense reconstruction, we have used the method Clustering Views for Multi-View Stereo (CMVS)/Patch-based Multi-View Stereo (PMVS). The CMVS software analyzes the sparse point cloud and creates multiple clusters as well as provides input files for feeding into PMVS. After that, PMVS software runs dense reconstruction from the clusters producing dense point clouds. The binaries are available from the CMVS/PMVS web page.[6] Note that VisualSFM application generates the parameters for CMVS/PMVS [14], which are stored in a `nv.ini` file. The user can manage these parameters according to the dataset, particular requirement and hardware constraints. In our experiments, the crucial parameters, namely, `minAngle`, `minNumOfConsistentCams` (`grow`), and `minNumOfConsistentCams` (`filter`) are set to 3.0, 6, and 2, respectively.

4.2 Evaluation

The result of 3D reconstruction depends on the size of the dataset and image resolution. A good number of images (approx. 500) for a particular example may produce satisfactory results. However, to process those number of images with high resolution, we need sufficient hardware resources. Due to our limited hardware resources, we could not utilize all the images in the datasets for 3D reconstruction. We consider only 150–200 images with distinct poses (for different viewpoints) from each of the datasets. Figure 2a–j show the results of different steps of 3D reconstruction for Jor Bangla and Nandalal temple datasets. The figures show that our datasets consist of good quality images to generate, analyze and further manipulate the 3D dense point cloud. Although the datasets are sufficient to reconstruct the high-quality dense estimation, the roofs of the temples are not estimated accurately due to insufficient number of images of the roofs of the temples. More results of 3D reconstruction for our datasets are available at http://www.isical.ac.in/~bsnpr/3DGeometry.php.

4.3 Possible Research Directions

In the previous sections, we have demonstrated the ability of the proposed dataset for experimenting with 3D reconstruction. Moreover, as it is tailored to the images only of terracotta carving temples and most of the temples in the dataset have quite symmetric surface, this dataset would be an ideal choice for the evaluation of specialized

---

[6]http://www.di.ens.fr/pmvs/.

algorithms in a number of directions. Here, we list a number of research directions related to 3D multiview geometry where our dataset could be useful.

- Automatic 3D inpainting [35]: To digitally restore the damaged portion of a 3D rendered temple, a similar textured/patterned region can be exploited.
- Exploring 3D symmetries in structure from motion [8]: Removing ambiguous pairwise matching for SFM and reconstruct only with the correct matches.
- Initialization-free reconstruction: Current structure from motion pipeline requires a lot of careful analysis and an iterative incremental Bundle Adjustment to fine-tune the reconstruction and camera pose. However, a direct method with random initialization of Bundle Adjustment is still a challenging problem.

5   Image Inpainting for Damaged Artifacts

Image inpainting restores a damage or a missing region of an image by copying suitable visual information from the known part of the image. This technique was proposed for different applications such as digital restoration of old photographs, antique documents and old paintings. In these applications, the algorithms mainly deal with different types of artifacts like water blotches [42, 43] and cracks [16, 17]. Nowadays, many image processing and computer vision researchers try to restore damaged heritage objects in digital space. Here, we present a large number of images of temples of Bishnupur to test and evaluate image inpainting methods to restore damages in heritage artifacts. Our main focus is on three temples, Jor Bangla, Madan Mohan, and Shyamrai, which are rich in terracotta decoration. The task is to digitally restore the damaged, missing, or broken terracotta parts of these temples (e.g., Fig. 3). Most of the sample images contain complex textures (macro) and structures for which inpainting becomes a challenging problem for these images.

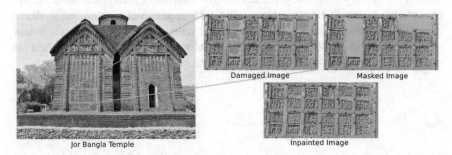

Fig. 3 An example of image inpainting for the damaged image captured from Jor Bangla temple

5.1 Some State-of-the-Art Methods

Several image inpainting methods [5, 10, 12, 15, 24, 32] are available in literature for natural images. These methods are different with respect to the optimization methods used for image inpainting. Next, we discuss some of them in brief and present their performance in our dataset.

Patch Priority-based Inpainting: One of the most popular image inpainting methods is exemplar (patch)-based, where the common goal is to infer the damaged or missing region patch by patch in such a way that the inpainted region is consistent with the rest of the image in terms of texture and structure. Initially, the idea is employed for texture synthesis [13] in order to generate high-resolution image from the corresponding low-resolution texture image. Later, structure propagation becomes more important for filling up large blob type target region (e.g., object removal) in natural scene images where several textures may be separated by simple (line) or complex (curvilinear) structures. To propagate line structure, Criminisi et al. [10] proposed a gradient-based patch *priority* term that determines the filling order of the patches in the damaged region based on isophote (e.g., edge) strength. The patch with maximum priority value is selected as target patch for filling first. The unknown pixels of the target patch is filled-in by either a single candidate patch or a set of candidate patches from the known region. Here, sum of square differences (SSD) is considered as distance measure between two patches. This method is greedy in nature since it replaces the target patches with the predicted patch sequentially. So significant error in patch prediction, at any stage, may propagate without any bound till the completion.

MRF-based Global Optimization: The Markov random field (MRF)-based image inpainting methods [24, 34] assign an optimal patch $Q_p \in \mathcal{M}_p$ (a set of candidate patches) to each target patch P_p in such a way that the following energy function $\mathcal{L}$ is minimized:

$$\mathcal{L}(Q) = \sum_{p \in \zeta} V_s(Q_p) + \sum_{(p,q) \in \mathcal{N}_4} V_p(Q_p, Q_q) \tag{1}$$

where $V_s(Q_p)$ and $V_p(Q_p, Q_q)$ denote the single node potential and pairwise potential, respectively. By this method, the target region is divided into overlapping patches representing the nodes of a graph and for each node (target patch), multiple candidate patches are selected. Then, out of these patches, it assigns an optimal patch to the corresponding node depending on the node's *belief*. The method is known as *priority belief propagation* (p-BP), and it consists of three steps: (i) assigning node *priority*, (ii) *label pruning*, and (iii) *inference*. The priority of an MRF node is determined by the number of eligible patches (in terms of belief) for that node. Lower the number, higher is the priority. In label pruning, the nodes are visited in the order of their priority and some candidate patches are selected from the known (non-damaged) region discarding rest of the patches. In inference step, a priority scheduling message passing algorithm [24] is used to visit each MRF node and the messages of the neighboring nodes are collected for determining its own belief. This method preserves global as well as neighborhood consistency in order to produce visually plausible inpainted image.

Coherence-based Optimization: The main idea of coherence-based method is to facilitate the search of the nearby patches by the result of the current query patch. So, it jointly searches the candidate patches for all query patches by sharing information to each other. This helps to converge the system to a local minimum, and it is also fast compared to others. This concept is incorporated into the objective function of image inpainting [32]. It combines the coherence property with the texture synthesis technique [13] by

$$\mathcal{F}(\hat{I} \mid I \setminus T) = \sum_{p \in T^*} \max_{q \in I \setminus T} sim\left(\mathbf{P}_p, \mathbf{P}_q\right) \tag{2}$$

where $\hat{I}$ is the inpainted image corresponding to the input image I, and $I \setminus T$ is the known region; and T^* is the estimated target region corresponding to the missing region T. $\mathbf{P}_p, \mathbf{P}_q$ are the target patch and the known or candidate patch at locations p and q, respectively. The above objective function is optimized by successively running two steps [44]: (i) *patch search* and *patch voting*. First, for the overlapping target patches in the unknown region, corresponding similar (well-matched) candidate patches are found from the known region ($I \setminus T$) in patch search step. Then in the voting step, these patches are blended together to infer the missing pixels of each overlapping region of the neighboring patches. Barnes et al. [5] proposed a fast randomized patch search algorithm called PatchMatch to provide optimum candidate patches maintaining the coherence property. They have used different geometric transformations in patch similarity measure to locate the best suitable candidate patch. This method provides a robust solution in patch selection, preserves global consistency and removes the pitfalls of local inconsistencies.

Transform Domain Approximation: An image completion method [15] has been proposed by using patch approximation in transform domain and kd-tree-based nearest neighbor field (NNF) computation in pyramidal framework. This method initializes the lowest scale by higher order singular value (HOSVD) in transform domain and up-samples the low-resolution image by kd-tree-based higher resolution patch searching. This method minimizes the energy function

$$\Phi(T, I \setminus T) = \sum_{p \in T} \min_{q \in I \setminus T} (d(\mathbf{P}_p, \mathbf{P}_q) + \lambda d(\nabla \mathbf{P}_p, \nabla \mathbf{P}_q)), \tag{3}$$

where ∇P_p and ∇P_q denote the gradients of target patch and known patch, respectively; and d is the SSD distance computed over the color and gradient channels. The gradient features are weighted by λ with respect to the color channels.

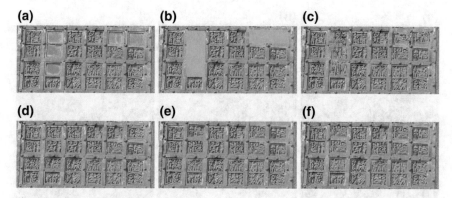

Fig. 4 Results of inpainting an image of Jor Bangla temple: **a** original image with damaged portion, **b** masked image, and result of **c** priority-based [10], **d** MRF-based [24], **e** coherence-based [32] and **f** HOSVD-based [15]

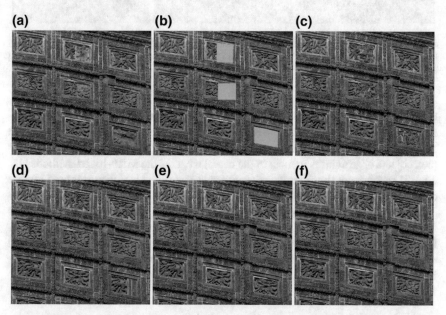

Fig. 5 Results of inpainting an image of Madan Mohan temple: **a** original image with damaged portion, **b** masked image, and result of **c** priority-based [10], **d** MRF-based [24], **e** coherence-based [32] and **f** HOSVD-based [15]

5.2 Evaluation

The performance of the image inpainting methods is tested on several images captured from the temples of heritage site in Bishnupur. Some of them are presented in Figs. 4, 5 and 6. The figures show the qualitative comparison of the image inpainting

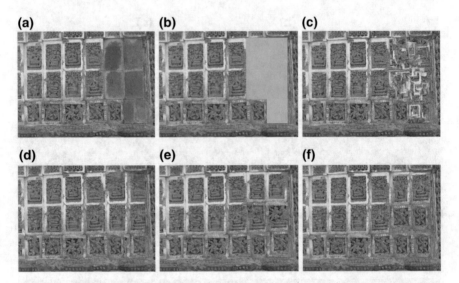

Fig. 6 Results of inpainting an image of Shyamrai temple: **a** original image with damaged portion, **b** masked image, and result of **c** priority-based [10], **d** MRF-based [24], **e** coherence-based [32] and **f** HOSVD-based [15]

methods based on patch priority [10], p-BP [24], coherence-based [32] and HOSVD-based [15]. The target or damaged region(s) in the image is marked by green color. It is clear from the figures that the priority-based method [10] fails to synthesize complex objects or structures in most of the cases, whereas the MRF-based methods [15, 24, 32] reconstruct those structures quite successfully. Also, they preserve texture clarity in the damaged region perfectly.

These sample images may have different panels depicting mythological stories from "Puranas". Reconstruction of proper panels/figures preserving the actual story is beyond the scope of the methods. These methods mainly concern about the visual quality of the inpainted image not about the semantic information carried in the image.

6 Temple Texture Classification

Texture analysis is a well-known problem in computer vision community. Researchers have tried with different types of textures starting from material to surface texture [6, 21, 29, 37]. To the best of our knowledge, this is the first attempt on temple texture analysis. The motivation of temple textures comes from the preservation of Indian digital heritage. India has a great history of heritage temples architectures. Each temple contains huge ancient artworks includes pictures and textures. Each texture highlights the art and cultures in its own identities. In this work, we have collected some texture data from the famous terracotta artwork on temples of Bishnupur. Here, our goal is not only to preservation the temple texture but also to highlight this as a general texture analysis problem in the related community. In the next subsection, we describe our temple texture data collection process.

6.1 Temple Texture Dataset

According to the local witness at Bishnupur, all the temples at Bishnupur were decorated with terracotta art and texture. But at present most of the work has been damaged and only three temples contain some terracotta artwork. We have used same four cameras as previously mentioned to capture the texture images. Since each image contains different types of textures, we have cropped each particular texture and manually grouped them into *16* different types of textures. Initially, all the texture are of different resolution but later we fixed the resolution to the average width of 121 and the average height of 128. We have collected total 2008 texture images of 16 different types of textures. Table 2 shows the dataset statistics and some samples from each group are shown in Fig. 7. For evaluation purpose, we divide the whole data into the training, validation and the testing set. First, we divide the data into 2:3 ratio as training and testing set. Then out of training data, we further divided it in 9:1 ratio as training and validation set. Finally, the partitioned data contains 723 training, 82 validation, and 1203 testing samples. We have a plan to update this dataset in future and update will be available at [4]. Based on the current partition we have evaluated our dataset using some state-of-the-art texture features as described in the next subsection.

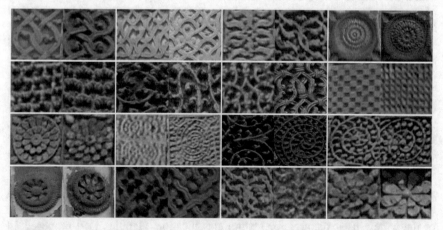

Fig. 7 Some examples of the texture images in our dataset. The first two images are the two samples from a group, and accordingly, the next two consecutive images belong to another group

Table 2 Texture image statistics in each group

Group	1	2	3	4	5	6	7	8
Number of samples	234	75	110	158	291	240	124	117
Group	9	10	11	12	13	14	15	16
Number of samples	44	37	54	54	138	140	98	94

6.2 Some State-of-the-Art Methods

In texture analysis, researchers mainly focus on two types of problems: texture classification and synthesis. This dataset is all about temple texture classification. So, we discuss some of the state-of-the-art texture classification techniques, and we evaluate our dataset by these techniques. Most of the work for texture classification has been focused on efficient feature representation. Initially, people started with some handcrafted features [9, 11, 19, 28, 30] and currently due to advancement of machine learning, people are trying to learn the efficient features from the training data. One of the popular feature learning techniques is based on deep convolution neural network (DCNN). Here, we first briefly describe one state-of-the-art DCNN model called Alex net [25] and then some of the handcrafted features as well. Finally, we present some results of each of the methods in Sect. 6.3.

Deep Convolution Neural Network (DCNN)-based Feature: Deep convolution neural network is a modification of traditional multilayer neural network consists of convolution, pooling, and some nonlinear operation in the different layer. DCNN learn important features using huge numbers of convolution filters and some non-linear operations sequentially. We train a state-of-the-art DCNN architecture called Alex net [25] for our temple texture classification. Alex net [25] contains a sequence of *convolution, nonlinearity, pooling, regularization, and normalization* operations. They have used five convolution layers followed by two fully connected layers. After each convolution and fully connected layer, they have used nonlinear, pooling, normalization and regularization operations. For details of this network architecture, the reader may go through the original work [25]. To train this network, we resize our texture image to 224×224 and use the last fully connected layer output as our feature representation which is of 4096 dimensions.

Haralick Texture Feature (HTF): Initially, researchers have tried with different types of low-level image features, and the feature proposed by Haralick [19] is one of the widely used features for texture classification. Haralick [19] proposed 14 different statistical measurements based on gray-level co-occurrence image matrix: a square matrix of size same as the number of gray levels in the image. Each element of the matrix is considered to be the probability that a pixel with value (row) is adjacent to a pixel (corresponding column). For our evaluation, we have used the same 14 different statistical measurements: (1) angular second moment, (2) total energy, (3) contrast, (4) correlation, (5) sum of variances, (6) inverse difference moment, (7) sum average, (8) sum variance, (9) sum entropy, (10) entropy, (11) difference variance, (12) difference entropy, (13) information measure of Correlation-1 and (14) information measure of Correlation-2 with 64 different gray levels in gray-level co-occurrence image matrix. The mathematical formulation of 14 different measures has been described in [19].

Segmentation-based Fractal Texture Analysis Feature (SFTAF): Fractal dimension is a powerful measure of texture complexity and shape. Costa et al. [9] proposed a fractal dimension-based feature for texture classification. They first generate some binary images from the input grayscale image based on different gray-level thresholds (L). They have proposed a two-threshold binary decomposition (TTBD) method to create a set of binary images from a grayscale image. For each binary image, they calculate the fractal dimension of the outer boundary of the segmented region. In addition to that, they have calculated the area (number of pixels) and mean gray level of the segmented region and finally get a $6 \times L$ dimension feature vector. We have used author's [9] suggested gray-level threshold value $L = 8$ and get a 48-dimensional feature vector.

Histograms of Oriented Gradients (HOG): Histogram of oriented gradients [11] is one of the popular handcrafted features for object classification and detection. There are various types of HOG proposed in the literature. Most successful one [11] divides the image into some cells and calculates the image pixel gradient magnitude histogram for each cell. They calculate a normalized 36-dimensional gradient histogram for each cell and concatenate them to represent the final descriptor. Here, we have used HOG implementation of [48] which gives 32-dimensional histogram for each cell. We have used the HOG cell size as 8 and get a feature vector of length $5824 (= 13 \times 14 \times 32)$.

Bag-of-Visual-Words (BOVW) and Fisher Vector (FV) Encoding of Local Features: A document can be classified based on the word frequency within that document. In computer vision, a similar type of idea has been applied for image classification. For image classification, people detect some local important features from an image and they call it as visual words. From the collection of visual words, they learn a visual vocabulary using a clustering algorithm (e.g., k-means). The center of each cluster is considered as a visual word of the vocabulary and the set containing all the cluster centers named as Bag-of-Visual-Words. Then, each image is described by this learned vocabulary using nearest neighbor encoding and a fixed size feature vector is obtained, whose length is same as the number of words in the vocabulary. We have used the similar type of method to represent our texture image. For local feature representation in each image, we densely sample N points and each point is described by the SIFT [28] descriptor. For our experiment, we take 200 samples from each training image and build a vocabulary of size 500. Each image is divided into *four* blocks and each block is described using the learned vocabulary to get a feature vector of dimension $2000 (= 4 \times 500)$.

Table 3 Comparison of baseline methods for texture classification

Methods	HTF	SFTAF	HOG	BOVW	GIST	FV	Alex net
Accuracy (%)	57.61	74.31	74.64	80.54	86.03	89.13	90.61

Also, we have used Fisher vector [31] encoding scheme to represent the texture image and got better result compared to the above nearest neighbor encoding. Here, we learned our vocabulary using Gaussian mixture model of size M (for our experiment $M = 64$) and use a spatial pyramid-based FV encoding scheme for final feature representation of length $65536 (= 4 \times 16384)$.

GIST Features: GIST is a popular global scene descriptor was introduced by Oliva and Torralba [30]. It calculates the global image statistics by applying Gabor filter in different scale and orientation. They use 32 different Gabor filters in four different scales and eight different angles. Finally, they average the Gabor feature maps into $16(= 4 \times 4)$ different cells and get a 512-dimensional feature representation. We have used the author's [30] implementation for our texture classification.

6.3   Evaluation and Discussion

We evaluate our temple texture dataset using the abovementioned features. To increase the training and validation data, we use some data augmentation on our main training and validation set. We flip each image horizontally and vertically and get 2169 (=3 × 723) images for training and 246 (=3 × 82) images for validation. On each type of features, we train a multi-class linear support vector machine (SVM) in one-vs-rest approach. As different types of features have the different dimensions, we choose the SVM cost parameters (c) based on the validation set. Based on these experimental settings, Table 3 shows the results of different state-of-the-art features. The comparison table highlights the superiority of DCNN-based feature over the traditional handcrafted features. Also, we have seen that there are enough scope to work with this dataset, and we hope this data will be helpful in the future for texture analysis researchers.

7   Content-Specific Figure Spotting and Retrieval

The walls of Bishnupur temples are decorated with bas-relief made of terracotta which depicts various events from "Puranas" as well as social life. The dataset contains a large number of such temple wall images. Content-specific figure spotting and retrieval technique can be used to detect/locate panels in the wall or a whole image that contains a specific sub-image or a figure. This panel/sub-image/figure may depict a specific event from the "Puranas". This can be posed as the problem of spotting or detecting a specific image (i.e., query image) in a larger image (i.e., target image). Note that, more than one instance of the query image may also be present in the target image and the method should report all of them. In our dataset, there are 66 large images that can be used for spotting and 1100 sub-images or figures in panels to be spotted on the former images. These 1100 images may also be used to evaluate traditional content-based image retrieval (CBIR) algorithms.

Quite a few methods have been proposed to solve this figure spotting problem [23, 36, 38]. Here, we have used the work of Seo and Milanfar [36] to show some results on our dataset. This method tries to detect content from a single target image given a single query image.

7.1 Baseline Method

The method of Seo and Milanfar [36] consists of three main steps as follows:

1. Computation of normalized local steering kernels (LSK) that produces salient feature matrices,
2. Comparison of the feature matrices using Matrix Cosine Similarity measure, and
3. Thresholding, followed by non-maxima suppression to get the final output.

In the first step, the method computes local steering kernels on the query image, as well as on each target patch of the target image. Local steering kernels robustly capture local structure information based on estimated gradients. In each patch of the image (i.e., query image and each of the target patch) the local steering kernel (LSK) is densely computed and normalized. The normalization ensures invariance to illumination changes. However, these LSKs are not used directly for matching purpose. PCA is applied to reduce the dimension of the features, and thereby the computational complexity is reduced. This also enhances the discriminating power of the features. As noted by the authors, the use of PCA for dimensionality reduction is not critical for the method. Other methods like Kernel PCA, LLE may also be used. Usually, two or three largest principal components are sufficient to retain the distinctive character of the data. The dimension reduced version of the normalized LSKs are used as features. The features obtained from each patch are column stacked to produce a matrix. So, we obtain feature matrix for the query image and also for each target patch of the target image. These matrices are used in the subsequent steps to compute the match.

After computation of the feature matrices, the similarity is computed between the feature matrix of the query image and that of each target patch. This is obtained by computing "Matrix Cosine Similarity" (also known as "vector correlation") defined as

$$\rho(\mathbf{F}_Q, \mathbf{F}_{T_i}) = \text{trace}\left(\frac{\mathbf{F}_Q^T \mathbf{F}_{T_i}}{||\mathbf{F}_Q||_F ||\mathbf{F}_{T_i}||_F}\right). \tag{4}$$

where $\mathbf{F}_Q$ is the feature matrix of the query image, $\mathbf{F}_{T_i}$ is the feature matrix of the i-th target patch and $||.||_F$ is Frobenius norm. The next step is to generate a "resemblance map" (RM) which indicates the likelihood of similarity between the query and the target. This is computed using the following function:

$$\text{RM}: f(\rho_i) = \frac{\rho_i^2}{1 - \rho_i^2}, \text{where}, \rho_i \equiv \rho(\mathbf{F}_Q, \mathbf{F}_{T_i}) \tag{5}$$

This resemblance map is thresholded in the next step to obtain the matching.

Two thresholds τ_o and τ is used by the method for the detection process. The threshold τ_o is used to check the existence of a match and τ is used for detecting the possibility of multiple matches in the target image. Then, non-maximal suppression is used to eliminate the possibility of multiple detections of the same object.

7.2 Evaluation

We evaluate the images from our dataset selected specifically keeping this application in mind. Note that in our dataset ground-truth for this application is not available. The results of the method shown in Figs. 8, 9 and 10 are evaluated manually. The first two figures show the results of content-specific figure spotting, and the last figure shows the results of content-specific figure retrieval. For the figure spotting results, color coded bounding box is used to identify and depict similarity, where red means most similar and blue means least similar. In Fig. 10, we have presented two sets of results for content-specific figure retrieval from the database containing 1100 images. The

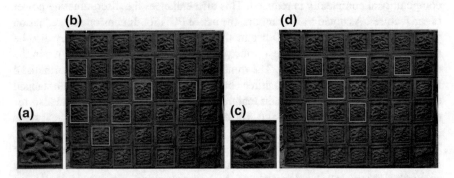

Fig. 8 Result of content-specific figure spotting and retrieval. **a** Query figure. **b** Temple wall image with presence of query figure marked. **c** Query figure. **d** Results obtained on the same temple wall image with different query figure. Red means most similar and blue means least similar

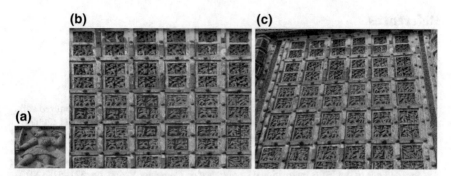

Fig. 9 Result of content-specific figure spotting and retrieval. **a** Query figure. **b** Temple wall image (fronto-parallel view) with presence of query figure marked. **c** Temple wall image (perspective view) where the method fails. Red means most similar and blue means least similar

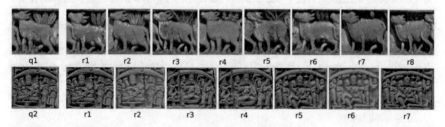

Fig. 10 Two example results of traditional CBIR obtained using our database. q denotes the query image and r denotes images retrieved from the database. Only some of the retrieved results are reported

figure shows only top few results obtained by the given method. In all the cases, the panel identified by the method as the most similar one is same as the one that we have used as the query image.

8 Conclusion

Here, we present an image dataset (publicly available and online accessible) [4] of Bishnupur terracotta temples. We believe that this dataset will be a major resource for a wide area of research in digital heritage. These image datasets are collected for various computer vision applications. Here, we present four separate applications (though not limited to) and analyze them to establish the usefulness of the dataset. We also mention some potential future research directions. We believe this dataset will encourage the research work toward the digital preservation and archiving of the world heritage sites. In future, we shall include images of more temples along with archaeological paintings, murals and 3D scans of different objects in the datasets.

References

1. http://whc.unesco.org/en/tentativelists/1087/
2. http://www.bankura.gov.in/Gazet/Chapter_2.PDF
3. http://www.asikolkata.in/bankura.aspx
4. http://www.isical.ac.in/~bsnpr/
5. Barnes, C., Shechtman, E., Finkelstein, A., Goldman, D.B.: Patch-match: a randomized correspondence algorithm for structural image editing. ACM Trans. Graph. **28**(3), 1–11 (2009)
6. Caputo, B., Hayman, E., Mallikarjuna, P.: Class-specific material categorisation. In: ICCV (2005)
7. Chatterjee, A., Madhav Govindu, V.: Efficient and robust large-scale rotation averaging. In: Proceedings of the IEEE International Conference on Computer Vision, pp. 521–528 (2013)
8. Cohen, A., Zach, C., Sinha, S.N., Pollefeys, M.: Discovering and exploiting 3D symmetries in structure from motion. In: 2012 IEEE Conference on Computer Vision and Pattern Recognition (CVPR), pp. 1514–1521. IEEE (2012)
9. Costa, A.F., Mamani, G.H., Traina, A.J.M.: An efficient algorithm for fractal analysis of textures. In: SIBGRAPI (2012)
10. Criminisi, A., Perez, P., Toyama, K.: Region filling and object removal by exemplar-based inpainting. IEEE TIP **13**(9) (2004)
11. Dalal, N., Triggs, B.: Histograms of oriented gradients for human detection. In: CVPR (2005)
12. Darabi, S., Shechtman, E., Barnes, C., Goldman, D.B., Sen, P.: Image melding: combining inconsistent images using patch-based synthesis. ACM Trans. Graph. (TOG), **31**(4), 82:1–82:10 (2012)
13. Efros, A., Leung, T.: Texture synthesis by non-parametric sampling. In: ICCV, vol. 2, pp. 1033–1038 (1999)
14. Furukawa, Y., Ponce, J.: Accurate, dense, and robust multi-view stereopsis. IEEE TPAMI **32**(8), 1362–1376 (2010)
15. Ghorai, M., Mandal, S., Chanda, B.: Image completion assisted by transformation domain patch approximation. In: Proceedings of the 2014 Indian Conference on Computer Vision Graphics and Image Processing, p. 66. ACM (2014)
16. Giakoumis, I., Nikolaidis, N., Pitas, I.: Digital image processing techniques for the detection and removal of cracks in digitized paintings. IEEE Trans. Image Process. **15**(1), 178–188 (2006)
17. Giakoumis, I., Pitas, I.: Digital restoration of painting cracks. In: Proceedings of the 1998 IEEE International Symposium on Circuits and Systems, 1998. ISCAS'98, vol. 4, pp. 269–272. IEEE (1998)
18. Halder, S., Halder, M.: Temple Architecture of Bengal: Analysis of Stylistic Evolution from Fifth to Nineteenth Century. Urbee Prakashan, Kolkata (2011)
19. Haralick, R.M., Shanmugam, K., Dinstein, I.: Textural feature for image classification. IEEE TSMC **3**(6), 610–621 (1973)
20. Hartley, R., Zisserman, A.: Multiple View Geometry in Computer Vision. Cambridge university press (2003)
21. Hayman, E., Caputo, B., Fritz, M., Eklundh, J.-O.: On the significance of real-world conditions for material classification. In: ECCV (2004)
22. Heinly, J., Schonberger, J.L., Dunn, E., Frahm, J.-M.: Reconstructing the world* in six days*(as captured by the Yahoo 100 million image dataset). In: Proceedings of the IEEE Conference on Computer Vision and Pattern Recognition, pp. 3287–3295 (2015)
23. Kim, T.K., Wong, S.F., Cipolla, R.: Tensor canonical correlation analysis for action classification. In: 2007 IEEE Conference on Computer Vision and Pattern Recognition, pp. 1–8, June 2007
24. Komodakis, N., Tziritas, G.: Image completion using efficient belief propagation via priority scheduling and dynamic pruning. IEEE TIP **16**(11) (2007)
25. Krizhevsky, A., Sutskever, I., Hinton, G.: Imagenet classification with deep convolutional neural networks. In: *NIPS* (2012)

26. Krizhevsky, A., Sutskever, I., Hinton, G.E.: Imagenet classification with deep convolutional neural networks. In: Advances in Neural Information Processing Systems, pp. 1097–1105 (2012)
27. Levoy, M., Pulli, K., Curless, B., Rusinkiewicz, S., Koller, D., Pereira, L., Ginzton, M., Anderson, S., Davis, J., Ginsberg, J., et al.: The digital Michelangelo project: 3D scanning of large statues. In: CGIT, pp. 131–144 (2000)
28. Lowe, D.G.: Distinctive image features from scale-invariant keypoints. IJCV **60**(2), 91–110 (2004)
29. Maji, S., Cimpoi, M., Kokkinos, I., Mohamed, S., Vedaldi, A.: Describing textures in the wild. In: CVPR (2014)
30. Oliva, A., Torralba, A.: Modeling the shape of the scene: a holistic representation of the spatial envelope. Int. J. Comput. Vis. (IJCV) **42**(3), 145–175 (2001)
31. Perronnin, F., Sanchez, J., Mensink, T.: Improving the fisher kernel for large-scale image classification. In: ECCV (2010)
32. Purkait, P., Chanda, B.: Digital restoration of damaged mural images. In: ICVGIP (2012)
33. Remondino, F.: Heritage recording and 3D modeling with photogrammetry and 3D scanning. Remote Sens. **3**(6), 1104–1138 (2011)
34. Ruzic, T., Pizurica, A.: Context-aware patch-based image inpainting using Markov random field modeling. IEEE Trans. Image Process. **24**(1), 444–456 (2015)
35. Sahay, P., Rajagopalan, A.: Geometric inpainting of 3D structures. In: Proceedings of the IEEE Conference on Computer Vision and Pattern Recognition Workshops, pp. 1–7 (2015)
36. Seo, H.J., Milanfar, P.: Training-free, generic object detection using locally adaptive regression kernels. IEEE Trans. PAMI **32**(9), 1688–1704 (2010)
37. Sharan, L., Liu, C., Rosenholtz, R., Adelson, E.H.: Recognizing materials using perceptually inspired features. IJCV **103**(3), 348–371 (2013)
38. Shechtman, E., Irani, M.: Matching local self-similarities across images and videos. In: 2007 IEEE Conference on Computer Vision and Pattern Recognition, pp. 1–8, June 2007
39. Simonyan, K., Zisserman, A.: Very deep convolutional networks for large-scale image recognition. arXiv:1409.1556 (2014)
40. Snavely, N., Seitz, S.M., Szeliski, R.: Photo tourism: exploring photo collections in 3D. In: ACM TOG, vol. 25, pp. 835–846. ACM (2006)
41. Snavely, N., Seitz, S.M., Szeliski, R.: Modeling the world from internet photo collections. IJCV **80**(2), 189–210 (2008)
42. Stanco, F., Tenze, L., Ramponi, G.: Virtual restoration of vintage photographic prints affected by foxing and water blotches. J. Electron. Imaging **14**(4), 043008–043008 (2005)
43. Stanco, F., Tenze, L., Ramponi, G.: Technique to correct yellowing and foxing in antique books. IET Image Process. **1**(2), 123–133 (2007)
44. Wexler, Y., Shechtman, E., Irani, M.: Space-time completion of video. IEEE TPAMI **29**(3), 463–476 (2007)
45. Wilson, K., Snavely, N.: Robust global translations with 1DSfM. In: European Conference on Computer Vision, pp. 61–75. Springer (2014)
46. Wu, C.: VisualSFM: A visual structure from motion system. http://ccwu.me/vsfm/ (2011)
47. Wu, C.: Towards linear-time incremental structure from motion. In: 3DV (2013)
48. Yang, Y., Ramanan, D.: Articulated human detection with flexible mixtures of parts. IEEE Trans. Pattern Anal. Mach. Intell. **35**(12), 2878–2890 (2013)
49. Zhang, Z.: A flexible new technique for camera calibration. IEEE TPAMI **22**(11), 1330–1334 (2000)

A Dataset of Single-Hand Gestures of Sattriya Dance

Mampi Devi, Sarat Saharia and D. K. Bhattacharyya

1 Introduction

Dance gesture recognition is a challenging problem in pattern recognition. Dance gesture recognition refers to the linguistic treatment of human motion where gestures are used to communicate drama artistically. The dataset introduced in this paper contains 1450 hand gesture images of 29 hastas from six individuals. From the original images, we have explored three sets of data, i.e. grey image data, binary image data and boundary data. Then, we applied feature extraction method on these data towards generation of a feature dataset. Unlike other datasets, in addition to these images, the numeric dataset is also available which is generated using special feature extraction method. Here, we extract three types of feature values, such as Hu's moments, Zernike moments and Legendre moments. We present initially an overview of our approach used to create the Sattriya dance single-hand gesture dataset. The hand gestures used in classical dance form are known as mudras, whereas in Sattriya dance, they are referred to as hastas. Predominantly, hastas are symbolic hand gestures which are used during dance performance to convey various expressions. Also, in this paper, we explore the performance of five benchmark classifiers using our own dataset in terms of accuracy.

M. Devi · S. Saharia (✉) · D. K. Bhattacharyya
Department of Computer Science and Engineering, Tezpur University, Tezpur, India
e-mail: sarat@tezu.ernet.in

M. Devi
e-mail: mampi@tezu.ernet.in

D. K. Bhattacharyya
e-mail: dkb@tezu.ernet.in

© Springer Nature Singapore Pte Ltd. 2018
B. Chanda et al. (eds.), *Heritage Preservation*,
https://doi.org/10.1007/978-981-10-7221-5_14

1.1 Motivation

Indian classical dance recognition has achieved popularity all over the world. There are eight different officially recognized classical dances in India. The Indian classical dances where most of the research on gesture recognition has been carried out are Bharat Natyam [1, 2] and Odissi [3, 4]. Sattriya dance is a fifteenth-century major Indian classical dance form and one among the eight Indian classical dances. To the best of our knowledge, neither there is any standard dataset available nor there is any significant research on gesture recognition reported in the literature for dance gestures of this dance form. One of the motivations of dance gesture recognition research is to create a universal communication environment for a dance drama, independent of language of the associated song. It has also applications in dance self-assessment and e-learning of dances. For any kind of dance learning, hand gestures are first and the foremost step for learning because of its flexibility and utility. Since there is no dataset available in the repository to investigate in this domain systematically, our objective is to create one dataset of Sattriya dance using single-hand gestures to support validation of recognition research in this domain.

1.2 Problem Formulation

The problem is to generate an unbiased dataset for Sattriya dance by extracting various invariant features of single-hand gestures images. The dataset should fulfil all the required characteristics of a benchmark dataset.

1.3 Contribution

This work has contributed a robust, unbiased and labelled feature dataset for Sattriya dance to support validation of classification performance. The dataset includes a large number of invariant features extracted from 29 hastas of Sattriya dance.

1.4 Organization of Paper

The rest of the paper is organized as follows: Sect. 2 discusses the importance of several asamyukta hastas datasets. Section 3 provides the detail about the development of the Sattriya dance single-hand gestures dataset. Section 3.4 reports the performance evaluation of well-known classifiers using our dataset and finally, the concluding remarks are given in Sect. 4.

2 Importance of Dataset

To begin any research on recognition system in computer vision, it is necessary to have standard dataset for performance analysis of different methods and algorithms. Though several research works on recognition of hand gestures of Indian classical dance forms, particularly Bharat Natyam and Odissi, are reported in the literature, there is no feature dataset of hand gestures of these dance forms available in any online repository. Therefore, the creation of a dataset in this domain will benefit the research community working in this area. The primary objective of our research is to develop an unbiased dataset of asamyukta hastas (single-hand gesture of Sattriya dance) and make it publicly available for performance evaluation of classifiers. Moreover, this dataset will also be relevant to other classical dances because several hand gestures of Sattriya dance, included in this dataset, are similar to hand gestures of other Indian classical dance forms with minor variation. In the next subsection, we give a brief description of Sattriya dance to provide readers a better understanding of the proposed dataset.

2.1 About Sattriya Dance

Sattriya nritya (dance) is a major Indian classical dance form having its origin in the Krishna-centred Vaishnavism monasteries, called Satras, of the Indian state of Assam. Though it was originated in the fifteenth century by the mediaeval polymath Srimanta Sankardev, it got official recognition as a classical dance form only in the year 2000 by Sangeet Natak Akademi of India. The core of Sattriya nritya was mythological stories and act of drama. However, with the growth of this tradition, it expresses in dance form. Now, this nritya is not confined in the Sattras only, and it has achieved a wide range of recognition throughout the world.

2.2 Data Labels

Hastas are defined as the combination of hand gestures by which viewer can understand the sequence meaning of dances. In general, 29 asamyukta hastas of Sattriya dance were adopted from four Indian classical dance books, viz. (i) Natya Sastra, (ii) Abhinaya Darpan, (iii) Sangeet Ratnakar and (iv) Srihasta Muktawali. Out of these 29 hastas, the dataset includes 20 hastas found similar in all the four books, three hastas from Abhinaya Darpan, four hastas from Sri-Hasta Muktaboli and two hastas from Kalikapuran and Abhinaya Darpan (The Mir'or of the gestures) Grantha [5]. Therefore, this dataset is also relevant to other classical dance forms of India. Further, the dataset includes 29 classes of these hastas. A sample of each of hastas is shown in Fig. 1.

Fig. 1 Twenty-nine asamyukta hastas

Table 1 List of related hand gesture datasets

Dataset name	Year	Url
Hand Posture and Gesture Datasets	1996, 1999– 2001	http://www.idiap.ch/resource/gestures/
Australian Sign Language Dataset	2002	https://archive.ics.uci.edu/ml/ datasets/Australian+Sign+Language+signs
Two-Handed Datasets	2005	http://www.idiap.ch/resource/twohanded
The NUS Hand Posture Datasets I, II	2010	https://www.ece.nus.edu.sg/stfpage/elepv/ NUS-HandSet
American Sign Language Dataset	2011	http://iims.massey.ac.nz/research/letters
Polish Sign Language ('P') and American Sign Language ('A')	2012, 2013	http://sun.aei.polsl.pl/mkawulok/gestures

2.3 Other Related Datasets

From our survey, six different related datasets have been found, which are reported in Table 1. Most of these datasets either have no accessible images or possess very less number of images. In addition to these datasets, there are few other datasets which are not publicly available.

(a) **Hand Posture and Gesture Dataset**: The hand posture and gestures dataset is available in four versions and introduced during 1996, 1999, 2000 and 2001. Out of these versions, two of them are for static hand postures [6, 7] and other two are dynamic hand postures databases [8, 9]. They use combination of different feature types at the graph node which is known as Elastic Graph Matching algorithm for their recognition purpose.

(b) **Australian Sign Language Dataset**: This dataset consists of sample of Auslan (Australian Sign Language) signs. In their dataset, 95 signs were collected from five signers with a total of 6650 sign samples. The source of the data is the raw measurements from a Nintendo PowerGlove. It was interfaced through a PowerGlove Serial Interface to a Silicon Graphics 4D/35G workstation. This dataset is available in UCIML repository [10].

(c) **Two-Handed Dataset**: This dataset consists of seven different two-handed gestures (rotations in all the 6 directions and a 'push' gesture). Seven persons have performed these gestures during two sessions with five records per gesture. Four persons have been used for training and the three others for testing.

(d) **The NUS Hand Posture Datasets (I & II)**: The NUS hand posture dataset is available in two versions: Dataset I and Dataset II. The version-I consists 10 classes of postures with 24 sample images per class, which are captured by varying the positions and sizes of the hand within the image frame. Both greyscale and colour images are available (160×120 pixels) [11]. The version-II is a 10-class hand posture dataset. The postures are captured in and around National University of Singapore

(NUS), against complex natural backgrounds, with various hand shapes and sizes. The postures are performed by 40 subjects, with different authenticities, against different complex backgrounds. The subjects include both males and females in the age range of 22 to 56 years. The subjects are with 10 hand postures where each posture is taken five times [12].

(e) **American Sign Language Dataset**: A New 2D Static Hand Gesture colour image dataset for ASL Gestures [13] reveals how a dataset of standard American Sign Language (ASL) hand gestures containing 2425 images from five individuals, with variations in lighting conditions and hand postures is generated with the aid of image processing techniques.

(f) **Polish Sign Language ('P') and American Sign Language ('A') Dataset**: This dataset for hand gesture recognition (HGR) contains the gestures from Polish Sign Language ('P' in the gesture's ID) and American Sign Language ('A') [14, 15]. In addition, it includes some special signs ('S') as well. The database consists of three series (termed HGR1, HGR2A and HGR2B) which include the subsequent data: original RGB images, ground truth binary skin presence masks and hand feature points location.

3   Our Single-Hand Gesture Dataset

To create this dataset, we captured 1450 images of 29 hand gestures (hastas) from six dancers. For each hasta, 50 images were taken with different viewing angles of the camera. The images were preprocessed to subtract the background and noise removal is done by applying Gaussian filter size 25×25. From each of the preprocessed image, we obtain grey image, binary image and boundary image to get three datasets. In the next step, three types of invariant moment feature vectors, viz. Hu's moment invariants, Zernike moments and Legendre moments were extracted. All the extracted features were tested on five types of benchmark classifier to classify the hastas into 29 classes. The hand gestures or hastas of Sattriya dance are defined as combinations of hand gestures by which viewer can understand the sequence meaning of dances. There are 76 hastas in Sattriya dance [5]. These hastas are grouped into three categories known as asamyukta (single-hand gesture) hasta, samyukta hasta (double-hand gesture) and nritya hasta. Nritya hastas are also double hand gestures which have no specific pattern and they vary from dance to dance. However, samyukta hastas and nritya hastas both are derived from asamyukta hasta. Therefore, asamyukta hastas are basis of all hastas. This dataset has been created based on asamyukta hastas only.

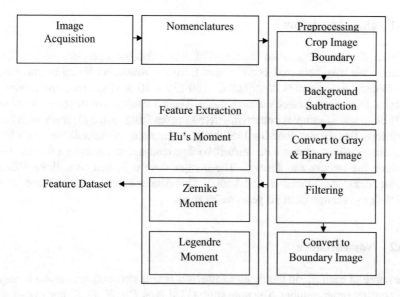

Fig. 2 Framework for dataset creation

3.1 Testbed Setup

The images were acquired as follows: volunteer dancers in standard Sattriya dance gestures, close to a simple 13 megapixel digital camera, uniform background. The images are captured from various directions, simulating a natural environment. The dancers who contributed to the images for the training set were wearing a wristband of colour similar to the background colour to make the segmentation of the hastas from the body part easy. Once the hands are segmented, they can be used for training directly.

3.2 Conceptual Framework

The overall process for creation of single-hand postures dataset of Sattriya dance for human–computer interaction is shown in Fig. 2. Each of the steps described below.

3.3 Major Steps

There are four major steps involved in creating this dataset. Each of them is explained in the following subsection.

3.3.1 Data Acquisition

Data acquisition refers to the collection of asamyukta hand gestures from different dancers. We have collected 1450 images from six volunteers for 29 hastas. Out of six dancers, four dancers contributed 1160 ($29 \times 10 \times 4$) samples comprising 10 samples from each dancer for each hasta. The remaining two dancers contributed 290 ($29 \times 5 \times 2$) samples comprising five samples from each dancer for each hasta. Therefore, this dataset contains 1450 images containing 50 samples for each hasta. The images were captured with uniform background and maintaining a fixed distance between the camera and dancers. The images were collected from three different Satras: Nikamul, Kamalabari and Auniati. One dancer is male and others are female, and their ages range from 16 years to 26 years.

3.3.2 Nomenclature

The name of each file in the dataset follows a simple convention to make it easy to refer during programming. The convention [13] is as $Pn\_N\_T\_R$. jpg where

- Pn: Person number (n = 1,2,3,4).
- N: Name of classes like pataka, padmokosha ($0 < N <= 29$).
- T: Captured on day or night, for day = d and night = n.
- R: Repetition ranging from 1,2, ..., 10.
- Jpg: Image format.

Example: P1_ Alpadma_d_1.jpg.

3.3.3 Annotation Database

Annotated details of the hastas are provided in a file named 'AnnotationDatabase.pdf' separately along with the dataset.

3.3.4 Preprocessing

The preprocessing phase plays a vital role in classification problem. The tasks performed in the preprocessing phase are shown in Fig. 3 and briefly described below

1. Crop and Size Normalization: In the first step of preprocessing, the acquired images were cropped at the boundary of the hand gestures. The cropped images are resized to 200 X 200 pixels.

2. Background Subtraction: Background subtraction of collected images had done using Gaussian mixture model (GMM) [16].

3.a. RGB Image to Grey Conversion: The cropped background subtracted RGB images are converted to grey images using the Matlab function 'rgb2gray'.

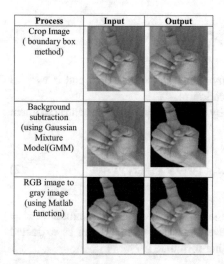

Process	Input	Output
Crop Image (boundary box method)		
Background subtraction (using Gaussian Mixture Model(GMM)		
RGB image to gray image (using Matlab function)		

Process	Input	Output
Gray image to Binary (automatic threshold value)		
Noise removal (using Gaussian 25X25 filter)		
Binary to boundary (Matlab function)		

Fig. 3 Preprocessing tasks of hand gesture

3.b. Grey Image to Binary Conversion: The grey images are converted to binary using threshold value determined by multiplying 1.6 with automatic grey threshold value of the Matlab function '$rgb2gray$'. In these binary images, object pixels are represented by '1' and others by 0.

4. Filtering: After conversion of binary images, the remaining noise of the images were removed by applying 25×25 Gaussian filter with sigma value 15 which gives a better result than other sigma values.

5. Binary Image to Boundary Conversion: From the binary images, the boundary images are extracted by using the matlab function '$bwboundaries(binary-image)$' to find out the global features.

3.3.5 Features Extraction

The next step is to extract various shape-based features from the images. The extracted features can be represented by some mathematical values. In the past decades, a large number of feature extraction methods have been evolved. In this work, we have extracted three types of moments features, namely, FS1, FS2 and FS3 consisting Hu's seven invariant moments [17, 18], Zernike moments [17, 19] and Legendre moments [20, 21], respectively.

1. FS1: Hu's Invariant Moments: Hu's seven invariant features were extracted based on the third-order central moments. These feature sets were computed on three different datasets (grey image dataset, binary image dataset and boundary dataset). The geometric moments of two-dimensional image '$M \times M$' with density distribution function f(x, y) can be defined as [17, 18] follows:

$$m_{pq} = \sum_{x=0}^{M-1} \sum_{y=0}^{M-1} x^p y^q f(x, y) \tag{1}$$

where 'p+q' represent the order of the moments and values of p and q vary as $0, 1, 2, \ldots$ and (x, y) denotes the pixel location.

When the function $f(x, y)$ is translated by an amount (x', y') then central moment can be written as

$$\mu_{pq} = \sum_{x=0}^{M-1} \sum_{y=0}^{M-1} (x - x')^p (y - y')^q f(x, y) \tag{2}$$

Here, (x', y') represents the centroid of the image which can be defined as $x' = m_{10}/m_{00}$ and $y' = m_{01}/m_{00}$. The Hu's seven invariant moments can be extracted from geometric moments using the following formulae [17]:

$$\phi_1 = \mu_{20} + \mu_{20} \tag{3}$$

$$\phi_2 = (\mu_{20} - \mu_{20})^2 + 4\mu_{11} \tag{4}$$

$$\phi_3 = (\mu_{30} - 3\mu_{12})^2 + 3(\mu_{21} - \mu_03)^2 \tag{5}$$

$$\phi_4 = (\mu_{30} + \mu_{12})^2 + (\mu_{21} + \mu_03)^2 \tag{6}$$

$$\phi_5 = (\mu_{30} - 3\mu_{12})(\mu_{30} + \mu_{12})[(\mu_{30} + \mu_{12})^2 - 3(\mu_{21} + \mu_{03})^2] \,|$$
$$+ 3(\mu_{21} - \mu_{03})(\mu_{21} + \mu_{03})[3(\mu_{30} + \mu_{12})^2 - (\mu_{21} + \mu_{03})^2] \tag{7}$$

$$\phi_6 = (\mu_{20} - \mu_{02})[(\mu_{30} + \mu_{12})^2 - (\mu_{21} + \mu_{03})^2] - 4\mu_{11}(\mu_{30} + \mu_{12})(\mu_{21} + \mu_{03}) \tag{8}$$

$$\phi_7 = (3\mu_{21} - \mu_{03})(\mu_{30} + \mu_{12})[(\mu_{30} + \mu_{12})^2 - 3(\mu_{21} + \mu_{03})^2]$$
$$- (\mu_{30} + 3\mu_{12})(\mu_{21} + \mu_{03})[3(\mu_{30} + \mu_{12})^2 - (\mu_{21} + \mu_03)^2] \tag{9}$$

As an example, the seven Hu's moment invariant for binary images of Alpadma hastas are shown in Fig. 4.

2. FS2: Zernike Moments: Shape analysis using Zernike moment has been found to have potential in pattern recognition and image analysis problem for their invariance and orthogonal property. Zernike moment is based on Zernike polynomial. If (ρ, θ) is a polar coordinate, the Zernike polynomial can be defined as [17]

$$R_{pq}(\rho) = \sum_{s=0}^{\frac{(p-|q|)}{2}} (-1)^s \frac{(p-s)!}{s!\left(\frac{(p+|q|)}{2} - s\right)!\left(\frac{(p-|q|)}{2} - s\right)!} \tag{10}$$

Hu's moment Features set(hf1, hf2, ..., hf7)							Images
0.226307	0.002844	0.000857	0.000615	0	0.000033	-1E-06	 P1_alpadma_n_1
0.231371	0.002896	0.001408	0.000676	0	0.000036	-1E-06	 P1_alpadma_n_8
0.231833	0.002599	0.001547	0.000651	0	0.000033	-1E-06	 P1_alpadma_n_10

Fig. 4 Example of seven invariant features set of Hu's moment

Here, p represents the non-negative integer and q is an integer with constraint $(p - |q|)$ is even. Here, $q < p$ and p and q denote the order of Zernike basis function.

In addition, to compute the Zernike moments, the range of Zernike moments are initially converted into unit circle. The centre of the circle equals the image centre and the pixels outside the circle are discarded. Here, the Zernike moments are implemented on binary image dataset with resolution 200×200. Mathematically, $V_{pq}(\rho, \theta))$ can be defined over unit disc as

$$V_{pq}(\rho, \theta)) = R_{pq}(\rho)^{(jp\theta)} \, where \, \rho <= 1 \tag{11}$$

Finally, the Zernike moments up to tenth order have been extracted from the images using the given formula.

$$Z_{(pq)} = \frac{(n+1)}{\pi} \int_0^{2\pi} \int_0^1 V^*_{pq(\rho,\theta)f(\rho,\theta)} \tag{12}$$

Zernike moments rotation invariant, robust with respect to noise and minor variation and have no information ambiguity. Example of Zernike moment features is shown in Figure 5.

3. FS3: Legendre Moments: Legendre polynomial was introduced by Teague [21]. The Legendre moments of order p + q is defined as follows [17, 20, 21]:

$$L_{pq} = \frac{(2p+1)(2q+1)}{4} \int_{-1}^{1} \int_{-1}^{1} P_p(x)P_q(y)f(x,y)dxdy \tag{13}$$

where the function $P_p(x)$ denotes the Legendre polynomial of order p. If $f(i, j)$ represents the pixel value at the (i, j)th pixel of a $N \times N$ image, then the Legendre moments can be approximated by the following equation:

Zernike moments features set(zf_00, zf_11, zf_20, zf_22.., z_10,8 zf_10,10)					Images
0.172431	0.028302	0.173894	0.31329	0.13100	
0.074291	0.113188	0.15827	0.055803	0.137155	
0.078724	0.04778	0.075533	0.0603	0.08723	
0.055142	0.051437	0.059085	0.050106	0.026837	
0.010276	0.024235	0.088369	0.088417	0.116435	
0.053791	0.021734	0.022582	0.04972	0.04494	
0.031011	0.034657	0.018418	0.039866	0.1106596	P1_alpadma_n_1
0.021857					
0.183429	0.029496	0.173753	0.281164	0.129841	
0.0376	0.109026	0.141683	0.063923	0.147185	
0.018467	0.014684	0.074058	0.06774	0.084874	
0.063923	0.062294	0.079642	0.039269	0.085826	
0.051286	0.036128	0.012923	0.062103	0.100207	
0.017034	0.028398	0.061205	0.110265	0.070097	
0.04184	0.067717	0.018404	0.054212	0.0944695	P1_alpadma_n_10
0.106535					

Fig. 5 Example of 36 features set of Zernike moments

$$L_{pq} = \frac{(2p+1)(2q+1)}{(N-1)^2} \sum_{i=1}^{N} \sum_{j=1}^{N} P_p(x_i) P_q(y_j) f(i,j) \tag{14}$$

Here, (x_i, y_j) represents the normalized pixel in the range $[-1, 1]$, given by $x_i = (2i/N) - 1$, $y_j = (2j/N) - 1$.

The Legendre polynomial $P_n(x)$ of order n is defined as

$$P_n(x) = \sum_{k=0}^{n} (-1)^{(n-k)/2} \frac{1}{2^n} \frac{(n+k)!x^k}{(\frac{n-k}{2})!(\frac{n+k}{2})!k!}, \tag{15}$$

Here, $|x| \leq 1$ and $(n-k)$ is even.

The recursive relation for Legendre polynomials can be written in simplified form as [17]

$$P_n(x) = \frac{(2n-1)x P_{n-1}(x) - (n-1) P_{n-2}(x)}{n} \tag{16}$$

Here, $P_0(x) = 1$; $P_1(x) = x$; $n > 1$.
Example of the Legendre moments of order 0 to 10 of two images is shown in Fig. 6 (Table 2).

3.4 Performance Evaluation of Classifiers Using Our Dataset

Classification means mapping the images into predefined classes, i.e. it is the function from input image feature to the output class. Classification consists of two stages: training and testing. Training stage refers to train the system with the extracted

Legendre-Moment Features Sets(lf_1, lf_2,......lf_66)					Images
0.55715	-0.24269	-0.34309	0.260251	-0.16117	
0.216378	0.135369	-0.29001	0.221406	0.379455	
-0.04498	-0.27579	-0.45886	0.155347	0.265961	
-0.17061	0.332198	-0.38218	-0.18008	-0.07141	
-0.06071	0.089528	0.14064	-0.08145	0.279011	
-0.3629	-0.08038	0.005706	0.13	-0.06903	
0.080343	-0.32578	0.341077	0.032694	0.021267	P1_alpadma_n_1
0.025678	-0.02177	-0.11558	0.124088	-0.33445	
0.255655	-0.1425	0.233067	-0.13065	-0.02946	
-0.06636	0.097534	-0.11631	0.275682	-0.00325	
-0.18003	-0.40015	0.418341	-0.17782	-0.1287	
-0.02326	0.000716	0.201391	0.109543	0.003137	
0.193929	-0.55	0.073072	0.233228	0.097782	
-0.19252					
0.539775	-0.17977	-0.22511	0.265304	-0.11936	
0.442221	0.015752	-0.248506	0.381235	0.332068	
-0.15343	-0.16915	-0.31591	0.375689	-0.01185	
-0.034064	0.233635	-0.41317	-0.01191	0.033154	
-0.05483	0.150877	-0.07764	0.081768	0.158677	
-0.27804	-0.10862	0.150451	-0.00196	-0.11221	
-0.03716	-0.122251	0.479702	0.038038	-0.35893	P1_alpadma_n_10
-0.0092	-0.04255	-0.06843	-0.14848	-0.2571283	
0.273294	-0.02722	0.511985	-0.36658	-0.21302	
-0.03597	0.042881	-0.047484167	0.216788	-0.27229	
-0.08266	0.232763	0.343635	0.050364	-0.16838	
-0.00544	0.124197	0.138278	-0.06389	0.14192	
0.232944	-0.6361	0.50301	-0.178423	0.08776	
-0.1827					

Fig. 6 Example of Legendre moments of order 0 to 10

Table 2 Description of general moment features [17]

Moment features	Symbol	Description
Zero-order function	M_{00}	Total intensity of an image and geometrical area for the image region
First-order function	$x_0 = M_{10}/M_{00}$, $y_0 = M_{01}/M_{00}$	Centroid of the image
Second-order function	$\mu_{20}, \mu_{02}, \mu_{11}$	μ_{20}, μ_{02} variance or distribution of horizontal and vertical projection, μ_{11} gives covariance measure
Third-order function	μ_{30}, μ_{03}	Skewness of the image projection, i.e. degree of deviation
Fourth-order function	μ_{40}, μ_{04}	Kurtosis of images, i.e. measure the flatness and peakness of images

Table 3 Results on Hu's moment invariants

Dataset	Classifier	Total instances	Correctly classified	Average	Kappa statistics	Mean absolute error	Root mean square error
Grey image dataset	K-nn (n = 5)	1015	704	69.4444	0.6857	0.0261	0.146
	Bayesian Network	1015	639	62.963	0.619	0.0314	0.114
	Nave Bayes	1015	516	50.9239	0.4952	0.0261	0.146
	Decision Tree	1015	742	73.1091	0.7109	0.0281	0.103
Boundary image dataset	K-nn (n = 4)	1015	786	77.4606	0.7666	0.0166	0.1231
	Bayesian Network	1015	631	62.173	0.6075	0.0341	0.1357
	Nave Bayes	1015	820	88.8853	0.8017	0.0179	0.0946
	Decision Tree	1015	971	95.7304	0.9524	0.0038	0.0434
Binary image dataset	K-nn (n = 5)	1015	727	71.6814	0.7076	0.0258	0.113
	Bayesian Network	1015	737	72.6647	0.7169	0.0237	0.1079
	Nave Bayes	1015	720	70.9359	0.7001	0.02659	0.143
	Decision Tree	1015	818	80.5911	0.8011	0.0159	0.0900

features and the testing stage refers to the matching the new input image features with the trained features value in the dataset using classifiers. In our experiment, all extracted moment features are trained and tested using different benchmark classifiers such as k-nearest-neighbour (k-NN), naive Bayes, Bayesian network, decision tree and support vector machine (SVM). The results of these classifiers are discussed in the next section.

3.5 Experimental Results

The Sattriya dance hand gesture dataset is initially preprocessed to for noise removal and background subtraction is done using a GMM model. From the preprocessed

Table 4 Classification accuracy on Hu's moment invariants

Classifier	Total no. of instances	Correctly classified instance	Accuracy (%)
K-nn (n = 5)	1015	727	71.68
Bayesian Network	1015	637	62.95
Nave Bayes	1015	720	70.93
Decision Tree	1015	818	80.59
SVM-Linear Kernel (c = 1, E = 1)	1450	986	68.00
SVM-Polynomial	1450	960	66.20
SVM-RBF (c = 9, gamma = 0.033)	1450	1031	71.10

Table 5 Classification accuracy on Zernike moments

Classifier	Total no. of instances	Correctly classified instance	Accuracy (%)
K-nn (n = 5)	1015	710	69.95
Bayesian Network	1015	380	35.17
Nave Bayes	1015	285	28.16
Decision Tree	1015	714	71.03
SVM-Linear Kernel (c = 1, E = 1)	1450	1013	69.86
SVM-Polynomial	1450	990	68.27
SVM-RBF (c = 9, gamma = 0.033)	1450	1044	72.00

images of the hand gestures, three datasets are created containing grey, binary and boundary images. Hu's moment invariant, Zernike moments and Legendre moments up to order 10 are computed from these three datasets. Further, different machine learning classifiers are applied to this dataset to find out the classification accuracy. For each classifier, 70% of data are used for training set and remaining 30% are used to validate the results. The results of Hu's invariant moments using five classifiers are shown in Table 3, and their comparison is shown in the graph of Fig. 7. Excluding the SVM, other four classifiers are experimented on all the three datasets, viz. grey image dataset, binary image dataset and boundary image dataset and the SVM classifier was used on binary image dataset only with three kernel functions such as linear kernel, polynomial kernel and the radial basis kernel (RBF). In this experiment, RBF kernel gives better result compared to other kernels.

To evaluate the accuracy of Hu's invariant features, we measure the value by Kappa statistics. Performance of the classifiers can be determined from Kappa statistics. The last two columns in the table show the classification error of the corresponding classifier in mean absolute error and root mean square error. Additionally, the feature

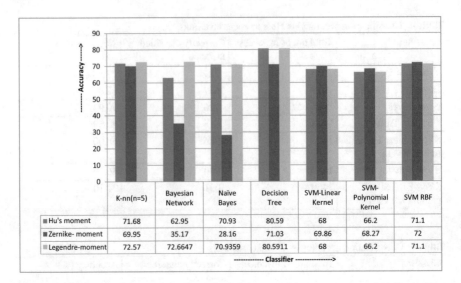

Fig. 7 Comparison of different classifiers with FS1

Table 6 Classification accuracy for Legendre moments

Classifier	Total no. of instances	Correctly classified instance	Accuracy (%)
K-nn (n = 5)	857	622	72.57
Bayesian Network	857	750	88.37
Nave Bayes	857	775	90.43
Decision Tree	857	823	96.03
SVM-Linear Kernel (c = 1, E = 1)	857	807	94.61
SVM-Polynomial	857	799	93.23
SVM-RBF (c = 9, gamma = 0.033)	857	779	90.90

set FS2 and feature set FS3 were extracted from the binary images only. The overall recognition rate for these datasets is shown in Tables 4, 5 and 6, respectively. From the results reported in the tables, we can observe that RBF kernel is more suitable for the proposed dataset. The different kernel parameters, i.e. C = 1 and E = 1 are setting for polynomial kernel. For this kernel, C denotes the complexity parameter and E is the exponent. Also, the parameters C and γ for RBF kernel were determined by Grid Search algorithm [22]. In this classifier, the parameter C controls the cost of miss-classification and γ represents the Gaussian kernel to handle nonlinear classification. It is graphically represented by a peak. A small γ gives a sharp peak in the higher dimension and large γ gives flat peak. Even though the recognition rate for each

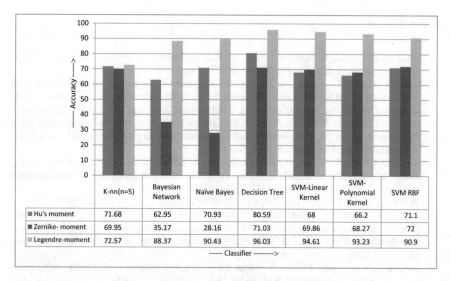

	K-nn(n=5)	Bayesian Network	Naïve Bayes	Decision Tree	SVM-Linear Kernel	SVM-Polynomial Kernel	SVM RBF
■ Hu's moment	71.68	62.95	70.93	80.59	68	66.2	71.1
■ Zernike- moment	69.95	35.17	28.16	71.03	69.86	68.27	72
▨ Legendre-moment	72.57	88.37	90.43	96.03	94.61	93.23	90.9

------ Classifier --------->

Fig. 8 Comparison of different classifiers on three feature sets

individual classifier is good, it is unable to fulfil our expectation. So, work is going on for further refinement. Figure 8 presents a comparison.

4 Conclusion and Future Remarks

A novel invariant feature dataset has been reported in this paper. The dataset includes 109 features, 1450 instances and 29 classes. The effectiveness of the dataset is established using five classifiers in terms of classification accuracy. The accuracies are good for some of the classifiers. The reason for low accuracy in the dataset may be because of the fact that most of the asamyukta hastas are very similar to each other and moments are good at capturing global features only. To classification accuracy can be improved by using feature extraction methods which capture local features along with global features, and we are working in this direction as part of our ongoing research. Also, we are planning to extend the dataset by including more instances and more features.

Acknowledgements We acknowledge the cooperation and help extended by Dr. Sunil Kothari, Padma Shri awardee, and Avinash Pasricha, famous photographer, for providing the images of Satriya dance hastas. We would also like to thank Mr. Ghanakanta Borah and Atul Kumar Bhuyan, two noted experts in the domain, for their continuous support during the creation of the dataset. Finally, we acknowledge the cooperation received from Auniati sattra and Nikamul sattra for producing knowledge on hand gestures.

References

1. Hariharan,D., Acharya, T., Mitra, S.: Recognizing hand gestures of a dancer. In: Pattern Recognition and Machine Intelligence, pp. 186–192. Springer (2011)
2. Saha, S., Ghosh, L., Konar, A., Janarthanan, R.: Fuzzy l membership function based hand gesture recognition for bharatanatyam dance. In: 2013 5th International Conference on Computational Intelligence and Communication Networks (CICN), pp. 331–335. Springer (2013)
3. Saha, S., Ghosh, S., Konar, A., Nagar, A.K.: Gesture recognition from Indian classical dance using kinect sensor. In: Fifth International Conference on Computational Intelligence, Communication Systems and Networks, pp. 3–8 (2013)
4. Saha, S., Ghosh, S., Konar, A., Janarthanan, R.: Identification of Odissi dance video using Kinect sensor. In: International Conference on Advances in Computing, Communications and Informatics (ICACCI), pp. 1837–1842. IEEE (2013)
5. Borah, K.: Sattriya Nrityar Rup darshan. Grantha-Sanskriti. Tarazan. Jorhat (2009)
6. Triesch, J., Malsburg, C.V.D.: Robust classification of hand postures against complex backgrounds. In: Proceedings of the Second International Conference on Automatic Face and Gesture Recognition, pp. 170–175. IEEE Computer Society Press, Killington, Vermont, USA, 14–16 Oct 1996
7. Jochen, T., Christoph, V.D.M.: A system for person-independent hand posture recognition against complex backgrounds. IEEE PAMI 23(12), 1449–1453 (2001)
8. Marcel, S.: Hand posture recognition in a body-face centered space. In: Proceedings of the Conference on Human Factors in Computer Systems (CHI) (1999)
9. Marcel, S., Bernier,O., Viallet, J.-E., Collobert, D.: Hand gesture recognition using input/output hidden Markov models. In: Proceedings of the 4th International Conference on Automatic Face and Gesture Recognition (AFGR) (2000)
10. Kadous, M.W.: GRASP: Recognition of Australian Sign Language using Instrumented Gloves, Honours thesis, School of Computer Science and Engineering, University of New South Wales (1995)
11. Pisharady, P.K., Vadakkepat, P., Loh, A.P.: Hand posture and face recognition using a fuzzy-rough approach. Int. J. Hum. Robot. 7(3), 331–356 (2010)
12. Pisharady, P.K., Vadakkepat P., Loh, A.P.: Attention based detection and recognition of hand postures against complex backgrounds. Int. J. Comput. Vis. 101(3), 403–419 (2013)
13. Barczak, A.L.C., Reyes, N.H., Abastillas, M., Piccio, A., Susnjak, T.: A new 2D static hand gesture colour image dataset for ASL gestures. Massey University (2011)
14. Kawulok, M., Kawulok, J., Nalepa, J., Smolka, B.: Self-adaptive algorithm for segmenting skin regions. EURASIP J. Adv. Signal Process. 170 (2014)
15. Nalepa, J., Kawulok, M.: Fast and accurate hand shape classification. In: Beyond Databases Architectures and Structures. CCIS, pp. 364–373. Springer, Berlin, Heidelberg (in press) (2014)
16. Mukherjee, S., Das, K.: An adaptive gmm approach to background subtraction for application in real time surveillance 2(1), 39–46 (2013). arXiv:1307.5800
17. Mukundan, R., Ramakrishnan, K.R.: Moment Functions in Image Analysis: Theory and Applications. World Scientific, Singapore (1998)
18. Clowes, M.B., Parks, J.R.: A new technique in automatic character recognition. Comput. J. 4(2), 121–128 (1961)
19. Ngan, K.N., Kang, S.B.: Fuzzy quaternion approach to object recognition incorporating Zernike moment invariants. In: 10th International Conference on Pattern Recognition Proceedings, pp. 288–290. IEEE (1990)
20. Saharia, S., Bora P.K., Saikia D.K.: Representation of printed characters with Legendre moments. In: Proceedings of 5th International Conference on Advances in Pattern Recognition 2003, Indian Statistical Institute, Kolkata, pp. 280–283, 11–13 Dec 2003
21. Teague, M.R.: Image analysis via the general theory of moments. JOSA 70(8), 920–930 (1980)
22. Hsu, C.-W., Chang, C.-C., Lin, C.-J.: A practical guide to support vector classification 1–16 (2003)

Analysis of Murals, Stucco Work, Relief Work and Textual Narratives for Understanding Clothing Styles of Vijayanagara Period

Mamata N. Rao

1 Introduction

There are a number of projects taken up in the recent decades in the area of cultural heritage. Most of these are in the domain of digitization and reconstruction. Some examples of such projects are as follows: the Theban mapping project [1]; the exhibits at Edo-Tokyo museum highlighting the lifestyle of Edo period [2]; the Roman Reborn [3] project an international initiative whose goal is the creation of 3D digital models illustrating the urban development of ancient Rome; the Digital Karnak Project [4] which puts together digital assets for Karnak, one of the largest temple complexes in the world; and Visualising Angkor is the visualization of the neighbourhood of Ankor Vat from 800 to 1400 AD [5]. Both architectural and social life reconstruction is seen for the work by Edo museum, Roman Reborn and Visualising Angkor. The Edo museum and the Visualising Angkor projects have looked at both architectural and social life digital reconstructions.

Our project looked at digital reconstructions of architectural and social life for bazaar streets of Hampi, a metropolis of Vijayanagara period. This was taken up under India Digital Heritage (IDH). This chapter will outline the process and methodology of arriving at visualizations of clothing style and material culture of Vijayanagara period, an important aspect that we took into consideration for the social life visualizations of bazaar street scenarios of Hampi, a metropolis of Vijayanagara period. Earlier studies on clothing styles of Vijayanagara period have mostly been textual descriptions, some with line diagram illustrations. Our work also focused on drawing colour and texture palate for the clothing styles of Vijayanagara period as digital documents.

M. N. Rao (✉)
National Institute of Design, Bengaluru Campus, 12 HMT Link Road,
Off Tumkur Road, Bengaluru 560022, India
e-mail: mamatarao@nid.edu

© Springer Nature Singapore Pte Ltd. 2018
B. Chanda et al. (eds.), *Heritage Preservation*,
https://doi.org/10.1007/978-981-10-7221-5_15

1.1 Historical Context of Vijayanagara Empire and Site Hampi

The metropolis of Hampi has an area of 25 km^2. Hampi, a UNESCO World Heritage site of Vijayanagara period (1327–1674 AD), located in South India. The city has two main zones:

- The **Royal enclosure** comprising palaces, administrative offices, houses for nobility along with a royal bazaar street and
- The **Sacred centre** comprising four temple complexes (Virupaksha, Vitthala, Krishna and Achyutaraya or Tiruvengalanatha) together with bazaar streets.

1.2 Historical Context of Vijayanagara Clothing Style and Material Culture

Description of Vijayanagara clothing style and material culture can be categorized into two broad categories:

1. **Textual narratives**: These are mostly text-based descriptions of lifestyle and clothing culture and can be seen as compilations in publications of research scholars. These are based on the detailed descriptions as seen in the travelogues of foreign visitors to Vijayanagara Empire. Descriptions of clothing style have also been compiled from the indigenous work of poets and writers of Vijayanagara period. One of the earliest published works on Vijayanagara kingdom was by Sewell, R. in his book titled 'A Forgotten Empire—Vijayanagar' [6] which detailed the history of this empire; described at length the city of Hampi along with the monuments of royal enclosure, the temple complexes, bazaar streets, the gateways along the roads; the lifestyle, clothing of royals and other people based on the travelogues of various foreign visitors to Vijayanagara kingdom. Thereafter, a number of other scholars such as Saletore [7], Mahalingam and Nilakantasastri [8], and Venkata Ramanayya [9] have written on the same lines of Robert Sewell but with more focus on Vijayanagara Empire, administration and social life. Filliozat [10] provides another interpretation to the work reported by Sewell [6]. All the above-mentioned publications provide various compilations of social life and clothing culture of Vijayanagara period as textual narratives. They also identify the foreign visitors and the poets/writers of Vijayanagara period who stated the descriptions.

2. **Visual interpretations based on Vijayanagara art/sculpture and textual narratives**: These are work by research scholars who have done primary work of looking at murals, relief work of Vijayanagara period, co-related with the textual narratives and given interpretations of the clothing style of this period with instances from the murals, relief work as examples to show and depict the clothing culture. The work of Reddappa [11] and Nirmala Kumari [12] has provided illus-

trations on clothing and material culture of Vijayanagara period by co-relating the textual narratives with the instances available in the art and sculpture of this period. Both these scholars have looked at the social life, clothing and material culture as reflected in sculpture and paintings of Rayala Seema. Verghese [13] has researched on the court attire of Vijaynagar based on study of five monuments at Hampi, namely, Mahanavami Dibba (the great platform), Hazara Rama temple (Ramachandra temple), Anjaneya temple all of which are found in the royal enclosure at Hampi and Krishna, Achyuta temple complexes (Tiruvengalanatha temple) belonging to the sacred centre at Hampi. This study looks at the male clothing style and the changes that occurred in the fourteenth, fifteenth and sixteenth centuries as depicted on these monuments with regard to the courts of Vijayanagar.

The history of clothing and material culture of Vijayanagara period can be obtained from a number of sources as listed below:

- Foreign travellers such as Abdur Razaak, Domingo Paes and Nicolo Conti.
- Poets and writers of Vijayanagara period such as Ahobala's 'Vasantotsava Champu', Kanakadasa's 'Mohanatarangini' and Krishnadevaraya's 'Amukta-malayada'.
- Art and architecture of Vijayanagara period.
- The early effort of capturing Hampi ruins done as pencil, pen and watercolour renderings by British officers, the important being the work by Colin Mackenzie which is available today on the British Library [14].
- Hampi ruins captured by early photographers such as Alexander Greenlaw in Michell [15] and Edmund [16].

Most research scholars have based their work on the textual narratives of foreign visitors, writers and poets; archaeological data from art and architecture of Vijayanagara period.

2   Premise of the Study

Our goal for the overall project under IDH was Architectural and social life reconstructions of bazaar streets of Hampi requiring visualizations of bazaar street scenarios with people clothed in the period style, with variations in colour and form of the clothing style for varied classes such as common people, the merchants, the royalty. This required a creation of a set of clothing style based on clothing terms of that period. A colour and texture palette along with the varied forms of wearing clothes was also needed.

The earlier work done in the area of clothing style and material culture of Vijayanagara has not captured the colour palette, texture and the varied forms of wearing clothes. There was a need to take up field study with focus on capturing colour palette, texture and varied forms of clothing styles. There were a number of mon-

uments in Hampi where archaeological data on clothing could be researched. The
following monuments were identified for conducting field study:

Monuments at Hampi for taking up field research:

- Gopurams of Krishna and Virupaksha temple complex for study of stucco work.
- Rangamantapa mural at Virupaksha temple.
- Relief work found in the bazaar street mantapas of Virupaksha, Vitthala and
  Krishna.
- Relief work found at Mahanavami Dibba.
- Murals of Lepakshi (this was the only one located outside of Hampi).

The methodology considered for the study and arriving at inferences of Clothing
style of Vijayanagara period is as detailed below.

2.1 Study of Literary Resources on Clothing Style and Material Culture of Vijayanagara

The work of Sewell [6], Saletore [7], Mahalingam [8] and Venkataramanayya [9] was
referred to for compiling the descriptions provided on clothing by foreign visitors,
poets and writers of Vijayanagara period. This together with the work of Reddappa
[11], Nirmala Kumari [12] and Verghese [13] provided the key clothing terms and
vocabulary of this period (Fig. 1).

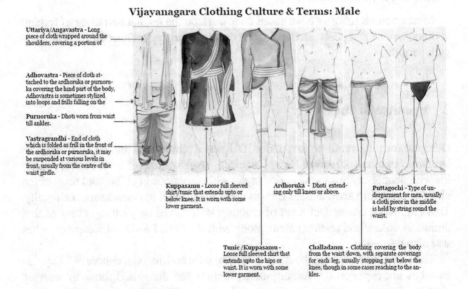

Fig. 1 Visualizations clothing styles of Vijayanagara period annotated with clothing terms

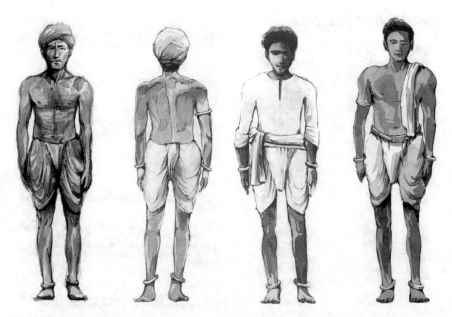

Fig. 2 Visualization of varied clothing form for common man based on Barbosa's description

Clothing as reported by Abdur Razaak, Domingo Paes, Nuniz and those from Amuktamalayada, Vasantotsava Champu were noted for various classes such as common people, royalty, nobility and brahmins and artistic sketches were visualized for each class. Some excerpts of selected descriptions are provided below as examples for common man (Figs. 2 and 3).

Common man

The common people wore *clothes as a girdle* below "wound very tightly in many folds and *short white shirt* of *cotton* or *silk* or *coarse brocade*" which were gathered between the thighs but were open in front. On their heads they carried *small turbans* while some wore *silk or brocade caps,* they wear their *rough shoes* on their feet (without stockings). They wear *large garments thrown over their shoulders* like *capes.* Barbosa [17], Reddappa [18]

"The common people go quite naked, with the exception of a *piece of cloth about their middle."* Varthema [19]

2.2 Study of Vijayanagara Murals for Clothing Style

The murals of Rangamantapa at Virupaksha temple Hampi and Veerabhadra temple, Lepakshi are one of the few surviving murals of Vijayanagara period. The work of Kotraiah [20] on Rangamantapa murals (paintings) dates these paintings to the early days of Vijayanagara Empire in the first half of sixteenth century executed under the patronage of Krishnadevaraya. Sivaramamurti [21] views the date to be around

Lion Cloth/Puttagōchi

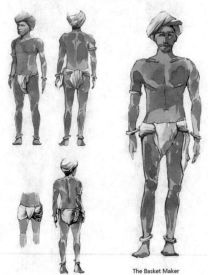

The common people go quite naked, with the exception of a piece of cloth about the middle.†

Varthema Jones

p 129, Google books, The Travels of Ludovico Di Varthema in Egypt, Syria, Arabia Deserta and Arabia Felix, in Persia, India, and Ethiopia, A. D. 1503 to 1508: Translated from the Original Italian Edition of 1510

The people used to wear a linen cloth round the body; he adds they could not wear more clothing on the account of the heat.

Nicolo Conti , Major, India, p 22

Rural Folks were bare bodied except for a cloth around their waist. '

Shorter than the form of dress mentioned, was 'Puttagōchi" or a lion cloth, which hardly covered the buttocks of a person. In 'Paramayōgi Vilāsamu' there is a reference to a basket maker who wore 'Puttagōchi' with garment's ends visible.

Jyotsna Kamat

The Basket Maker

Depiction of Social Life in Vijayanagara Sculptures, Jyotsna Kamat Paper presented in the National Seminar organized during Centennial occasion of the Depr. Of Archaeology, Mysore 1985

Fig. 3 Visualization of clothing for common man based on Varthema, Conti and Kamat's description

fifteenth century. Dallapicola [22] has referred to the work done by Cooper [23] who views settles the date for the ceiling paintings at Rangamantapa of Virupaksha temple Hampi to be between 1830 and 1840. Dallapicolla [22] states that the earliest surviving Vijayanagara painting to be of those in the Virabhadrasvami Temple at Lepakshi. These murals were studied by us to identify and map the clothing terms to the depictions shown in the panels for these murals.

Study and analysis of Rangamantapa murals: The description of Kotraiah [20] that identified various Hindu Gods, scenes from sthalapurana, other mythological stories, ten incarnations of Vishnu (Dasavatara), scene from epics such as Ramayana and Mahabharata showing Rama winning Sita and Arjuna winning Draupadi, a scene depicting royal party going for a hunt, a scene showing Vidyaranya's procession was mapped to the murals as textual annotations (Fig. 5). There are 13 main panels and many more sub-panels. Each panel was studied in detail identifying the characters depicted in the panel, the clothing terms along with the colour and texture palette for the clothing style were mapped in a table. The swatch was based on digital selections taken from the 1 GB stitched image of mural captured with Hasselblad camera (Fig. 4).

Study and analysis of Lepakshi murals: This study was taken up based on photographs on five main narrative panels and smaller panels taken by teams from IIACD and NID, respectively. The same methodology of identifying the characters

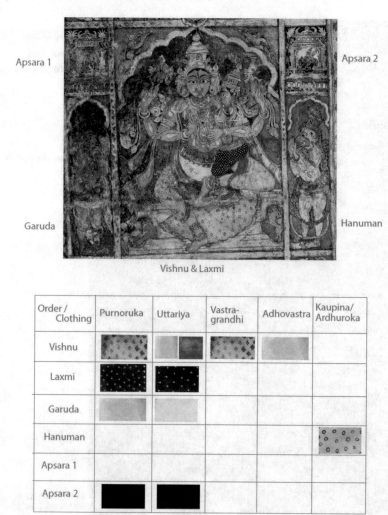

Fig. 4 Mapping of characters and clothing terms with colour and texture palette in a table

depicted in the panel, mapping the clothing terms along with the colour and texture palette in a table was followed for the main narrative panels and the smaller panels.

For both the Rangamantapa and Lepakshi murals, a conclusive chart of colour and texture palette was derived for each clothing term. Figure 6 shows the derivation of the chart for 'uttariya' an upper garment for men, based on analysis of Rangamantapa and Lepakshi murals.

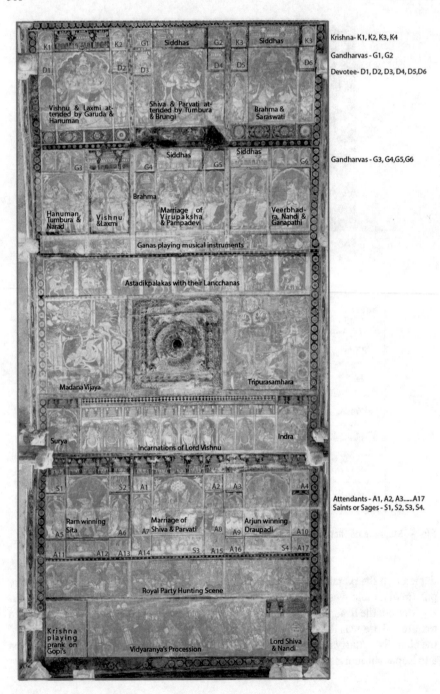

Fig. 5 Annotated information on Rangamantapa mural

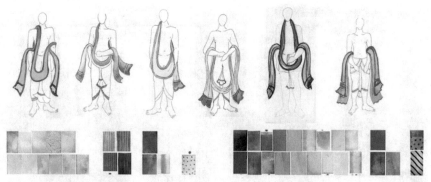

(a) Rangamantapa mural analysis for Uttariya, a male upper garment

Uttariya

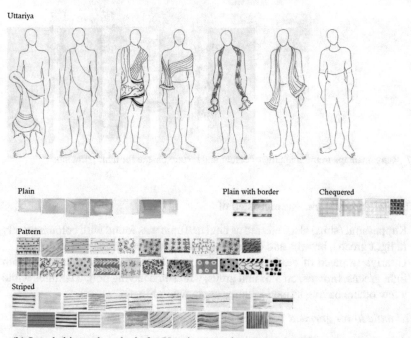

(b) Lepakshimural analysis for Uttariya, a male upper garment

Fig. 6 Varied forms of wearing an uttariya along with the colour and texture palette

The various clothing types found in Rangamantapa murals were of the following kind as shown in Fig. 7 for male garments and Fig. 8 for female garments:

320   M. N. Rao

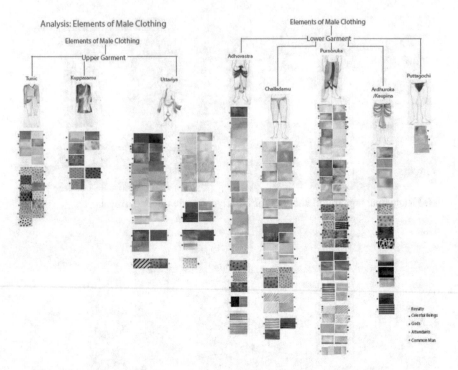

Fig. 7 Rangamantapa mural mapping of colour and texture palette for male garments

The *male upper garments* consisted of

(a) Kuppasamu (shirt) also referred as angi or Tunic was found with colours mostly in light greens, browns and creams, with some having dotted textures.
(b) Uttariya (a piece of cloth thrown across shoulders) had colour ranging from light greens, browns, creams and greys, with some having dotted textures while a few others having striped textures as shown in Fig. 6a.

The *male lower garment* consisted of

(a) Adhovastra (a waist cloth) with colour ranging from light greens, browns, creams and greens; some had dotted, striped and other organic textures.
(b) Challadamu (breeches) with colour ranging from greens, browns and creams; some had dotted, striped and wave-like textures.
(c) Purnoruka (long dhoti) and Ardhoruka (short dhoti) were found with colour ranging from greens, browns and creams; some had dotted, striped, floral and other organic textures.
(d) Puttagochi (a loincloth held by a string) was found in very few instances with pale green and light blue colours.

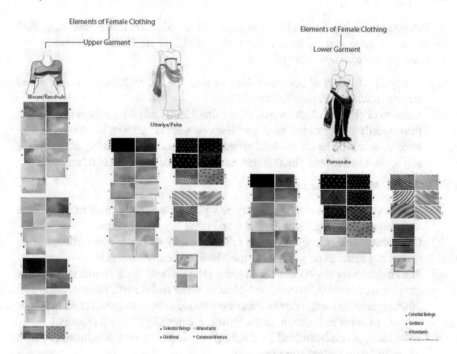

Fig. 8 Rangamantapa mural mapping of colour and texture palette for female garments

The *headgear* consisted of

(a) Turbans (a short form of headgear) in varied forms with colours ranging from light greens, browns and a few with dotted, striped textures.

The *female upper garments* consisted of

(a) Ravike (blouse) also referred as Kanchuki worn either with the saree or the pavada (lower long skirt) had colour ranging from light greens, browns, greys and creams with dotted and cross hair-like textures.
(b) Paita/uttariya (a piece of cloth thrown across shoulders) was worn over the pavada (lower long skirt) had colour mostly in black and creams with dotted, chequered and curved thin/broad stripes as textures. There were those with plain colours in light green, cream and greys.

The *female lower garments* consisted of

(a) Saree (a long cloth wound around the body).
(b) Pavada (lower long skirt), a ghagra-like clothing style was worn over the pavada (lower long skirt). But it was not clear to identify and distinguish between the two forms. The colours ranged from blacks and creams with dotted, cross hair, chequered textures. There were also creams with think/broad stripes in crimson, black, grey curved stripes as well as straight stripes.

The various clothing types found in Lepakshi murals were of the following kind as shown in Figs. 8 and 9 for male garments and Fig. 10 for female garments:
The *male upper garments* consisted of

(c) Cabaya (long shirt almost knee-length) also spelled as Kabayi or was found mostly in white and pale yellow.
(d) Uttariya (a piece of cloth thrown across shoulders) had plain colours that ranged from mostly being white, greens or browns, with or without borders. The textured ones mostly had white background with chequered, floral/organic, straight and wave-like stripes. The textures were seen to be in a variety of colours.

The *male lower garment* consisted of

(e) Adhovastra (a waist cloth) had very few plain colours and most of them were textured in chequered, stripes, floral and other organic patterns.
(f) Challadamu (breeches) with plain colours mostly white or with dotted, or fine chequered textures on yellow, crimson looking like animal skin.
(g) Purnoruka (long dhoti) and Ardhoruka (short dhoti) were found with colour ranging from greens, browns and creams; some had dotted, striped, floral and other organic textures. A lot of them were found to have striped, floral and other organic patterns in crimson, black brown, green and yellowish colours.
(h) Puttagochi (a loincloth held by a string) was found in very few instances with white and pale yellow colours.

The *headgear* consisted of

(a) Kulayi (a long conical form of headgear) with colours ranging from light greens, browns and a few with dotted, striped textures.

The *female garments* consisted mostly of

(a) Saree (a long cloth wound around the body) mostly having textured patterns. The patterns were chequered in single or two colours, straight and curved stripes, floral and other organic ones in crimson, blue, black, brown colours on mostly white background (Fig. 11).

2.3   Study of Relief Work for Clothing Style

The relief work and iconography was studied for Virupaksha, Vitthala and Krishna bazaar street. The iconography was found as relief work on the shaft of the columns, door jambs of bazaar street mantapas and colonnades. We have taken photographs for each of the sides of the column, door jambs where iconography was found and for each of these, line drawings have been created using Adobe Illustrator that show the icons as line drawings. Figure 12 shows iconography study from Vittala bazaar street

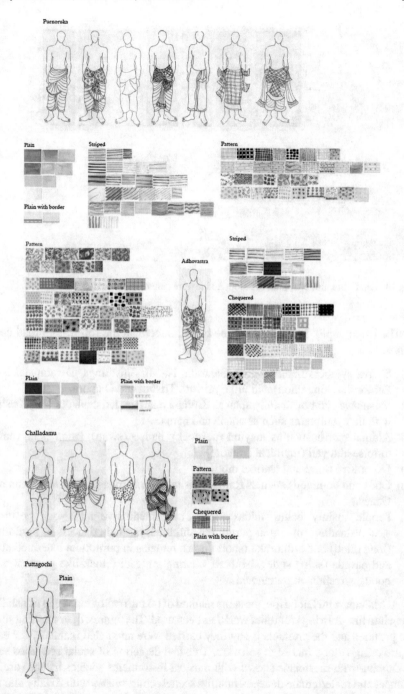

Fig. 9 Lepakshi mural mapping of colour and texture palette for male lower garments

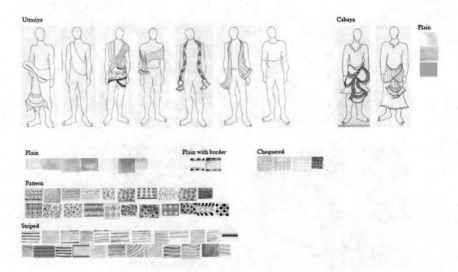

Fig. 10 Lepakshi mural mapping of colour and texture palette for male upper garments

The iconography found in the three bazaar street had the following broad categories:

(a) Shaiva symbols mainly being Ganesha, Nandi, Shivalinga, Dwarapalakas in Purnoruka (long dhoti) and uttariya, with Trishul and Damaru.
(b) Vaishnava symbols mainly such as Kalinga mardana Krishna, dancing Krishna with flute, emblems such as conch and nama.
(c) Animal motifs such as mayura (peacock), hamsa (swan), kamadhenu (cow), tortoise and yali (mythical creature).
(d) Decorative floral and leaflike motifs.
(e) Gods and demigods such as Rama, Krishna, Narasimha-Laxmi, Hanuman and Ganas.
(f) People mainly being siddas (ascetic) in meditative and yoga postures; seated/standing royalty in purnoruka and uttariya; male dancers in purnoruka (long dhoti) and ardhoruka (short dhoti); females in purnoruka like dhoti style and pavada (skirt) style; shepherd wearing gongadi (cloak-like garment with hood); wrestlers in puttagochi.

At Mahanavami Dibba too, the same method of taking photographs and translating them into line drawings for relief work has been used. The figures, their clothing style, the postures and the artefacts if any they carried were annotated manually for each figure using Adobe InDesign software. This had depiction of social scenarios such as dancing with musicians shown with musical instruments such as halage (drum), trumpet and male/female dancers, hunting scenes, court scenes with royalty and fan bearers, war scenes showing cavalry and soldiers, horse and camel traders. Figure 13 shows the categorization for different classes for phase 2 of Mahanavami Dibba.

Saree

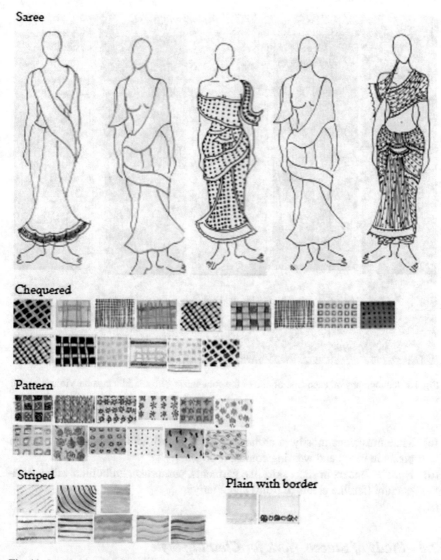

Chequered

Pattern

Striped   Plain with border

Fig. 11 Lepakshi mural mapping of colour and texture palette for female garment, saree

The relief work iconography found had the following broad categories:

(a) Royals in seated postures and nobles standing with closed hands. The royals seem to have purnoruka (ankle-length dhoti). The nobles seem to be wearing Cabaya (long knee-length shirt) and short conical hats.

(b) Royals in standing posture shown with purnoruka, adhovastra, uttariya and wearing long conical headgears or Kulayi.

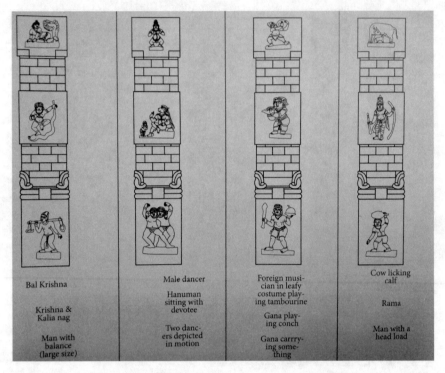

Fig. 12 Iconography on each side of one of the columns in Kalyana Mantapa on Vitthala bazaar street

(c) Male musicians mostly in ardhoruka (short dhoti) with vastragrandhi (fanlike pleats in front) and wearing conical headgears.

(d) Female dancers in short skirt like garments, purnoruka, ardhoruka with vastra-grandhi (fanlike pleats in front) and uttariya.

2.4 Study of Stucco Work for Clothing Style

The stucco work on the outer and inner gopurams, main shikhara, mahamantapa and parapets was considered for Virupaksha and Krishna temple complexes. Verghese and Dallapicola [24] have stated that the outer eastern gopuram (hiriya gopuram) and the inner goupram (Raya Gopuram), and the Balakrishna temple (Krishna) were constructed during the time of Krishnadevaraya. The work by Mitchell and Wagoner [25] dates the stucco work of Virupaksha temple outer East Gopuras to a later date and state '…this part of the gopura appears to be substantially rebuilt especially on the east and north where the mouldings are crude in execution'.

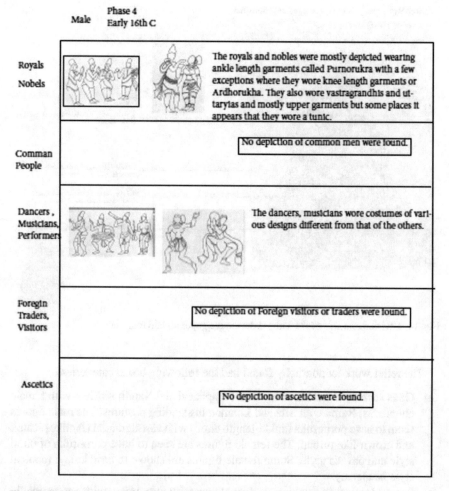

Fig. 13 Relief work on Mahanavami Dibba categorized by class in phase 4

For each of these structures for the study, all the four sides such as north (N), south (S), east (E) and west (W) were considered. Each side was divided into tiers (I, II, III), and each tier was divided into one central (C), many right (R) and left panels (L) with nomenclature. Each of the individual panel was annotated for the figure/figures with details of what they wore and held in their hands (Figs. 14 and 15).

The stucco work at Virupaksha and Krishna temple complexes depicted figures of Gods and Goddesses, Royals, Nobles, Ascetics, Dancers and common people. Most of the figures were standing ones with Anjali hasta (folded hands in salutations), some seated figures of ascetics and royalty or nobles. Most of the figures were human figures wearing varied clothing styles. The various human figures found are categorized as below.

Stucco work analysis of Outer Eastern Gopuram

c) Northern face of the Gopuram :

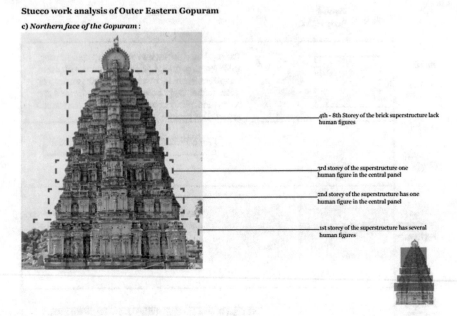

4th - 8th Storey of the brick superstructure lack human figures

3rd storey of the superstructure one human figure in the central panel

2nd storey of the superstructure has one human figure in the central panel

1st storey of the superstructure has several human figures

Fig. 14 Division of a side of the Virupaksha temple gopuram into four tiers

The relief work iconography found had the following broad categories:

(e) Gods such as Ganesha; Shiva with Pampadevi and Nandi; Krishna with female attendants; Rama with Sita and Laxman in standing postures. The male figures seem to have purnoruka (ankle-length dhoti) with vastragrandhi (fanlike pleats); and crown-like turban. The female figures are seen to have purnoruka of dhoti style and pavada style. Some female figures are shown to have kulayi (conical style headgear).

(f) Royals (males) in standing posture shown with purnoruka, with vastragrandhi (fanlike pleats) uttariya and wearing long conical headgears or Kulayi.

(g) Royals (females) in standing posture seen to have purnoruka of dhoti style and pavada style, uttariya or paita. Some female figures are shown to have kulayi (conical style headgear).

(h) Ascetics in puttagochi, knee and ankle length wrap.

(i) Female dancers in short skirt like garments, purnoruka, ardhoruka with vastragrandhi (fanlike pleats in front) and uttariya.

Virupaksha Temple Stucco Work Analysis

Nomenclature for 1st storey superstructure with human figures is detailed as under

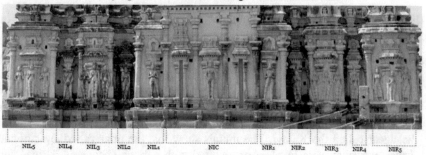

Legend

I - 1st storey, II - 2nd storey, III - 3rd storey
NC - Northern (N) face, Central (C)panel
NL1 - Northern (N) face, Left (L), Panel no. 1
NR1 - Northern (W) face, Right (R), Panel no. 1

Virupaksha Temple Stucco Work Analysis

**Eastern Gopuram, Northern Face,
Tier 1 - Left: NIL5 panel**

Standing **male figure** and two female figures could belong to royalty. The female figures could also be attendants of the royal male figure. All the figure are in samabhanga posture. The clothing style and jewellary are as under:

- *Purnoruka* (lower garment upto ankles) of kaccha style for the male figure and one female figure with vastragrandhi (fan shaped pleats) in the front. The other female figure has purnoruka of langa/ pavadai (skirt) form.
- *Kamarabandha* (waist band) of jewelled band type for all the figures.
- *Jewellary* on ear, neck, armlet, hand and waist. Both male and female figures have anklets.
- Both female figures have *hair bun* tied in two different styles.

Fig. 15 Division of each tier into central, right and left panels and annotations for each panel with information on clothing style

3   Conclusions

The findings for analysis of murals, relief work, stucco work and textual narratives on clothing styles of Vijayanagara period is categorized for different classes as follows:

- Royal males—They had purnoruka, ankle-length dhoti; ardhoruka of ankle-length dhoti, or a wrap style as lower garment. The lower garment in some cases had vastragrandhi (fanlike pleats) in the front and sometimes with adhovastra, a waist cloth. They wore an upper garment like Kuppasamu (short shirt) or sometimes were bare with only an uttariya. Most of the times they had a conical form of headgear called the Kulayi. The murals show that the uttariya, adhovastra and lower garments were in plain or textured with various chequered, stripes and organic patterns in crimson, black, green and blue on white background. These could have been embroidered textures as described by foreign travellers and writers of Vijayanagara period.
- Royal/Noble females—They had purnoruka, ankle-length dhoti or like a long skirt called pavada; most of the times as the lower garment. The lower garment in some cases had vastragrandhi (fanlike pleats) in the front. They wore an upper garment like Ravike (blouse) with only an uttariya called as the paita. Only sometimes, they had a conical form of headgear called the Kulayi. Sometimes they are seen wearing sarees. The murals show that the purnoruka and sarees could be plain or textured with various chequered, stripes and organic patterns in crimson, black, green and blue on white background. These could have been embroidered textures.
- Noble males—Most of the nobles are seen to be wearing clothing very similar to royals and in many instances are shown wearing an upper garment Cabaya or Kabayi, a long shirt that is beyond knee-length.
- Common men—They seem to have worn either purnoruka, ardhoruka both in dhoti style or like a wrap. Most of the times, they wore a very short ardhoruka much above the knees and puttagochi (a loincloth held by a string).
- Common women—They seem to have mostly worn sarees slightly above knee-length and many times without a ravike (blouse).

The colour and texture palette are based on digital selections from captured image or sometimes watercolour renders of patterns very close to the digital screen image. In future, one might need to look and factor the change in colour of murals due to weathering effects and ageing, for much more precise knowledge on the colour and texture of clothing in Vijayanagara period.

Acknowledgements We thank the Department of Science and Technology, Government of India for funding the project 'Representation of Art, Artifacts and Architecture of Hampi Bazaars from a Design Perspective' DST No: NRDMS/11/1586/09/Phase-II/Project No 15. The author would like to thank National Institute of Design (NID) for all the institutional support, facilities and the various project appointees who worked at Digital Hampi Lab at NID. We would like to thank the Director NID, Prof. Pradyumna Vyas for all the encouragement in taking this project up at our Institute. I would also like to thank Prof. S. Settar for providing valuable comments; Prof. Santanu Chaudhury (IIT-Delhi) and Prof. S. Ranganathan (NIAS-Bengaluru) for all the support as the Coordinators of India Digital Heritage (IDH) Project.

References

1. The Theban Mapping project. http://www.thebanmappingproject.com/
2. Edo Museum in Tokyo. https://www.edo-tokyo-museum.or.jp/en/p-exhibition/
3. The Roman Reborn project. http://romereborn.frischerconsulting.com/
4. The Digital Karnak project. http://dlib.etc.ucla.edu/projects/Karnak
5. Visualising Angkor. http://infotech.monash.edu/research/groups/3dg/projects/visualising-angkor.html
6. Sewell, R.: A Forgotten Empire—Vijayanagar. Asian Educational Services, New Delhi (1900)
7. Saletore, B.A.: Social and Political Life in the Vijayanagara Empire (AD 1346–AD 1646). BG Paul & Co. (1934)
8. Mahalingam, T.V., Nilakantasastri, K.A.: Administration and Social Life under Vijayanagar, vol. 1 (1940)
9. Venkataramanayya, N.: In: Nilakanta Sastri, K.A. (ed.) Studies in the History of the Third Dynasty of Vijayanagara, Madras University Historical Series-11. Ananda Press, Madras (1935)
10. Filliozat, V.: Vijayanagara. National Book Trust (1997)
11. Reddappa, K.: Material Culture Depicted in Vijayanagara Temples. Bharatiya Kala Prakashan (2003)
12. Nirmala Kumari, Y.: Social Life as Reflected in Sculptures and Paintings of Later Vijayanagara Period (AD 1500–1650). T.R Publications (1995)
13. Verghese, A.: Court attire at Vijayanagara (from a study of monuments). Q. J. Myth. Soc. **92**, 43–63 (1991)
14. British Library. https://www.bl.uk/
15. Michell, G. (ed.): The Alkazi Collection of Photography—Vijayanagara Splendour in Ruins (Alexander Greenlaw Photographs). Mapin Publishing, Ahmedabad (2008)
16. Edmund, L. http://www.bl.uk/onlinegallery/onlineex/apac/photocoll/r/zoomify61689.html
17. Barbosa, D.: Book of Duarte Barbosa—An Account of the Countries Bordering the Indian Ocean, Coasts of East Africa. Asian Educational Services (reprint 1989, 2002)
18. Reddappa, K.: Material Culture Depicted in Vijayanagara temples. Bharatiya Kala Prakashan, p. 284 (2003)
19. Varthema, J.: The Travels of Ludovico Di Varthema in Egypt, Syria, Arabia Desert and Arabia, in Persia, India and Ethiopia, AD 1503–1508: Translated from the Original Italian Edition of 1510. Google Books
20. Kotraiah, C.T.M.: Vijayanagara Paintings. Q. J. Myth. Soc. **92**, 49(4), 228–237 (1959)
21. Sivaramurti C.: Vijayanagara Paintings. Publications Division (1985)
22. Dallapicola, A.L.: Vijayanagara and Nayaka Paintings. In: Verghese, A., Dallapicola, A.L. (eds.) South India Under Vijayanagara—Art and Archeology, pp. 273–281. OUP, India (2011)
23. Cooper, I.: Vijayanagara or Victoria? The Ceiling of the Virupaksha Temple at Hampi. South Asian Stud. **13**, 67–69 (1997)
24. Verghese, A., Dallapicola, A.L.: Archaeological Work at Hampi. In: Verghese, A., Dallapicola, A.L. (eds.) South India Under Vijayanagara—Art and Archeology. OUP, India (2011)
25. Michell, G., Wagoner P.B.: Vijayanagara Architectural Inventory of the Sacred Centre, vol. 1, p. 135. Text and Maps, Manohar Publishers, New Delhi (2001)

Visually Reconstructed Krishna Temple, Hampi, Karnataka

Meera Natampally

1 Background

The Hindu temple architecture is a typical trabeated style of construction based on precise grid design and symmetry. The Vijayanagara architecture is said to be a culmination of Dravidian temple building tradition, a foremost temple building style of southern India. The marvelous architectural design of the temple complex and its elements with the structural system using stone is an impeccable synergy between structural innovation and architectural expressions. The foundation of Vijayanagara Empire was laid in 1336 AD, ruled by three dynasties Sangama, Saluva, Tuluva.

Hampi was the capital of the Vijayanagara Empire, and it is a village in Bellary district, Karnataka surrounded by lush greenery. The essential elements of the style are sacred, precise, and harmonious geometry. Hampi is recognized by the UNESCO and 56 out of the many monuments are protected by UNESCO.

2 Objective

The objective is to visually reconstruct the missing parts of the temple complex in detail, which is an attempt to restore its original glory digitally. The objective of the research is to digitally interpret Hampi/Vijayanagara architecture for interaction and understanding by commoners. Also, to create an open access digital cultural knowledge bank with digital archives on the evolution of temples architecture of Hampi, where data can be constantly updated by other interested researchers practitioners

M. Natampally (✉)
PRINCIPAL ARCHITECT SEKOS architecture firm, Bengaluru, India
e-mail: mn.architect@gmail.com

© Springer Nature Singapore Pte Ltd. 2018
B. Chanda et al. (eds.), *Heritage Preservation*,
https://doi.org/10.1007/978-981-10-7221-5_16

and broader public. Besides, to represent the temple complexes and temple elements graphically, pictorially, and digitally and in turn making it navigational and participatory to all users.

3   Introduction

3.1   Planning of Vijayanagara Temples

The Vijayanagara Empire made a significant remark in the history of temple architecture during its reign 1336–1565CE was a notable period of temple architecture that developed during their rule. The empire built temples, monuments, and planned towns. In addition to this, they also made modifications to the existing monuments and structures across South India.

3.2   Elements of Vijayanagara Style of Architecture

- It is a combination of Chalukya, Hoysala, Pandya, and Chola styles which evolved earlier in the centuries (Fig. 1a). Vijayanagara period was associated with sculptures (Fig. 1b) and paintings (Fig. 1c) apart from developing temple architecture.

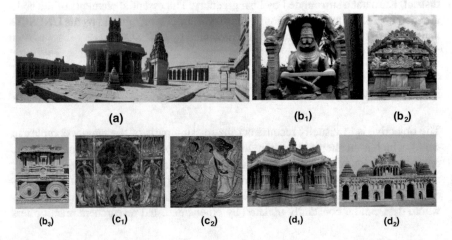

Fig. 1 **a** Panoramic view of vittala temple, **b** Sculptures of Hampi, **c** Paintings of Hampi, **d** Granite structures of Hampi

- The sculptures are much defined with less ornamentation and high proportions (Fig. 1b). Western Chalukyas preferred sandstone but Vijayanagara used granite as it helped to reduce the density of the sculptures and is durable (Fig. 1d).
- Temples are covered with strong enclosures where the huge granite stones were used, granite gave a more crude rugged appearance as it was sharply cut and skillfully modeled (Fig. 2a). Granites are placed one above the other without mortar joints and sheer self-weight of the stone makes it stand as strong enclosures (Fig. 2b).
- Small shrines consist of a cell and porch (Fig. 2c) and the medium- sized shrines consist of a cell, antechamber/antarala leading to a mantapa, which is an enclosed pillar called ardha mantapa, which has 2 entrances on its sides and along the axis of the cell the entrance leads to a maha mantapa (Fig. 2d), an open-pillared hall which has 3 entrances.
- In the Krishna temple, especially the east gopuram is very elaborate with brick and stucco work and it stands as one of the largest gopurams in Hampi (Fig. 3a). Larger in scale and higher than the main temple, this structure forms an impressive entrance to the complex. The gopuram is covered with detailed stucco figures of warriors, probably depicting the conquest of Orissa (Fig. 3b).
- The plinth is very defined with a carved frieze about 4–5 ft high (Fig. 3c) with ornated-stepped entrances on all the 4 sides supported by ornate pillars (Fig. 3d). There are double plinths in some of the mantapas.
- The columns have rampant horse and rider supported by other animals (Fig. 4a) and figure-sculptured panels, miniature panels is a favorite Vijayanagara era motif and 8- or 16-sided bands. The capitals are usually banana flower motifs (Fig. 4b).
- The sun shades are stone carved, sometimes doubly carved are also noticed (Fig. 4c). The parapet is constructed with brick and lime mortar are very ornate and sometimes brick and lime mortar sculptures are noticed in the niches Fig. 4d. Stepped tanks are constructed using chlorite slabs (Fig. 4e).

4 Research

This temple was built by the king (Krishnadevaraya) in 1513 AD to celebrate the conquest of the eastern kingdom of Udayagiri. The main deity installed in the temple was the figure of Balakrishna. Description for all the structures in Krishna temple is as below (Fig. 5).

- This temple has 2 strong enclosures with the outer enclosure having 2 entrances and the inner enclosure with 3 entrances. The temple faces east with a garba-griha/a sanctum sanctorum followed by antarala, ardha mantapa, maha mantapa,

Fig. 2 **a** Strong wall, **b** Enclosure granite blocks are placed one above the other, **c** Smaller shrine, **d** Plan and view of maha mantapa

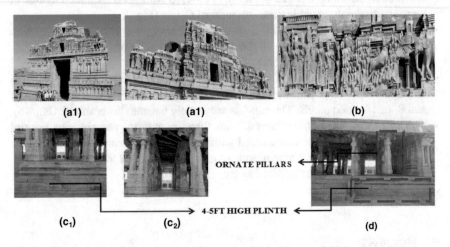

Fig. 3 **a** East gopuram, **b** Stucco figures of warriors **c** Maha mantapa **d** Maha mantapa

and a large eastern gopuram all along the same axis. The sanctum sanctorum and the antarala are enclosed to circumambulation at the lower level, which depicts Ramayana sculpture panels and very ornate pilasters and niches attached to the garbagriha. The artha mantapa has 4 pillars and 2 entrances on north and south flanked by yali motifs (Fig. 6).

Fig. 4 **a** Yali motifs and columns supported with pillars, **b** Cad drawing of pillars, **c** Stone-carved sunshades, **d** Parapet constructed with brick and lime mortar, **e** Stepped tank

Fig. 5 **a** Plan of krishna temple, **b** Aerial view of krishna temple, **c** East elevation of maha mantapa, **d** Small shirine and north gopuram seen at near

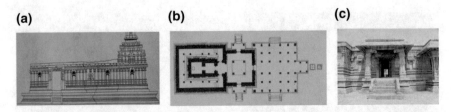

Fig. 6 **a** Section of Balkrishna temple, **b** Plan of Balkrishna temple, **c** Entrance of Balkrishna temple

Fig. 7 **a** Ramayana sculpture panels, **b** Ornate pilasters and niches, **c** Plan of the maha mantapa, **d** Columns at the periphery of maha mantapa, **e** Portion of the ceiling of maha mantapa

- The sanctum sanctorum and the antarala are enclosed to circumambulation at the lower level which depicts Ramayana sculpture panels (Fig. 7a) and very ornate pilasters and niches attached to the garbagriha (Fig. 7b). The maha mantapa also has 2 entrances here and the third entrance as we find usually along the axis is blocked with the mantapa (Fig. 7c). Here mantapa has 16 free standing columns at the center and at the periphery (Fig. 7d). The cells on either side of the maha mantapa are highly proportionate with a conical roof filled with ornate brick and lime mortar sculptures (Fig. 7e).

Fig. 8 **a** Plan of the Secondary Goddess Temple, **b** Columns with triple block of carvings, **c** View of the Secondary Goddess Temple

4.1 Secondary Goddess Temple

- On the northwestern side of the main temple is a temple dedicated to the goddess which has a sanctum sanctorum, antarala, and maha mantapa. In addition to this, a small cell facing the south opens to the maha mantapa (Fig. 8a).
- There are 2 more cells to the southwest of the garbagriha, one facing east and the other facing north where superstructure of these two are missing (Fig. 8b).
- Here the temple complex has 2 levels; the southeast is lower than the rest of the area (Fig. 8c). It has 3 sides colonnade housing few mantapas.
- Joints between the mandapa basement and the upapithas of the two structures indicate that the hall is a later insertion: it is built in two stages.
- Columns have triple blocks of carvings separated by polygonal sections, with beveled brackets above. Beveled brackets carry beams and an angled eave.

4.2 North and South Gopuram

- Above their granite entrance pathway, gopuras feature ascending storeys built with wood, brick, and plaster stucco figures, which are undoubtedly a Vijayanagara inception inspired from the smaller Chola and Pandya gopuras and styles (Fig. 9a).

(a)   (b)   (c₁)   (c₂)

Fig. 9 **a** North gopuram, **b** Stuco figures, **c** South gopuram

Most of the ruins have lost their towers or superstructures above the roof, as they were mainly made out of woodwork and red bricks with lime stone mortar and sculptures made of plaster stucco figures, as we can make out of this ruined entrance tower (Fig. 9b).

They are less durable and weaker than their rocky counterparts. Over time, they have collapsed and decayed due to weather and negligence, with the granite pathways or gateways beneath left almost intact (Fig. 9c). There is no doubt that the ruined tower was once lofty and beautiful, with a typical Dravidian shala roof, a half barrel-shaped top section.

4.3   Kitchen and Storage Granary

- A walled-in-kitchen is built into the south east corner of the enclosure. Plain walls rise on east corner of the enclosure (Fig. 10a). Plain walls rise on kapota, gala, and undecorated kapota, with a similar kapota serving as a cornice. There is a doorway on the west. The interior has three by four bays, with half-columns engaged into the walls. The roof over the east three bays is raised up to create an open clerestory (Fig. 10b).
- In the outer enclosure, there is a domed structure to store granary on the southern side. There are pavilions and a tank in this enclosure (Fig. 10c) Opposite to the east entrance is the Krishna bazaar with colonnade and a large tank.

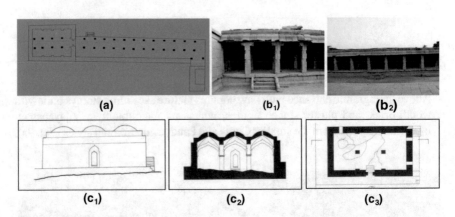

(a)   (b₁)   (b₂)

(c₁)   (c₂)   (c₃)

Fig. 10   a Plan of kitchen, **b** Side view of kitchen, **c** Elevation of storage granary, section of storage granary, plan of storage granary

4.4 Pushkarni and Ruined Bazaar

- The pushkarni which also means sacred stepped water tank, has a small empty shrine at the center. The shrine is ornated with a dome-like structure with shikhara made of brick and mortar. The dome is decorated with plastered sculptures. The plaster is weathered over time. During festivals, the utsava murthy is placed in the empty shrine. There is a ruined bazaar before the Krishna complex, this area is modernized and now is known as the Krishna temple bazaar. The ruined colonnaded bazaar stretches up to half a kilometer (Fig. 11).

5 Visual Reconstruction—Krishna Temple

The visual reconstruction of Krishna temple involves different stages:

1. Documentation of the whole temple physically and pictorially by measure drawing it and producing 2D AutoCAD drawings as existing and photograph of the past and present study.

Fig. 11 **a** Stepped water tank, **b** Ruined bazaar—Krishna temple

Fig. 12 Reconstruction of the east gopuram in digital space using historical evidence: **a** Existing east gopuram, **b** Greenlaws picture, **c** Visually reconstructed image

Fig. 13 Reconstruction of the shrine in digital space using historical evidence: **a** Existing small shrine, **b** Greenlaws picture, **c** Visually reconstructed image

(a₁)   **(a₂)**

(b₁)   **(b₂)**   **(c)**

Fig. 14 Reconstruction of the north gopuram in digital space using historical evidences: **a** Existing north gopuram, **b** Greenlaws picture, **c** Visually reconstructed image

2. Thorough literature study, history and studying the prototypes, applying architectural principles like proportion, scale, grammar, etc, consulting sthapatis [temple sculptors] and art historians.
3. With the above data the missing parts of the structures were visually reconstructed by using SketchUp software. 3D models are made to resemble the original as closely as possible with trial and error methods.
4. The 3D model is applied with texture and walk through is made so that an attempt is made to resemble the temple to its original glory (Figs. 12, 13, 14, 15 and 16)

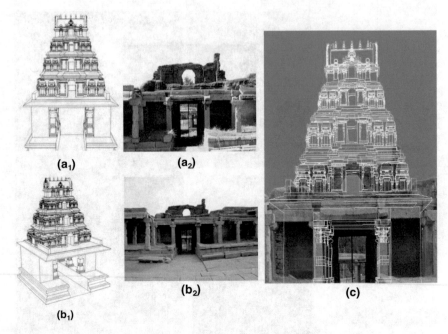

Fig. 15 Reconstruction of the south gopuram in digital space using historical evidence: **a** Existing south gopuram, **b** Greenlaws picture, **c** Visually reconstructed image

Fig. 16 Reconstruction of the garbhagriha in digital space using historical evidence: **a** Existing garbhagriha view, **b** Greenlaws picture, **c** Visually reconstructed image

Acknowledgements The author likes to thank Saiyed Umer, Manavi Puligal, Pooja S., Shruthi N., Arjun K. S., Reshma Shetty, and Namrata S. H. for their help in preparing this manuscript.

References

1. Mitchell, G., Wagoner, P.B.: Vijayanagara Architectural Inventory of the Sacred Centre, vols. 1, 2 and 3. Manohar Publishers, New Delhi (2001). Alexander Greenlaw Vijayanagara splendor and ruins
2. https://c1.staticflickr.com/7/6190/61103868100166c1ca0eB.jpg
3. http://www.trayaan.com/2016/02/hampiruinsvijayanagaramonument-world-heritage-bellary-karnataka-part-2.html#. W OI aY tK GO1s
4. https://www.flickr.com/photos/mukulb/611039707

Printed in the United States
By Bookmasters

Printed in the United States
by BookMasters

Printed in the United States
By Bookmasters